Mastering Event-Driven Microservices in AWS

Design, Develop, and Deploy Scalable, Resilient, and Reactive Architectures with AWS Serverless Services

Lefteris Karageorgiou

www.orangeava.com

First Published: August 2024
Published By: Orange Education Pvt Ltd, AVA™
Address: 9, Daryaganj, Delhi, 110002, India

275 New North Road Islington Suite 1314 London,
N1 7AA, United Kingdom

ISBN (PBK): 978-81-97396-69-4
ISBN (E-BOOK): 978-81-97396-67-0

Scan the QR code to explore our entire catalogue

www.orangeava.com

Dedicated To

*To My Wonderful Wife, Angelina, and Our Adorable
Children, George and Nasia, Who Inspire Me
Every Day and Give My Life Profound
Meaning and Purpose*

About the Author

Lefteris Karageorgiou is a proud Greek family man who treasures every moment spent with his wonderful wife and two adorable children. From an early age, he was captivated by the fascinating world of video game development, devouring programming books on C++ and even writing his first program at the age of 15.

Armed with a Master's degree in Computer Science and a Bachelor's in Mathematics, Lefteris embarked on an incredibly rewarding 16-year journey in software engineering. He's worn many hats along the way, working as a developer, lead, and architect across diverse industries like trading, gaming, and maritime. His expertise extends to a wide array of programming languages, including Java, .NET, Python, NodeJS, React, and Angular. One of Lefteris's proudest achievements was successfully leading the migration of large monolithic systems to event-driven microservices architectures.

Not one to keep his knowledge to himself, Lefteris has shared his expertise as an AWS Tech Instructor for 4 years, training over 200 students on the AWS cloud platform. He's also a published Technical Author for the hugely popular blog, allowing him to indulge his passion for technical writing.

Currently, Lefteris works as a Solutions Architect at Amazon Web Services, guiding customers on their journey to the AWS Cloud. He's a serverless expert, advocating for serverless concepts through numerous high-profile presentations and events.

Moreover, Lefteris has co-founded a startup, assuming the role of the CTO, and played a pivotal role in successfully launching a MarTech platform, where he single-handedly developed the infrastructure, backend, and part of the frontend, all hosted on serverless services on AWS.

Beyond his professional life, Lefteris embraces an active lifestyle filled with workouts, swimming, and running. He dreams of one day retiring to a breathtaking Greek island, soaking up the sun and treasuring the vibrant Greek summers he loves so much.

About the Technical Reviewer

Prasant Samal has 12 years of experience in solutioning and designing web applications, deployed both on-premises and in the cloud. Prasant has worked across various industries, including insurance, fintech, and airlines. A results-oriented Solution Architect with AWS certification, Prasant has excelled in delivering scalable applications in the insurance and investment domains over the past five years, showcasing a proven track record in end-to-end development lifecycle management.

Currently serving as a Solution Architect, Prasant has led successful migrations and modernizations of on-premises applications to AWS for clients. With certifications in AWS, Kubernetes, and multi-cloud networking, and a background of diverse roles in multiple organizations, Prasant demonstrates a comprehensive ability to translate complex requirements into technical specifications, mentor teams, and deliver solutions using both agile and waterfall methodologies.

Acknowledgements

Writing this book has been an incredible journey, and it wouldn't have been possible without the support and contributions of many individuals.

First and foremost, I would like to express my sincere gratitude to my family for their unwavering encouragement and understanding throughout the writing process. Their belief in me kept me motivated, even during the most challenging times.

I owe a debt of gratitude to my colleagues and peers in the industry who generously shared their knowledge and experiences with me. Their insights and expertise have been invaluable in shaping the content of this book, ensuring its accuracy and relevance.

I would also like to extend my appreciation to the team at Orange AVA for their professionalism and guidance. Their support and commitment to bringing this book to completion have been truly remarkable.

Finally, I would like to thank the broader AWS community for their passion and enthusiasm for cloud computing and event-driven architectures. Their continuous exploration and innovation have been a constant source of inspiration for me.

This book is the culmination of countless hours of research, experimentation, and dedication. I hope it will serve as a valuable resource for developers and architects alike, helping them navigate the exciting world of event-driven microservices in AWS.

Finally, I extend my gratitude to you, the readers, for selecting this book as your guide to acquiring knowledge. May it prove to be an indispensable companion as you embark on your quest to become proficient in event-driven microservices in AWS and navigate the realm of serverless computing on the AWS cloud.

Preface

In his AWS *re: Invent* 2022 keynote address, Dr. Werner Vogels, the esteemed Chief Technology Officer of Amazon, eloquently expounded upon the advantages of constructing asynchronous, loosely coupled systems and how the event-driven architectural paradigm serves as a potent enabler for such systems. His insights underscored the growing importance of embracing this architectural approach in the ever-evolving landscape of modern software development.

Welcome to *Mastering Event-Driven Microservices in AWS*, a book that promises to elevate your proficiency in the art of building and operating event-driven microservices within the powerful ecosystem of Amazon Web Services (AWS). This comprehensive volume stands as a beacon, guiding you through the intricacies of event-driven architectures and equipping you with the knowledge and skills necessary to harness the full potential of AWS's serverless services.

Comprising ten chapters, each a self-contained module, this book serves as an invaluable companion on your journey to *Mastering Event-Driven Microservices in AWS*. Its pages encompass a vast array of topics, ranging from foundational concepts to advanced techniques, ensuring a comprehensive exploration of this architectural paradigm. Whether you are a seasoned developer or Cloud architect seeking to expand your horizons, or a newcomer eager to immerse yourself in the realm of event-driven microservices within AWS, this book promises to be an indispensable resource, catering to individuals of all levels of expertise.

Chapter 1. Introduction to Event-Driven Microservices: The chapter introduces you to the concept of microservices and event-driven architectures. Understand the advantages of microservices over monoliths, the drawbacks of the synchronous nature of microservices, and the benefits of event-driven architectures.

Chapter 2. Designing Event-Driven Microservices in AWS: The chapter delves into the realm of event-driven architectures, leveraging the power of AWS serverless services. Learn how to build microservices using AWS Lambda, craft APIs with Amazon API Gateway, and create distributed, event-driven workflows with Amazon SQS, Amazon SNS, Amazon EventBridge, AWS Step Functions, and Amazon Kinesis.

Chapter 3. Messaging with Amazon SQS and Amazon SNS: The chapter focuses on building microservices that interact with each other using messaging patterns, including point-to-point messaging, publish/subscribe messaging, and fan-out. Learn how to use Amazon SQS and Amazon SNS to build scalable, reliable, and secure distributed systems on AWS.

Chapter 4. Choreography with Amazon EventBridge: The chapter provides a comprehensive guide to leveraging Amazon EventBridge to implement common choreography patterns such as event sourcing, CQRS, scheduler pattern, and claim check pattern.

Chapter 5. Orchestration with AWS Step Functions: The chapter provides a thorough overview of building orchestration workflows with AWS Step Functions. Understand the Amazon States Language and learn how to use the Step Functions Workflow Studio to build common orchestration patterns such as SAGA and circuit breaker.

Chapter 6. Event Streaming with Amazon Kinesis: The chapter delves into the three Amazon Kinesis services employed in the creation of event streaming systems. Learn how to use Amazon Kinesis Data Streams for streaming data ingestion, Amazon Data Firehose for data pipelines, and Amazon Managed Service for Apache Flink for real-time analytics.

Chapter 7. Testing Event-Driven Systems: The chapter explores various testing methodologies for event-driven microservices, encompassing unit testing, integration testing, end-to-end testing, contract testing, and performance testing. Explore how to leverage tools such as AWS SAM, Step Functions Local, Localstack, and Artillery to streamline and automate the testing process within the AWS ecosystem.

Chapter 8. Monitoring and Troubleshooting: The chapter guides you through the essential practices of monitoring and troubleshooting event-driven microservices on AWS. Learn how to log and monitor with Amazon CloudWatch, track account activity with AWS CloudTrail, and troubleshoot distributed systems with AWS X-Ray.

Chapter 9. Optimizations and Best Practices for Production: The chapter concentrates on enhancing performance, reducing costs, and implementing best practices for systems operating in a production environment.

Chapter 10. Real-World Use Cases on AWS: The chapter explores practical applications of event-driven microservices in AWS across various industries including e-commerce, Internet of Things (IoT), financial services, media and entertainment, logistics and transportation, and healthcare and life sciences.

This book is a practical guide filled with hands-on examples, real-world use cases, and industry best practices. It aims to empower you with the knowledge and skills to build event-driven microservices on the AWS cloud. This journey through event-driven architectures and AWS serverless services will enhance your abilities in the rapidly evolving field of cloud-native application development. Happy coding and deploying!

Downloading the code bundles and colored images

Please follow the links or scan the QR codes to download the
Code Bundles and Images of the book:

https://github.com/ava-orange-education/Mastering-Event-Driven-Microservices-in-AWS

The code bundles and images of the book are also hosted on
https://rebrand.ly/4d2f98

In case there's an update to the code, it will be updated on the existing
GitHub repository.

Errata

We take immense pride in our work at **Orange Education Pvt Ltd,** and follow
best practices to ensure the accuracy of our content to provide an indulging
reading experience to our subscribers. Our readers are our mirrors, and we
use their inputs to reflect and improve upon human errors, if any, that may
have occurred during the publishing processes involved. To let us maintain the
quality and help us reach out to any readers who might be having difficulties
due to any unforeseen errors, please write to us at :

errata@orangeava.com

Your support, suggestions, and feedback are highly appreciated.

DID YOU KNOW

Did you know that Orange Education Pvt Ltd offers eBook versions of every book published, with PDF and ePub files available? You can upgrade to the eBook version at **www.orangeava.com** and as a print book customer, you are entitled to a discount on the eBook copy. Get in touch with us at: **info@orangeava.com** for more details.

At **www.orangeava.com**, you can also read a collection of free technical articles, sign up for a range of free newsletters, and receive exclusive discounts and offers on AVA™ Books and eBooks.

PIRACY

If you come across any illegal copies of our works in any form on the internet, we would be grateful if you would provide us with the location address or website name. Please contact us at **info@orangeava.com** with a link to the material.

ARE YOU INTERESTED IN AUTHORING WITH US?

If there is a topic that you have expertise in, and you are interested in either writing or contributing to a book, please write to us at **business@orangeava.com**. We are on a journey to help developers and tech professionals to gain insights on the present technological advancements and innovations happening across the globe and build a community that believes Knowledge is best acquired by sharing and learning with others. Please reach out to us to learn what our audience demands and how you can be part of this educational reform. We also welcome ideas from tech experts and help them build learning and development content for their domains.

REVIEWS

Please leave a review. Once you have read and used this book, why not leave a review on the site that you purchased it from? Potential readers can then see and use your unbiased opinion to make purchase decisions. We at Orange Education would love to know what you think about our products, and our authors can learn from your feedback. Thank you!

For more information about Orange Education, please visit **www.orangeava.com**.

Table of Contents

Unleashing the Power of AWS Event-Driven

CHAPTER 1
Introduction to Event-Driven Microservices

Introduction

This chapter provides an introduction to monolithic architectures, microservices, and event-driven architectures. First, we will briefly explore the history behind the rising popularity of microservices and compare the benefits of microservices over traditional monolithic architectures. We will also discuss some of the disadvantages of the synchronous nature of microservices and how an event-driven approach can help address these drawbacks. Next, we will dive deep into the benefits and key components of event-driven architectures. Finally, we will give a short introduction to the large e-commerce platform that will be built throughout the book to demonstrate microservices and event-driven architectures in action.

Structure

In this chapter, we will discuss the following topics:

- Introduction to Monolithic Architectures
- Defining Microservices
- Brief History of Microservices
- Benefits of Microservices Over Monolithic Architectures
- Defining Event-Driven Architectures
- Benefits and Key Components of Event-Driven Architectures
- Combining Microservices and Event-Driven Architectures
- Difference Between Event-Driven Architecture and Traditional Architecture
- Building Our First Event-Driven Microservices System

Introduction to Monolithic Architectures

In the world of software development, the choice of architectural design can have a significant impact on the flexibility, scalability, and overall success of a project. One of the most fundamental architectural styles is monolithic architecture, also known as monolith, which has been widely used for decades.

A monolithic architecture is a software application where all the components - the user interface, the business logic, and the data access layer - are tightly coupled and developed as a single cohesive unit. This means that the entire application is built, deployed, and scaled as a single standalone entity.

In a monolithic architecture, the various components of the application are typically packaged together and deployed as a single executable file or container. This allows for a simplified development process, as the different components can be easily integrated and tested together. Additionally, the tight coupling of the components can make it easier to maintain and update the application, as changes to one component can be easily propagated throughout the entire system.

Some key characteristics of monolithic architectures include:

- **Single codebase**: A monolithic application is built as a single, indivisible unit, containing all the components and functionalities within a single codebase. This means that any changes or updates to the application require rebuilding the entire codebase.

- **Tightly coupled components**: In a monolithic architecture, the different components of the application, such as the user interface, business logic, and data access layers, are tightly coupled and interdependent. Changes in one component can potentially affect other components, making it harder to isolate and modify specific parts of the application.

- **Shared resources**: All components within a monolithic application share the same resources, such as the application server, database, and memory space. This can lead to potential resource contention and performance issues as the application scales.

- **Monolithic deployment**: Monolithic applications are typically deployed as a single unit, meaning that any change or update requires redeploying the entire application. This can lead to longer deployment cycles and potential downtime during updates or maintenance.

Monolithic architectures can be particularly well-suited for smaller, less complex applications or for applications where the development team is relatively small and the requirements are well-defined. Additionally, monolithic architectures can be a good starting point for new projects, as they can provide a solid foundation for building and iterating on the application over time.

Adopting a monolithic architectural approach offers multiple benefits, including:

- **Simple development and deployment**: Monolithic architectures are relatively simple to develop and deploy, especially for smaller applications or projects with a limited scope. The single codebase and deployment unit make it easier to manage and maintain the application.

- **Easier testing and debugging**: Testing and debugging a monolithic application can be more straightforward since all components are contained within a single unit, reducing the need for complex integration testing.

- **Tight integration**: With all components tightly coupled within the same codebase, monolithic applications often have better performance and fewer integration issues compared to distributed architectures.

- **Cross-cutting concerns**: Handling cross-cutting concerns like logging, security, and caching can be easier in a monolithic architecture since they can be centralized and applied consistently across the entire application.

However, as applications grow in complexity and scale, monolithic architectures can also present some challenges. As more features and functionality are added to the application, the codebase can become increasingly complex and difficult to manage. This can make it challenging to scale individual components of the application independently, as the entire system needs to be scaled as a whole.

Monolithic architectures can encounter various challenges, such as:

- **Scalability**: As an application grows in complexity and user base, monolithic architectures can become difficult to scale effectively. Scaling individual components or handling increased load can be challenging due to the tightly coupled nature of the codebase.

- **Complexity**: Over time, monolithic applications can become increasingly complex and accumulate technical debt, making it harder to maintain, extend, or refactor the codebase.

- **Deployment**: Deploying updates to a monolithic application requires redeploying the entire codebase, which can be time-consuming and increase the risk of introducing bugs or downtime.

- **Resilience and fault tolerance**: If one component of a monolithic application fails, it can potentially bring down the entire system, making it less resilient and fault-tolerant compared to architectures that isolate components.

- **Technology lock-in**: Monolithic architectures often rely on a specific technology stack or programming language, making it difficult to adopt new technologies or programming paradigms without rewriting significant portions of the codebase.

While monolithic architectures have their advantages, especially for smaller projects or applications with limited complexity, they can become challenging to maintain and scale as the application grows. As a result, many modern applications are shifting towards more modular and distributed architectures, such as microservices, to address scalability, maintainability, and technology independence concerns.

Defining Microservices

Microservices is an architectural style that structures an application as a collection of small autonomous services, modeled around a *business domain*. Each service is self-contained and implements a single business capability.

Microservices are loosely coupled, communicating through well-defined APIs, usually REST *over* HTTP, rather than sharing data or dependencies. This modular approach allows each service to be developed, deployed, and scaled independently. Since services are decoupled, teams can choose the best tools and languages for each one.

Microservices enable continuous delivery and deployment of large, complex applications. The decentralized nature also brings complexity like *distributed transactions* and infrastructure overhead.

Some key characteristics of microservices include:

- **Small and focused**: Each microservice is focused on implementing one specific functionality or business capability. They are small in size to keep them focused.

- **Autonomous**: Microservices are independent of each other and can be deployed, scaled, and updated independently. Each has its own database and technology stack as needed.

- **Loosely coupled**: Microservices interact with each other via simple APIs, usually REST APIs with lightweight protocols like HTTP/JSON. There is minimal coordination between services.

- **Owned by small teams**: Microservices empower small, cross-functional development teams to develop, deploy, and operate them independently.

- **Services own their own data**: Each microservice manages its own database and data persistence. This encourages a decentralized data management approach.

- **Infrastructure automation**: Microservices architectures lend themselves to infrastructure automation techniques like containerization and orchestration to manage massively scalable deployments.

- **Designed for failure**: Microservices are designed to gracefully handle failures of other services. If one service fails, the system remains operational.

In a typical microservices architecture, as depicted in *Figure 1.1*, a client sends a request to the backend system through an **API Gateway**. The API Gateway serves as the entry point to the backend and routes the request to the appropriate microservice.

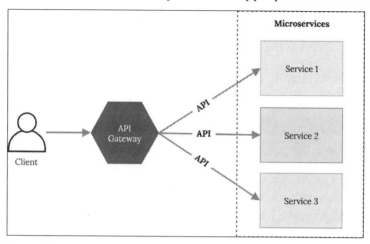

Figure 1.1: *An API Gateway routes requests to different microservices*

For example, when a user logs in to amazon.com, the website makes requests to various backend microservices. For instance, a request is sent to the recommendation microservice to suggest items based on the user's preferences. Another request goes to the order microservice when the user wants to purchase an item. In this way, *amazon. com* leverages different microservices to handle specific tasks behind the scenes.

Note: *To ensure high availability of services, multiple instances of the same microservices are deployed. To evenly distribute traffic and requests across these redundant microservice instances, you should use a **load balancer**. The load balancer enables smooth scaling and fault tolerance by routing traffic away from failed or overloaded instances. This load-balancing architecture helps prevent service disruptions and improves the overall performance and reliability of the system.*

Load balancers and API Gateways serve different purposes. Load balancers distribute incoming requests across multiple servers to optimize performance and availability. API gateways, on the other hand, act as a single entry point for APIs. They provide more advanced functionality than load balancers, including authentication and authorization of clients ensuring that only legitimate requests can access the services, rate limiting to protect the system from being overwhelmed by too many requests, data transformations such as converting between different data formats or applying data masking for security purposes and response caching to improve performance and reduce the load on downstream services. While API Gateways can leverage load-balancing capabilities, their main role is API traffic management, security, and governance rather than just request routing.

Some architectures have an API Gateway that sends requests to a shared load balancer, which then distributes the traffic across all microservices. Other architectures use a separate load balancer for each microservice that receives traffic directly from the API gateway.

Brief History of Microservices

The concept of **microservices** emerged in the early 2010s as a new architectural approach to building software systems. It evolved as an alternative to **monolithic application** architectures, which can become large, complex, and difficult to maintain and scale over time.

Some of the early pioneers and advocates of microservices included companies like Netflix, Amazon, and Uber, which adopted microservices to handle the massive scale and complexity of their operations. Netflix, in particular, played a major role in popularising microservices through its adoption of its video streaming platform starting around 2011-2012.

By 2014, there was a rise in conferences, meetings, blogs, and open-source tools related to microservices, indicating its growing popularity. Terms like **microservices architecture** became more common. By breaking large monolithic applications into smaller, loosely coupled services, proponents argued that microservices enable greater agility, scalability, and ability to continuously deliver new features through faster, independent development and deployment of individual services.

Over time, common principles and best practices emerged for building microservices. These include decentralized data management, lightweight communication protocols like REST, containerization, infrastructure automation, and organizing services around business capabilities. Increased use of **Docker containers** and orchestration systems like **Kubernetes** further accelerated microservices adoption by providing a standard way to deploy them. Over the next several years, many major tech companies migrated their monolithic applications to microservices. This included the likes of Uber, Airbnb, Twitter, Spotify, and others.

Today, microservices have become a widely used architectural style for building modern applications, especially in the cloud. Their benefits around flexibility and speed of innovation have made them a popular choice for companies undergoing digital transformation initiatives. However, microservices also introduce complexity around managing a distributed system. Striking the right balance continues to be an ongoing area of focus.

Note: *Contrary to popular belief, the origins of microservices architecture can be traced quite far back in history. The microservices architecture is analogous to the* **Unix** *philosophy of having small and focused tools that do one thing well and can be combined to accomplish larger tasks. In Unix, simple tools are composed using pipes to create powerful pipelines. Similarly, microservices are composed together over APIs and messaging to build complex applications.*

Both approaches emphasize building simple and modular components that encapsulate specific functions. Small microservices, like Unix tools, focus on their own separate concerns. This makes them easier to develop, deploy, scale, and maintain independently. Loose coupling through APIs/messaging allows combining and reusing microservices flexibly.

The Unix philosophy encourages writing programs that work together. Microservices also enable integrating diverse systems by abstracting functionality behind APIs and communicating over lightweight protocols. Both aim for small building blocks that connect together, avoiding large monolithic applications.

Like Unix processes, microservices often represent long-running stateless functions. Their lightweight nature allows spinning up more instances as needed to scale horizontally. Microservices can also leverage container technology like Docker, which utilizes OS-level virtualization features similar to those found in Unix. Overall, the microservices architectural style reflects Unix influences in its emphasis on decomposition, composability, concurrency, and optimizing for change.

Ken Thompson, the designer of the original Unix operating system (~1970), said:

The Unix philosophy emphasizes building short, simple, clear, modular, and extendable code that can be easily maintained and repurposed by developers other than its creators.

Benefits of Microservices Over Monolithic Architectures

Microservices and monolithic architectures are two different approaches to designing and implementing software systems. The key differences between the two are the architecture, scalability, development and deployment, fault tolerance, communication, and modularity and reusability. Next, we will take a closer look at these key differences.

Architecture

Monolithic architecture: In a monolithic architecture, the entire application is built as a single unit, with all components tightly coupled and interdependent. This means that changes to one part of the application can have a ripple effect on other parts, making it more difficult to maintain and update.

Microservices: Microservices architecture involves breaking down a large application into smaller and independent services, each with its own specific purpose and functionality. These services are designed to be loosely coupled and can be developed, deployed, and scaled independently.

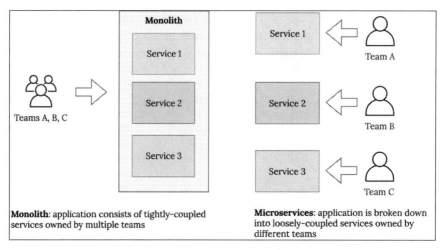

Figure 1.2: Monolith vs. microservices: Architecture

Scalability

Monolithic architecture: Monolithic applications are typically more challenging to scale, as the entire application needs to be scaled, even if only a small part of it is experiencing high demand. This can result in inefficient resource utilization and higher costs.

Microservices: Microservices are designed to be highly scalable and can be easily scaled up or down by deploying additional instances of individual services or by removing instances, respectively. This allows for better resource utilization and improved performance under high loads.

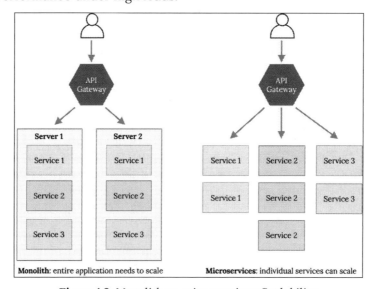

Figure 1.3: Monolith vs. microservices: Scalability

Development and Deployment

Monolithic architecture: In a monolithic architecture, the entire application needs to be rebuilt and redeployed whenever changes are made, which can be time-consuming and complex, especially for large applications.

Microservices: Microservices architecture promotes a decentralized development approach, where different services can be developed and deployed independently by different teams. This allows for faster development cycles and easier integration of new features and technologies.

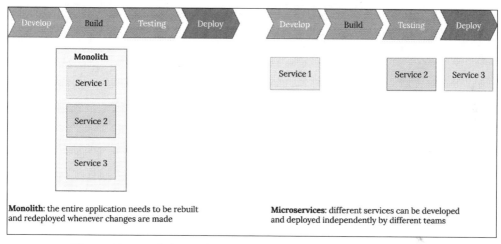

Figure 1.4: *Monolith vs. microservices: Development and Deployment*

Fault Tolerance

Monolithic architecture: In a monolithic architecture, a single point of failure can bring down the entire application, as all components are tightly coupled.

Microservices: Microservices are designed to be fault-tolerant, as each service is independent and can handle failures gracefully. If one service fails, it does not bring down the entire system.

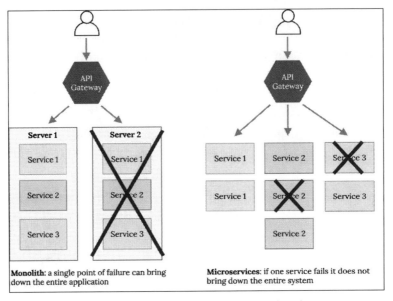

Figure 1.5: *Monolith vs. microservices: Fault Tolerance*

Communication

Monolithic architecture: Communication within a monolithic application is typically done through internal calls to other components within the same codebase.

Microservices: Communication between microservices is typically done through APIs or event channels, allowing for loose coupling and independent evolution of services.

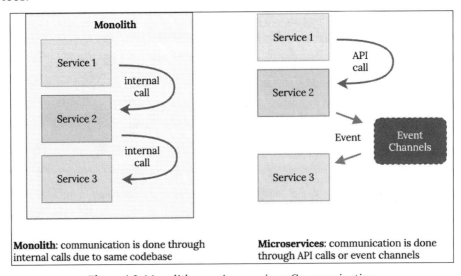

Figure 1.6: *Monolith vs. microservices: Communication*

Modularity and Reusability

Monolithic architecture: Monolithic applications are typically less modular and less reusable, as components are tightly coupled and difficult to extract and reuse in other contexts.

Microservices: Microservices promote modularity and reusability, as each service has a specific purpose and can be easily reused in other contexts.

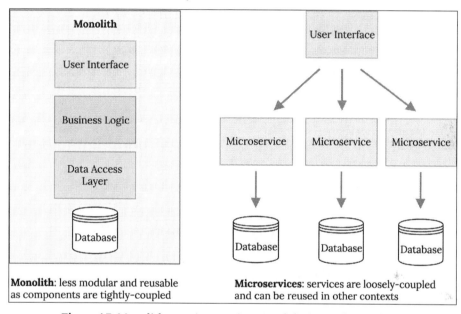

Figure 1.7: *Monolith vs. microservices: Modularity and Reusability*

Advantages of Microservices

One of the key benefits of microservices is that they enable teams to develop, deploy, and scale different services independently. This makes development faster since teams can work in parallel on different services. It also enables easier scaling, since individual services can be scaled based on demand rather than scaling the entire monolithic application.

In addition, microservices promote loose coupling between different components, so changes to one service do not necessitate changes to other services. This enhances flexibility and maintainability.

Microservices are also designed to be resilient, so if one service fails, the application as a whole continues to function. The loose coupling and independent nature of microservices also make it easier for different services to use different technologies best suited for their specific functions.

Here are some key advantages of using microservices:

- **Modularity**: Microservices are modular and loosely coupled, allowing different services to be developed, deployed, and scaled independently. This makes continuous development and deployment easier.

- **Scalability**: Services can be scaled horizontally by deploying instances as needed, allowing for high scalability. Resources can be allocated to specific services as needed.

- **Maintainability**: Code is organized around business domains rather than technology layers, making the codebase easier to understand and maintain. Individual services are also smaller and faster to change.

- **Flexibility**: Services can be implemented using different programming languages, frameworks, and data stores based on what fits their specific requirements rather than having to fit a monolithic architecture.

- **Resilience**: Issues with one service are less likely to bring down other services. The overall system is less fragile and failures can be isolated.

- **Reusability**: Services are designed to be independently deployable and platform agnostic, making them reusable across different projects and platforms.

Overall, microservices provide faster development, easier scaling, enhanced maintainability, and resilience compared to monolithic architectures.

Project Time: Introducing Our E-commerce Platform

In this book, we will work together to build a large e-commerce platform, using an event-driven microservices architecture, which we will call **Shopme**. The goal is to combine theoretical concepts with practical examples, so you can see how the ideas apply in the real world. We will build **Shopme** from scratch and add new components over time, improving the architecture as we go. By the end of the book, you will have hands-on experience with advanced event-driven microservices architectural patterns and techniques.

We are very optimistic that **Shopme** will become an extremely successful global e-commerce platform, processing millions of purchases daily. To achieve this, we must build a system that is scalable, always available, and easily extensible without compromising stability. There is much exciting work ahead as we start building the foundation of Shopme. We will begin by looking at some core services and functionality.

E-commerce platforms require an *ordering system* and so does Shopme. We will begin by building our first use case using a simple microservices architecture. The microservices of the ordering system could include:

- **Order Service**: Receives and processes orders
- **Inventory Service**: Manages product inventory count and availability
- **Payment Service**: Handles payments
- **Fulfilment Service**: Manages order shipping and fulfilment

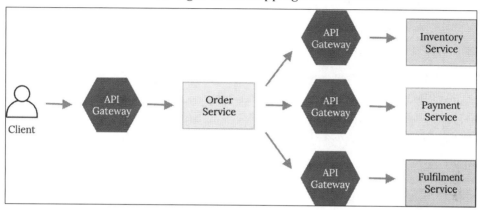

Figure 1.8: *Synchronous request-response microservices architecture*

The architecture flows such that when a user places an order through the user interface, a new API call is sent to the Order Service to process the order. The Order Service then calls the Inventory Service to check the availability and update the product inventory count, followed by the Payment Service to handle payment, and finally the Fulfilment Service to ship the order to the user.

Shopme utilizes a synchronous **request-response** architecture for communication between its services. A request-response architecture is a communication model in which a client sends a request to a server, and the server responds with a response. This model is commonly used in web applications and other distributed systems.

While the request-response architecture is a widely used and effective communication model, it does have some disadvantages that must be considered when designing distributed systems such as:

- **Latency**: The request-response model can introduce latency due to the time it takes for the server to process the request and generate a response. This can be particularly problematic in distributed systems where the server and client are located in different geographical locations.
- **Scalability**: The request-response model can be difficult to scale, as the server must handle each request individually. This can lead to bottlenecks and performance issues as the number of requests increases.
- **Blocking**: The client has to wait for the server's response before continuing. This can result in performance bottlenecks if the server cannot handle concurrent requests efficiently.

- **Complexity**: The request-response model can be complex to implement, as it requires the development of a server-side application that can handle requests and generate responses. This can increase the development time and cost.

- **Tight coupling**: The request-response model introduces tight coupling between clients and servers. Clients directly call specific server endpoints, creating dependencies. Changes to the server require changes on the client side.

A solution that can help us overcome those challenges is **event-driven architecture**. In the following section, we will explore the specific challenges that event-driven architectures aim to tackle.

The Rise of Event-Driven Architectures

Event-driven architectures emerged as a response to the growing complexity and scalability challenges faced by traditional monolithic applications. In traditional monolithic architectures, different components of an application are tightly coupled, making it difficult to scale individual components independently. As the application grows, scaling the entire monolith becomes a daunting task, leading to performance bottlenecks and increased maintenance costs. Event-driven architectures address this issue by decoupling components into smaller and independent services that communicate with each other through events. This loose coupling allows each service to scale independently, improving overall system scalability and resilience.

Furthermore, event-driven architectures provide better support for distributed systems and microservices architectures. In a microservices environment, services need to communicate and coordinate their actions. Event-driven architectures facilitate this communication by enabling services to publish and subscribe to events, ensuring that relevant information flows seamlessly between components. This loose coupling between services reduces dependencies and promotes greater flexibility and agility in the system.

Another benefit of event-driven architectures is their ability to handle asynchronous processes more effectively. Traditional request-response architectures can struggle with long-running tasks or situations where immediate responses are not required. Event-driven architectures decouple the producer of an event from the consumer, allowing for asynchronous processing and better utilization of system resources. This is particularly useful in scenarios such as message queuing, data streaming, and real-time event processing.

Moreover, event-driven architectures enable better fault tolerance and resiliency. Since components are decoupled, failures in one component do not necessarily affect the entire system. Events can be persisted and replayed, ensuring that no data is lost in case of failures. Additionally, event-driven architectures often employ patterns like circuit breakers and retries, further enhancing the system's ability to recover from failures.

The upcoming sections will provide an in-depth exploration of event-driven architectures.

Defining Event-Driven Architecture

Event-driven architecture (EDA) is a software architecture pattern that promotes the production, detection, consumption, and reaction to events. In **EDA**, software components called event producers generate **events** and publish them. Other components called event consumers subscribe to events of interest and execute logic upon receipt of those events. This loose coupling between event producers and consumers enables flexible and scalable architectures.

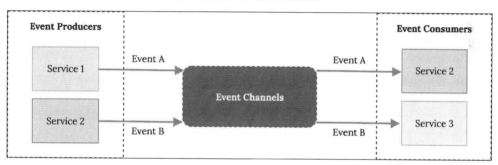

Figure 1.9: *Producers publish events to channels, which are delivered to consumers*

The key aspects of EDA include:

- Components interact by emitting and reacting to **events**. An **event** is any significant change in state that components need to be aware of.

- **Events** are published to an **event channel**, which delivers them to subscribed components. The publishers of events don't know or care which components will handle the events.

- Subscribing components handle the **events** asynchronously by listening on the **event bus** and taking action when relevant events occur. This avoids complex dependencies and coupling between components.

- **EDA** promotes loose coupling, scalability, and flexibility by allowing you to evolve components independently as long as they conform to the established events. Components can be added or removed without affecting the rest of the flow.

- **Events** serve as triggers for taking action, but they also act as a log of state changes for the whole system, like an **audit trail**.

EDA is well-suited for distributed systems that need to react to events coming from many different sources, like websites reacting to user interactions or microservices processing transactions. The decentralization and asynchronous event handling make the architecture scalable and resilient.

Key Components of Event-Driven Architectures

As shown in *Figure 1.9*, the key components of event-driven architectures are as follows:

- **Events**: An event is a change in state that is significant within a system. It captures something that happened in the system at a specific point in time. Events can be triggered by user actions, sensors, schedules, and more.

- **Event producers**: An event producer is any component of the system that generates and publishes events. Examples producers include user interfaces, IoT devices, API calls, and more. Producers create and publish event data into the system. For example, a button click produces a *"button clicked"* event.

- **Event consumers**: An event consumer is any component of the system that listens for and reacts to events. Consumers subscribe to certain events and take action when those events occur, such as executing business logic. Example consumers include application servers, analytics engines, and more.

- **Event channels**: The channels that events are published through. This allows producers and consumers to communicate without tightly coupling them. For example, an event bus or message queue.

Benefits of Event-Driven Architectures

Event-driven architectures are gaining popularity as an alternative to traditional request-response models for building scalable, high-performance applications. EDA comes with several benefits as an architectural style. Here are some:

- **Loose coupling**: Components are loosely coupled since they communicate indirectly through events rather than directly calling each other's APIs. This makes the system more modular and flexible.

- **Scalability**: It's easy to scale out event processing across multiple nodes since events can be distributed via a message queue. New instances just need to subscribe to the event queue.

- **Flexibility**: New event sources and event consumers can be added independently without affecting existing flow. This supports agile development.

- **Real-time processing**: Events are processed as they occur rather than in batches. This enables real-time decision making.

- **Auditability**: Events provide an audit trail that can be replayed to reconstruct what happened in the system for debugging or analysis.

- **Responsiveness**: Systems can react to events as they happen for faster response times.

- **Asynchronous communication**: Event producers don't block while emitting events. Consumers can process events asynchronously at their own pace.

- **Fault tolerance**: If an event consumer goes down, events can be replayed to it upon recovery without losing data.

Having covered the fundamental principles and advantages of microservices and event-driven architectures, we will now explore how these two approaches can be integrated.

Combining Microservices and Event-Driven Architectures

Microservices and **event-driven** architecture can work very well together. As discussed previously, microservices are small and independent services that focus on specific business capability, which makes them loosely coupled, flexible, and scalable. Event-driven architecture uses events to trigger actions and communications between decoupled services.

For example, when one microservice updates a customer record, it can publish an event. Other microservices subscribe to events and take action when certain events occur. This allows different microservices to react to business events without tight coupling between the services.

An **event channel** handles publishing and subscribing to events. Overall, an event-driven approach helps enable communication and coordination between decoupled microservices. It promotes loose coupling by acting as an intermediary between services. Events allow services to broadcast notifications and updates globally across a system. This event-driven approach complements the focused and modular nature of microservices very well.

Event-driven microservices are well-suited for many modern applications that need to respond to events happening across distributed systems in **real-time**. Some of the most common use cases include delivering personalized user experiences, implementing complex business workflows, integrating heterogeneous systems, and building reactive applications.

For example, an e-commerce site could use event-driven microservices to update a user's cart in real-time as they add or remove items, trigger notifications when an item goes on sale, and process orders asynchronously using event queues. Ride-sharing and food delivery apps also rely on events like driver location updates and order statuses to coordinate the state of their systems. Beyond consumer apps, supply chain systems can leverage events for tracking inventory across locations.

Event-driven architecture helps enterprise integration by standardizing events from disparate sources into a unified stream for downstream services to consume. Overall, event-driven microservices enable scalable and flexible architectures by decoupling services and avoiding direct dependencies between them. The lightweight nature of events makes them perfect for modern distributed applications.

Companies like Netflix, Amazon, Uber, eBay, Twitter, Spotify, PayPal, and many others use event-driven microservices to decompose large applications into independently scalable and manageable services. This helps with agility, scalability, and maintainability.

Difference Between Event-Driven Architecture and Traditional Architecture

Event-driven architecture is a software design paradigm that differs significantly from traditional request-response architectures. In a request-response architecture, a client sends a request to a server, which processes the request and sends back a response. The client waits for the response and then continues its processing.

In contrast, EDA is based on the **publish-subscribe pattern**, where events are published and subscribed to by different components. Events are data objects that represent things that have happened or will happen in the system. These events are typically stored in an **event queue** or a **message broker**, which acts as a central hub for communication between different components.

The components of the system, known as event handlers or event-driven services, subscribe to events of interest and process them as they occur. This allows for more real-time and responsive systems, as components can react to events as they happen, rather than waiting for a request from another component.

EDA also promotes loose coupling between components, as they don't need to know about each other explicitly. They only need to be aware of the events they are interested in. This makes the system more scalable and flexible, as adding or removing components can be done without affecting the rest of the system.

EDA is commonly used in distributed systems, microservices, and cloud-native applications due to its scalability, flexibility, and ability to handle complex event-driven workflows.

Deciding When to Use or Avoid Event-Driven Architecture

Event-driven architecture has numerous advantages, but it also has some limitations that make it unsuitable for certain use cases. Event-driven systems work best for asynchronous, decoupled domains with complex event-based processing needs. Simpler and synchronous processing may be better served by other architectures. Here are some guidelines on when event-driven architecture is useful and when it may not be the best choice.

Use event-driven architecture when:

- You need to *decouple* different components of the system. Events allow loose coupling between event producers and consumers.
- You need *high scalability and flexibility*. It's easy to add new event producers/ consumers without affecting others.
- You want to implement *reactive programming models* that react to events asynchronously.
- You need to audit or log events like user actions, state changes, and more. The event log provides an audit trail.
- You want to *integrate or orchestrate* multiple systems by listening to events from each one.

Avoid event-driven architecture when:

- Your domain has simple requirements and not much asynchronous processing. An event-driven system can add unnecessary complexity.
- You need highly predictable processing and guaranteed order of operations. Event handling can be less deterministic.
- Your team is inexperienced with event-driven programming. It requires a different approach to design and testing.
- Low latency is a key requirement. Synchronous communication may be faster for some use cases.
- Events are not natural or frequent in your problem domain. Forcing an event-driven style can feel unnatural.

Project Time: Migrating Our E-commerce Platform to Event-Driven

When we first designed **Shopme**, our major e-commerce platform, we utilized a microservices request-response architecture. However, we noticed some clear drawbacks with this approach over time. We have now decided to transition **Shopme** to an event-driven architecture, which we expect will provide certain advantages compared to our initial design.

Figure 1.10 illustrates the new event-driven architecture for the ordering system, which uses asynchronous communication between microservices. Instead of direct synchronous calls, the microservices now communicate by sending and receiving events over an event channel. This decouples the microservices and allows them to react to events independently.

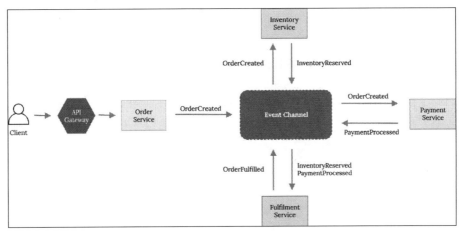

Figure 1.10: *Event-driven architecture for the ordering system*

The architecture flow has now changed to:

- The **Order Service** publishes an `OrderCreated` event to the event channel when a user places an order.

- The `OrderCreated` event triggers the **Inventory Service** to reserve product inventory. If the product inventory reservation is successful, it publishes an `InventoryReserved` event.

- The `OrderCreated` event also triggers the **Payment Service** to process payment and publishes a `PaymentProcessed` event.

- The `InventoryReserved` and `PaymentProcessed` events trigger the **Fulfilment Service** to ship the order to the user which then publishes an `OrderFulfiled` event.

The ordering system utilizes an event-driven architecture, which enables the microservices to be loosely coupled, non-blocking, and scalable. However, we have not yet examined how users are notified when a new payment must be processed or when an order is successfully placed. We will explore those notification mechanisms in depth in the upcoming chapters.

Conclusion

Event-driven microservices are a modern architectural approach that can help developers build scalable, resilient, and flexible applications. By splitting monoliths into independently deployable services and connecting them via asynchronous events, teams can reap many benefits. Event-driven microservices provide loose coupling, scalability, flexibility, fault tolerance, and performance benefits over synchronous request/response architectures.

Originally, we designed our large e-commerce platform using a basic request-response microservices architecture. Later, we migrated to an event-driven architecture and observed clear benefits. In the next chapter, we will explore various event-driven architectural patterns and apply them to our platform using AWS services to demonstrate event-driven microservices in practice.

CHAPTER 2

Designing Event-Driven Microservices in AWS

Introduction

This chapter covers designing event-driven architectures using AWS serverless services. We will start by defining serverless computing and discussing how AWS serverless provides automated scalability and availability. Then, we will look at implementing the microservices business logic with AWS Lambda and building APIs with Amazon API Gateway. After that, we will discuss AWS integration services for creating distributed, event-driven workflows, including Amazon SQS, Amazon SNS, Amazon EventBridge, AWS Step Functions, and Amazon Kinesis. We will also cover serverless-friendly data storage options like Amazon S3 and Amazon DynamoDB. By the end of the chapter, you will understand how to leverage AWS serverless to implement event-driven patterns like point-to-point messaging, publish/subscribe, fan-out, event sourcing, CQRS, event streaming, and more. In subsequent chapters, we will build examples of the patterns covered here.

Structure

In this chapter, we will discuss the following topics:

- Serverless in AWS
- Microservices and APIs with AWS Lambda and Amazon API Gateway
- Messaging with Amazon SQS and Amazon SNS
- Choreography with Amazon EventBridge
- Orchestration with AWS Step Functions
- Streaming with Amazon Kinesis

- Data Stores with Amazon S3 and Amazon DynamoDB
- Event-Driven Design Patterns: Point-to-Point Messaging, Publish/Subscribe, Fan-out, Event Sourcing, CQRS, Scheduler, Claim Check, Circuit Breaker, SAGA, Streaming Data Ingestion, Data Pipeline, Real-Time Analytics

Defining Serverless

This book guides you through creating **event-driven microservices** use cases using **Amazon Web Services (AWS)** serverless offerings. We will begin by explaining the concept of **serverless**. After that foundation is set, we can delve into the specifics.

Serverless, also known as **serverless computing,** refers to cloud computing architectures where the provider manages the servers and infrastructure for you. Serverless abstracts away server management and *lets developers focus just on their application code.* It provides *automatic scaling* and *pay-per-use billing,* making it attractive for many workloads. The cloud provider handles provisioning and managing servers.

The key characteristics of serverless architectures are:

- **No need to provision or manage servers**: The cloud provider handles this automatically for you.
- **Pay-per-use pricing**: You only pay for the resources used when your code is executed, and you don't pay for idle capacity.
- **Auto-scaling**: The system scales up and down automatically based on demand.
- **Highly available**: The system has built-in high availability.
- **Built-in security**: The security is managed by the cloud provider.
- **Event-driven**: Code can be triggered to run in response to events like HTTP requests, database changes, queue messages, and so on.

The AWS serverless services covered in this book can be grouped into three main categories:

- **Compute**: AWS Lambda
- **Integration**: Amazon API Gateway, Amazon SQS, Amazon SNS, Amazon EventBridge, AWS Step Functions, Amazon Kinesis
- **Data stores**: Amazon S3, Amazon DynamoDB

Note: *This is not an exhaustive list of AWS serverless offerings. We will focus on only some key services in this book. Other notable AWS serverless services not covered here include* **AWS Fargate,** *a serverless compute engine for containers that works with* **Amazon Elastic Container Service (ECS)** *and* **Amazon Elastic Kubernetes Service (EKS),** **Amazon Aurora Serverless,** *a serverless relational database compatible with MySQL and*

PostgreSQL, *and* **Amazon Managed Streaming for Apache Kafka (MSK)**, *a serverless version of Apache Kafka.*

Next, we will examine how the AWS serverless services attain high availability and scalability.

High Availability and Scalability of AWS Serverless

AWS operates *data centers* around the world to provide a *highly available* and *low latency* experience for customers. AWS divides its infrastructure into **Regions** and **Availability zones**.

Regions are located in different areas of the world. Each Region contains multiple isolated locations known as Availability Zones. At the time of writing, there are more than 30 geographic AWS Regions, including *North America, Europe, Asia Pacific, South America,* and the *Middle East.*

The Availability Zones within a Region provide inexpensive, low-latency network connectivity between zones but are isolated from failures in other Availability Zones. Each Availability Zone runs on its own physically distinct and independent infrastructure. The Availability Zones have redundant power, networking, and connectivity designed to be highly reliable. This allows customers to operate production applications and databases that are more highly available, fault-tolerant, and scalable than would be possible from a single data center.

The AWS infrastructure provides customers with the scale and availability needed to deploy applications across geographic Regions with high availability, fault tolerance, and low latency.

The AWS serverless services provide native high availability capabilities through *multi-AZ* (multi–Availability Zone) redundancy. The services handle replication, failovers, and scaling, relieving developers of these tasks. For example, **AWS Lambda** achieves high availability by running functions across multiple Availability Zones in a Region automatically. Even if one zone goes down, Lambda will redistribute functions to healthy zones. Lambda also scales out dynamically to handle load changes. So, if demand increases, Lambda will rapidly provision additional capacity across Availability Zones to process events.

Similarly, **Amazon API Gateway** provides high availability by deploying API endpoints across multiple Availability Zones automatically. Even if an entire zone goes down, API Gateway will direct traffic to the healthy zones without any interruption. It also scales seamlessly as traffic increases to maintain high performance.

Now, let's explore AWS Lambda and Amazon API Gateway in detail since these services will play a central role in our architecture.

Microservices with AWS Lambda

AWS Lambda is an ideal AWS serverless service for event-driven microservices. Lambda removes the hassle of installing runtimes, application servers, and other dependencies just to run a web application. With Lambda, you simply write your code and AWS handles deploying and running it for you. This serverless approach allows you to focus on writing code without worrying about infrastructure. Lambda's *auto-scaling* and *pay-per-use pricing* make it a very compelling service for modern applications.

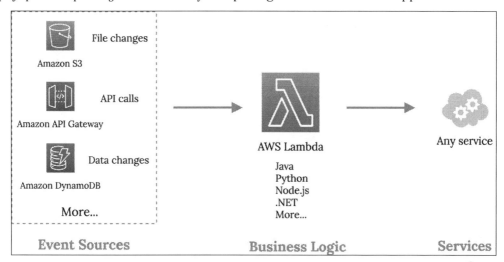

Figure 2.1: *AWS Lambda is triggered in response to events, contains business logic, and supports various programming languages*

Here are some key things to know about AWS Lambda:

- **Serverless**: Lambda allows you to run code without having to provision or manage servers. AWS handles all the server and infrastructure management.

- **Event-driven**: Lambda functions are invoked in response to events such as changes to data in Amazon S3 or Amazon DynamoDB, as illustrated in *Figure 2.1*.

- **Pay per use**: You are charged based on the number of requests served and the runtime of your functions. There is no charge when your functions are not running.

- **Scalable**: Lambda automatically scales to meet demand without any additional configuration.

- **Stateless**: Lambda functions are independent and isolated stateless functions.

- **Various languages**: Lambda supports a variety of languages, including Java, Node.js, Python, .NET, and more.

- **Integration**: Lambda integrates with many other AWS services like Amazon

API Gateway, Amazon Kinesis, Amazon S3, Amazon DynamoDB, and so on, making it useful for serverless applications.

Here are some common use cases and examples of how AWS Lambda can be used:

- **Serverless APIs**: Build REST APIs that run code in response to HTTP requests without having to manage servers. This is useful for lightweight microservices and API backends.

- **Data processing**: Run code to transform or process data as it comes into AWS services like Amazon S3, Amazon DynamoDB, Amazon Kinesis, and so on. This allows on-demand processing without servers.

- **Automated tasks**: Schedule Lambda functions to run code on a regular schedule (*cron jobs*) or trigger them in response to custom events to automate workflows.

- **Real-time file processing**: Process uploads to Amazon S3 by automatically triggering a Lambda function to run code every time a new object is uploaded. This is useful for transforming data, image analysis, and so on.

- **IoT backends**: Execute Lambda functions in response to IoT events, such as data streams from IoT sensors or custom events from IoT applications.

- **Chatbots and Alexa skills**: Run code in response to chatbot interactions or Alexa voice commands by integrating Lambda with services like Amazon Lex, Amazon Connect, and Alexa Skills Kit.

- **Serverless websites**: Build entire websites hosted on Amazon S3/Amazon CloudFront that run Lambda functions for dynamic page generation or API endpoints. It removes all backend servers.

Overall, **AWS Lambda** is a simple, cost-efficient, and powerful service to run your code without thinking about servers. The serverless architecture enabled by Lambda is revolutionizing how modern applications are built today.

AWS Lambda: Working Under the Hood

AWS introduced **AWS Lambda** in 2014 as a **serverless computing** service where AWS handles all server management and customers pay only for resources used. Initially, Lambda was built using traditional VMs, which provide strong isolation between customers but add computational overhead versus containers.

As customers requested faster scaling, lower latency, and features like provisioned concurrency, AWS realized traditional VMs limited these capabilities. So, they built **Firecracker**, released in 2018, which combines the security of hardware virtualization with the efficiency of containers.

Firecracker's stripped-down virtual machine monitor (VMM), with just 50,000 lines of secure **Rust** code (versus over 1 million in traditional VMs), allows for the creation of **lightweight microVMs** extremely quickly. This is a significant efficiency gain over traditional VMs.

Firecracker achieves simplicity by removing unneeded devices and instead uses optimized **virtio** interfaces for guest OS communication. Virtio is a virtualization standard for device drivers that provides a mechanism for efficient communication between virtual machines and their host systems. By utilizing virtio interfaces, Firecracker avoids resource-intensive emulation of complex physical devices. Instead, it relies on optimized virtio interfaces for essential functionality like networking and storage. As serverless workloads don't require complex hardware, Firecracker omits those features.

Building APIs with Amazon API Gateway

As mentioned earlier, a microservices architecture relies on an API gateway to serve as the sole entry point to the backend system. **Amazon API Gateway** is an API gateway service offered by AWS that can fulfill this role.

Amazon API Gateway is a fully managed service that makes it easy for developers to create, publish, maintain, monitor, and secure APIs at any scale. Amazon API Gateway integrates seamlessly with many AWS services, including AWS Lambda, as illustrated in *Figure 2.2*.

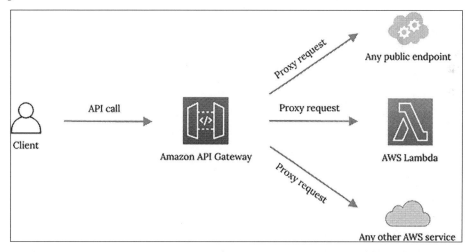

Figure 2.2: *Amazon API Gateway triggers and proxies requests to any public endpoints and AWS services including AWS Lambda*

Some key features of Amazon API Gateway include:

- **API creation**: Easily create REST, HTTP, and WebSocket APIs. Developers can import existing API definitions or create them from scratch.

- **Deployment and management**: API Gateway handles all the tasks involved in deploying and running your APIs, including provisioning, access control, monitoring, and version/environment management. APIs can be deployed to multiple stages like test, dev, prod, and so on.

- **Security**: API Gateway provides various security features, such as API keys, OAuth 2.0, AWS IAM permissions, CORS, throttling, and so on, to safeguard your API infrastructure and backend systems.

- **Scalability**: API Gateway is designed to scale seamlessly to handle increasing traffic on your APIs. It can handle requests in the range of hundreds of thousands per second.

- **Monitoring**: Detailed metrics and dashboards are provided by API Gateway to monitor API calls and trace errors. Amazon CloudWatch integration allows logging API execution logs.

- **API Caching**: Caching of API responses is supported to reduce calls made to backend and improve latency. Caching can be customized for each stage.

- **Throttling**: API Gateway includes rate limiting and burst capabilities, allowing you to control the maximum number of requests per second and the initial burst of requests that can be processed before enforcing the rate limit.

Note: *How **AWS Lambda** autoscales when triggered by **Amazon API gateway**?*

Lambda functions automatically scale to handle concurrent requests triggered by Amazon API Gateway or any other event source. API Gateway can receive thousands of requests per second and invoke Lambda to execute the function for each request.

Lambda provides a secure and isolated execution environment for running Lambda functions. When a Lambda function is invoked, Lambda provisions an execution environment specifically for that function instance. The execution environment contains the runtime implementation for the programming language used to develop the function and other components needed to run the code.

Lambda functions are stateless, so they can rapidly scale horizontally. When requests increase, Lambda automatically provisions additional execution environments to run concurrent instances of the function in parallel.

You do not have to manually provision infrastructure. Lambda and API Gateway manage all the scaling in real-time based on traffic patterns. When requests decrease, Lambda scales down by shutting down unused execution environments that are no longer needed, minimizing cost during periods of low traffic.

The auto-scaling allows the Lambda functions to handle a massive volume of concurrent requests. The time required to initialize new execution environments, known as cold starts, and the maximum request throughput depend on how fast Lambda can scale to meet increasing demand from API Gateway.

The Popularity of Amazon API Gateway

Over the past few years, **Amazon API Gateway** has emerged as a leading API management service, experiencing rapid adoption and growth. Amazon API Gateway was first announced by AWS in 2015 and has become one of the most popular offerings within AWS's portfolio. API Gateway has handled tremendous growth in API call volume since its launch and now powers APIs for thousands of customers.

The growth of Amazon API Gateway reflects the expanding adoption of APIs across industries. Companies are recognizing the benefits of API-led connectivity for unlocking business value. Amazon API Gateway removes the complexity of API management and accelerates API deployments. With its continuing evolution and integration with other AWS services, Amazon API Gateway is poised to remain a leading API management platform.

Event-Driven Integration Services in AWS

In this book, we will explore several AWS offerings used to decouple services, including **Amazon SQS**, **Amazon SNS**, **Amazon EventBridge**, **AWS Step Functions**, and **Amazon Kinesis**. Because these services are serverless, we do not need to provision servers or manage scaling manually.

With the exception of **AWS Step Functions**, these services use an **event channel** for communication between producers and consumers. The event channel allows events to be published in a decoupled manner, avoiding tight coupling between producers and consumers.

AWS offers three types of event channels to enable event-driven architectures: **message queues**, **event routes**, and **data streams**. Each channel serves a different purpose and is supported by a distinct AWS service. Let's examine each event channel more closely.

Message Queues

Message queues are a *data structure* that enable *asynchronous event processing* by decoupling event producers and consumers. Events are added to a queue by producers and pulled off by consumers for handling. The queue acts as a *buffer*, storing events until they can be processed.

Queues store events in **first-in, first-out (FIFO)** order. New events are added to the end of the queue, while consumers remove events from the front, as shown in *Figure* 2.3. This ordering prevents events from being missed or handled out of sequence.

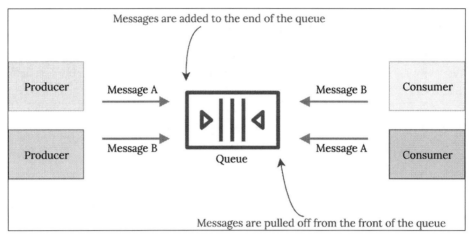

Figure 2.3: *In message queue systems, each message can only be processed by a single consumer*

A key benefit of queues is that they decouple producers and consumers. Producers can rapidly generate events without concern for how busy consumers are, while consumers can handle events at their own pace. The queue buffers events safely until consumers are ready.

Queues help prevent consumers from falling behind on event handling. The size of the queue can be tuned to provide sufficient buffering without excessive memory usage. Multiple consumers can also pull from a queue in parallel, allowing the queue to *load balance* work across a consumer group.

Common queue implementations in AWS include **Amazon SQS**, a serverless message queuing service, and **Amazon MQ**, a managed message broker service that supports **Apache ActiveMQ** and **RabbitMQ**. This book focuses solely on Amazon SQS and does not cover Amazon MQ, as at the time of writing, Amazon MQ does not offer a serverless version.

Event Routes

Event routes allow you to *match* incoming events and automatically send them to one or more *targets*. A route consists of a *matching rule* and a *target*.

The rule matches events based on *event pattern* matching or filtering by source. For example, you can create a rule that matches any events from Amazon S3 starting with *images*.

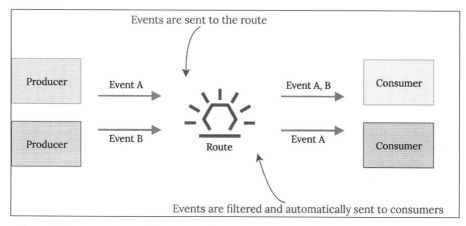

Figure 2.4: *Event routes allow a single event to be distributed to multiple consumers*

The target dictates where to send events when a rule is triggered. Targets can include AWS Lambda functions, Amazon Kinesis streams, Amazon SQS queues, and more. You can send events to multiple targets at once.

Common route implementations in AWS include **Amazon EventBridge**, a serverless event bus service, and **Amazon SNS**, a serverless notification service.

Data Streams

A **data stream** is a *sequence of events* that are organized into an *immutable append-only* log. Once events are added to a stream, they stay there forever in the order they were added. New events can only be appended to the end of the stream: earlier events in the stream cannot be changed or deleted.

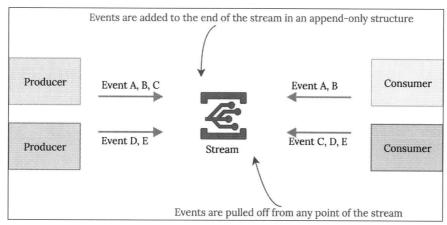

Figure 2.5: *Data streams allow consumers to process a stream of events in the order they arrive*

The immutable and ordered nature of streams allows them to capture a complete history of events over time. Since streams are durable, the entire event history remains available for replay even if consumers temporarily disconnect. Multiple different consumers can subscribe to the same stream, and each will receive and process the events in the same order, but consumers do not have to process events at exactly the same time.

The *append-only structure* makes streams well-suited for capturing event histories that can then be processed, analyzed, audited, and so on. Consumers can join the stream at any point and process new events as they are added, *rewind* and *replay* historical events, *fast-forward* to the latest event, or consume the stream in various other ways. By subscribing to a stream, consumers get durable, ordered, replayable access to a complete event history.

Common stream implementations in AWS include **Amazon Kinesis** and **Amazon Managed Streaming for Apache Kafka (MSK)**. This book will focus exclusively on Amazon Kinesis and will not include coverage of Amazon MSK.

Event-Driven Design Patterns

Table 2.1 provides a list of common event-driven design patterns covered in the book, along with the AWS services used to implement each pattern.

Architecture/ Design pattern	Description	AWS Services
Microservices	Decoupled services that contain business logic	AWS Lambda
API Gateway	Serves as the entry point to the microservices	Amazon API Gateway
Point-to-point messaging	Messages are sent from one sender to one receiver	Amazon SQS
Publish/subscribe	Messages are published to multiple receivers	Amazon SNS
Fan-out	Same message is sent to multiple receivers	Amazon SQS Amazon SNS
Event sourcing	Publish domain events that represent state changes	Amazon EventBridge
CQRS	Separates read and write operations for a data store	Amazon EventBridge Amazon DynamoDB
Scheduler	Trigger workflows on a schedule	Amazon EventBridge
Claim check	Send large payloads to receivers	Amazon EventBridge Amazon S3
Circuit breaker	Stop processing events if too many are failing	AWS Step Functions

SAGA	Manage long-running business transactions	AWS Step Functions
Streaming data ingestion	Continuously ingest high volumes of data	Amazon Kinesis Data Streams
Data pipeline	Pass data between services	Amazon Kinesis Firehose
Real-time analytics	Process and analyze streams in real-time	Amazon Managed Service for Apache Flink

Table 2.1: *Event-Driven Design Patterns covered in this book*

In the previous chapter, we explored microservices and API Gateways using AWS Lambda and Amazon API Gateway. Now, we will take a deeper look into messaging in AWS.

Messaging with Amazon SQS and Amazon SNS

Messaging is a key component of many applications and services today. It allows different components of an application to communicate *asynchronously* and *decouple processes*. AWS provides several managed services for messaging that make it easy to add messaging capabilities to applications without running your own messaging infrastructure. The AWS services that we will examine are **Amazon Simple Queue Service (Amazon SQS)** and **Amazon Simple Notification Service (Amazon SNS)**.

Amazon SQS

Amazon Simple Queue Service (Amazon SQS) is a fully managed message queuing service that enables the decoupling and scaling of microservices, distributed systems, and serverless applications. SQS allows users to send, store, and receive messages between software components through a **queue model**. It enables asynchronous messaging and decoupling application components so they can run independently.

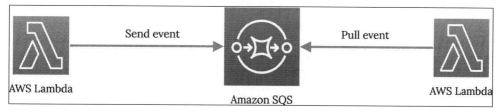

Figure 2.6: *Amazon SQS is a pull-based messaging service and integrates seamlessly with AWS Lambda*

Here are some key features of Amazon SQS:

- **Managed message queues**: SQS handles all the infrastructure and management required to run highly available queues.
- **Scalable**: SQS queues can handle virtually any throughput load and automatically scale to meet demand.
- **Reliable**: Messages are stored redundantly across multiple servers and data centers.
- **Message visibility timeout**: Provides a timeout period for processing a message during which it won't be returned to other consumers.
- **Message retention**: Messages can be retained in the queue for up to 14 days.
- **Delay queues**: Set a delay period before a message becomes available in the queue.
- **FIFO queues**: Preserve the exact order in which messages are sent and received with no duplicates, making them useful when order is critical.
- **Dead letter queues**: Redirect messages that can't be processed to a dead letter queue.
- **Pricing**: Pay-as-you go pricing with no upfront costs.

Common use cases for Amazon SQS include:

- **Decoupling applications**: SQS allows you to decouple application components so they can run independently, making applications more resilient.
- **Work distribution**: SQS can be used to distribute tasks and process data in parallel by multiple components.
- **Scaling microservices**: SQS queues can help scale individual microservices independently to meet demand.
- **Smooth out traffic spikes**: Queues can help handle temporary traffic spikes by buffering requests for processing during traffic dips.
- **Retry logic**: Failed messages can be automatically retried using SQS queues.
- **Job workflow**: SQS queues can coordinate and manage sequences of jobs and steps in a workflow.

Amazon SQS is a reliable, scalable, and flexible message queuing service. It takes care of the underlying infrastructure and helps developers build asynchronous, event-driven architectures. SQS integrates well with other AWS services and is commonly used for decoupling application components across a microservices architecture.

Amazon SNS

Amazon Simple Notification Service (Amazon SNS) is a managed service that provides message delivery from publishers to subscribers (also called producers and consumers). SNS works on a **publish/subscribe** model where the publishers publish messages to **topics,** and subscribers who are interested can subscribe to those topics to receive the messages.

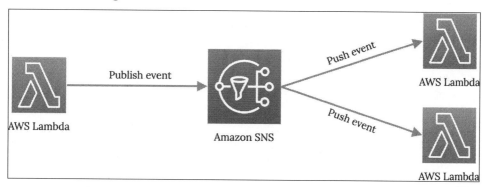

Figure 2.7: *Amazon SNS is a push-based messaging service and integrates seamlessly with AWS Lambda*

Here are some key features of SNS:

- **Push notifications**: SNS allows you to send push notifications to various endpoints like *Apple Push Notification Service* (APNS), *Google Cloud Messaging* (GCM), SMS, email, SQS queues, HTTP/S *webhooks*, and so on.

- **Topic-based pub/sub**: SNS allows publishers to send messages to a topic, and subscribers can subscribe to the topics they are interested in. This decouples the publishers and subscribers.

- **Access control**: SNS provides fine-grained access controls to allow and restrict publishers/subscribers from certain topics.

- **Reliability**: SNS stores the messages across multiple AZs to provide high availability and prevent message loss.

- **Scalability**: SNS is designed to scale to billions of messages per day without any degradation in performance.

- **Flexible message delivery**: Messages can be delivered over multiple transport protocols like SMTP, SMS, HTTP/S, and so on. Delivery retries and back-off timings can be configured.

- **Pricing**: You only pay for what you use, with no upfront fees.

Some common use cases for Amazon SNS include:

- **Application notifications**: Send notifications to users of an application, such as new messages, friend requests, appointment reminders, and so on.

- **System alerts and notifications**: Get notified for issues like a server going down, high CPU usage, errors, and so on. This allows you to respond quickly.

- **Email and SMS subscriptions**: Allow users to subscribe to topics and receive notifications via email or SMS when new messages are published.

- **Push notifications to mobile devices**: Send push notifications to apps on iOS, Android, Fire OS, and Windows devices.

- **Event publishing and fan-out**: Publish messages to SNS topics, which then *fan-out* and deliver to multiple subscribed endpoints like SQS queues, Lambda functions, HTTP webhooks, and so on.

- **Monitoring applications**: Applications can publish custom metrics and events to SNS, which can trigger alarms and workflows.

Amazon SNS provides a managed, highly scalable publish/subscribe messaging service that has broad use cases for event notifications, pub/sub messaging, mobile push notifications, and more. Its flexibility, reliability, and simple pricing make it easy to adopt.

Now, let's explore some messaging design patterns and AWS services that can be utilized to implement them.

Messaging Design Patterns

When architecting a distributed system, it is important to consider different messaging patterns and choose one that fits your use case. In the following sections, we will explore some common messaging design patterns: **point-to-point messaging**, **publish/subscribe messaging**, and **fan-out**. Let's examine the specifics of each pattern more closely, including when it is suitable to apply each one.

Point-to-Point Messaging

The **point-to-point messaging** pattern is a commonly used architecture for asynchronous messaging systems. It involves sending messages from one producer to one consumer via a message broker.

With point-to-point messaging, messages are *persisted* in a queue by the message broker. The messages in the queue can only be retrieved and processed by a single consumer. Once the message is consumed, it is removed from the queue.

This differs from publish/subscribe messaging where messages are broadcast to multiple subscribers. In point-to-point, there is a one-to-one relationship between the producer and consumer.

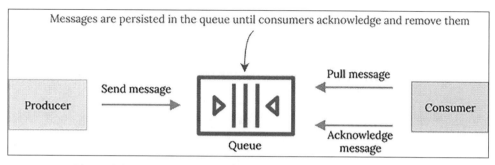

Figure 2.8: *In point-to-point messaging, a consumer acknowledges and removes a message from the queue after processing it*

Some key characteristics of point-to-point messaging:

- **Direct communication between two parties**: Messages are sent from one sender to one receiver.

- **Asynchronous and non-blocking**: The sender does not need to wait for the receiver to be available or ready before sending a message. The message is stored until the receiver can process it.

- **Persistent storage**: Messages are stored reliably, often in a queue, until the receiving party retrieves them. This prevents message loss if there is a system failure.

- **Message ordering**: Messages are typically kept in order as per the sending sequence. Newer messages are held until older ones are consumed first.

- **Acknowledgment and confirmation**: The system often confirms receipt and successful processing of the message. If a message fails, it can be redelivered.

- **Load balancing**: Messages may be distributed across multiple consumers/ receivers to balance the load.

Point-to-point messaging is commonly used for:

- **Workflow processing**: A message triggers the next step in a business process. Steps are decoupled and scaled independently.

- **Order processing**: An order message is consumed and processed only once, even if multiple consumers exist.

- **Integration**: Different applications are integrated via asynchronous messaging. Loose coupling reduces dependencies.

- **Batch processing**: Messages are stored during the day and processed in batches at night.

Amazon SQS provides a fully managed message queuing service that enables point-to-point communication between services in AWS.

Let's examine one approach for implementing point-to-point messaging: **asynchronous APIs**.

Asynchronous APIs

In modern application architectures, it is common to need to handle *asynchronous workloads* and *background processing* triggered by API *requests*. A simple and scalable way to enable this is to use an **API Gateway** with a **message queue**.

When an API request comes into API Gateway, instead of handling the request synchronously, API Gateway can be configured to send the request payload to a message queue. This allows the request to be processed asynchronously by consumers of the queue, as illustrated in *Figure 2.9*.

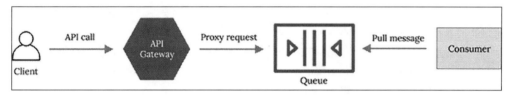

Figure 2.9: *With asynchronous API requests, the message queue allows the requests to be handled asynchronously rather than making the client wait for a response*

Some key benefits of this architecture:

- **Improved user experience**: The API client does not need to wait for potentially long-running processing. The client simply triggers the work and moves on.

- **Decoupled components**: The API gateway is just responsible for ingesting requests and forwarding them to the queue. The consumers of the queue handle processing asynchronously.

- **Scalability**: Message queues make it easy to scale up consumers and handle bursts of traffic.

- **Resiliency**: Requests are persisted in the queue until processed so they are not lost. Failed processing can be retried.

- **Auditability**: Requests and responses are logged through the message queue.

To implement this architecture in AWS, **Amazon API Gateway** should send the requests to **Amazon SQS** instead of directing them to the microservices.

Publish/Subscribe Messaging

Publish/subscribe messaging, also known as **pub/sub**, is a communication pattern in which senders of messages, known as publishers, do not send the messages directly to specific receivers, but instead send them to a distribution service, which is responsible for delivering the messages to interested receivers, known as *subscribers*.

This allows subscribers to subscribe to specific topics and receive notifications for new messages that are sent to those topics. Publishers do not have to know the identity of the subscribers, and the subscribers do not have to explicitly request to receive messages from specific publishers.

The distribution service acts as a mediator, routing messages to interested subscribers based on their interests, and allowing publishers to focus on sending messages without worrying about who will receive them.

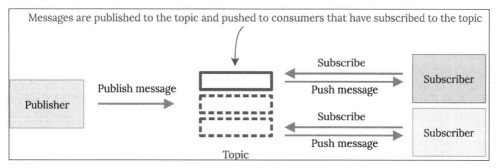

Figure 2.10: *The publish/subscribe messaging pattern requires that subscribers register their interest in a particular topic in order to receive messages published to that topic*

Some key characteristics of pub/sub messaging include:

- **Asynchronous communication**: Publishers and subscribers do not interact directly.

- **One-to-many messaging**: A single published message can be sent to multiple subscribers.

- **Decoupled architecture**: Publishers and subscribers are fully independent and unaware of each other.

- **Topic-based routing**: Subscribers receive only messages classified as relevant to the topics they subscribe to.

- **Message filtering**: Message brokers can filter messages based on content or rules to only send to appropriate subscribers.

- **Persistent storage**: Message brokers often store messages durably so they are not lost if subscribers are offline.

Pub/sub messaging is commonly used for *event notifications* in event-driven architectures. We will utilize **Amazon SNS** for implementing publish/subscribe messaging in AWS.

Fan-out Pattern

The **fan-out** pattern is a useful integration pattern for processing messages from a messaging system and routing them to multiple destinations. The fan-out pattern provides a way to take a single message from a *topic* and republish it to *multiple queues*, *topics*, or *services* for further processing. This allows different parts of a system to consume and process the same message independently and in parallel.

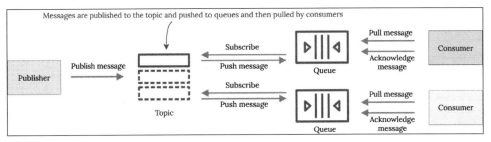

Figure 2.11: *The fan-out pattern involves publishing messages to a topic, which then distributes the messages to multiple queues*

The key benefits of the fan-out pattern are:

- **Reduced load on source system**: The source only sends data to one place, fanning it out from there.

- **Flexibility**: It's easy to add new destinations without changing the source system.

- **Reliability**: If one destination goes down, the source is unaffected.

- **Asynchronous processing**: Destinations can consume data on their own schedules.

- **Broadcasting ability**: Efficient for getting data to multiple places.

The fan-out pattern in AWS can be implemented by sending messages to an **Amazon SNS** topic, which then distributes the messages to multiple **Amazon SQS** queues. The messages in the SQS queues can then be processed in parallel by consumers pulling from each queue independently. This allows for scalable parallel processing of messages published to the SNS topic.

Now that we have examined different messaging patterns, the next section will delve deeper into **choreography** in AWS.

Choreography with Amazon EventBridge

Amazon EventBridge is a serverless event bus service that makes it easy to build event-driven applications at scale. EventBridge allows different services to react to events from other AWS services or custom applications. This enables an event-driven architecture called **choreography** where decoupled services can asynchronously communicate with each other via events.

In **choreography**, services produce events in response to state changes. Other downstream services consume these events and react to them. The producer and consumer services don't call each other directly. Rather, they exchange events through an event bus like EventBridge.

This loose coupling between services provides several benefits, including:

- Services can evolve independently without *tightly coupling* to each other's APIs. As long as events comply with a contract, services can be changed without impacting others.

- Services can react to events *asynchronously* and *in parallel.* The event producer doesn't wait for reactions to complete.

- Events are durable and can trigger multiple reactions. If a downstream service is unavailable, events are buffered until it comes back online.

- It's easy to add new event consumers over time. New services can react to events by subscribing to the event bus.

EventBridge supports both custom events from your own applications as well as over 20 built-in events from AWS services. For example, AWS Lambda functions can publish events to EventBridge when they execute. An application could react to these events by invoking another Lambda function to process the event data, as shown in *Figure 2.12.*

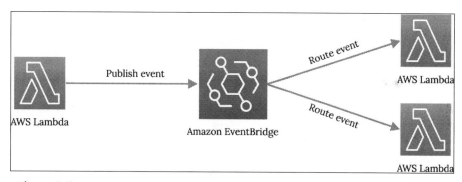

Figure 2.12: *Amazon EventBridge is a push-based messaging service and can route a single event to multiple AWS Lambda functions*

With EventBridge, you create **event buses** that act as the intermediaries between event producers and consumers. Rules match events to routes that distribute events to target services. EventBridge schemas and payloads provide a consistent way to pass event data between decoupled services.

Some key features of Amazon EventBridge include:

- **Reliability**: EventBridge is highly available and durable with *replay* options in case you miss an event.

- **Flexibility**: Support for all kinds of events like clicks, purchases, file uploads, or custom application events. Works with SaaS, applications, AWS, and on-premises apps.

- **Scalability**: EventBridge can handle millions of events per second, growing as you grow.
- **Serverless**: No servers to manage. EventBridge is fully managed by AWS.

Here are some common use cases used with EventBridge:

- **Application integration**: EventBridge can be used to connect different applications together by allowing them to react to events from each other. For example, updating a customer record in one app could emit an event to trigger related actions in other apps.
- **Serverless workflows**: EventBridge allows building serverless workflows that stitch together multiple AWS services based on events. For example, uploading a file to Amazon S3 could trigger a Lambda function to process that file.
- **Scheduled automation**: EventBridge has cron scheduling capabilities to trigger tasks at specific times, like running backups or analytics jobs.
- **Third-party integration**: EventBridge can ingest events from third-party apps, SaaS tools, and so on. This allows reacting to events outside of AWS.
- **Operational monitoring**: Events for things, such as auto-scaling, deployments, error alerts, and so on, can be routed to EventBridge and used to provide operational visibility.
- **Log processing**: Amazon CloudWatch Logs can stream logs to EventBridge, which then allows processing and reacting to the log data.
- **Audit trailing and compliance**: Critical system events can be audited and traced using EventBridge. For example, privileged user sign-ins, security group changes, and so on.

Next, we will explore design patterns that are commonly used with Amazon EventBridge.

Design Patterns Used with Amazon EventBridge

Some key design patterns used with Amazon EventBridge are **Event sourcing**, Command Query Responsibility Segregation **(CQRS)**, **Scheduler pattern,** and **Claim check pattern**. To start, we will take a look at event sourcing and how it works.

Event Sourcing

Event sourcing is a software design pattern that focuses on capturing all changes made to an application state as a *sequence of events*. Instead of storing just the current state, event sourcing persists the full series of actions that led to the current state.

In a traditional application, the current state of the data is stored in a database. With event sourcing, whenever the application performs an action, an event object is created that contains details about that action. The event is appended to an event log or event store, which acts as the system of record.

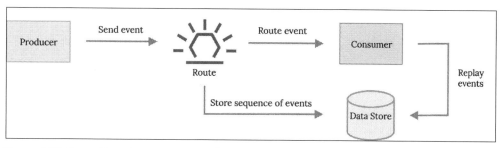

Figure 2.13: *Event Sourcing captures each state change as a sequence of immutable events over time rather than directly mutating an entity's state*

Some key principles of event sourcing include:

- **Immutability**: Events are immutable once written, meaning they cannot be changed.
- **Persistence**: Events are durably persisted to an event store. This ensures the full series of changes are captured.
- **Replayability**: The application can rebuild its current state by replaying the events from the beginning.
- **Auditability**: The event log is an audit trail that can be analyzed to understand system behavior over time.
- **Granularity**: Events can represent minor or major changes in the application. The level of granularity is configurable.

Event sourcing offers several benefits, including:

- **Full audit trail**: The sequence of events provides detailed insight into system changes over time.
- **Easy error recovery**: Errors can be corrected by rolling back events or applying compensating events.
- **Debugging capabilities**: Bugs can be debugged by replaying the event sequence leading up to an error.
- **Flexibility**: With only event data, the application can generate different views of the data for different purposes.

Overall, **event sourcing** provides powerful auditing, debugging, and recovery capabilities by taking a log-centric approach to data. It is best suited for applications that need to analyze changes over time or recover from errors easily.

Amazon EventBridge and **Amazon DynamoDB** can be used together in AWS to implement event sourcing. EventBridge replaces the routing component, while DynamoDB serves as the data store.

CQRS

CQRS stands for **Command Query Responsibility Segregation**. It is an architectural pattern that separates read and write operations for a data store, and it is typically used with the **event sourcing** pattern. The goal of CQRS is to scale the application better and allow the system to optimize each side.

In a traditional **CRUD** (Create, Read, Update, Delete) application, the same data model is used to query and update a database. With CQRS, we split that into two separate models:

- The **write model** accepts commands that modify state.
- The **read model** projects data for queries.

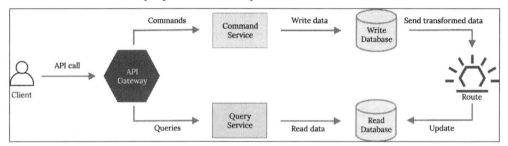

Figure 2.14: CQRS *separates read and write operations for a data store*

The benefits of CQRS are as follows:

- **Scaling**: CQRS allows scaling the read and write sides independently. You can have more read instances than write instances, allowing you to scale the read side as needed to meet demand.

- **Optimized data models**: The write model can use a normalized data model optimized for updates and inserts. The read model can *denormalize* the data for fast reads and projections.

- **Security**: It's easier to secure the write side as only the command side talks to the database. The read side can be opened up more widely.

- **Separation of concerns**: Segregating the read and write sides can result in cleaner code and better maintainability. Developers can focus on the specific requirements of each side.

- **Event sourcing**: By persisting changes as a sequence of events, CQRS naturally lends itself to event-sourcing approaches. This gives more flexibility in querying past events.

CQRS is a valuable pattern when you need to scale write and read operations independently. It does add complexity, so use it judiciously based on your system's requirements. However, for large-scale applications, it can be a lifesaver in scaling the data tier.

Amazon EventBridge and **Amazon DynamoDB** can be used to implement CQRS in AWS. EventBridge replaces the router to dispatch events to appropriate services, while DynamoDB provides separate databases for writes and reads.

Scheduler Pattern

The **scheduler** pattern is a design pattern that allows tasks or operations to be scheduled for execution at a certain time or periodically. It decouples the scheduling and execution of tasks from the components that generate the tasks.

Some key characteristics of the scheduler pattern are as follows:

- There is a scheduler component that manages a queue of tasks and determines when they should execute based on scheduled times or intervals.
- The scheduler runs periodically and checks if there are any tasks ready for execution. If tasks are ready, it executes them.
- Tasks are generated by other components in the system and added to the scheduler's queue to await execution. The components generating tasks don't need to know about scheduling logic.
- The scheduler provides an abstraction between task generation and task execution. Components can generate tasks whenever needed without worrying about when they will actually run.
- Tasks contain some action or set of operations to perform. This is usually represented by a callback method or passing in code via a functional interface.
- Tasks can be one-time tasks scheduled for a certain time in the future, or recurring tasks that run periodically.

Some common uses of the scheduler pattern include:

- Scheduling background tasks like cleaning up files or aggregated data.
- Performing recurring maintenance operations like database cleanup.
- Scheduling timed jobs like sending emails.
- Running tasks periodically like batch processing jobs.
- General deferring of work to be done later.

The scheduler pattern helps create robust and scalable applications by offloading timing and scheduling concerns from other components. It enables loose coupling since components don't need direct dependencies on each other to generate and execute tasks.

In AWS, **Amazon EventBridge** gives you the ability to schedule tasks to run at specific times or intervals.

Claim Check Pattern

The **claim check** pattern is a useful design pattern in programming that can help reduce memory usage when working with large objects.

The claim check pattern involves separating large data objects from the main application memory and storing a **claim check** or pointer to that data instead. The large objects are stored in an external service or data store, while the application only maintains a reference to them.

When the application needs to access or work with large data, it passes the claim check to the service storing the data, which looks up the object by its ID and returns it. The application can then work with the full object temporarily before releasing it to be garbage collected. The claim check acts as a lightweight reference instead of the application having to hold the entire data object in memory.

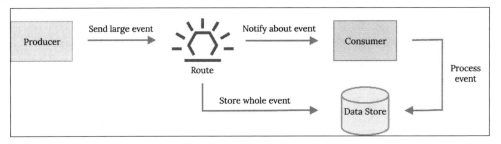

Figure 2.15: *With claim check, large events are stored externally and replaced with a reference to access them, allowing more efficient message passing*

Some key benefits of claim check pattern include:

- **Reduces memory usage**: Only claim checks need to be stored instead of full large objects.
- **Improves performance**: Less data to serialize when persisting or passing data around.
- **Flexibility**: Data can be stored externally in a place optimized for large data.
- **Caching**: Claims can have expiration times for automatic caching of data.

The **claim check** pattern can be implemented in AWS by using **Amazon EventBridge** to route events to consumers and **Amazon S3** to store large event payload data.

Having explored several design patterns used with Amazon EventBridge, we will now dive deeper into orchestration using **AWS Step Functions** in the next section.

Orchestration with AWS Step Functions

AWS Step Functions is a serverless **orchestration** service that allows you to easily coordinate components of distributed applications and microservices using visual workflows. With Step Functions, you can build and run *workflow-driven* applications in AWS.

AWS Step Functions allow you to visualize and test your application as a series of steps. The steps can be integrated with other AWS services, such as AWS Lambda, Amazon SNS, Amazon SQS, Amazon DynamoDB, and more.

Step Functions provide a graphical console to arrange and visualize the components of your application as a *series of steps*, as shown in *Figure 2.16*. This eliminates the need to write code for coordination and state management. The Step Functions workflow engine executes each step in order. It tracks the state of each step and retries when there are errors.

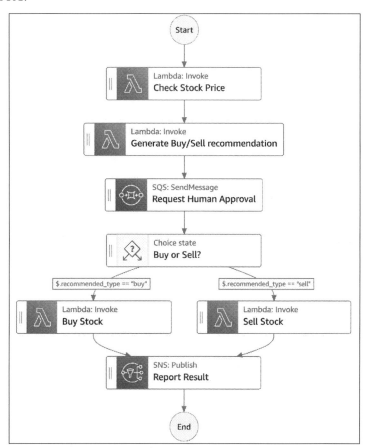

Figure 2.16: *AWS Step Functions example for a serverless stock trading workflow using AWS Lambda, Amazon SQS, and Amazon SNS*

Some key benefits of using Step Functions include:

- **Visual workflow creation**: Easily build and iterate workflows using the graphical interface.
- **Distributed application coordination**: Orchestrate up to hundreds of AWS services.
- **Error handling**: Automatically retry and catch errors in your application logic.
- **Audit history**: Log each step to monitor and visualize workflow executions.
- **No servers to manage**: Fully managed service, no servers to provision

Here are some examples of how Step Functions are used:

- **Data processing**: Run a series of Lambda functions to transform and analyze data.
- **Web applications**: Call APIs, perform calculations, and integrate with databases.
- **IoT applications**: Ingest, process, and analyze telemetry data from devices.
- **Logistics and order fulfillment**: Track and process orders across various systems.
- **Media transcoding**: Encode, segment, and distribute videos.

AWS Step Functions provide a serverless and visual way to orchestrate distributed applications in AWS. By using pre-built states and integrations with other AWS services, Step Functions makes it easy to create workflows that are robust, scalable, and reusable. The graphical console simplifies building and visualizing your workflows. Step Functions handle error handling, retries, and state management automatically.

Design Patterns Used with AWS Step Functions

We will now examine two design patterns often utilized with AWS Step Functions: the **circuit breaker** and **SAGA**.

Circuit Breaker

The **circuit breaker** pattern is a software design pattern that allows a system to detect when a downstream service is failing and prevent repeated requests from overwhelming it. This pattern can improve the stability and resiliency of distributed systems that rely on external services.

The circuit breaker acts as a *proxy* for operations that might fail. It monitors for failures, and when a threshold of failures is reached, the circuit trips and stops allowing calls. This gives the downstream service time to recover without being bombarded with requests.

The circuit breaker has three states, explained as follows:

- **Closed**: The circuit allows requests to go through to the downstream service. It monitors for failures.

- **Open**: The circuit is tripped after a threshold of failures is reached. All requests fail immediately, without trying to call the downstream service.

- **Half-open**: After staying open for a set amount of time, the circuit goes into a half-open state to test if the downstream service has recovered. A limited number of test requests are let through to see if they succeed. If requests succeed, the circuit goes back to being closed. If requests still fail, the circuit reverts to being open.

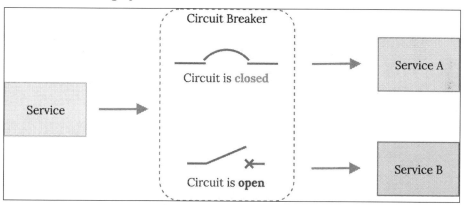

Figure 2.17: *The Circuit Breaker pattern prevents an application from repeatedly trying to execute an operation that is likely to fail*

The circuit breaker can prevent cascading failures in distributed systems. By quickly failing and stopping requests, overload situations can be avoided on downstream services that are having trouble. This allows the services time to recover.

The circuit breaker pattern is commonly used in microservices architectures to prevent chain reactions when one service fails. It's also useful for any distributed system that relies on remote services.

Some key benefits include:

- Improved stability by preventing cascading failures
- Faster failure detection and recovery times
- Reduced load and stress on failing services
- Simple implementation

The circuit breaker helps create robust systems by adding resilience when integrating with services that can fail. It's a simple but powerful pattern for handling failures in distributed systems. In AWS, you can implement the circuit breaker pattern with **AWS Step Functions**.

SAGA

In a microservices architecture, a single business transaction can span multiple services. This creates a challenge when one service fails: how do you rollback the entire transaction? Enter the **SAGA pattern**.

A SAGA is a *sequence of local transactions* where each transaction updates data within a single service, as illustrated in *Figure* 2.18. The SAGA coordinates these transactions to achieve a global outcome.

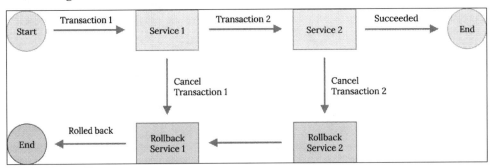

Figure 2.18: *The SAGA pattern is a way to manage long-running business transactions and compensate operations through a sequence of local transactions that can be reversed to undo partial work*

SAGAs maintain data consistency across services without using distributed transactions. So, if one service fails, the SAGA executes compensating transactions that counteract the previous transactions. This lets you rollback failed transactions without rolling back the entire global transaction.

A SAGA is coordinated by a Saga Coordinator, which manages Saga lifecycle and transaction log. Here's how a SAGA works:

1. The Saga Coordinator begins a new Saga to achieve a global transaction.

2. The Saga Coordinator sends requests to participate in the Saga to each service.

3. Each service runs its local transaction and updates its database. It reports back success or failure to the Saga Coordinator.

4. If all services succeed, the Saga completes. If any service fails, the Saga Coordinator starts compensating transactions.

5. The Saga Coordinator sends requests to rollback previous transactions to each service.

6. Services run compensating transactions to undo their previous actions and report back to the coordinator.

7. Once all compensations succeed, the Saga is rolled back.

SAGAs provide several benefits, including:

- Maintain data consistency without distributed transactions
- Decouple services by managing transactions out-of-process
- Better fault tolerance: A single failure doesn't cause the entire transaction to fail
- Transactions across multiple databases, domains, and technologies

The SAGA pattern is useful for implementing eventual consistency and fault tolerance in a microservices architecture. By coordinating local transactions across services, SAGAs allow large business transactions to be executed atomically and rolled back on failure. The SAGA pattern can be implemented in AWS by using **AWS Step Functions**.

Now that we have examined design patterns used with AWS Step Functions, we will delve further into event streaming with **Amazon Kinesis** in the final section for event-driven design patterns.

Event Streaming with Amazon Kinesis

Event streaming is a method of *capturing and analyzing real-time data* from event sources like applications, devices, and systems. The goal is to understand what is happening right now, so you can respond and take action immediately.

Amazon Kinesis is a managed service provided by AWS for ingesting and processing real-time streaming data. Kinesis enables you to continuously capture and store terabytes of data per hour from hundreds of thousands of sources, such as website clickstreams, database event streams, financial transactions, social media feeds, IT logs, and location-tracking events. The data collected is available in milliseconds to enable real-time analytics use cases such as real-time dashboards, real-time anomaly detection, dynamic pricing, and more.

Kinesis has three main components, explained as follows:

- **Kinesis Data Streams**: This is the core component that enables you to ingest and process data streams in real-time. Data streams are divided into *shards* that allow parallel processing.

- **Data Firehose**: This component automatically loads streaming data into data stores like Amazon S3, Amazon Redshift, Amazon OpenSearch, and so on. It takes care of tasks like data transformations with minimal configuration.

- **Managed Service for Apache Flink**: This component performs real-time analytics on streams using SQL queries. The results can be piped to dashboards, reports, or other data stores.

Here are some of the key benefits of using Amazon Kinesis:

- **Real-time data streaming**: Kinesis allows you to ingest and process large streams of data in real-time with sub-second latency. This enables real-time analytics and reactions to information.

- **Scalability**: Kinesis can handle any amount of streaming data and throughput you need by scaling stream capacity up or down. This allows you to easily adapt to changes in data volume.

- **Durability**: Data is replicated across multiple Availability Zones to prevent data loss. Kinesis streams are highly available.

- **Integration**: Kinesis integrates nicely with many other AWS services, like AWS Lambda, Amazon Redshift, Amazon OpenSearch, and so on. This makes it easy to build full data pipelines.

Some common use cases with Amazon Kinesis are:

- **Real-time metrics and reporting**: Analyze application metrics, clicks, and usage patterns as they occur.

- **Real-time anomaly detection**: Identify anomalies in financial transactions, network monitoring, and other areas as they happen to spot issues.

- **Analytics on IoT data**: Process data streams from IoT devices to better understand equipment performance.

- **Log analysis**: Analyze log data in real-time to identify errors and issues instantly.

- **Real-time segmentation**: Analyze customer behavior data to segment and engage customers in the moment.

Amazon Kinesis makes real-time stream processing accessible for many applications. Its capabilities for scalability, security, and integration with other AWS services make it a go-to-choice for organizations seeking real-time insights from their data streams.

Design Patterns Used with Amazon Kinesis

Next, let's explore some design patterns used with Amazon Kinesis: **streaming data ingestion**, **data pipeline**, and **real-time analytics**.

Streaming Data Ingestion

With the rapid growth of data in recent years, **streaming data ingestion** has become an important part of many organizations' data infrastructure. **Streaming data ingestion** refers to the process of capturing, processing, and storing real-time data that is generated continuously from various sources, such as application logs, IoT sensors, website traffic, social media, and more.

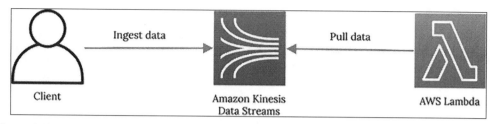

Figure 2.19: *Amazon Kinesis Data Streams can be used to ingest streams of data from any source, which can then be processed by AWS Lambda*

Some key benefits of streaming data ingestion are:

- **Low latency**: Streaming ingestion allows data to be available for use within milliseconds or seconds rather than waiting for batch processing. This enables real-time analytics and reactions.

- **Flexible scaling**: Streaming systems can easily scale up or down based on data volume. This allows optimizing infrastructure costs.

- **Continuous processing**: Streaming ingestion allows continuous data flow rather than periodic batches. This enables uninterrupted real-time analytics.

- **Handling variety of data**: Streaming can handle different formats like JSON, AVRO, Protobuf, and so on. This provides flexibility for varied data sources.

- **Replayable streams**: Streaming systems allow replaying streams in case of failures. This provides fault tolerance.

Overall, **streaming data ingestion** provides valuable capabilities for today's real-time analytics needs. With careful system design and the right technologies, streaming ingestion's benefits can be realized while overcoming its challenges. In AWS, **Amazon Kinesis Data Streams** can be used for streaming data ingestion.

Data Pipeline

Data pipeline is a common architectural pattern used in software engineering to move and process data between different services, applications, or microservices. It provides a reliable and scalable way to ingest, transform, store, and analyze data as it flows through multiple steps.

A data pipeline is a set of processes and storage that transport data from one system to another. It's like an assembly line, where each stage adds value to the data and pipes it to the next destination.

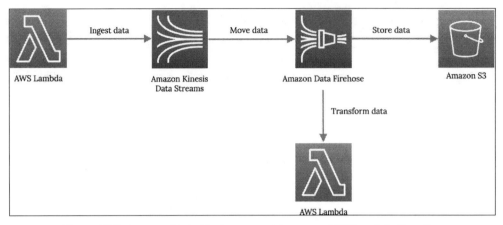

Figure 2.20: *Amazon Data Firehose can trigger an AWS Lambda function to transform data streams sent to Amazon Kinesis Data Streams and automatically load the processed data to Amazon S3*

The main components of a data pipeline are:

- **Data sources**: This is where data enters the pipeline. Common sources include databases, APIs, log files, IoT devices, and so on.

- **Data processing**: The raw data is cleaned, filtered, aggregated, enriched, or transformed as needed. This might involve scripts, ETL tools, stream processing, and so on.

- **Temporary storage**: Data is held temporarily between steps. This can be a caching layer, message queues, buffers, and so on.

- **Permanent storage**: The final destination for persisted data, usually a data warehouse, lake, or database.

- **Data consumption**: Where the processed, analytical data is consumed by applications, reports, dashboards, and users.

Some benefits of using data pipelines are:

- **Automation**: Pipelines move and process data automatically on a schedule or trigger. This frees developers from manual data wrangling.

- **Reliability**: If part of the pipeline fails, data can be replayed from the beginning to resume where it left off. This makes the system robust and fault-tolerant.

- **Scalability**: Data pipelines can handle increasing data volumes by scaling horizontally and distributing work across more resources.

- **Reusability**: Logic coded into the pipeline gets reused as more data flows through over time. This saves duplicate efforts.

- **Auditability**: Data lineage from source to destination is visible. This provides transparency and traceability.

The optimal implementation depends on the data volume, complexity of processing, existing infrastructure, and team skills. Well-designed data pipelines allow efficient movement of data between systems and power data-driven applications.

Amazon Data Firehose is used in AWS to process data in a data pipeline.

Real-Time Analytics

In today's fast-paced business environment, companies need to be able to make decisions quickly in order to stay competitive. This is where real-time analytics comes in. **Real-time analytics** refers to the ability to continuously analyze and process data as it is generated, allowing businesses to understand what is happening right now instead of looking at past trends.

Real-time analytics enables organizations to identify opportunities and risks in real-time and take timely actions. For example, an e-commerce company can monitor sales data, web traffic, server loads, and other metrics as they occur. Or a sports company can show live game dashboards to analyze player behavior, game metrics, and in-game events as they happen.

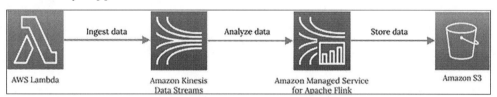

Figure 2.21: *Amazon Managed Service for Apache Flink can perform real-time analytics on data streams sent to Amazon Kinesis Data Streams and store the processed data to Amazon S3*

Here are some key benefits of real-time analytics:

- **Faster insights and decision making**: With real-time data, companies can analyze information and act on it within minutes or seconds rather than waiting for reports to be generated. This agility allows businesses to capitalize on fleeting opportunities.

- **Increased operational efficiency**: By linking analytics directly to business operations, companies can automate more processes and optimize resource allocation based on real-time data. For instance, adjusting staffing levels based on current sales or traffic data.

- **Rapid anomaly detection**: Real-time monitoring makes it possible to swiftly detect anomalies, problems, and risks so companies can take corrective actions before small issues become big problems. Whether it's a technical glitch, supply chain disruption, or sudden change in customer behavior, organizations can respond promptly.

- **Enhanced customer experience**: Customer-facing employees can use real-time data to improve customer service and support. For example, accessing a customer's most recent transactions and activity to provide personalized services.

The ability to garner insights and make data-driven decisions quickly is becoming a key competitive advantage across industries. Though real-time analytics comes with big data challenges, the right infrastructure and analytical tools can help companies reap the benefits of agile decision making. Organizations that leverage real-time data will be able to outmaneuver and outperform their slower-moving competitors.

Amazon Data Firehose is used in AWS to analyze streams of data in real-time using SQL *queries*.

Choosing Between SQS, SNS, EventBridge, and Kinesis

In the previous sections, we covered AWS serverless offerings that enable event-driven integration: Amazon SQS, Amazon SNS, Amazon EventBridge, and Amazon Kinesis. When building applications on AWS, selecting the right integration service is crucial to meet your specific needs. Evaluating the queue, pub/sub, event routing, and streaming capabilities of each service will guide you in choosing the right AWS event-driven service. Let's recap the services and the most common use cases for each one.

Amazon SQS is a fully managed message queuing service that enables decoupling and scaling of distributed systems and microservices. Amazon SQS is used for:

- **Decoupling applications**: SQS allows you to decouple application components and process data asynchronously. This improves scalability, reliability, and performance.

- **Message queuing**: SQS provides a message queueing service to store messages while waiting for a component to process them. This enables asynchronous message processing workflows.

- **Buffering requests**: SQS can buffer requests before forwarding them to another component. This smooths out spikes in workloads and prevents overloading. For example, buffering requests before sending them to a worker fleet.

Amazon SNS is a pub/sub messaging service that allows sending one-to-many messages to subscribers. Amazon SNS is used for:

- **Pushing notifications to end users**: SNS can send push notifications to mobile apps, SMS messages, and email to alert users about new information relevant to them. This is useful for notifying users of new updates, promotions, account activity, and so on.

- **Broadcasting messages to clients**: SNS can fan out messages to a large number of subscribed endpoints for simultaneous delivery. This allows publishing messages to multiple subscribers like distributed systems to notify them of state changes.

- **Logging and monitoring**: SNS can send notifications about critical events happening in your infrastructure to trigger alarms, log events, or initiate workflows. For example, it can publish messages to an SQS queue when there are errors that need processing.

Amazon EventBridge allows reacting to state changes and events from AWS services and your own applications. Amazon EventBridge is used for:

- **Application integration**: EventBridge makes it easy to connect different applications together by allowing one application to react to events from another. For example, you could have an e-commerce application publish events to EventBridge when a new order is placed, and trigger a billing application to charge the customer.

- **Serverless workflows**: EventBridge is useful for coordinating serverless workflows and functions. For example, you could have a video processing workflow where EventBridge invokes different Lambda functions for transcoding, thumbnail generation, and so on based on events emitted during the workflow.

- **Third-party integration**: EventBridge provides an easy way to react to events from third-party SaaS applications and AWS services. For example, you could ingest events from services like Zendesk or Shopify into EventBridge and then trigger actions in your own application based on those events.

Amazon Kinesis is a real-time streaming service for processing large streams of data. Amazon Kinesis is used for:

- **Streaming data ingestion**: Kinesis can be used to continuously ingest and process high volumes of data from many sources like website clickstreams, IoT devices, or financial transactions. The data is durably stored in shards and can then be processed and analyzed.

- **Real-time analytics**: The data in Kinesis streams can be analyzed in real-time to derive insights. For example, analyze clickstream data to get visitor trends or use IoT sensor data to detect anomalies. Kinesis enables real-time analytics and reactions to incoming data.

- **Data pipeline and ETL**: Kinesis can be used to securely and durably land data before processing it further and loading it into data warehouses, lakes, and so on. The data pipeline can preprocess, transform, and aggregate before loading for downstream analytics. This replaces batch ETL processes.

Data Store Services Used in Event-Driven Architectures in AWS

In an event-driven architecture, when an event occurs, some processing is done and data may need to be persisted. Choosing the right data store is critical for performance and scalability. AWS provides several serverless data store services that are well-suited for these types of applications. Two key AWS services that can enable event-driven workflows are **Amazon Simple Storage Service (Amazon S3)** and **Amazon DynamoDB**.

Amazon S3 and **Amazon DynamoDB** are highly scalable, resilient data stores that can also serve as event sources for event-driven architectures. Specifically, S3 can generate events to notify about *file changes*, while DynamoDB can publish *item-level table modifications*. In the following sections, we will examine these event notification capabilities of S3 and DynamoDB in greater detail.

Amazon S3

Amazon Simple Storage Service (Amazon S3) is a cloud-based storage service that offers scalable and flexible object storage. S3 enables users to store and retrieve data from anywhere via web service interfaces. With S3, you can upload, download, and manage your data easily from any device.

Some key features of Amazon S3 include:

- **Scalable storage**: You can store as much data as you want and access it from anywhere. S3 offers unlimited storage space and auto-scaling capabilities.

- **Object-based storage**: Data is stored as objects in buckets, which you can organize via folders and metadata. This allows you to upload files of any format, like images, videos, documents, and so on.

- **Security and access management**: S3 supports robust security features like access control lists, bucket policies, and encryption for data security. You can control who can access which objects.

- **High durability and availability**: Amazon S3 stores data across multiple *Availability Zones*. It guarantees 99.999999999% durability and 99.99% availability of objects.

- **Low latency and high throughput**: S3 is optimized to deliver low latency and high data transfer speeds. It supports massive parallel downloads and uploads for fast data access.

- **Integrations and APIs**: S3 seamlessly integrates with various AWS services. It also provides simple REST for programmatic access using AWS SDKs.

- **Flexible pricing**: You only pay for what you use with no upfront costs. S3 offers a range of storage classes optimized for different use cases, like frequent access, infrequent access, or archival storage.

With its pay-as-you-go model, **Amazon S3** is ideal for anyone looking for a reliable and scalable cloud storage solution. Use cases include backup and recovery, big data analytics, mobile/web apps, IoT devices, media hosting, and more. Overall, Amazon S3 provides a versatile, secure, and efficient way to store any amount of data in the cloud.

Amazon S3 Event Notifications

Amazon S3 can act as an *event producer* in an event-driven architecture. S3 buckets can publish events to AWS Lambda, Amazon SQS, Amazon SNS, and Amazon EventBridge whenever files are created, deleted, or changed in the bucket. For example, you could have an S3 bucket that receives uploaded image files. Whenever a new object is added to that bucket, an event can trigger a Lambda function to process the image and add metadata, as illustrated in *Figure 2.22*.

Figure 2.22: *Uploading a file to Amazon S3 can trigger an AWS Lambda function to extract the metadata about the uploaded file and save it to an Amazon DynamoDB table*

With **Amazon S3 event notifications**, you can enable powerful workflows and processing that react to changes in your S3 buckets. The granularity, supported targets, and near real-time delivery allow for many use cases in data analysis, serverless applications, and more.

Amazon DynamoDB

Amazon DynamoDB is a fully managed NoSQL database service provided by AWS. DynamoDB enables developers to create databases that provide reliable performance at any scale without having to manage servers or deal with database administration tasks.

Some key features of DynamoDB include:

- **Fully managed service**: As a fully managed cloud database, DynamoDB removes the operational burdens of scaling, replication, software patching, hardware provisioning, setup, and configuration, so developers don't have to worry about any of that.
- **Fast performance**: DynamoDB is optimized for fast, predictable performance

at any scale. It supports *single-digit millisecond* response times for accessing and updating data.

- **Highly scalable**: DynamoDB is highly scalable and can handle massive workloads while maintaining low latency and predictable performance. Tables can scale up or down automatically based on demand.

- **Durable data storage**: Data is stored redundantly across multiple *Availability Zones* and automatically replicated across Regions for high availability and durability.

- **Powerful query capabilities**: DynamoDB provides a rich set of query capabilities, including key-value lookups, scans, and complex queries to filter data.

- **Integrated security**: DynamoDB offers encryption *at rest* and *in transit*, fine-grained access controls, and integration with AWS Identity and Access Management.

- **Low cost**: DynamoDB charges based on provisioned throughput capacity and storage used per month with no minimum fees and no upfront costs. This makes it a very cost-effective database option.

Amazon DynamoDB is a great choice for modern serverless applications that need a fully managed, highly scalable database with millisecond latency. Its flexibility and seamless scalability make it ideal for gaming, e-commerce, social media, and IoT applications.

Amazon DynamoDB Streams

Amazon DynamoDB tables can also integrate into event-driven workflows using **DynamoDB streams**. When data is modified in a DynamoDB table, a stream of events can be published that reflects the changes. Other applications can listen to these streams and take action based on the events.

For example, you could have a DynamoDB table that tracks user signups. A Lambda function could be triggered by a stream insertion event to send a welcome email to new users using Amazon SNS, as shown in *Figure 2.23*. Or a stream update event could indicate a user's email was changed, triggering a Lambda to update associated data.

Figure 2.23: *When a new user is added to Amazon DynamoDB, an AWS Lambda function can be triggered to publish an event to Amazon SNS, which then sends an email to the new user about their registration*

DynamoDB streams open up many possibilities for asynchronous workflows based on data changes. The streams provide an ordered sequence of events that other systems can subscribe to.

Conclusion

In this chapter, we have explored how AWS serverless enables building event-driven architectures. By automating infrastructure management, serverless computing allows developers to focus on business logic while achieving scalability, availability, and operational efficiency.

We looked at implementing microservices with AWS Lambda functions triggered by events from various sources. Amazon API Gateway provides a way to expose these functions through REST APIs. To coordinate distributed services, AWS offers a range of integration services for messaging, notifications, workflow, and streaming data processing. Amazon SQS, Amazon SNS, Amazon EventBridge, AWS Step Functions, and Amazon Kinesis enable the implementation of common integration patterns such as publish/subscribe, fan-out, event sourcing, event streaming, and more in a serverless way. Data can be persisted in serverless stores like Amazon S3 and Amazon DynamoDB.

By leveraging these managed AWS services, developers can quickly build and iterate on event-driven systems. The services integrate seamlessly while abstracting away infrastructure complexities, enabling faster innovation and reduced time to market. In the upcoming chapter, we will reinforce these concepts by developing concrete examples of event-driven architectures using AWS serverless services.

CHAPTER 3

Messaging with Amazon SQS and Amazon SNS

Introduction

This chapter focuses on designing and implementing microservices that interact with each other using messaging patterns. We will explore how to use Amazon SQS and Amazon SNS to build scalable, reliable, and secure distributed systems. We will also discuss the prerequisites for building on AWS, such as creating an account and setting up an IAM user. First, we will dive into the details of Amazon API Gateway and AWS Lambda, which are essential for building microservices that can be accessed via REST APIs. Then, we will examine messaging patterns, including point-to-point messaging, publish/subscribe messaging, and fan-out. We will also delve into the features of Amazon SQS and Amazon SNS, such as standard vs. FIFO queues/topics, short and long polling, message filtering, and dead-letter queues. By the end of this chapter, you will have a solid understanding of how to design and implement scalable microservices using AWS messaging services.

Structure

In this chapter, we will discuss the following topics:

- Getting Started with AWS: Create an Account and IAM User, Install Programming Languages and Tools
- Microservices with Amazon API Gateway and AWS Lambda
- Messaging Patterns with Amazon SQS and Amazon SNS: Point-to-Point Messaging, Publish/Subscribe Messaging, Fan-out
- Amazon SQS Features: Standard vs. FIFO Queues, Visibility Timeout, Message

Retention Period, Delivery Delay, Message Size, Short and Long Polling, Dead-Letter Queues, Encryption

- Amazon SNS: Standard vs. FIFO Topics, Message Archiving/Replay/Analytics, Message Filtering, Delivery Policy, Encryption, SMS Messaging, Mobile Push Notifications, Email Notifications

Getting Started with AWS

To get started with building event-driven microservices on AWS, you first need an **AWS account** and an **IAM (Identity and Access Management)** user configured with appropriate access permissions. This will allow us to access AWS services programmatically and via the management console. You also need to install the **AWS CDK** for provisioning cloud resources, **Java** for implementing the application logic, and any other required tools. With the fundamentals in place - the AWS account, IAM credentials, AWS CDK, Java, and tools - you will have the necessary building blocks to begin developing event-driven microservice architectures hosted on AWS. Let's begin by creating an AWS account.

Creating an AWS Account

To start using **AWS**, you first need to create an account. Creating an AWS account is quick and easy to do. First, go to the AWS website **https://aws.amazon.com/** and click on the **Create an AWS Account** button. You will need to provide some basic personal information like your name, email address, phone number, and password to secure your account. AWS will ask for a credit card, but you can select the **Free Tier,** which allows you access to certain AWS services for 12 months without incurring any costs. Once your account is created, you will have access to the entire suite of AWS cloud computing services using the **root user** to build cloud-based applications.

Note: *AWS offers a **Free Tier** that provides free usage of certain AWS services for 12 months after signing up or is always free. This allows users to explore and try out select AWS services at no cost. Some of the popular services included in AWS Free Tier are **AWS Lambda**, **Amazon API Gateway**, **Amazon S3**, and more. For example, the AWS Free Tier includes 1 million free requests per month for up to 12 months for API Gateway APIs and 1 million free requests per month that can be used to run Lambda functions for always. The free tier is meant to be an easy way for new customers to get hands-on with AWS services without having to worry about costs. It's useful for learning, prototyping applications, and even running small workloads at no cost. Keep in mind that certain practical labs included in this book may involve some expenses. Make sure to closely monitor usage and billing as charges will start accruing as soon as you launch services. You can do that by visiting the **Billing** dashboard from the AWS management console.*

Creating an IAM User on AWS

To enhance security, it is advisable to refrain from utilizing your AWS account's root user, which you created in the previous step, for routine activities. A better approach is to configure **IAM (Identity and Access Management)** users with suitable permissions and use them to interact with AWS services and resources. IAM allows you to securely control access to AWS. By making IAM users for daily tasks rather than relying on the powerful root user, you reduce risk and follow security best practices.

To create an IAM user, go to the AWS management console **https://console.aws. amazon.com/** and sign in as the *root user* with your AWS account credentials you used during the account creation. Go to the IAM dashboard and follow the steps to create a user under the **Users** page. The user you will create can access AWS resources and services through the AWS management console. If you want to provide programmatic access to the user then you have to create an **access key ID** and **secret access key** which will serve as the credentials that the IAM user can use to make AWS API calls programmatically. You can create these from the IAM page of the user you have created.

Tip: *In AWS IAM, **least privilege** is an important concept that refers to granting users the minimum permissions they need to perform their jobs and nothing more. Implementing least privilege improves security by limiting the blast radius if credentials are compromised or if users inadvertently access resources they should not. To apply the least privilege, you carefully assess what a user needs to access and grant only those specific permissions through IAM policies.*

For testing purposes, you have created a user with AdministratorAccess to have full access. However, in a production environment, the principle of least privilege should be followed – users should be granted the minimum permissions necessary to provision the AWS resources needed for their role.

Understanding the AWS IAM Permissions

AWS IAM is a powerful service that allows you to control access to your AWS resources. With IAM, you can specify which actions can be performed on those resources.

IAM roles are a key concept in IAM, and they allow you to define a set of permissions that can be assigned to users or services. An IAM role is essentially a bucket of permissions that can be assumed by a service or a user, and it provides short-term credentials to access other services. It defines what actions can be performed on AWS resources.

IAM policies, on the other hand, are the rules that define what actions can be performed on AWS resources. Policies are associated with IAM roles, and they specify the permissions that are granted to the role.

Throughout this book, you will be creating roles and policies and integrating them with AWS services. It's crucial to understand how these components work together, so it is recommended to refer to the official AWS documentation for IAM roles to gain a deeper understanding:

https://docs.aws.amazon.com/IAM/latest/UserGuide/id_roles.html.

Amazon Resource Name (ARN)

To utilize certain AWS services in this chapter, we will need to locate the Amazon Resource Name (ARN) associated with those services. **Amazon Resource Names (ARNs)** are unique identifiers used to identify AWS resources in your account. An ARN allows you to specify any AWS resource unambiguously across all of AWS.

The ARN of a service has the following format: `arn:aws:service:region:account-id:resource`.

For example, the ARN of a Lambda function named *order-service* in the Frankfurt region (*eu-central-1*) would be `arn:aws:lambda:eu-central-1:<account id>:function :order-service`.

You can find the ARN for a resource on the AWS management console by selecting the resource and viewing the details panel.

Programmatically Provisioning AWS Resources

To provision the AWS resources discussed in this book, you can utilize the example code available on *GitHub*. Using this code requires having **Java 21** installed, as it is the programming language used for the **Lambda functions** and the **AWS Cloud Development Kit (CDK)**. The AWS CDK is an open-source framework that allows defining cloud infrastructure as code and deploying it on AWS. You will also need **Apache Maven** installed to build the Lambda functions. It is also recommended to install the **AWS Command Line Interface (AWS CLI),** which is a unified tool to manage your AWS services and will be utilized throughout this book.

Note: *To run the Java 21 code examples provided in this book, you can use* **Amazon Corretto 21** *which is Amazon's no-cost, multiplatform, production-ready distribution of* **OpenJDK 21**. *It is designed as a drop-in replacement for Java 21 that provides long-term support (LTS) with quarterly security updates as well as performance enhancements and bug fixes. Corretto 21 supports Linux, Windows, and macOS platforms and it is fully compatible with the Java 21 standard while delivering improved reliability, availability, and manageability compared to other OpenJDK distributions.*

Getting Started with Our E-commerce Project

Let's revisit **Shopme**, our large e-commerce platform that we started designing in *Chapter 1, Introduction to Event-Driven Microservices*, and see how we can apply the architectures and design patterns discussed in *Chapter 2, Designing Event-Driven Microservices on AWS*.

Shopme aims to be a successful e-commerce platform built with an event-driven microservices architecture. So far, we have designed the *ordering system* with four microservices: **NewOrder**, **ReserveInventory**, **ProcessPayment**, and **FulfilOrder**. We also used an API Gateway as the entry point to the microservices and an event channel to decouple the microservices, allowing them to react to events independently.

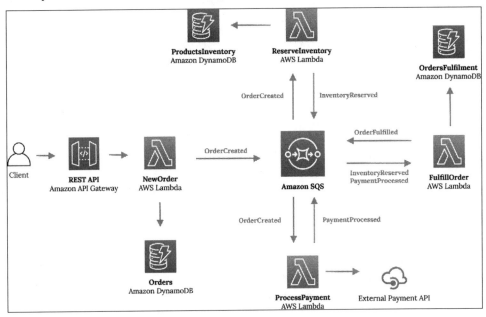

Figure 3.1: *Event-driven microservices architecture for the ordering system in AWS*

In this chapter, we will implement the architecture of our e-commerce platform using messaging services on AWS. As shown in Figure 3.1, the flow of the architecture would be:

1. The backend system will be accessed through a REST API entry point created using API Gateway. Clients will invoke this API to connect to the backend.

2. When an order is placed, API Gateway invokes the **NewOrder** service, implemented as a Lambda function, to process the order. The **NewOrder** service validates the order details and saves them to the **Orders** DynamoDB

table. If the order is successfully created in DynamoDB, the **NewOrder** service publishes an **OrderCreated** message to SQS to notify other services that a new order is ready for further processing.

3. When an **OrderCreated** message is received, it triggers the **ReserveInventory** Lambda function. The **ReserveInventory** service reserves product inventory for new orders and saves data about the inventory quantities of the new orders in the **ProductsInventory** DynamoDB table. If the product inventory reservation is successful, the **ReserveInventory** service publishes an **InventoryReserved** message to SQS.

4. The **OrderCreated** message also triggers the **ProcessPayment** Lambda function. The **ProcessPayment** service calls an external payments API in order to process the payment. If the payment is successfully processed by the external API, the **ProcessPayment** service then sends a **PaymentProcessed** message to SQS.

5. The **InventoryReserved** and **PaymentProcessed** messages trigger the **FulfillOrder** Lambda function. This service fulfills the orders and logs details about each fulfillment in the **OrdersFulfilment** DynamoDB table. After an order is successfully fulfilled, the service publishes an **OrderFulfilled** message to SQS. Other microservices that we have not yet built into our architecture can consume these messages from the queue.

The architectural design patterns covered in this chapter, which can implement the architecture discussed include:

- **Microservices with AWS Lambda and Amazon API Gateway**: Create a REST API with API Gateway and Lambda functions for the microservices.

- **Point-to-point messaging with Amazon SQS**: Use SQS for asynchronous communication between the microservices.

- **Asynchronous APIs with Amazon SQS**: Use SQS between API Gateway and the microservices to scale the system.

- **Pub/sub and fan-out with Amazon SNS:** Use SNS to send a single message to multiple recipients.

We will begin by examining how to integrate an API Gateway REST API with the microservices implemented as Lambda functions.

Microservices with AWS Lambda and Amazon API Gateway

Amazon API Gateway and AWS Lambda work together to help us create robust and scalable API endpoints. API Gateway sits in front of the Lambda functions and handles the API requests and responses. When an HTTP request comes into an API Gateway endpoint that is configured to invoke a Lambda function, the API Gateway translates the request into a JSON payload that gets passed to the Lambda function. The Lambda function runs the application code to process the request and generate a response. This response gets handed back to API Gateway, which can transform it and return it as the HTTP response to the initial API request.

This integration allows the Lambda functions to focus on the application logic while API Gateway handles all the API management, scaling, security, and monitoring. Together they provide a convenient way to develop, deploy, and manage APIs that can invoke serverless functions written in languages like Node.js, Python, Java, and so on.

Project Time: Building a REST API and Microservices

We will begin building the ordering system by creating a new REST API in the API Gateway that sends requests to the *NewOrder* service implemented as a Lambda function. The **NewOrder** service will validate the requests and store them in a DynamoDB table, as shown in *Figure 3.2*.

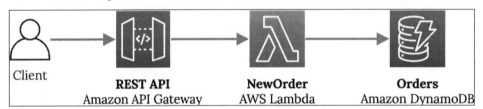

Figure 3.2: *Synchronous integration between Amazon API Gateway, AWS Lambda, and Amazon DynamoDB*

Creating Our First Lambda Function

To start with, let's create the Lambda function for the **NewOrder** service from the AWS management console:

1. From the list of services, search for *lambda* and go to the **AWS Lambda** dashboard.

2. From the **Lambda** dashboard, on the left sidebar click **Functions** and then click the **Create function** button.

3. Select **Author from scratch** and give the function the name **new-order-service**, choose the runtime **Java 21,** and **x86_64** for the architecture, as shown in *Figure 3.3*.

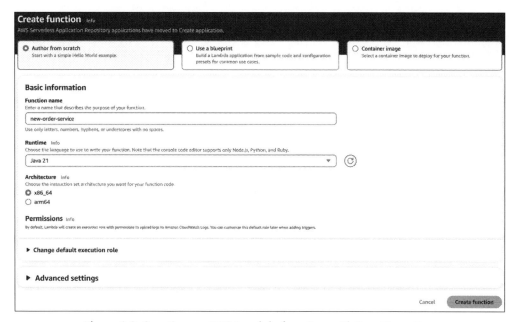

Figure 3.3: *Creating an AWS Lambda function with Java 21 runtime*

4. Use the default settings for the remaining options and click the **Create function**.

We have successfully created a Lambda function but have not yet added any code to it. We will now examine how a Lambda function executes when invoked.

Note: *Lambda functions can be configured in various ways, such as changing the memory allocation, adding environment variables, updating the concurrency level, and more. Some of these configuration options are useful for optimizing Lambda performance. For now, we will not modify the default Lambda configuration. In later chapters, we will explore Lambda configuration settings in more detail.*

Understanding the Lambda Handler Method

As discussed previously, Lambda allows you to run code without provisioning or managing servers. You upload your code and Lambda takes care of everything required to run and scale your code with high availability. When Lambda runs your code, it invokes a **handler** function that you define in your code. The **handler** is the method in your code that processes events. When your **Lambda** function is invoked, **Lambda** runs the code in the handler method. The **handler** receives the event data as input and returns a response.

You specify the name of the **handler** method when you upload your code to **Lambda**. The **handler** method should have two parameters: an **event** object and a **context** object. The **event** object contains information about the event that triggered the invocation, such as the request data for an API call. The **context** object contains metadata about the invocation, like the function name and execution time. Writing a **handler** function gives you full control over how Lambda responds to events.

Since we are integrating API Gateway with a **Lambda** function written in Java, the **Lambda handler** method will receive two parameters - an **APIGatewayProxyRequestEvent** object containing the request data, and an **APIGatewayProxyResponseEvent** object for constructing the response to return from the Lambda function.

Let's now see how to create our **Lambda handler** method for the **NewOrder** service in Java, which saves new orders to a DynamoDB table and then returns a successful response to API Gateway:

```java
public class LambdaHandler implements RequestHandler<APIGatewayV2HTTP
Event, APIGatewayV2HTTPResponse> {


        private DynamoDbClient ddb = DynamoDbClient.builder()
                .region(Region.EU_CENTRAL_1)
                .build();


        private Gson gson = new Gson();


        private SimpleDateFormat sdf = new SimpleDateFormat("yyyy/MM/dd
hh:mm:ss");


        @Override
        public APIGatewayV2HTTPResponse handleRequest(APIGatewayV2HTTP
Event event, Context context) {
                System.out.println("Received order request from API Gate-
way");


                // get order event
                var order = toOrder(event);


                // save Order to DynamoDB
                HashMap<String,AttributeValue> itemValues = new HashMap<>();
                itemValues.put("orderId",  AttributeValue.build-
er().s(order.getOrderId()).build());
```

```
            itemValues.put("customerId",   AttributeValue.build-
er().s(order.getCustomerId()).build());

            itemValues.put("orderDate",   AttributeValue.build-
er().s(sdf.format(order.getOrderDate())).build());

            itemValues.put("status",   AttributeValue.build-
er().s(order.getStatus().toString()).build());

            itemValues.put("items",   AttributeValue.builder().
ss(order.getItems()).build());

            itemValues.put("total",   AttributeValue.builder().n(order.
getTotal()).build());


            var request = PutItemRequest.builder()
                    .tableName("orders")
                    .item(itemValues)
                    .build();


            ddb.putItem(request);


            // return response to APIGW
            APIGatewayV2HTTPResponse response = new APIGateway-
V2HTTPResponse();
            response.setStatusCode(HttpStatusCode.CREATED);
            response.setBody(order.getOrderId());
            return response;
        }


    private Order toOrder(APIGatewayV2HTTPEvent event) {
            var orderRequest = gson.fromJson(event.getBody(), OrderRe-
quest.class);
            var order = new Order();
            order.setOrderId(UUID.randomUUID().toString());
            order.setCustomerId(orderRequest.getCustomerId());
            order.setOrderDate(new Date());
            order.setStatus(OrderStatus.PLACED);
            order.setItems(orderRequest.getItems());
```

```
                order.setTotal(orderRequest.getTotal());

                return order;

        }

}
```

The preceding **Lambda handler** method in Java uses two important libraries: **aws-lambda-java-core** and **aws-lambda-java-events**. The **aws-lambda-java-core** and **aws-lambda-java-events** libraries provide useful tools and utilities for developing Lambda functions using Java. The **aws-lambda-java-core** defines the **Lambda Context** object as well as interfaces that Lambda accepts, for example, the **RequestHandler**. The **aws-lambda-java-events** library builds on top of the core library and provides easy serialization and deserialization of common AWS event sources like Amazon API Gateway, Amazon S3, Amazon DynamoDB, and Amazon Kinesis. These libraries handle the translation between raw Lambda event formats and Java POJOs, so developers can focus on writing their business logic. Using these officially supported AWS SDK libraries makes it much easier to develop Lambda functions in Java compared to working directly with the Lambda APIs and raw JSON event formatting.

The **APIGatewayProxyRequestEvent** contains information about the HTTP request sent from the API Gateway, including headers, path parameters, query string parameters, and the request body. The **APIGatewayProxyResponseEvent** is used to return a response object back to the API Gateway with the HTTP status code, headers, and body. A typical Lambda handler would get data from the request event, perform some processing or integration with other services, and return a response using the **APIGatewayProxyResponseEvent**. This provides a simple way to connect API Gateway and Lambda to create a serverless API backend. The handler method must have a *public access modifier* and return an **APIGatewayProxyResponseEvent** object.

Uploading the Lambda Code

The next step is to build the **NewOrder** service code and deploy it to Lambda. We will use **Apache Maven** to handle the build process. It will compile the code and package it as a **jar** file, which will be output to the **target** folder in your local project directory. Once we have the jar file, we can import it into Lambda:

1. From the **AWS Lambda function** dashboard, open the **Code** tab and click on **Upload from .zip or .jar file**.

2. From the popup, find the **new-order-service.jar** file from the **target** folder of your project and click **Save**.

3. As soon as the jar file is uploaded, you will see a **Successfully updated the function new-order-service** message on top of the **Lambda** function.

4. Finally, you have to update the handler method to point to the **LambdaHandler** Java class we have created. From the **Code** tab, find the **Runtime settings**

section and click on **Edit**. There add **com.example.LambdaHandler** for the **Handler** input, as shown in *Figure 3.4*. Click **Save**.

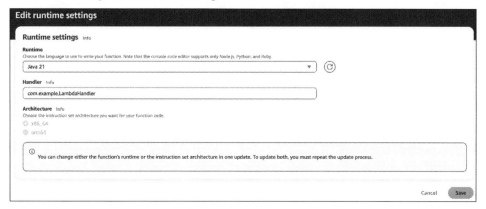

Figure 3.4: *Editing the runtime settings of an AWS Lambda function*

The **NewOrder** Lambda function has been created and deployed but does not yet have permission to write data to DynamoDB. The principle of least privilege is applied to all AWS services by default, meaning Lambda functions start out with minimal permissions. In the next section, we will update the permissions granted to the *NewOrder* Lambda function to allow it to save new orders to DynamoDB when triggered.

Updating the Lambda Function Permissions

In order for the **NewOrder** service Lambda function to save data to DynamoDB, we have to update the IAM role with the correct permissions:

1. From the **Lambda** dashboard of the **new-order-service** function, go to the **Configuration** tab and click on **Permissions** from the left sidebar.

2. From the **Execution** role section, find the role name and click on it to take you to the **IAM Roles** page. The role name should be **new-order-service-role-<id>**.

3. From the **IAM Roles** page, go to the **Permissions** tab and find the **Policy name** that starts with the name **AWSLambdaBasicExecutionRole**. When you click on it, you will be directed to the **IAM Policies** page.

4. Select the **Permissions** tab and click **Edit** to modify the permissions.

5. Find the ARN of the **orders** DynamoDB table and, on the **Policy editor** add a new statement that will only apply to the DynamoDB **orders** table:

```
{
        "Effect": "Allow",
        "Action": [
                "dynamodb:PutItem"
```

```
        ],
        "Resource": [
                "arn:aws:dynamodb:eu-central-1:<account id>:table/
    orders"
        ]
    }
```

6. Click **Next** and review the new permissions added. Finally, click **Save changes**.

The next step is to create the DynamoDB table that will store the orders data.

Creating the DynamoDB Table

To store new orders, the **NewOrder** service will utilize a **DynamoDB** table named **orders**. DynamoDB is a serverless database offering excellent performance. To create the **DynamoDB** table:

1. From the list of services, search for **dynamo** and click on **DynamoDB** to go to the **DynamoDB** dashboard.

2. On the left sidebar, click **Tables** and then click the **Create table** button.

3. Enter **orders** for the *Table name* and **orderId** for the **Partition Key**, as shown in *Figure 3.5*.

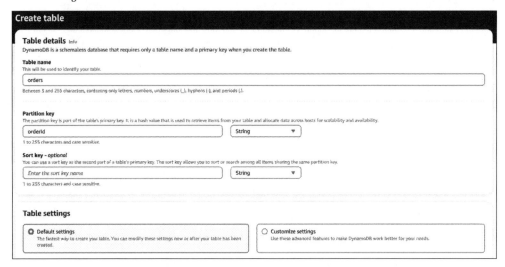

Figure 3.5: *Creating an Amazon DynamoDB table*

4. Use the default settings for the remaining options and click **Create table**.

The **DynamoDB** table will be provisioned within seconds. Next, we will build the REST API using API Gateway, which will serve as the event source for the **NewOrder** service.

Building the REST API With Amazon API Gateway

Amazon API Gateway allows the creation of APIs with three different endpoint types: *REST, HTTP*, and *websockets*. REST APIs allow building *RESTful* APIs that support common *HTTP* verbs like **GET**, **POST**, **PUT**, and **DELETE** for *CRUD* operations. *HTTP* APIs provide a simple way to create APIs that integrate with AWS Lambda functions and are good for high-performance requirements. *Websocket* APIs allow real-time bidirectional communication between the API and connected devices/clients. While *REST* APIs are the most fully featured, *HTTP* APIs offer faster performance and lower costs. *Websocket* APIs enable real-time capabilities not possible with REST or HTTP.

To start with, let's create a REST API with API Gateway:

1. From the list of services, search for *api* and click on API Gateway to go to the **API Gateway** dashboard.

2. Click on **Create API** and select **REST API** for the API *type*. Give your API the name **ordering-platform-api**, optionally a description, and select the *API endpoint type* to be **Regional,** as shown in *Figure 3.6*.

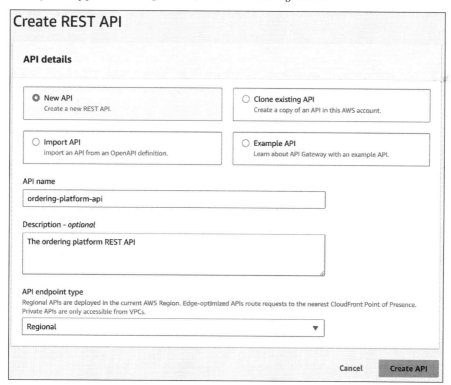

Figure 3.6: *Creating a REST API with Amazon API Gateway*

Note: *API Gateway supports deploying APIs in three ways – regional, private, and edge-optimized. Regional APIs are public APIs accessible over the internet and deployed in a region, providing high availability. Private APIs are accessible only within a Virtual Private Cloud (VPC) using a secure connection. An edge-optimized API is accessible over the public internet but caches API responses in Amazon CloudFront, a content delivery network (CDN) service, and edge locations for fast performance.*

3. Click **Create API** and wait for the **Successfully created REST API ordering-platform-api** message.

The REST API for order creation has been set up. The next step is to integrate it with the **NewOrder** service to allow new orders to be placed through the API. This involves creating an API resource such as **/orders** that define the endpoint structure, configuring the supported HTTP methods like GET to retrieve orders, and POST to create orders, and connecting the API methods to backend integrations like Lambda functions.

By defining the API resources, methods, and integrations, we will enable placing orders through calls to the REST API:

1. From the API Gateway dashboard, click on **Resources** in the left menu to see the root resource (/) that was automatically created.

2. Make sure the root resource (/) is selected and click on **Create resource**.

3. Give the new resource the name **orders** and click **Create resource**.

4. The new **/orders** resource will appear under the root resource.

5. Now that we have our first resource, we have to create a method for it to define the API functionality. Make sure the **/orders** resource is selected and click on the **Create method** on the right.

6. Select **POST** for the **Method type**, **Lambda** function for the **Integration type** and check the **Lambda proxy** integration, as illustrated in *Figure* 3.7. Search for the **new-order-service** Lambda function we created in the previous section. The ARN of the **new-order-service** will be displayed immediately after you select it.

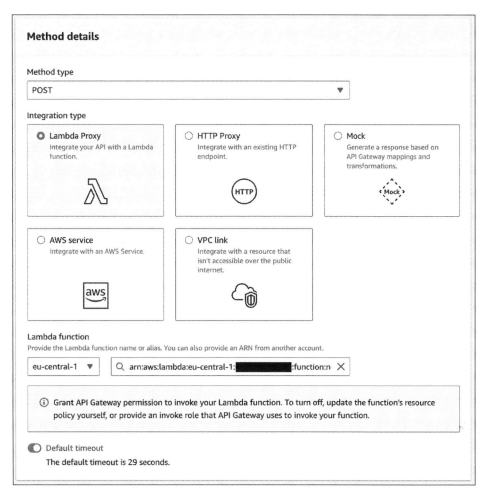

Figure 3.7: *Creating a resource method in Amazon API Gateway*

7. After you click on the **Create** method, you will see the new method created under the **/orders** resource.

A new method has been added which integrates with the **NewOrder** service. When the POST **/orders** HTTP request is made to API Gateway, it will now invoke the **NewOrder** service. Before calling this new endpoint, the API changes need to be deployed to a new stage, for example, **dev** or **prod**, in API Gateway. Stages allow having multiple versions of the API configured and deployed separately.

1. Click on **Deploy** API.

2. From the popup, select ***New stage*** for the stage, **dev** for the **Stage name**, and add an optional description, as shown in *Figure* 3.8.

Figure 3.8: *Deploying an API to a new stage in Amazon API Gateway*

3. Click on **Deploy** to deploy the API changes.

You now see that a new **dev** stage has been created under the **Stages** section. There you should find the **Invoke URL** of the ordering platform API we deployed, which is the endpoint exposed by API Gateway for our API, as well as other configurations such as rate, burst, API cache, logs and tracing and others.

Testing the Backend System

We will now test the REST API and **Lambda** function we have created. To test the API, we will use the **curl** command from a terminal, calling the **Invoke** URL:

```
$ curl -X POST <API Gateway Invoke URL >'/orders' \
  --header 'Content-Type: application/json' \
  --data-raw '{
    "customerId": "123",
    "items": ["item1", "item2", "item3"],
```

```
        "total": "74.5",
        "paymentDetails": {
            "paymentMethod": "CARD",
            "paymentTransactionId": "FDS232SGFDF341934"
        },
        "shippingDetails": {
            "receiverName": "John Doe",
            "receiverPhoneNumber": "123-456-7890",
            "shippingAddressLine1": "123 Main St",
            "shippingAddressLine2": "Apt 101",
            "shippingCity": "Anytown",
            "shippingState": "CA",
            "shippingZipCode": "12345",
            "shippingCountry": "USA"
        }
    }
}'
```

The response from API Gateway includes the **order ID** for the order that was created. You can also locate the newly created order by checking the DynamoDB items from the console or by running an AWS CLI command:

```
$ aws dynamodb scan --table-name orders --region eu-central-1
```

Understanding Lambda Cold Starts

When you first invoked the API Gateway endpoint that triggered the **NewOrder Lambda** function, you might have noticed it took several seconds to complete. On subsequent invocations, the response time was much faster. This is because of the **cold starts** that **Lambda** functions experience.

Lambda functions are stateless and therefore a new container needs to be spun up to serve each invocation. This adds additional latency compared to reusing an existing warm container. This is referred to as a cold start and occurs when a **Lambda** function is invoked for the first time or after a period of inactivity. It's a trade-off for the autoscaling and cost benefits of Lambda.

During a cold start, the Lambda runtime environment and your function code need to be loaded before the invocation can begin executing. This can take up to several seconds. Factors that affect cold start latency include the runtime, size of the deployment package, complexity of dependencies, and others.

Cold starts can be mitigated by optimizing your functions, keeping containers warm with regular invocations, using *provisioned concurrency*, using Lambda layers to separate out dependencies, and others. In upcoming chapters, we will examine some of those techniques more closely, as minimizing cold starts is crucial in an event-driven microservices architecture to avoid adding latency to the system.

Using IaS to Provision AWS Resources

As your infrastructure and application needs grow in production environments, it becomes increasingly important to manage your AWS resources in a structured, repeatable way. Provisioning resources manually through the AWS console works well at first, but can quickly become difficult to track, replicate, and control access. This is where **Infrastructure as Code (IaC)** tools like **AWS Cloud Development Kit (CDK)** come in.

The following code shows how to create the example we used previously using the CDK, a REST API integrated with a **Lambda** function, and DynamoDB for data storage, as opposed to manually configuring each component through the console, as in the previous example.

```
// create Lambda function

var lambda = Function.Builder.create(this, "Lambda_NewOrderService")
                .functionName("new-order-service")
            .runtime(Runtime.JAVA_21)
            .memorySize(512)
            .timeout(Duration.seconds(15))
            .code(Code.fromAsset("<path for jar file>"))
            .handler("com.example.LambdaHandler")
            .build();


// create REST API
var restApi = LambdaRestApi.Builder.create(this, "ApiGateway_Ordering-
PlarformApi")
            .restApiName("ordering-platform-api")
            .proxy(true)
            .build();


// add resource method
var apiResource = restApi.getRoot().addResource("orders");
```

```
apiResource.addMethod("POST", new LambdaIntegration(lambda));

// create DynamoDB table
var table = Table.Builder.create(this, "DynamoDB_OrdersTable")
                .tableName("orders")
                .partitionKey(Attribute.builder()
                    .name("orderId")
                    .type(AttributeType.STRING)
                    .build())
                .build();

// grant permissions to Lambda to write data to Dynamo
table.grantReadWriteData(lambda);
```

Point-to-Point Messaging with Amazon SQS

We previously created a synchronous integration between the REST API and the **NewOrder** service. To notify other microservices about new orders, our event-driven architecture will use **point-to-point messaging** to send order events. With this approach, a message is sent from one sender to one receiver, allowing each message to be processed by a single recipient.

To implement point-to-point messaging on AWS, we can use **Amazon Simple Queue Service (SQS)**. Amazon SQS is a fully managed message queuing service that enables you to decouple applications and services, allowing them to communicate with each other without needing to be tightly coupled. With SQS, you can send and receive messages between independent software components, such as microservices, and easily integrate with other AWS services like AWS Lambda, Amazon Kinesis, and Amazon SNS.

SQS will enable the *NewOrder* service to publish order events that other microservices can then consume individually via queues. This event-driven workflow aligns with our architecture while allowing the *NewOrder* service and consuming services to scale independently.

Some key features of Amazon SQS that we will discuss throughout this chapter include standard vs. FIFO queues, short and long polling, dead-letter queues, visibility timeout, and more. Let's begin by examining the differences between standard and FIFO queues.

Amazon SQS Standard vs. FIFO Queues

There are two types of queues available in Amazon SQS: **standard** queues and **FIFO (First-In-First-Out)** queues. We will discuss the differences between these two types of queues, their use cases, and how to choose the right queue for your needs.

Standard queues are the most commonly used type of queue in Amazon SQS. They are designed to provide a reliable and highly available messaging system for a wide range of use cases. Standard queues are optimized for high throughput and can handle a large number of messages. They also provide features such as long-term message storage, deduplication, and content-based routing.

Here are some key features of Standard queues:

- **High throughput**: Standard queues can handle a nearly unlimited number of messages per second, making them suitable for high-traffic applications.

- **At-least-once delivery**: Messages are guaranteed to be delivered at least once, but there is a chance that some messages may be delivered more than one time.

- **Best-effort ordering**: Messages are typically delivered in the order they were sent, but occasionally the order may not be preserved.

FIFO (First-In-First-Out) queues are designed for use cases where message order is important. They provide a strict order guarantee, ensuring that messages are processed in the order they are received. FIFO queues are optimized for low latency and high throughput, making them suitable for real-time applications.

Here are some key features of FIFO queues:

- **High throughput**: FIFO queues can handle a large number of messages per second, up to 3000 messages per second with batching, or up to 300 messages per second.

- **Exactly-once processing**: FIFO queues ensure messages are delivered exactly once and remain available until processed and deleted by a consumer. Duplicate messages are never introduced.

- **First-in-first-out delivery:** The sequence in which messages are sent and received is strictly maintained in the order they were added to the queue.

If your workload requires strict message ordering and no duplicates, use FIFO queues. If loose ordering is acceptable or duplicates are not an issue, standard queues can provide better throughput scalability.

Project Time: Asynchronous Messaging for the Microservices

So far, the **ReserveInventory**, **ProcessPayment**, and **FulfilOrder** services have not been notified when new orders are created in the *NewOrder* service. In this section, we will update the **NewOrder** service to send messages about new orders to a new SQS queue and create the **ReserveInventory** service which will subscribe to this queue and receive order-created messages, as shown in *Figure 3.9*.

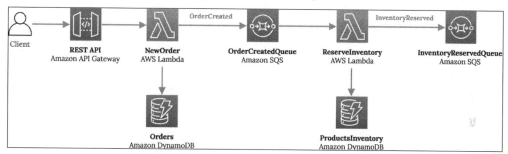

Figure 3.9: *Point-to-point messaging between microservices using Amazon SQS*

By having the **NewOrder** service send events about new orders, we can decouple the microservices. Other microservices can independently scale to process increased loads when order volumes grow, without impacting the *NewOrder* service. This event-driven architecture enables loose coupling and scalability across services.

Creating an SQS Queue

First, we need to create an SQS queue:

1. From the list of services, search for *sqs* and click on **Simple Queue Service** to go to the **Amazon SQS** dashboard.

2. On the left sidebar, click **Queues** and then click the **Create queue** button.

3. Select **Standard** for the **Type** and enter **OrderCreatedQueue** for the queue name, as shown in *Figure 3.10*.

Figure 3.10: *Creating an Amazon SQS queue*

4. Take note of the several configuration options. Use the default settings for the remaining options and click **Create queue**.

In just a few easy steps, you have set up a serverless queue that is now ready for use. The queue you created is a standard queue with these default settings:

- **Visibility timeout**: 30 seconds
- **Message retention period**: 4 days
- **Delivery delay**: 0 seconds
- **Maximum message size**: 256 KB
- **Receive message wait time**: 0 seconds

Further on in this chapter, we will examine the configuration options more closely.

Updating the Lambda Function to Send Messages to the SQS Queue

Next, we need to update the **NewOrder** service to send the new order messages to the SQS queue we created. The **ReserveInventory** service in our microservices architecture will then pick up those messages from the queue. After saving a new order item to DynamoDB, the **NewOrder** service will send a message to the SQS queue, as shown in the following code:

```
// Retrieve the queue
var getQueueRequest = GetQueueUrlRequest.builder()
        .queueName("OrderCreatedQueue")
        .build();


var queueUrl = sqsClient.getQueueUrl(getQueueRequest).queueUrl();


// Send the message to the queue
var sendMsgRequest = SendMessageRequest.builder()
        .queueUrl(queueUrl)
        .messageBody(gson.toJson(order))
        .build();


sqsClient.sendMessage(sendMsgRequest);
```

The **NewOrder** service should also be updated to grant the necessary permissions to send messages to SQS. For that, we need to update the IAM role of the **NewOrder** service like we did previously:

1. Find the IAM Role of the **new-order-service** and open the Policy editor of the **AWSLambdaBasicExecutionRole**, as we saw previously. Add a new statement that will allow the NewOrder service to send messages to the **NewOrderQueue** queue:

```
{
    "Effect": "Allow",
    "Action": [
        "sqs:GetQueueUrl",
        "sqs:SendMessage"
    ],
    "Resource": [
        "arn:aws:sqs:eu-central-1:<account id>:OrderCre-
atedQueue"
    ]
}
```

2.   Click **Next** and review the new permissions added. Finally, click **Save changes**.

The **NewOrder** service has been updated to publish a message to a new SQS queue upon the successful creation of a new order. The next step is to develop the **ReserveInventory** service, which will subscribe to this SQS queue and reserve inventory for new orders.

Creating the Lambda Function for the ReserveInventory Service

The **ReserveInventory** service will also be implemented as a **Lambda** function. It will listen for **OrderCreated** messages sent by the *NewOrder* service to the **OrderCreatedQueue** queue, using the **SQSEvent** Java class from the **aws-lambda-java-events** library we saw earlier.

Upon receiving an order message, **ReserveInventory** will reserve the required inventory by storing reservation data in DynamoDB. It will then send an *InventoryReserved* message to the **InventoryReservedQueue** SQS queue. Let's see what the Lambda handler method for the *ReserveInventory* service looks like:

```java
public class LambdaHandler implements RequestHandler<SQSEvent, Void> {


        private DynamoDbClient ddb = DynamoDbClient.builder()
                .region(<region>)
                .build();


        private SqsClient sqsClient = SqsClient.builder()
                .region(<region>)
                .build();


        @Override
        public Void handleRequest(SQSEvent event, Context context) {
                for (var message : event.getRecords()) {

                        // convert the message body to order event
                        var order = gson.fromJson(message.getBody(), Order.
class);

                        // save reserved inventory to DynamoDB
```

```
                    HashMap<String,AttributeValue> itemValues = new
HashMap<>();

                    itemValues.put("orderId",  AttributeValue.build-
er().s(order.getOrderId()).build());


                var request = PutItemRequest.builder()
                    .tableName("products-inventory")
                    .item(itemValues)
                    .build();


                ddb.putItem(request);


                // send InventoryReserved message to SQS
                var getQueueRequest = GetQueueUrlRequest.builder()
                    .queueName("InventoryReservedQueue")
                    .build();


                var queueUrl = sqsClient.getQueueUrl(getQueueReq-
uest).queueUrl();


                var sendMsgRequest = SendMessageRequest.builder()
                    .queueUrl(queueUrl)
                    .messageBody(message.getBody())
                    .build();


                sqsClient.sendMessage(sendMsgRequest);
            }
            return null;
        }
    }
```

The *SQSEvent event* object in the code contains all the unprocessed messages sent by
the *NewOrder* service to the *OrderCreatedQueue* queue. The *ReserveInventory* service
needs to process these messages in a loop and reserve the items in a new DynamoDB
table. For each message that is processed, the *ReserveInventory* service should send a

new message to the *InventoryReservedQueue* queue, indicating that the inventory has been reserved.

Adding SQS as an Event Source for Lambda

We will now add the **OrderCreatedQueue** queue as an event source for the **ReserveInventory** service. To enable **Lambda** to get messages from SQS, we need to provide the **Lambda** function with the necessary permissions. Specifically, the IAM role for the **Lambda** function should have permissions to receive, delete, and get attributes for messages from the SQS queue:

1. Find the *IAM Role* of the **inventory-service** and open the *Policy editor* of the **AWSLambdaBasicExecutionRole**, as we saw previously. Add a new statement that will allow the **NewOrder** service to send messages to the **OrderCreatedQueue** queue:

```
{
        "Effect": "Allow",
        "Action": [
                "sqs:ReceiveMessage",
                "sqs:DeleteMessage",
                "sqs:GetQueueAttributes"
        ],
        "Resource": [
                "arn:aws:sqs:eu-central-1:<account id>:OrderCreated-
Queue"
        ]
}
```

2. Click **Next** and review the new permissions added. Finally, click **Save changes**.

The **ReserveInventory** service has been granted permission to receive messages from the **OrderCreatedQueue** queue. The next step is to add the **OrderCreatedQueue** queue as an event source for the **ReserveInventory** service:

1. From the **Lambda** dashboard of the **inventory-service** function, go to the **Configuration** tab and click on **Triggers** from the left sidebar. Click **Add trigger**.

2. Select the **OrderCreatedQueue** queue, as shown in *Figure 3.11*. Use the default settings for the remaining options and click **Add**.

Figure 3.11: *Adding Amazon SQS as an event source for AWS Lambda*

Tip: The **Batch size** *option enables messages to build up in an SQS queue before triggering a Lambda function invocation. The batch size can be configured up to 10,000 messages. Additionally, the* **Batch window** *option specifies the maximum amount of time Lambda will wait after receiving a message from an SQS queue before invoking a function to process that message. This waiting period can be set up to 5 minutes. Enabling batching and setting a longer wait time reduces the number of Lambda invocations, which helps optimize cost. This batching approach works best for workloads that are not highly time-sensitive.*

3. You will now see a **Creating** state for the SQS trigger, which will change to **Enabled** after some seconds. You might need to refresh the page to see the changes.

The event source for the `ReserveInventory` service has been updated to retrieve messages from the `OrderCreatedQueue` queue. With this change implemented, the `ReserveInventory` service is configured to process new order messages published by the *NewOrder* service to the `OrderCreatedQueue` as they become available.

The rest of the microservices will be implemented in subsequent sections.

Note: *Lambda polls messages from SQS synchronously. There is a Lambda option to add a destination service, for example, SQS or SNS, but that is only applicable to asynchronous invocations. If Lambda and SQS integration were asynchronous, we could have used this destination service and not updated the code to send messages to new queues.*

Testing the Backend System

To evaluate the new architecture, execute the same *curl* command from the previous example again. Then, verify the item was inserted into DynamoDB by running an AWS CLI command to retrieve the item:

```
$ aws dynamodb scan --table-name products-inventory --region eu-central-1
```

Amazon SQS Features

When we created the SQS queues, we saw some configuration options that control key aspects of how Amazon SQS works. These options included `visibility timeout`, `message retention period`, `delivery delay`, `message size`, and `receive message wait time` related to `short and long polling`. Let's take a closer look at what each of these options means and how they impact our architecture.

Visibility Timeout

In Amazon SQS, `visibility timeout` is the duration for which a message is invisible to other receiving applications after it is received by a consumer. The `visibility timeout` defines the duration for which a message is stored in the queue and not read by a consumer.

`Visibility timeout` is an important parameter in Amazon SQS because it allows you to control the lifecycle of messages in the queue. You can use `visibility timeout` to ensure that messages are consumed within a specific timeframe, preventing them from accumulating in the queue and causing congestion.

The default `visibility timeout` is 30 seconds for all messages in a queue. Typically, the visibility timeout should be set to the maximum amount of time your application needs to fully process and delete a message. This ensures messages are not redelivered to other consumers if they are still being processed.

Here are some best practices for configuring `visibility timeout` in Amazon SQS:

- **Set a reasonable visibility timeout**: The `visibility timeout` should be set based on the expected consumption rate of messages and the amount of time it takes for a consumer to process a message.

- **Monitor message age**: Monitor the age of messages in the queue to ensure that messages are not being left in the queue for an extended period of time.

- **Use a short visibility timeout for high-priority messages**: If you have high-priority messages, consider using a short visibility timeout to ensure that these messages are consumed quickly.

- **Use a long visibility timeout for low-priority messages**: If you have low-priority messages, consider using a long visibility timeout to ensure that these messages are not consumed too quickly.

Message Retention Period

The `message retention period` in Amazon SQS determines how long messages are retained in the queue before they are automatically deleted. This feature allows you to control the lifespan of messages in your queue, ensuring that messages are not retained for longer than necessary.

When a message is sent to an Amazon SQS queue, it is stored in the queue until it is consumed by a worker or until the message retention period expires. For example, if the message retention period is set to 7 days, and a message is sent to the queue on Monday, it will be automatically deleted from the queue on the following Monday, assuming it has not been consumed by a worker before then.

The default message retention period in Amazon SQS is **4 days** and can be configured from **1 minute** up to **14 days**.

Here are some best practices for using the message retention period in Amazon SQS:

- Set the message retention period based on the needs of your application. For example, if your application can process messages quickly, you may want to set the retention period to a shorter value to avoid storing messages for longer than necessary.

- Consider using a message retention period that is longer than the time it takes for your workers to process messages. This will ensure that messages are not automatically deleted before they can be processed.

- Monitor the size of your queue and adjust the message retention period as needed to prevent the queue from growing too large.

- Consider using Amazon SQS's *Dead Letter Queue* feature to send messages that are not processed after a certain amount of retries to another queue.

Delivery delay

The **`delivery delay`** feature in Amazon SQS allows you to specify a delay period for messages before they are delivered to a queue. When a new message is sent to a queue with a delivery delay configured, that message will be made invisible to consumers for the duration of the configured delay period. This feature can be useful when you want to introduce a delay between message processing steps.

For example, suppose you have a multi-step workflow that processes a message, and you want to ensure that the next step in the workflow does not start until a certain amount of time has passed. You can use the delivery delay feature to specify a delay period, and the message will be held in the queue until the delay period has elapsed.

The default and minimum delay for an Amazon SQS queue is **0 seconds**, which means messages are processed right away, and the maximum is **15 minutes**.

The delivery delay feature in Amazon SQS can help you build more robust and scalable applications in several ways:

- **Introduce delays between message processing steps**: The delivery delay feature can also be used to introduce delays between message processing steps. This can be useful if you want to ensure that messages are not processed too quickly or if you want to allow for manual intervention or other processing steps to occur before the next message is processed.

- **Handle message processing failures**: If a message processing step fails, you can use the delivery delay feature to ensure that the message is not delivered to the next step until it has been successfully processed. This can help you avoid the need for manual intervention or retry mechanisms.

- **Improve message routing and processing**: By using the delivery delay feature, you can improve the routing and processing of messages in your application. For example, you can use the delay period to ensure that messages are processed in a specific order or to allow for manual intervention before the next message is processed.

Message Size

Amazon SQS supports messages of various sizes, ranging from 1 KB to 256 KB. The message size is determined by the producer when the message is sent to the queue.

The message size can have significant implications for the performance and efficiency of the queue. Here are some factors to consider:

- **Throughput**: The message size can affect the throughput of the queue. Larger messages can result in slower throughput, as they take longer to transmit and process.

- **Latency**: The message size can also affect the latency of the queue. Larger messages can result in longer latency, as they take longer to transmit and process.

- **Cost**: The message size can affect the cost of using the queue. Larger messages can result in higher costs, as they require more storage and processing resources.

- **Reliability**: The message type can affect the reliability of the queue. Delayed messages can be more reliable, as they are stored in the queue for a longer period of time before they are made available to consumers.

Short and Long Polling

In SQS, two main polling strategies can be used to receive messages from a queue: **short polling** and **long polling**. The main difference between these two strategies is the amount of time that the receiving application spends waiting for new messages to arrive. This time is specified in the `receive message wait time` configuration we saw when creating the SQS queue.

Short polling is a technique where the receiving application periodically checks the queue for new messages, typically instantly (`0 seconds`, which is the default) or every few seconds. This approach is useful when the application needs to process messages quickly and cannot afford to wait for a long time for new messages to arrive.

The advantages of short polling are:

- **Faster response time**: The application can process messages more quickly, which can improve the overall performance of the system.
- **Lower latency**: The application can respond to messages more quickly, which can improve the user experience.

Long polling is a technique where the receiving application waits for a longer period of time, typically 20 seconds, which is the maximum you can set, before checking the queue for new messages. This approach is useful when the application can afford to wait for a longer time for new messages to arrive, and the system can handle a higher volume of messages.

The advantages of long polling are:

- **Lower overhead**: The application needs to check the queue less frequently, which can reduce the overhead and improve the efficiency of the system.
- **Lower resource usage and cost**: The application needs to maintain a connection to the queue for a shorter period of time, which can reduce the resource usage and cost of the API calls to SQS.

The choice of polling strategy depends on the specific requirements of the application and the system. If the application needs to process messages quickly and cannot afford to wait for a long time for new messages to arrive, short polling may be the better choice. However, if the application can afford to wait for a longer time for new messages to arrive and the system can handle a higher volume of messages, long polling may be the better choice.

Understanding How Lambda Scales with SQS

When a Lambda function subscribes to an SQS queue, it polls the queue and waits for messages to arrive. Lambda processes messages in batches, starting with 5 concurrent executions of the function.

If there are additional messages in the queue, Lambda automatically scales up the concurrency, adding up to **300 executions per minute** up to a maximum of **1,250 concurrent executions**. This allows Lambda to scale dynamically based on the length of the SQS queue.

This auto-scaling behavior is managed by AWS and cannot be changed. To process more SQS messages, you can optimize the Lambda function for higher throughput in several ways:

- Increase the memory allocated to Lambda

- Configure the reserved concurrency to Lambda

- Use SQS features like visibility timeout, dead-letter queues, and batching

In later chapters, we will explore these strategies for increasing Lambda throughput in more detail when processing high volumes of SQS messages. The auto-scaling capabilities make Lambda a flexible compute option for consuming SQS queues, but there are configuration choices that allow you to fine-tune throughput.

Project Time: Asynchronous APIs with Amazon API Gateway, Amazon SQS, and AWS Lambda

Earlier, we built a synchronous integration from Amazon API Gateway to AWS Lambda. API Gateway calls the *NewOrder service* directly and waits for the response. This works well at low traffic volumes. However, as traffic increases, the synchronous model creates a scaling bottleneck.

At the time of writing, API Gateway has a regional account limit of 10,000 *concurrent API executions*. On the other hand, Lambda has a regional account limit of 1,000 *concurrent requests*. That means that for the region we selected in the AWS account, the API Gateway can process up to 10,000 concurrent requests at the same time. Meanwhile, Lambda can handle up to 1,000 concurrent requests simultaneously in that region.

This synchronous model essentially couples the scaling limits of API Gateway and Lambda together. If more requests come to either API Gateway or Lambda, then these get *throttled*, which results in errors for the end users.

To resolve this issue, we can decouple the scaling limits of API Gateway and Lambda by putting Amazon SQS in between so that API Gateway puts requests onto an SQS queue instead of invoking Lambda directly, as shown in *Figure 3.12*. Then the *NewOrder* Lambda function polls the queue and processes requests asynchronously. SQS queues can handle nearly *unlimited* inbound traffic and queue up requests. This prevents API Gateway from throttling. Requests are processed asynchronously and in parallel. Latency is higher, but overall throughput increases.

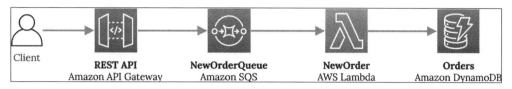

Figure 3.12: *Add Amazon SQS between Amazon API Gateway and AWS
Lambda for asynchronous APIs*

With SQS as a buffer, API Gateway and Lambda can scale independently. API Gateway is protected from throttling errors while Lambda can consume as much parallel traffic as its resources and scaling policies allow. The asynchronous queue model is essential for large-scale, high-throughput APIs.

Next, let's see how to integrate SQS with API Gateway and Lambda.

Note: *The quotas of 10,000 concurrent API requests for API Gateway and 1,000 concurrent requests for Lambda that we talked about are initial limits that can be increased as needed. Customers can request higher quotas from AWS Support to scale up these resources over time based on growing demand. This provides flexibility to expand capacity without being constrained by predefined hard limits.*

Integrating SQS With Lambda

The steps to integrate a new SQS queue with the **NewOrder** service mirror those we previously completed when integrating an SQS queue with the **ReserveInventory** service. Specifically, we need to:

1. Create an SQS queue named **NewOrderQueue**.

2. Update the execution role of the **NewOrder** service to allow the **NewOrderQueue** as an event source:

```
{
        "Effect": "Allow",
        "Action": [
                "sqs:ReceiveMessage",
                "sqs:DeleteMessage",
                "sqs:GetQueueAttributes"
        ],
        "Resource": [
                "arn:aws:sqs:eu-central-1:<account id>:NewOrder-
Queue"
        ]
}
```

3. Add the **NewOrderQueue** as a new trigger to the *NewOrder service*.

4. Update the Lambda code with the new **SQSEvent**.

5. Remove the API Gateway trigger.

We have successfully replaced the event source of the **NewOrder** service from API Gateway to the **NewOrderQueue** queue.

Integrating SQS with API Gateway

The next step would be to replace the direct integration of API Gateway with Lambda with an integration using SQS as an intermediary between API Gateway and Lambda. For that, we have to create a new IAM Role, which would grant API Gateway the necessary permissions to send messages to **NewOrderQueue**:

1. From the **IAM** dashboard, go to the **Policies** page from the left sidebar, and click **Create policy.**

2. Select **SQS** for the *Service*, **SendMessage** for the *Actions allowed*, and select the ARN of the **NewOrderQueue** queue, as shown in *Figure 3.13*. Click **Next**.

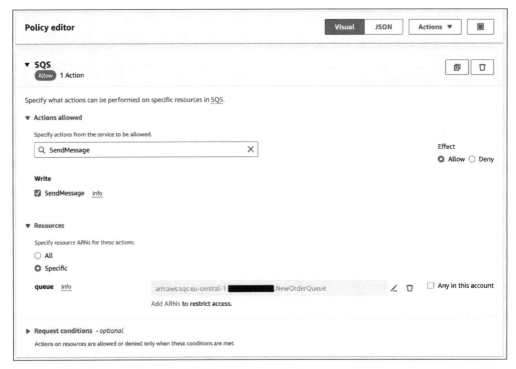

Figure 3.13: *Granting Amazon API Gateway permissions to send messages to Amazon SQS*

3. Enter **OrderingPlatformAPINewOrderQueuePolicy** for the **Policy name** and optionally a description. Click **Create policy.**

4. From the **IAM** dashboard, go to the **Roles** page from the left sidebar, and click **Create role**.

5. Select **Custom trust policy** for the **Trusted entity type** and add the **Custom trust** policy.

```
{
    "Version": "2012-10-17",
    "Statement": [
        {
            "Effect": "Allow",
            "Principal": {
                "Service": [
                    "apigateway.amazonaws.com"
                ]
            },
            "Action": [
                "sts:AssumeRole"
            ]
        }
    ]
}
```

6. Click **Next**. Select the **OrderingPlatformAPINewOrderQueuePolicy** policy we created earlier. Click **Next**.

7. Give the role the name **OrderingPlatformAPINewOrderQueueRole** and, optionally, a description. Review the permissions and click **Create role**.

We will now add a new resource to the API Gateway to asynchronously call the **NewOrder** service using the **NewOrderQueue** queue:

1. From the **API Gateway** dashboard of the **ordering-platform-api**, click on **Resources** from the left sidebar.

2. Click on the **root resource/** and click **Create resource**.

3. Enter **orders-async** for the **Resource name** and click **Create resource**.

4. Select the **/orders-async** resource you created and click **Create method**.

5. Select **POST** for the **Method type**, **AWS service** for the **Integration type**, the AWS region **eu-central-1**, and **Simple Queue Service (SQS)** for the AWS

service, as illustrated in *Figure 3.14*. Leave the **AWS Subdomain** blank. For the **HTTP method**, choose **POST**. For *Action Type*, choose `Use path override`. For **Path override** - *optional*, enter `<account_id>/NewOrderQueue`. For the Execution role, enter the ARN of the **OrderingPlatformAPINewOrderQueueRole** IAM role that you created previously. Click **Create method**.

Figure 3.14: *Integrating Amazon API Gateway with Amazon SQS*

6. From the resources, select the **POST** method you created and click on the **Integration request** tab. Click **Edit** next to the *Integration request settings*.

7. Scroll down and select **Never** for the **Request body passthrough**. Scroll down and open the **URL request header parameters**. Add a new request header parameter and enter **Content-Type** for the **name** and **'application/x-www-form-urlencoded'** for **Mapped from**. Do not forget to add the single quotes otherwise, you will get an error. Click **Save**.

8. From the same **Integration request** tab, scroll down and find the **Mapping templates** section. Click **Create template**.

9. For the **Content type**, enter **application/json**, for the **Generate template**, select **Empty**, and for the **Template body**, enter **Action=SendMessage&MessageBody=$input.body**. Click **Create template**.

10. Click **Deploy API** to the **dev** stage to deploy the changes.

The integration between API Gateway, SQS, and Lambda has been successfully completed.

Testing the Integration

Let's now test the integration and confirm that the integration between API Gateway, SQS and Lambda works. We will call the same API, we did previously, but for the **/ orders-async** method now:

```
$ curl -X POST <API Gateway Invoke URL >'/orders-async' \
  --header 'Content-Type: application/json' \
  --data-raw '{
    "customerId": "123",
    "items": ["item1", "item2", "item3"],
    "total": "74.5",
    "paymentDetails": {
        "paymentMethod": "CARD",
        "paymentTransactionId": "FDS232SGFDF341934"
    },
    "shippingDetails": {
        "receiverName": "John Doe",
        "receiverPhoneNumber": "123-456-7890",
        "shippingAddressLine1": "123 Main St",
        "shippingAddressLine2": "Apt 101",
        "shippingCity": "Anytown",
        "shippingState": "CA",
        "shippingZipCode": "12345",
        "shippingCountry": "USA"
    }
}'
```

The response you receive now will not include the **order ID** that was previously provided by the **NewOrder** service. The communication is now asynchronous, meaning the response is simply an acknowledgment from SQS confirming that it has successfully added the message to its queue. You will no longer get the **order ID** in the response since the processing happens asynchronously after SQS queues the message rather than synchronously, while the request is still open. A sample response from SQS would be:

```
{
  "SendMessageResponse": {
    "ResponseMetadata": {
      "RequestId": "f7668386-041c-505f-96b3-de67667cee1d"
    },
    "SendMessageResult": {
      "MD5OfMessageAttributes": null,
      "MD5OfMessageBody": "a63d9a2189bb96c034057f6855f81762",
      "MD5OfMessageSystemAttributes": null,
      "MessageId": "b4308ce6-34fa-493e-9748-ef586d8397eb",
      "SequenceNumber": null
    }
  }
}
```

To confirm that the new order has been successfully saved to DynamoDB, you should either locate the items in the DynamoDB *Orders* table dashboard or run a CLI command:

```
$ aws dynamodb scan --table-name orders --region eu-central-1
```

Amazon SQS Features (Continued)

Previously, we discussed some key features of Amazon SQS that are relevant to our architecture. In the following sections, we will examine another two Amazon SQS capabilities in more detail to understand how they can be useful for our needs: **dead-letter queues** and **encryption**.

Dead-Letter Queues

Amazon SQS has a feature called a **dead-letter queue,** which is a separate SQS queue used for storing messages that could not be processed from the original queue. If a consumer fails to process a message from the main queue, that message gets moved to the **dead-letter queue** for storage. The **dead-letter queue** allows failed messages to be isolated rather than blocking the main queue while still providing an opportunity to debug or re-process them if needed.

There are a couple of reasons why a message might be moved to a dead-letter queue, including:

- **Message expiration**: If a message expires before it can be processed, it will be moved to the dead-letter queue.

- **Message rejection**: If a message is rejected by the intended recipient, it will be moved to the dead-letter queue.

Once a message is in the **dead-letter queue**, it can be processed by a different system or at a later time. For example, a **dead-letter queue** might be monitored by a separate system that can process the messages in the queue.

Using dead-letter queues in SQS provides several benefits, including:

- **Improved reliability**: Dead-letter queues help to ensure that messages are not lost if they cannot be processed by the intended recipient.

- **Fault tolerance**: Dead-letter queues provide a way to handle messages that cannot be processed due to system failures or other issues.

- **Message recovery**: Dead-letter queues allow messages to be recovered and processed at a later time, even if the original system is no longer available.

Tip: *For production systems, it is best practice to configure dead-letter queues for all message queues. This helps ensure that no messages are lost and that any failed messages are routed to the dead-letter queue for later analysis. Monitor the dead-letter queues regularly to verify that messages are processed correctly overall.*

To set up a dead-letter queue for an existing SQS queue, you have to create a new SQS queue that will serve as the dead-letter queue. Then, open the settings for the original SQS queue you want to attach a dead-letter queue to and there select the SQS queue you created as the dead-letter queue, as shown in *Figure 3.15*.

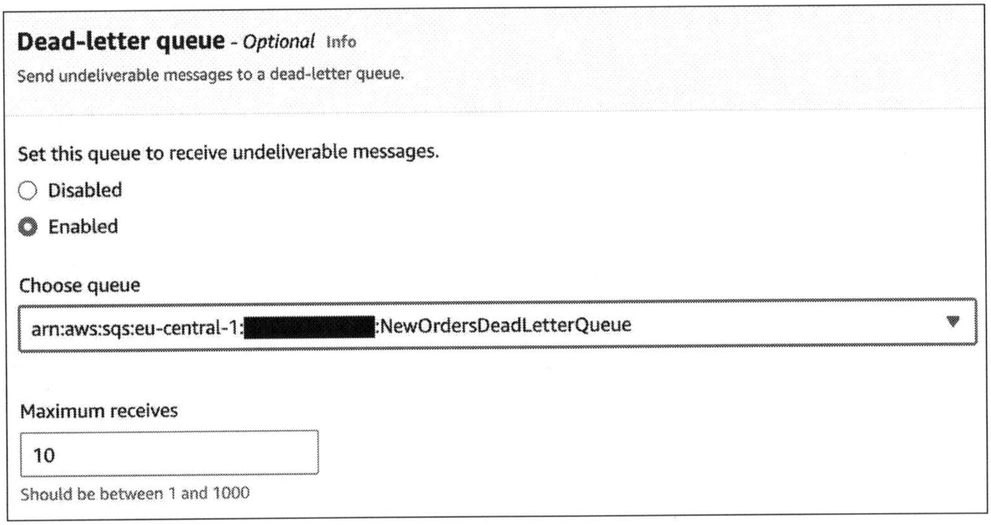

Figure 3.15: *Configuring a dead-letter queue for an Amazon SQS queue*

This configures the dead-letter queue so that messages that fail processing on the original queue will be sent to the dead-letter queue you created rather than being discarded.

Encryption

Encryption is a critical aspect of data security, and it's essential to ensure that your data is protected from unauthorized access, especially when it's in transit or at rest. Amazon SQS provides two server-side encryption options to ensure the security of your data, including **SSE-SQS** and **SSE-KMS**.

Server-Side encryption with **SSE-SQS** encrypts messages with keys fully managed by Amazon SQS. When you send a message to an SQS queue with SSE-SQS enabled, the message body is encrypted on the server side with an SQS-owned encryption key before the message is stored. The same key is used to decrypt the message when retrieving it from the queue. Enabling SSE-SQS requires no action on your part other than selecting the encryption option when creating or modifying your queue. There are no additional charges for enabling SSE-SQS. The encryption and decryption happen transparently on the SQS service side.

Server-Side encryption with **AWS Key Management Service (SSE-KMS)** allows you to create and manage the keys used to encrypt your SQS messages within AWS KMS. The SQS queue is associated with an AWS KMS customer master key (CMK) which is used to encrypt messages when they are stored in the queue. When enabling SSE-KMS, you need to first create a CMK in KMS or use an existing CMK that you manage. There are additional charges for using AWS KMS keys in SQS encryption.

An advantage of using SSE-KMS over SSE-SQS is more control over encryption keys, including the ability to create, rotate, and disable the CMK keys. However, there is more complexity involved in managing AWS KMS keys.

To enable encryption on our SQS queues, we can go to the **SQS** dashboard, select the queue we want to encrypt, open the queue settings, and choose either SSE-SQS or SSE-KMS as the encryption option, as illustrated in *Figure 3.16*.

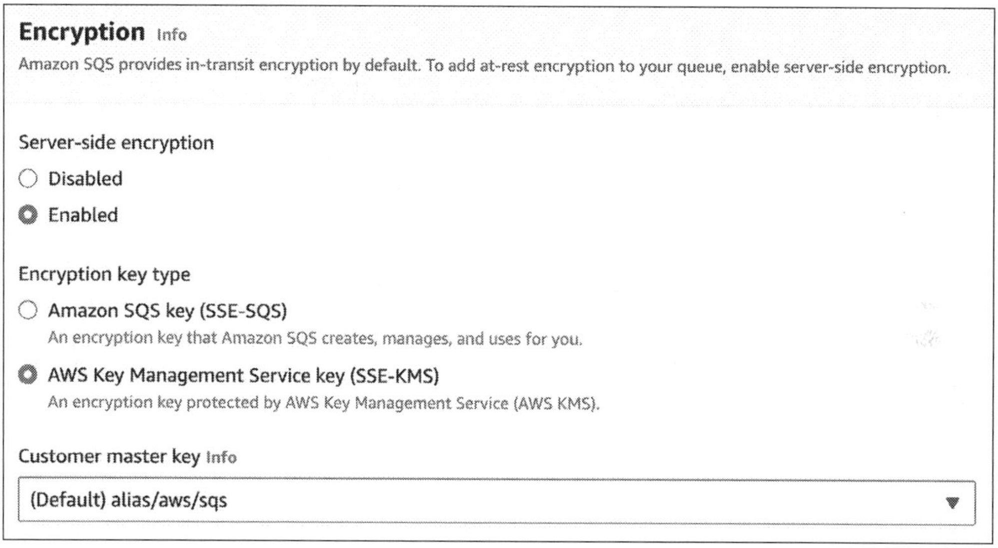

Figure 3.16: *Selecting the encryption key type for an Amazon SQS queue*

Pub/sub and Fan-out with Amazon SNS

Previously, we discussed how the *NewOrder service* sent new order messages to the `ReserveInventory` service through SQS. However, SQS only allows a message to be processed by a single receiver. To send the same message to multiple recipients, we can utilize the **Amazon Simple Notification Service (SNS)**.

Amazon SNS is a managed messaging service that enables applications, end-users, and devices to communicate with each other. SNS allows you to send notifications to subscribers via multiple protocols, including HTTP/S, email, SMS, SQS queues, and mobile push notifications. SNS is a push-based service and messages are sent to topics. Similar to SQS, SNS also supports FIFO topics and encryption is done the same way. SNS supports a variety of subscribers, including Amazon SQS, AWS Lambda, SMS, Email, HTTP(s), and more.

By using SNS instead of SQS in our architecture, the `NewOrder` service can publish a new order message once and have it be processed by the `ReserveInventory` service as well as the `ProcessPayment` service through two new SQS queues that will be subscribed to SNS. Next, let's modify our architecture and introduce SNS to it.

Sending the Same Message to Multiple Recipients

In our current architecture, the **NewOrder** service publishes new order events to the **OrderCreatedQueue** queue, which is then consumed by the **ReserveInventory** *service* for processing. However, we also need the **ProcessPayment** service to consume these events to process payments in parallel. One option to implement that would be to update the **NewOrder** service to send the same message to another SQS queue consumed by the **ProcessPayment** service. However, that requires code changes in the **NewOrder** service and creates a tight coupling between services. Also, if more services need that event, we would have to repeatedly update the **NewOrder** service.

Instead, we can have the **NewOrder** service publish the message to an SNS topic, which will fan out the message to multiple recipients subscribed to that topic, as illustrated in *Figure* 3.17. This avoids modifying the **NewOrder** service each time a new consumer is added. Any service needing the event can simply subscribe to the SNS topic without any changes to the **NewOrder** service. This decouples services and avoids coordination between teams when new consumers are added.

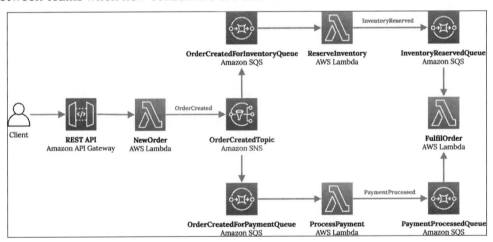

Figure 3.17: *Fan-out messaging pattern with Amazon SNS*

Next, we will look at the necessary steps to modify our architecture and utilize Amazon SNS.

Creating an SNS Topic

First, we need to create the SNS topic where the messages will be sent to:

1. From the list of services, search for *sns* and click on **SNS** to go to the **Simple Notification Service** dashboard.

2. On the left sidebar, click **Topics** and then click the **Create topic** button.

3. Select **Standard** for the *Type* and enter **OrderCreatedTopic** for the name, as shown in *Figure 3.18*.

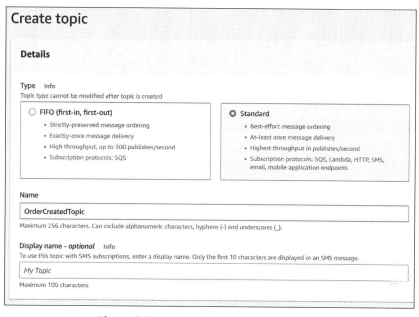

Figure 3.18: *Creating an Amazon SNS topic*

4. Use the default settings for the remaining options and click **Create topic**.

The serverless SNS topic has been set up and is now ready to receive messages. The next step will be to update the **NewOrder** service to publish messages to the SNS topic we created, rather than sending them to the SQS queue. This will allow the **NewOrder** service to fan messages out to multiple endpoints through the SNS topic subscriptions.

Updating Lambda to Send Message to SNS

First, we need to update the IAM role for the **NewOrder** service to grant the necessary permissions to send messages to SNS.

1. Find the IAM Role of the **NewOrder** service and open the **Policy editor** of the **AWSLambdaBasicExecutionRole**, as we saw previously. Add a new statement that will allow the **NewOrder** service to send messages to the **NewOrderQueue** queue:

```
{
        "Effect": "Allow",
        "Action": [
                "sns:Publish"
        ],
```

```
        "Resource": [
            "arn:aws:sns:eu-central-1:<account id>:OrderCreated-
Topic"
        ]
    }
```

2. Click **Next** and review the new permissions added. Finally, click **Save changes**.

Next, we will have to update the **NewOrder** service code to send messages to SNS rather than SQS. This is fairly simple to do with the classes provided by the SDK:

```
// Create a new SNS client
SnsClient snsClient = SnsClient.builder()
          .region(<region>)
          .build();


// Publish message to SNS
var pubRequest = PublishRequest.builder()
        .topicArn("<ARN of OrderCreatedTopic>")
        .message(<Order message DTO>)
        .build();


snsClient.publish(pubRequest);
```

The **NewOrder** service has been updated so that it now sends a message to the **OrderCreatedTopic** topic instead of the **OrderCreatedQueue** queue when an order is created. The **ReserveInventory** service previously received order-created messages from the **OrderCreatedQueue**. To enable the **ReserveInventory** service to continue receiving these order-created messages, the **OrderCreatedQueue** queue needs to be subscribed to the **OrderCreatedTopic** topic. This subscription will forward messages published from **OrderCreatedTopic** to **OrderCreatedQueue** for consumption by the **ReserveInventory** service.

Subscribing Queue for the Topic

Let's now configure the **OrderCreatedQueue** queue to subscribe to the **OrderCreatedTopic** topic that we previously created:

1. Go to the **OrderCreatedQueue** dashboard, select the **SNS subscriptions** tab, and click **Subscribe to Amazon SNS topic**.

2. Select the **OrderCreatedTopic**, as shown in *Figure* 3.19, and click **Save**.

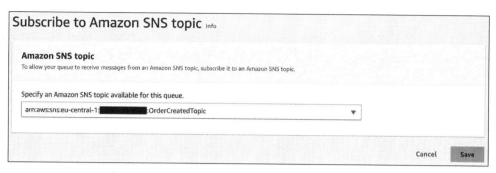

Figure 3.19: *Subscribing an SQS queue to an SNS topic*

And that's it! The **OrderCreatedTopic** publishes events for any subscribers, such as the **OrderCreatedQueue** queue. The **ReserveInventory** service consumes events from that queue to process them. Next, we need to create another SQS queue for the **ProcessPayment** service and have it subscribe to the **OrderCreatedTopic** as well. This will allow the **ProcessPayment** service to consume the same events published to the **OrderCreatedTopic**.

Creating a New SQS Queue and the **ProcessPayment** Service

The **ProcessPayment** service will have an implementation similar to the **ReserveInventory** service. Its event source will be a new SQS queue that subscribes to the **OrderCreatedTopic** topic. The full implementation details are available in the *GitHub repository*, but we will not cover them here.

Testing the Backend System

Finally, we will have to test the updated architecture to verify the new order message is being sent correctly to the **ReserveInventory** and **ProcessPayment** services. Run the same *curl* command again that you previously executed and then search for the DynamoDB items that were created.

Amazon SNS Features

Now let's explore in detail some of the main capabilities of SNS, such as standard vs. FIFO topics, SNS subscribers, message archiving, replay, and analytics, message filtering, delivery policy, and encryption.

Standard vs. FIFO topics

When using Amazon SNS, you need to choose between **standard** or **FIFO** topics. The main differences between standard and FIFO SNS topics are:

- **Throughput**: Standard topics support very high throughput and can handle a nearly unlimited number of messages per second. FIFO topics have lower throughput limits to support strict ordering. FIFO topics support up to 300 messages or 10 MB per second.

- **Ordering guarantees**: Standard topics provide *best-effort* ordering, which means messages are generally delivered in the order they are sent, but occasional out-of-order delivery is possible. FIFO topics guarantee that messages are delivered exactly in the order they are sent by individual publishers.

- **Deduplication**: Standard topics may have some *message duplication*. If a message is sent more than once to a standard topic, there is a small chance a subscriber may receive it more than once. FIFO topics ensure each message is delivered once and only once for each subscriber. No message duplication can occur.

Standard topics work well for most typical publish-subscribe and fan-out use cases, such as sending notifications, updates, streams of data, and more. FIFO topics are ideal for messaging requiring strict sequencing, such as financial transactions, log writes, or operations that must happen sequentially.

SNS Subscribers

Amazon SNS supports various subscribers, including AWS Lambda, Amazon SQS, Amazon Data Firehose, HTTP(s), SMS, push notifications, and email. The AWS services and HTTP(s) are straightforward, so let's examine SMS, push notifications, and email in more detail.

Amazon SNS provides a highly scalable and reliable **SMS messaging service** to over 200 countries, with built-in redundancy across multiple providers. You can control the originating identity using sender IDs, long codes, or short codes. The SNS sandbox allows testing SMS workflows before deploying them into production.

For mobile apps, Amazon SNS enables simple, cost-effective fan-out **push notifications** to iOS, Android, Fire, Windows, and Baidu devices. These mobile notifications can be triggered by user actions or business logic flows. The notifications are delivered via native platforms like *Amazon Device Messaging (ADM)*, *Apple Push Notification Service (APNs)*, *Baidu Cloud Push (Baidu)*, *Firebase Cloud Messaging (FCM)*, *Microsoft Push Notification Service for Windows Phone (MPNS)*, and *Windows Push Notification Services (WNS)*.

Additionally, Amazon SNS supports `email notifications` from subscribed topics for various use cases - application alerts, and DevOps workflow notifications when specific events occur like new Amazon S3 object uploads or CloudWatch alarms breaching thresholds.

Message Archiving, Replay, and Analytics

Amazon SNS offers integration with Amazon Data Firehose for standard topics, enabling message storage in services like Amazon S3, Amazon Redshift, Amazon OpenSearch, and MongoDB. This allows message archiving in analytics services such as Datadog, New Relic, and Splunk. For FIFO topics, SNS provides an in-built option to store and replay messages without needing to set up a separate archival system. This enhances the durability of event-driven applications and helps recover from downstream failures.

Message Filtering

By default, an Amazon SNS topic subscriber receives all messages published to that topic. To only receive a subset of the messages, a subscriber can apply a filter policy to the topic subscription. A filter policy is a JSON object with properties that determine which messages the subscriber will receive. Amazon SNS supports filter policies that evaluate either the message attributes or the message body based on the scope set for the subscription. Filter policies for the message body assume the message payload is a well-formed JSON object. If a subscription has no filter policy, the subscriber gets all messages posted to the topic. When publishing a message to a topic with a filter policy, Amazon SNS checks the message attributes or body against the policy properties for each subscription. If any message attributes or body properties match, Amazon SNS sends the message to that subscriber. Otherwise, Amazon SNS does not send the message to that subscriber.

Delivery Policy

Amazon SNS has a delivery policy for each delivery protocol that defines how it retries message delivery when the endpoint system becomes unavailable. The policy has retry attempts across four phases:

1. **Immediate Retry Phase**: Retries immediately after the initial attempt, with no delay between retries.

2. **Pre-Backoff Phase**: Specifies the number of retries and delays between them before applying backoff.

3. **Backoff Phase**: Controls delay between retries using a backoff function that defines the minimum delay, maximum delay, and how the delay increases from minimum to maximum. The backoff function can be arithmetic, exponential, geometric, or linear.

4. **Post-Backoff Phase**: This is the final phase that specifies the number of retries and delays between them after the backoff phase.

Once the delivery policy is exhausted, Amazon SNS stops retrying and discards the message, unless a `dead-letter queue` is attached to the subscription.

The default delivery policy for Amazon SNS is:

- Immediate Retry Phase: 3 retries with no delay
- Pre-Backoff Phase: No retries specified
- Backoff Phase: Minimum and maximum backoff delay of 20 seconds; function: linear
- Post-Backoff Phase: No retries specified

Encryption

Similar to Amazon SQS, when data is traveling between Amazon SNS and other services within the AWS cloud, it is encrypted in transit by default using HTTPS/SSL. This also protects data as it moves over the public internet and between AWS services.

Amazon SNS also supports server-side encryption using **AWS Key Management Service (KMS)**. This encrypts messages before publishing them to SNS topics and decrypts them for subscribers. It provides an additional layer of security over the default HTTPS encryption.

Conclusion

In this chapter, we explored the design and implementation of microservices using AWS messaging services, including Amazon SQS and Amazon SNS. We discussed the prerequisites for building on AWS, such as creating an account and setting up an IAM user, and delved into the details of Amazon API Gateway and AWS Lambda, which are essential for building microservices that can be accessed via REST APIs. We also examined messaging patterns, including point-to-point messaging, publish/subscribe messaging, and fan-out, and explored the features of Amazon SQS and Amazon SNS, such as standard vs. FIFO queues/topics, visibility timeout, message retention period, short and long polling, message filtering, and dead-letter queues.

By now, you should have a solid understanding of how to design and implement scalable microservices using AWS messaging services. You should be able to create microservices that can communicate with each other using message queues and topics, and handle failures gracefully using features like dead-letter queues.

In the upcoming chapter, we will thoroughly explore the realm of choreography with Amazon EventBridge, delving into the most essential design patterns, such as event sourcing, CQRS, the scheduler, and the claim check pattern.

CHAPTER 4

Choreography with Amazon EventBridge

Introduction

This chapter provides a comprehensive guide to leveraging Amazon EventBridge to implement scalable, event-driven architectures. We begin with an overview of choreography and the key EventBridge concepts including events, event buses, rules, event patterns, and targets. Next, we explore common choreography patterns built with EventBridge such as event sourcing, CQRS, scheduler pattern, and claim check pattern. The chapter covers practical EventBridge functionality like third-party service integrations, archiving and replay capabilities, schemas and pipes. By the end of this chapter, you will have a solid understanding of how to design and implement event-driven architectures and the most commonly used choreography design patterns using Amazon EventBridge.

Structure

In this chapter, we will discuss the following topics:

- Introduction to Choreography
- Overview of the Amazon EventBridge Key Concepts: Events, Event Buses, Rules, Event Patterns, Targets
- Choreography Patterns with Amazon EventBridge: Event Sourcing, CQRS, Scheduler Pattern, Claim Check Pattern
- Amazon EventBridge Features: Third-Party Integrations, Archive and Replay, Pipes, Schemas, Event Retry Policy, Dead-Letter Queues

Choreography

In recent years, the concept of **choreography** has gained significant attention in the field of event-driven architectures. Choreography refers to the art of designing and coordinating movements and actions in a dance performance. In choreography, the coordination between different services is *decentralized*. This is in contrast to *orchestration*, where a central orchestrator controls the interactions between services.

Choreography is essential in event-driven architectures because it allows services to communicate with each other effectively, ensuring that the overall system behaves as expected. It enables services to react to changes in the system, adapt to new conditions, and respond to events in a timely and efficient manner. For example, when an order is placed on a website, an `OrderPlaced` event would be emitted. Several other components, such as the billing system, fulfillment system, and more, would listen for that event and handle their part of the order processing without coordination from a central system.

The use of choreography in event-driven architectures offers several benefits, including:

- **Improved agility**: Choreography enables services to respond quickly to changes in the system, allowing the overall system to adapt to new conditions and respond to events in a timely manner.

- **Better coordination**: Choreography ensures that services communicate effectively, reducing the risk of misunderstandings or misinterpretations that can lead to errors or system failures.

- **Increased efficiency**: Choreography optimizes the flow of events and actions, reducing unnecessary delays or duplication of effort, and improving the overall efficiency of the system.

- **Enhanced flexibility**: Choreography allows services to be developed and deployed independently, enabling the system to be scaled and modified more easily.

Applying choreography in event-driven architectures requires a systematic approach. Here are some steps to follow:

- **Identify the services**: Identify the services that will participate in the choreography. This includes defining the functionality of each service and the events that it will produce or consume.

- **Define the events**: Define the events that will be used to communicate between services. This includes defining the format of the events, the data they will contain, and the semantics of the events.

- **Define the flow**: Define the flow of events and actions between services. This includes defining the sequence of events, the triggers that will cause services to react, and the logic that will govern the flow of events.

- **Define the interactions**: Define the interactions between services, including the messages that will be exchanged and the format of the messages.

- **Test and refine**: Test the choreography by simulating the flow of events and actions. Refine the choreography as needed, iterating on the design until the desired behavior is achieved.

Amazon EventBridge

Amazon EventBridge is a serverless event bus service that makes it easier to build event-driven applications using choreography. EventBridge facilitates reliable messaging between distributed services by providing a flexible event bus with a number of useful capabilities.

In a choreography-based architecture built with EventBridge, services publish events when something notable happens, such as performing an action or reaching a state. Other services subscribe to events and trigger logic when an event is received.

This removes the need for a central orchestrator - the logic to handle an event is pushed into the subscriber services themselves. The event stream acts as a communication channel, allowing services to indirectly coordinate actions and distribute data as needed.

Some key capabilities EventBridge provides to support choreography patterns:

- Reliable event delivery with replay, retries, dead-letter queues, and batching
- Event rules and filtering to route events to target services
- Integration with a variety of event sources and targets like AWS services, SaaS apps, custom applications, and more.
- Scheduled events to trigger time-based workflows

These capabilities greatly simplify building reliable, asynchronous event flows between decoupled services, which serve as the backbone of choreography-based architectures.

Amazon EventBridge Key Concepts

Amazon EventBridge has five key concepts: **events**, **event buses**, **rules**, **event patterns**, and **targets**. Next, we will take a closer look at each one of those.

Events

An event in EventBridge represents a change in the environment or state. For example, an event could indicate that a new file was uploaded to Amazon S3, a payment transaction failed, and more. Events are represented as JSON objects and are the core building blocks of EventBridge functionality.

Let's see a sample structure of a custom event with minimum information when a new order is created:

```
{
  "source": "[com.example.new-order-service]",
  "detail-type": "[OrderCreated]",
  "detail": {
    "orderId": "DSY34BG29FGSD34D"
  }
}
```

The **source** field specifies the origin of the event and it is suggested that you use the **Java package-name** style to populate this field. The **detail-type** identifies the type of the event and the **detail** contains all the information needed about the event.

Apart from custom events, you can also listen to events that AWS services generate. For instance, Amazon S3 sends the following event when a new file is uploaded:

```
{
  "source": ["aws.s3"],
  "detail-type": ["Object Created"]
}
```

The source field in AWS event data indicates which AWS service generated the event. The source field begins with **aws** followed by the name of the service, such as **aws.lambda**, for AWS Lambda events or **aws.s3** for Amazon S3 events. There are other fields that you can add to an event such as **account**, **time**, **region**, and others. You can find them all in the official documentation of EventBridge:

https://docs.aws.amazon.com/eventbridge/latest/userguide/eb-events-structure.html

Event Buses

An **event bus** is an EventBridge component that acts as a router to receive events from sources such as AWS services or partner SaaS applications, like Datadog, GitHub, and others, and deliver them to destinations for processing. The events from SaaS partners will be examined more closely later in this chapter.

Event buses allow decoupling event sources from event destinations. You get a **default event bus** with your AWS account and can create additional custom event buses or partner event buses for more advanced routing.

Typically, you would create a new event bus in order to distribute traffic across different systems or to process events that include *personally identifiable information* (PII) such as credit card number or full name.

Rules

EventBridge rules match incoming events and route them to one or more targets. A target can be an AWS service such as AWS Lambda, Amazon Kinesis, or Amazon SQS. It can also be third-party services or your own applications. The rule defines the pattern of events to match and the target(s) to invoke when an event matches the pattern.

When creating a rule, you specify:

- **Event source and pattern**: The event source emits the events that you want to respond to. You also define a pattern that matches the events you're interested in. Some common event sources are AWS services, custom applications, and third-party SaaS applications.
- **Targets**: These are the services that are invoked when an event matches the pattern defined in the rule. Targets can include AWS Lambda functions, Amazon Kinesis streams, Amazon SNS topics, Amazon SQS queues, and built-in targets.

When an EventBridge rule matches an event, it distributes the event to the target. The target then performs an action in response to receiving the event, such as executing a Lambda function, putting data on a Kinesis stream, or capturing the event in an S3 bucket.

Event Patterns

Event patterns are rules that match against the fields and values in the event itself. They allow you to specify criteria to filter events and only send relevant events to your targets. For example, you could create a pattern that matches any API call event from API Gateway with an `HTTP 500 status code`.

Event pattern matching happens before the event is sent to your target. This prevents irrelevant events from triggering your downstream services unnecessarily.

Some options for creating patterns include:

- String/numeric matching on event attributes
- Filtering with prefix, suffix, or contains logic
- Regular expressions
- Logical AND/OR combinations of conditions

The syntax for event patterns is based on `JSONPath`. Some key concepts:

- Match on event fields using dot notation. For example, `detail.orderId`

- Comparators like *numeric equals*, *string equals*, and others to compare values
- Logical operators like **AND, OR, NOT** to combine checks
- Wildcards for partial string matches

Event patterns enable powerful filtering of events sent to your EventBridge targets. Combined with services integrating natively with EventBridge, it makes it easy to develop reactive, event-driven architectures.

Targets

Amazon EventBridge allows you to respond to events in your AWS environment and third-party services by triggering targets. **Targets** are the resources that are invoked by EventBridge when a certain event occurs. Some common event target types include:

- **AWS Lambda functions**: You can invoke Lambda functions to run serverless code in response to an EventBridge event.
- **Amazon SQS queues**: EventBridge events can trigger SQS queues to delay processing or create decoupled architectures.
- **Amazon SNS topics**: Using SNS topics as event targets allows EventBridge events to fan out and trigger multiple subscribers and endpoints.
- **Amazon Kinesis Data streams**: EventBridge can put event data into a Kinesis data stream for real-time processing.

Event targets are essential components of EventBridge that allow for flexible and automated responses to events across AWS services and custom applications. Choosing suitable targets lets you unlock powerful event-driven architectures.

EventBridge Integration with Third-Party Sources

Amazon EventBridge supports integrating events from many popular third-party sources out-of-the-box, making it easy to build event-driven architectures without having to set up and operate extra infrastructure. EventBridge offers integration with third-party sources through two key capabilities: **API destinations** and **partner event sources**. Next, we will examine those features more closely.

API Destinations

API destinations are endpoints that EventBridge can directly call when an event pattern matches. This allows your applications and services to react to events from AWS services and custom applications without having to set up an intermediary Lambda function.

When an event occurs that matches a configured rule, EventBridge makes an HTTPS request to the defined API destination. This request contains information about the event in its payload. Your service at the API destination endpoint can then process the event data and take any necessary actions.

There are several benefits to using API destinations:

- **Simplicity**: No need to write Lambda functions just to forward events to another endpoint. You can trigger your HTTP service directly.

- **Speed**: Invoking an API destination happens faster than invoking a Lambda function first. This reduces latency.

- **Cost**: With API destinations you only pay for the EventBridge events and HTTPS calls. No Lambda compute costs for intermediary functions.

- **Scale**: API destinations can handle high-load events and scale responses without capacity planning.

Some examples of good use cases for API destinations include:

- Send event data to **webhook** endpoints used by external services and applications.

- Log event information to logging and analytics services.

- Forward event data to internal HTTP APIs that trigger notifications, workflows, data pipelines, and more.

- Stream event data to third-party streaming and messaging platforms.

API destinations open up many possibilities for integrating AWS event streams with external applications and endpoints. They provide a simple and cost-effective method for reacting to all of your important event data.

Partner Event Sources

Amazon EventBridge allows you to connect your applications with data from third-party services using partner event sources. **Partner event sources** are pre-built integrations with SaaS partners like Stripe, Zendesk, and Datadog that automatically stream events from those services into EventBridge in real-time.

Some key benefits of using partner event sources include:

- **No coding** required to get events data into EventBridge. The integration is handled for you.

- **Real-time data streaming** from the partner service. As soon as something changes in the partner service, an event is streamed to EventBridge allowing you to trigger workflows, notifications, and more.

- **Structured**, easy-to-consume JSON data. The event data is normalized into a consumable JSON format.

EventBridge provides ongoing additions of new partner event sources. Refer to the following documentation to see available integrations and the roadmap for upcoming sources that will be added:

https://docs.aws.amazon.com/eventbridge/latest/userguide/eb-saas.html#eb-supported-integrations.

Leveraging partner sources allows streamlining complex workflows across AWS and SaaS tools.

Project Time: Introducing Amazon EventBridge to Our Architecture

In this section, we will revisit the architecture of Shopme, our large e-commerce project, and incorporate Amazon EventBridge to enable some key improvements. Specifically, we will make three major changes, as shown in *Figure 4.1*:

1. **Migrate from SNS to EventBridge**: All event notifications will now be routed through a central EventBridge event bus rather than SNS topics.

2. **Replace `ProcessPayment` service**: The existing `ProcessPayment` Lambda function will be deprecated. Instead, payment events will be configured as an API destination within EventBridge, leveraging **Stripe**, a third-party SaaS payment application.

3. **Add partner event source**: We will set up a partner event source with **Stripe** in EventBridge to ingest events from **Stripe**.

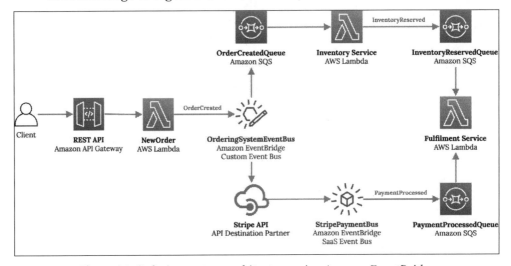

Figure 4.1: *Ordering system architecture using Amazon EventBridge*

These architectural changes aim to streamline event processing in Shopme by:

- Taking advantage of EventBridge more robust targeting options compared to SNS.

- Reducing cost, complexity, and latency by removing the **ProcessPayment** Lambda function.

- Enabling easier extensibility and integration with third-party services via EventBridge partner connectivity.

In the following section, we plan to modernize Shopme's architecture using EventBridge to simplify integration flows and enable direct integration with key SaaS applications.

Creating an EventBridge Custom Event Bus

First, we will create a custom event bus in Amazon EventBridge that will be used to route all events from the **Ordering system**. This dedicated event bus will serve as the central hub for the events generated by the **NewOrder** service.

1. From the list of services, search for **eventbridge** and click on **Amazon EventBridge** to go to the **Amazon EventBridge** dashboard.

2. On the left sidebar, click **Event buses** and then click the **Create event bus** button.

3. Enter **OrderingSystemEventBus** for the **event bus name**, as shown in Figure 4.2, and use the default settings for the remaining options. Click **Create**.

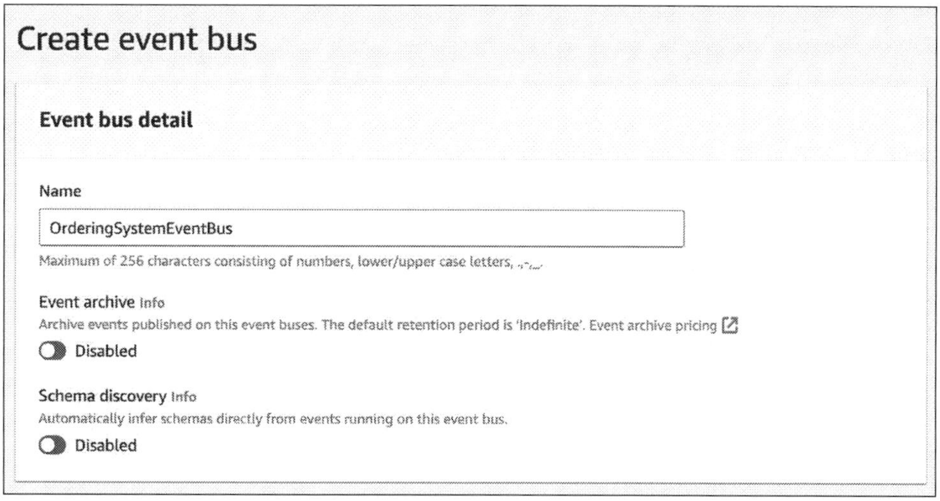

Create event bus

Event bus detail

Name

OrderingSystemEventBus

Maximum of 256 characters consisting of numbers, lower/upper case letters, .,-,_.

Event archive Info
Archive events published on this event buses. The default retention period is 'Indefinite'. Event archive pricing ↗
◉ Disabled

Schema discovery Info
Automatically infer schemas directly from events running on this event bus.
◉ Disabled

Figure 4.2: *Creating an Amazon EventBridge custom event bus*

The event bus will be instantiated right away and can be accessed in the **Custom**

event bus section. Additionally, note that there is a **default** event bus available in the **Default event bus** section.

Creating an EventBridge Rule

The next step is to create a rule that will match incoming events from the **NewOrder** service and then route those events to two destinations: the **OrderCreatedQueue** queue and the *API destination*. This rule will enable the custom event bus you set up to take the **NewOrder** events and send them to where they need to go to trigger inventory reservations and other downstream processes.

1. From the **Amazon EventBridge** dashboard, on the left sidebar, click **Rules** and then click the **Create rule** button.

2. In *Step 1 Define rule detail*, enter **OrderCreatedRule** for the *rule name*, and select the **OrderingSystemEventBus** for the *event bus*, as shown in *Figure 4.3*. Click **Next**.

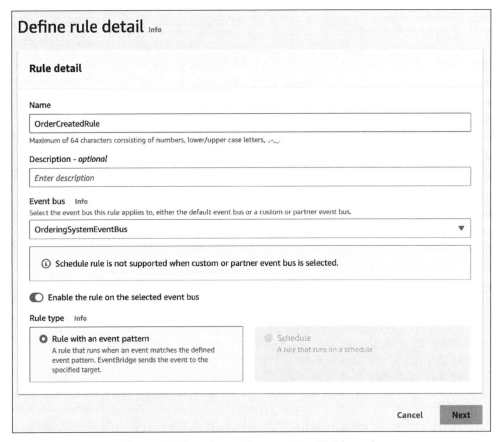

Figure 4.3: *Creating an Amazon EventBridge rule*

3. In *Step 2 Build event pattern*, select **Other** for the **Event source**, leave the **Sample event** empty, and add the following JSON for the **event pattern**. Click **Next**.

```
{
    "source": ["com.example.new-order-service"],
    "detail-type": ["OrderCreated"]
}
```

4. In *Step 3 Select target(s)*, select **AWS service**, select **SQS queue** for the **target**, and select **OrderCreatedQueue** for the **queue**, as illustrated in *Figure 4.4*. Click **Next**.

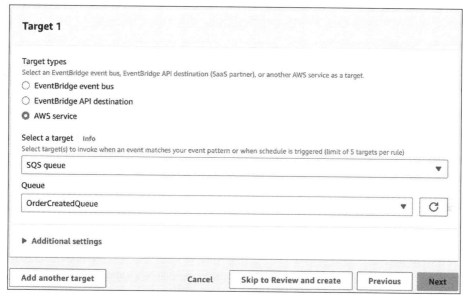

Figure 4.4: *Adding an SQS queue as a target to an Amazon EventBridge rule*

5. In *Step 4 Configure tags*, you can optionally add **tags**. Click **Next**.

6. In *Step 5 Review and create*, review the rule information and click **Create rule**.

The next step is to update the **NewOrder** service to publish these custom events to the EventBridge event bus you created instead of SNS. This will route the **NewOrder** custom events to the **OrderCreatedQueue** queue for processing through the EventBridge rule you set up.

Updating the Lambda Code to Send Events to EventBridge

The next step is to modify the **NewOrder** service to publish events to EventBridge instead of SNS. Using the SDK's provided classes, we can easily switch the integration from SNS to EventBridge with minimal code changes.

```
// Create a new EventBridge client
EventBridgeClient eventBridgeClient = EventBridgeClient.builder()
        .region(region)
        .build();


// Set the event source, detailType and the detail object
var entry = PutEventsRequestEntry.builder()
        .source("com.example.new-order-service")
        .detailType("OrderCreated")
        .detail(gson.toJson(order))
        .build();


// Send the event to EventBridge
var eventsRequest = PutEventsRequest.builder()
        .entries(entry)
        .build();


eventBridgeClient.putEvents(eventsRequest);
```

The **NewOrder** service has been updated to publish events to EventBridge whenever a new order is created. These events are then automatically delivered to the **OrderCreatedQueue** queue that we set up in the previous chapter. The **ReserveInventory** service still listens to the **OrderCreatedQueue** queue for new orders. The only change needed is that the SQS message body will now contain the EventBridge event payload instead of the previous message format. So, the **ReserveInventory** service will need a minor code update to process the new event payload structure sent from EventBridge. Other than parsing the new event data, the overall flow remains the same - **NewOrder** publishes events, EventBridge routes them to SQS, and **ReserveInventory** consumes order events from that queue.

Creating an API Destination

We will now create an API destination to replace the **ProcessPayment** service and handle payment processing. The API destination will be added as the second target to the rule we created earlier. For testing, we will use a fake *Stripe* API rather than the real *Stripe* API, which would require creating an account and obtaining credentials. The

API destination supports *Basic authentication* with username/password, *OAuth client credentials*, and *API keys* for authentication. Using a fake HTTP API allows us to test without needing real credentials. When ready for production, real Stripe credentials could be configured in the API destination.

We can use the AWS Management Console to set up an API destination:

1. From the **Amazon EventBridge** dashboard, on the left sidebar, click **API destinations** and then click the **Create API destination** button.

2. Enter **StripePaymentAPI** for the **name**, the Stripe payments API for the **API destination endpoint**, and **POST** for **HTTP method**, as shown in *Figure 4.5*.

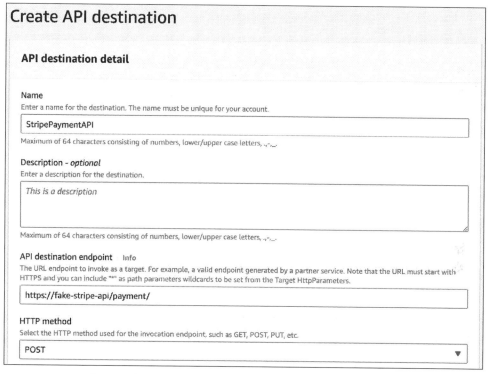

Figure 4.5: *Creating an Amazon EventBridge API destination*

3. Scroll down and click **Create a new connection**. Enter **StripePaymentAPIConnection** for the **Connection name**, select **Other** for the **Destination type**, and select the **Authorization type** supported by Stripe when you created the Stripe account, as shown in *Figure 4.6*. For testing purposes, we would use **Basic** with a dummy username and password. Click **Create**.

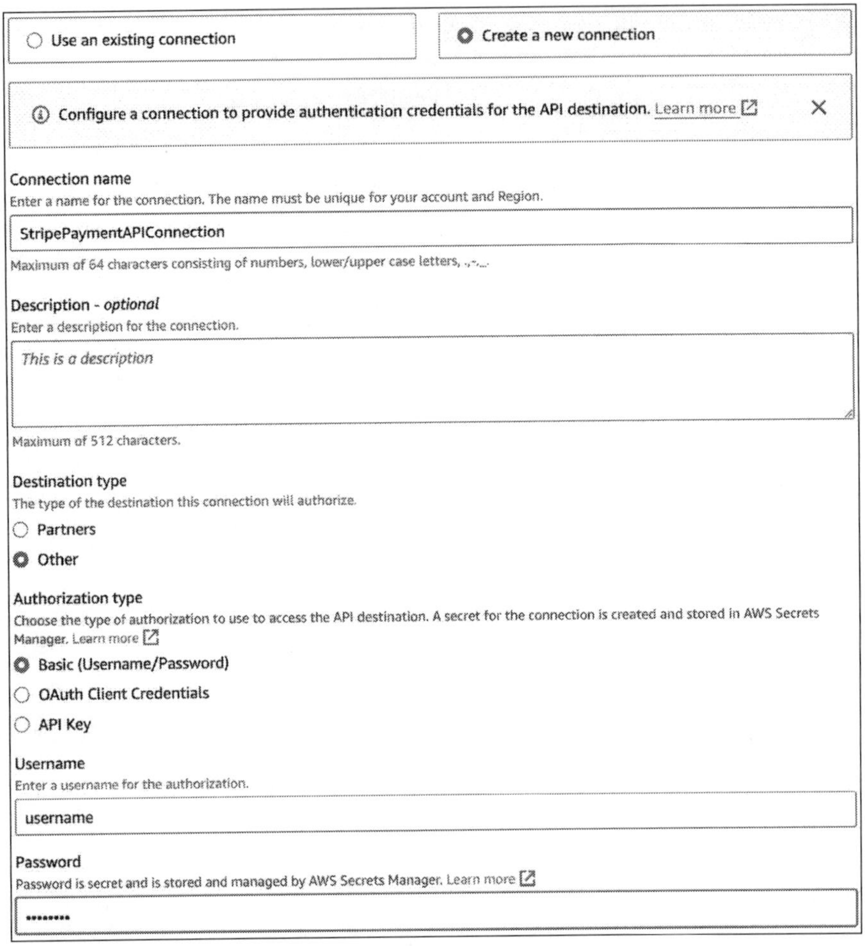

Figure 4.6: *Creating a connection for an Amazon EventBridge API destination*

Now that you have created the API destination, you need to add it as a target to the previously created rule.

1. From the **Amazon EventBridge** dashboard, on the left sidebar, click **Rules**, select the **OrderingSystemEventBus** event bus, select the **OrderCreatedRule**, and click **Edit**.

2. On the left sidebar, click *Step 3* **Select target(s)** and click on **Add another target** at the bottom left.

3. Select **EventBridge API destination** for the *Target type*, select **Use an existing API destination** for the **API destination**, select the **StripePaymentAPI** we created earlier, and enter **$.detail** for the **path parameter**.

4. Use the default settings for the remaining options, and click **Next**. Go to *Step 5* **Review and update** and click **Update rule**.

The rule has been updated to publish the same event to both the **OrderCreatedQueue** *queue* and the API *destination*. By leveraging the API *destination* capability of EventBridge, we eliminated the need for the **ProcessPayment** Lambda function. This reduced costs and latency before sending payments to *Stripe*.

However, our system still needs to know if *Stripe* successfully processed the payment. For this, *Stripe* can configure a partner event source - an event bus sending events to our account from *Stripe's* side. We can consume these partner events in our backend to check payment status. The partner event model allows services like *Stripe* to inform us of status changes through EventBridge event streams.

Creating a Partner Event Source

Stripe has seamless integration with EventBridge as a partner source. In just a few clicks, you can connect your *Stripe* account to EventBridge and enable real-time streaming of payment events and other activity data into EventBridge for further processing.

To set up *Stripe* as an event source:

1. From the **Amazon EventBridge** dashboard, on the left sidebar, go to **Partner event sources**.

2. Search for **Stripe** and click **Set up**.

3. Follow the prompts to create an event bus for Stripe into your account.

4. *Stripe* events will now start streaming into EventBridge in real-time.

After finishing all the steps, the new partner event bus will show up in the **Partner event sources** dashboard. You can now create a new rule that will send all the events from the partner event bus to the rest of the backend system, specifically to the **FulfilOrder** service that we haven't yet implemented.

Testing the Backend System

To test the new architecture, run the curl command from *Chapter 3, Messaging with Amazon SQS and Amazon SNS*, again to insert an item. Then, confirm the item was successfully added by the **ReserveInventory** service to DynamoDB by using the AWS CLI to retrieve the inserted item:

```
$ aws dynamodb scan --table-name products-inventory --region eu-central-1
```

Amazon EventBridge Archive and Replay

Amazon EventBridge has an **archive and replay** feature that gives users more management capabilities for their event streams. This capability enables archiving event streams and replaying them later.

EventBridge **archive** gives users the ability to automatically archive their EventBridge event streams to a durable store. This allows users to reliably store a copy of all events flowing through EventBridge for analysis or replay later.

The **replay** capability then allows users to replay the entire event stream or a filtered subset of events from the archive back into EventBridge. This essentially lets you rewind and replay your event stream to recreate previous scenarios or repeat processing on older event data.

Here are some of the key benefits of the EventBridge archive and replay feature:

- **Auditability**: Archive gives you an immutable event trail for auditing or compliance purposes. You have a reliable log of all events that occurred.
- **Reprocess events**: Replay allows you to reprocess event data in case you need to update your event processing logic or fix bugs in your application.
- **Replay for testing**: You can replay specific event streams or filtered event subsets into your applications to effectively recreate past scenarios for testing.
- **Debugging**: Replay events to diagnose or debug issues by analyzing the event trail leading up to a failure or unexpected output.
- **New analysis**: Perform new analytics or run updated machine learning models on archived event streams.

The archive and replay capability of EventBridge is valuable for implementing the **event sourcing** pattern, which we covered in *Chapter 2, Designing Event-Driven Microservices in AWS*. Next, we will explore using EventBridge to enable event sourcing in depth.

Event Sourcing with Amazon EventBridge

Event sourcing is a software design pattern that focuses on capturing all changes to an application state as a *sequence of events*. Instead of only storing the current state, event sourcing persists the full series of actions that led to the current state. This event log allows the application to reconstruct past states and provides an audit trail of changes.

The core idea behind event sourcing is that every change to an application state is captured as an event and appended to an event log. For example, when a user signs up for a new account, the `UserSignedUp` event would contain details like the `user ID`, `name`, `email address`, and `timestamp`. Every event represents something that happened in the system at a specific point in time.

So, in an event-sourced system, the current application state is calculated by replaying all the stored events in order. This differs from traditional systems, where only the latest data snapshot would be stored in a database. The event store is at the heart of an event-sourced architecture. It persists sequential streams of events in a durable way.

In event sourcing, events are immutable. Once written, an event cannot be changed or deleted. This append-only nature is what creates an accurate audit log of what happened over time.

To reconstruct the current state, the application replays events from the beginning, runs logic to apply events, and builds up-to-date projections of the state. This rebuild process lets you understand how the state has changed over time.

Old application states can also be reconstructed by replaying a subset of the events. This is useful for analytics or migrating old data to new data models.

Amazon EventBridge is a great fit for implementing event sourcing patterns. Here are some key benefits:

- **Event storage and replay**: EventBridge stores and replays events in chronological order and guarantees at-least-once delivery of events. This durable event storage makes it ideal for replaying event sequences to rebuild application state.

- **Decoupling**: EventBridge allows publishing events from one part of your architecture to be consumed by other components in a fully decoupled way through event rules and targets. This loose coupling is a key enabler for event-sourcing architectures.

- **Serverless integration**: EventBridge integrates natively with serverless services, such as AWS Lambda and AWS Step Functions, to drive business logic and state machines from event streams. This makes it easy to implement reactive event processing in serverless apps.

- **Audit trails**: The complete history of events delivered by EventBridge provides full audit traceability into changes for compliance needs. You get built-in transparency over all application actions.

EventBridge handles many of the complexities of managing, storing, and routing events that are critical for event sourcing. Its serverless capabilities allow focusing business logic on reacting to state changes rather than plumbing. In the next section, we will incorporate event sourcing into our project.

Project Time: Archiving and Replaying Events

Since we have set up EventBridge as the event store for our project, event sourcing is already enabled to some extent. However, to fully support event replay capabilities, we still need to turn on the archive feature in EventBridge. This will allow us to retrieve and replay historical events if needed.

Creating an EventBridge Archive

We will now set up an EventBridge archive to store and replay events sent to the custom event bus we previously created.

1. From the **Amazon EventBridge** dashboard, on the left sidebar, click **Archives** and click **Create archive**.

2. Enter **OrderingSystemEventBus_Archive** for the **Name**, select **OrderingSystemEventBus** for the **Source**, and select **Indefinite** for the **Retention period**, as shown in *Figure 4.7*. Click **Next**.

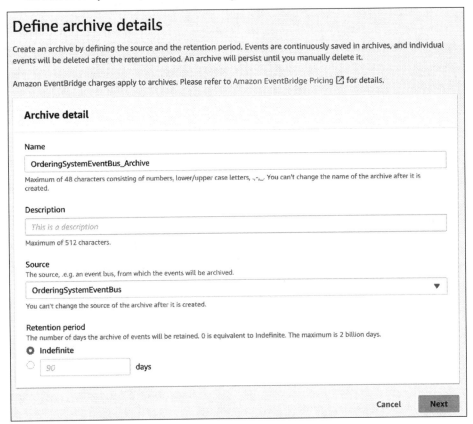

Figure 4.7: Creating an Amazon EventBridge archive for a custom event bus

3. Select **No event filtering** for the **Event pattern** and click **Create archive**.

The custom event bus now archives all events sent to it, allowing for later replay and analysis of those events. Events that were previously sent to the event bus are not automatically archived. In order to archive older events, you need to resend them to the event bus so that the archiving process can capture them.

Note: *There may be a delay between an event being published to an event bus and the event arriving in the archive. We recommend you delay replaying archived events for 10 minutes to make sure all events are replayed.*

Whenever you create a new archive, a new rule is created. If you go to the AWS Management Console and open the rules for the **OrderingSystemEventBus** bus, you will find a new rule created named **Events-Archive-OrderingSystemEventBus_Archive**. This rule is responsible for listening to the events sent to the custom event bus and archiving them. The event pattern for this rule is:

```
{
  "replay-name": [{
    "exists": false
  }]
}
```

When events are replayed, the **replay-name** attribute is added to the events, and this event pattern prevents any archives from being automatically replayed multiple times.

Replaying the Events

We will now replay the events that were recorded when we created the archive for our custom event bus.

1. From the **Amazon EventBridge** dashboard, on the left sidebar, click **Archives**. Find and click on the **OrderingSystemEventBus_Archive**.

2. Examine the **Event count** value to confirm if it is greater than 0, as shown in *Figure* 4.8. If the value is 0, wait for up to 10 minutes, checking periodically to see if the **Event count** has increased. Once the **Event count** is greater than 0, select the *Replays* tab and click the **Start new replay** button.

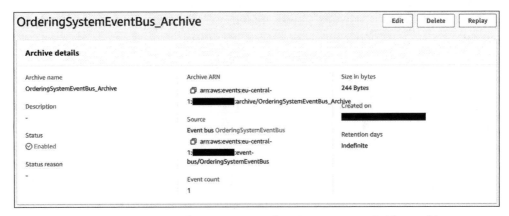

Figure 4.8: Examining the event count of an Amazon EventBridge archive

3. Enter `replay-1` for the **Name**, select the **OrderingSystemEventBus_Archive** for the **Source**, and select **All rules**, as shown in *Figure 4.9*.

Figure 4.9: Creating a replay from an Amazon EventBridge archive

4. Scroll down and select a timeframe for replaying the events. Click **Start Replay**.

After triggering the EventBridge events to be replayed, wait for several minutes to allow the replay to fully propagate through the system. Then, check DynamoDB to validate that the replayed events have successfully inserted new items, verifying that EventBridge replay capability is functioning as expected.

Note: *Keep in mind that an AWS account is limited to* **10 simultaneous replays** *running at a time per AWS Region.*

Amazon EventBridge Pipes: Routing Events Through Targets

EventBridge pipes is a feature in Amazon EventBridge that allows more control over how events flow from sources to targets. A pipe routes events from a single source to a single target. It contains logic to filter events based on specified criteria and enrich event data by adding information before routing the events to the target. The filtering and enrichment capabilities of pipes are two features that are not supported by EventBridge rules.

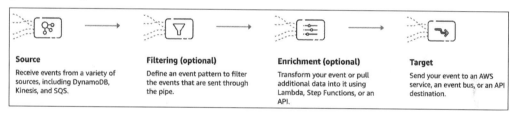

Figure 4.10: *Amazon EventBridge pipes key concepts*

Figure 4.10 illustrates the key concepts of EventBridge pipes:

- **Source**: EventBridge pipes ingest events from various sources including Amazon Kinesis, Amazon DynamoDB, Amazon SQS, and others that are not supported by EventBridge rules.

- **Filters**: EventBridge pipes have the ability to filter the events from a source and only process a subset of those events. This filtering is configured on a pipe by defining an event pattern that specifies which events the pipe should forward to the target. The pipe uses this event pattern to evaluate each event from the source and determine whether to send it on to the target for processing.

- **Enrichment**: EventBridge pipes allow you to enrich the data from a source before sending it to a target. For example, you may receive **OrderCreated** events that lack full order details. Using the enrichment capability, you can configure a Lambda function to get the order details from an API and retrieve the complete order data. The EventBridge pipe can then take that supplemented information and pass it along to the desired target. This enables you to enhance and customize the data to better meet the needs of the applications and services receiving the events.

- **Target**: After the filtering and enrichment of the event, it is sent to a target, which can be AWS Lambda, Amazon API Gateway, and others.

EventBridge pipes is a useful feature for implementing the CQRS design pattern. Next, we will examine CQRS more closely and look at how to apply it in our project.

CQRS Pattern with Amazon EventBridge and Amazon DynamoDB

The **CQRS (Command Query Responsibility Segregation)** pattern is an architectural pattern that separates read and write operations into different models. Implementing CQRS with Amazon EventBridge and Amazon DynamoDB allows building scalable and event-driven applications.

In simple terms, CQRS segregates operations into two categories:

- **Commands**: Used to modify state (`create`, `update`, `delete` operations). Commands emit events once they are completed.
- **Queries**: Used to read state (`fetch/get` operations). Queries subscribe to events to update read models and views.

By splitting into commands and queries, applications can scale the read and write sides independently. Commands can use a write-optimized data store, while queries use a read-optimized data store.

We can use Amazon EventBridge to propagate data changes from our write model to the read model in a CQRS implementation. Here is one way to implement CQRS with EventBridge and DynamoDB:

1. A Lambda function, which acts as the command service, inserts data to a DynamoDB table optimized for writes.

2. An EventBridge pipe ingests data from the DynamoDB write table and sends it to a Lambda function.

3. The Lambda function inserts the data to a DynamoDB table optimized for reads.

4. A Lambda function, which acts at the query service, uses the DynamoDB read table to fetch data.

This separation enables scaling reads and writes independently. Amazon API Gateway can be used to route commands and queries to the relevant services.

The CQRS pattern can be useful when:

- Your system uses the database-per-service pattern, resulting in data being spread across multiple microservices. CQRS allows querying across services.

- Your read-and-write operations have divergent non-functional requirements. For example, reads must scale to handle high traffic while writes require strong consistency guarantees. CQRS allows optimizing each pathway separately.

- You can tolerate eventual consistency for read queries. The read database used by CQRS often favors availability and performance over absolute up-to-date accuracy.

Next, we will incorporate CQRS into our project.

Project Time: Implementing CQRS

We will now add the CQRS pattern to our architecture. Since we expect a high volume of reads and writes to the database storing new orders, we will split these operations to prevent overloading. The write operations will go to one database optimized for writes. The read operations will use a separate database optimized for reads. This separation of workloads with CQRS will enable each database to scale better.

In our architecture, we have utilized an Amazon DynamoDB table called **Orders** to handle both read and write operations. Going forward, we will rename this existing *Orders* table to **OrdersWrite** and it will only be used for write operations. Additionally, we will create a new DynamoDB table called **OrdersRead** that will exclusively handle read operations for order data.

Amazon EventBridge pipes allow us to ingest data from the **OrdersWrite** table. We can then optionally filter and transform this data before sending it to the **Lambda** function, which will take the processed data and write it to the **OrdersRead** table, as shown in *Figure 4.11*.

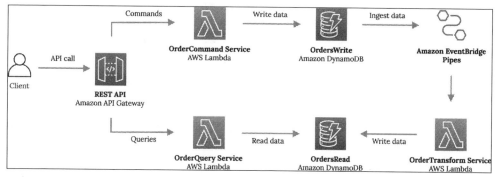

Figure 4.11: *CQRS pattern for the Ordering system using Amazon EventBridge pipes*

DynamoDB streams need to be enabled on DynamoDB tables for EventBridge pipes to ingest data changes from the tables. **DynamoDB streams** is a DynamoDB feature that continuously captures a time-ordered log of item-level changes made to any table which is retained for up to 24 hours. Enabling streams allows EventBridge pipes to capture DynamoDB data modification events like inserts, updates, and deletes and process them downstream.

We will now begin implementing CQRS in our project. Rather than setting up all components like DynamoDB tables and Lambda functions, we will focus specifically on enabling DynamoDB streams and creating EventBridge pipes to route events. The additional components can be created similarly to how we have done previously. This will establish the underlying infrastructure to enable CQRS while allowing us to add other pieces later.

Turning on DynamoDB Streams

To begin, you will need to turn on DynamoDB streams for the **OrdersWrite** table:

1. From the **Amazon DynamoDB** dashboard, select the **OrdersWrite** table and select the **Exports and streams** tab.

2. Scroll down to the **DynamoDB stream details** section and click **Turn on**, as shown in *Figure 4.12*.

Figure 4.12: *Turning on DynamoDB streams for a DynamoDB table*

DynamoDB streams have been enabled on the **OrdersWrite** table, allowing you to create an EventBridge pipe to process data changes.

Creating an EventBridge Pipe

We will now create the EventBridge pipe:

1. From the **Amazon EventBridge** dashboard, on the left sidebar, click **Pipes** and then click the **Create pipe** button.

2. From the **Source** tab, select **DynamoDB** for the **source** and the **stream** you have enabled.

3. From the **Target** tab, select **AWS Lambda** and select the **OrderTransform** Lambda function.

4. Click **Create pipe** and enter **NewOrdersPipe** for the pipe name.

5.   Click **Confirm and create pipe** to create the pipe.

The EventBridge pipe has been created and it will automatically route data from the **OrdersWrite** table to the **OrdersRead** table. As previously mentioned, a drawback of this approach is that your query patterns must be compatible with eventual consistency, as you may retrieve stale data as updates propagate through the system asynchronously.

Scheduler Pattern with Amazon EventBridge

The **scheduler pattern** is a common design pattern that allows you to schedule jobs or tasks to run at certain times or intervals. This can be useful for running cron jobs, workflows, notifications, backups, and more. **Amazon EventBridge scheduler** is a capability of Amazon EventBridge that allows you to schedule automated tasks that invoke targets at certain times or intervals.

When creating an EventBridge scheduler, you must specify:

- **Schedule**: The time or interval at which the scheduler triggers. Options include fixed times, intervals like every 5 minutes or 1 day, or cron expressions. The occurrence of the scheduler can be one-off or recurring and you can optionally configure the start and end date time of the scheduler.

- **Schedule group**: EventBridge scheduler allows you to create schedule groups to organize your scheduled events. You can alternatively use the *default* scheduler group that comes with your AWS account.

- **Target**: The AWS service that you want to invoke when the rule triggers. Target options include AWS Lambda functions, Amazon Kinesis streams, Amazon SQS queues, and more.

- **Input**: Any JSON input you want to pass to the target when the scheduler invokes it.

Once you create the scheduler, EventBridge will automatically begin triggering the target based on the defined schedule. Our next step will be integrating an EventBridge scheduler into our project.

Project Time: Create an EventBridge Scheduler

To test the **NewOrder** service in a test environment, we will create an Amazon EventBridge scheduler that triggers the **NewOrder** service to run every day at midnight. Configuring this daily scheduled execution will help validate that the **NewOrder** service functions properly.

1. From the **Amazon EventBridge** dashboard, on the left sidebar, click **Schedules** and then click the **Create schedule** button.

2. In the **Schedule name and description** section, enter **OrderServiceSchedule** for the **name**.

3. In the **Schedule pattern** section, select **Recurring schedule** for the **Occurrence**, enter **0 0 * * ? *** for the **Cron expression**, and select **Off** for the **Flexible time window**, as shown in *Figure 4.13*.

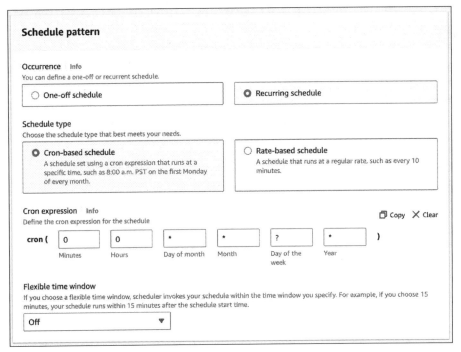

Figure 4.13: Defining the cron expression for an Amazon EventBridge scheduler

4. Leave the **Timeframe** section empty and click **Next**.

5. In the **Target detail** section, select **Templated targets** and select **AWS Lambda Invoke**.

6. In the **Invoke** section, select the **new-order-service** Lambda function. Enter the JSON we use for testing the backend system as a string within the **body** field, as shown in *Figure 4.14*. This JSON needs to be enclosed in the **body** field because the event passed to the **Lambda function** is an API Gateway request. Click **Next**.

Figure 4.14: *Specifying the input sent to a Lambda function configured as the target for an Amazon EventBridge scheduler*

7. Use the default settings for the settings, which will activate the scheduler right away and generate a new IAM role for the scheduler. Click **Next**.

8. Review the scheduler and click **Create schedule**.

The scheduler is configured to automatically trigger the **NewOrder** service at midnight every day, passing the JSON we provided as input to the **Lambda function**.

Note: *EventBridge schedulers cannot be manually triggered and will run based on their defined schedule. To run a scheduler earlier than its scheduled time, the schedule would need to be updated to an earlier time, such as to run in the next minute. The alternative is to wait for the originally scheduled runtime, such as waiting until midnight if that was the originally defined schedule.*

Claim Check Pattern with Amazon EventBridge and Amazon S3

Claim check is a pattern that uses a data store like Amazon S3 to pass large payload data between systems while only sending a *claim check* instead of the entire payload via EventBridge. The claim check contains metadata and instructions for retrieving the full payload from S3.

This helps in the following ways:

*   **Reduces cost**: Only small claim check events are sent via EventBridge instead

of large payloads. EventBridge charges based on the number and size of events sent.

- **Improves efficiency**: Your application does not need to process large unnecessary payloads when often only the metadata is needed initially. The payload can be retrieved from S3 when actually needed.

- **Message size limitation**: EventBridge messages have a size limit of 256 KB. Larger messages exceeding this limit cannot be published through EventBridge and will result in errors.

This is how claim check works with EventBridge and S3:

1. A client uploads a large payload to S3 and sends an EventBridge event with metadata and S3 pointers (claim check) instead of the payload.

2. EventBridge rules and targets listening to the event get the lightweight claim check only. This is fast and cost-efficient.

3. When an application actually needs the payload, it uses the S3 pointers provided in the claim check to retrieve the object from S3.

Some examples of using claim check with EventBridge and S3 include:

- Uploading large media files to S3 while allowing processing systems to efficiently react to the upload.

- Passing large dataset files between systems. Only a small claim check would flow through EventBridge.

- Having a distributed pipeline react to large file uploads without transferring unnecessary data between components.

By only passing small claim checks rather than large payloads over EventBridge, you can build more cost-effective and performant event-driven architectures. The full objects can still be retrieved from S3 when required by downstream consumers.

Project Time: Claim Check Pattern

We will now incorporate the claim check pattern into an example project using Amazon EventBridge and Amazon S3. Amazon S3 is an object storage service where you can create **buckets** that contain files, also known as **objects**. When creating a bucket, Amazon S3 exposes an *upload* URL endpoint that allows you to directly upload files to that bucket through the S3 API or one of the AWS SDKs. This allows you to bypass the need to have an API Gateway sit in front of the storage service. The claim check pattern involves storing a large payload in an S3 bucket and sending a smaller *claim check* representing that payload (for example, the S3 URL) through EventBridge. When you need to retrieve or display the large payload, you use the claim check to retrieve the payload from S3.

The architecture shown in *Figure* 4.15 shows how a client uploads a file to Amazon S3. This upload triggers an event notification that is sent through Amazon EventBridge. The event notification contains only a *claim check* with the S3 file location, not the actual file content. An AWS Lambda function subscribes to events from EventBridge, so it is invoked when the upload event is received. The Lambda function uses the S3 file location from the event payload to directly retrieve the file contents from Amazon S3. By having the Lambda function load the file itself rather than including the content in the event, only a small claim check needs to be sent through EventBridge rather than the potentially large file.

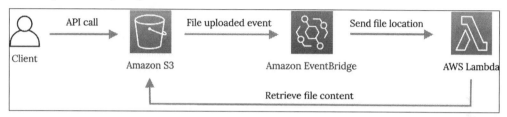

Figure 4.15: *Claim check pattern with Amazon EventBridge and Amazon S3*

Note: *Amazon API Gateway has a hard timeout limit of 29 seconds per request. This can cause issues when API Gateway is placed in front of Amazon S3 for file uploads, as large uploads may take over 29 seconds to complete. If the S3 upload does not finish within the 29-second time frame, API Gateway will terminate the connection and return a timeout error to the client. To avoid this, you can either directly upload files to Amazon S3 through the API or SDK or set up an asynchronous process for large file uploads that continues executing after the API Gateway timeout window.*

Next, we will demonstrate how this architecture can integrate smoothly with AWS services. Specifically, we will show how to configure Amazon S3 to publish events to **Amazon EventBridge**, and how to set up an EventBridge rule that allows a Lambda function to be triggered by those S3 events.

Enable Event Notifications on S3

To begin, you would need to turn on **Amazon S3 event notifications**. This feature allows you to get notified when certain events happen in your S3 buckets. S3 automatically sends events to EventBridge when certain activities occur in your S3 bucket such as an object is created or deleted. You don't need to manually select which event types to deliver to EventBridge. You can then create rules in EventBridge to route these events to additional targets for further processing and handling. So, EventBridge gives you a centralized way to react to and manage activities happening across your S3 buckets.

1. From the list of services, search for S3 and click on **S3** to go to the **Amazon S3** dashboard.

2. Assuming you have created an S3 bucket, click on the bucket and open the

Properties tab. Scroll down and find the **Amazon EventBridge** section. Click **Edit**.

3. Select **On** to send notifications to Amazon EventBridge for all events in this bucket, as shown in *Figure 4.16*, and click **Save changes**.

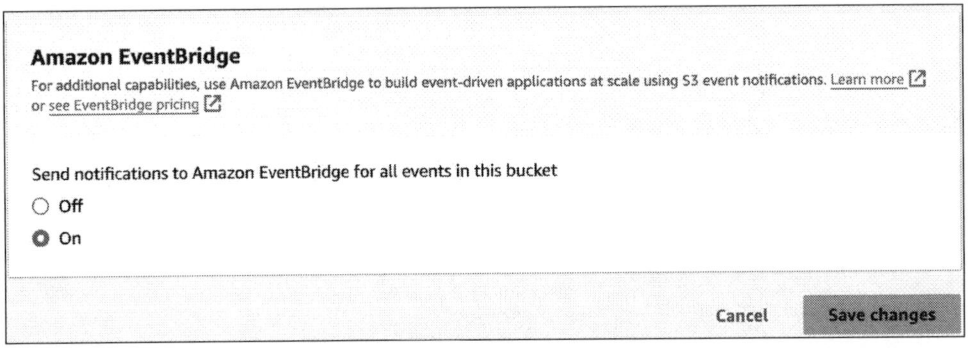

Amazon EventBridge

For additional capabilities, use Amazon EventBridge to build event-driven applications at scale using S3 event notifications. Learn more ⬚ or see EventBridge pricing ⬚

Send notifications to Amazon EventBridge for all events in this bucket

○ Off

◉ On

Cancel   Save changes

Figure 4.16: Turning on the Amazon S3 event notifications for Amazon EventBridge

The S3 bucket has been configured to send events to EventBridge. The next step is to create an EventBridge rule that routes those S3 events to a Lambda function for additional processing. This will allow the Lambda function to execute whenever a new object is created in the S3 bucket.

Creating EventBridge Rule to Listen to File Uploads on S3

Creating the EventBridge is fairly simple and is similar to what we have done before. Here are the steps:

1. From the **Amazon EventBridge** dashboard, on the left sidebar, click **Rules** and then click the **Create rule** button.

2. In *Step 1 Define rule detail*, enter **S3ObjectUploadedRule** for the **rule name**, and select the **OrderingSystemEventBus** for the **event bus**. Click **Next**.

3. In *Step 2 Build event pattern*, select **AWS events or EventBridge partner events** for the **Event source** and leave the **Sample event** empty.

4. In the **Event pattern** section, select **Simple Storage Service (S3)** for the **AWS service**, **Amazon S3 Event Notification** for the **Event type**, select **Specific event(s)** and find the **Object Created** event, select **Specific bucket(s) by name** and enter the S3 bucket name you have created, as shown in *Figure 4.17*. Click **Next**.

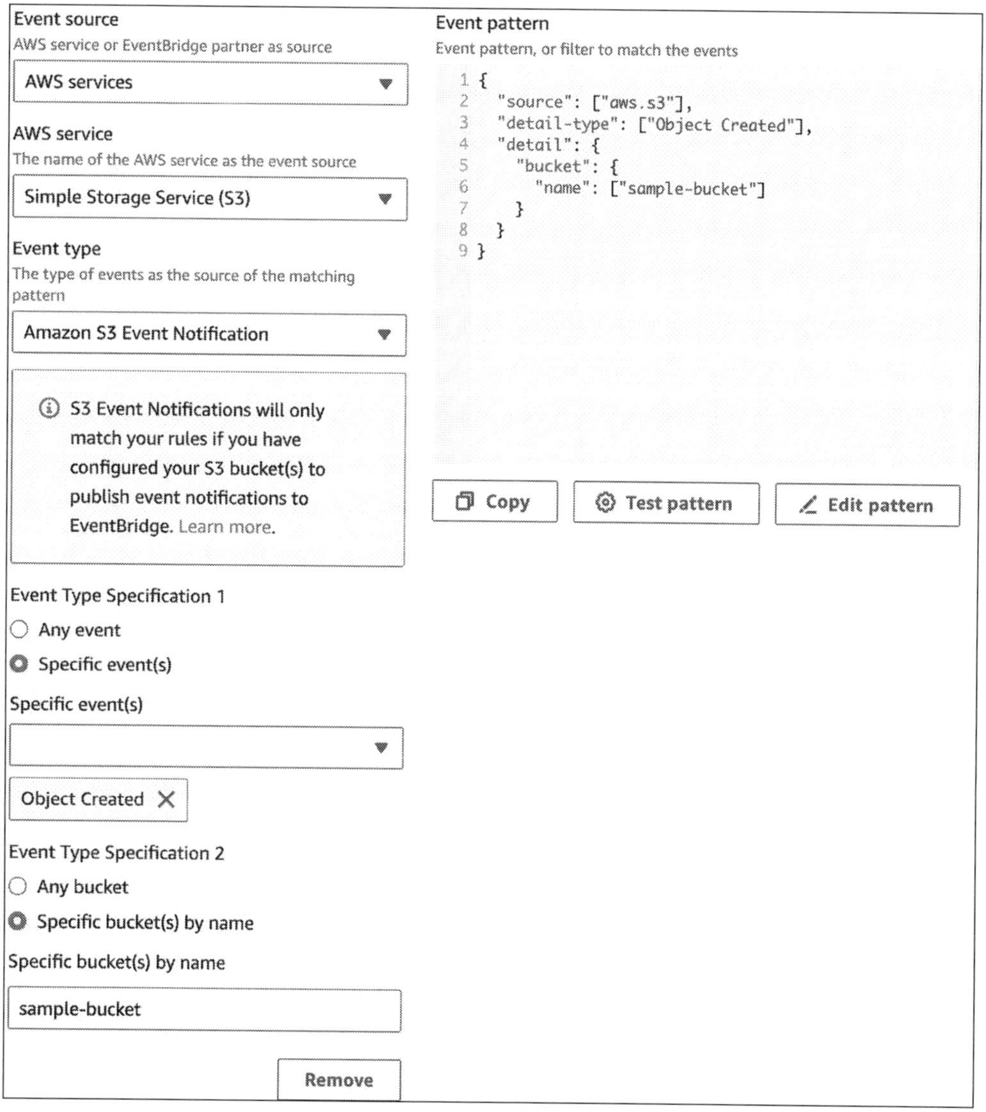

Figure 4.17: *Adding an event pattern to an Amazon EventBridge rule to match file-uploaded events from Amazon S3*

5. In *Step 3 Select target(s)*, select **AWS service**, select **Lambda function SQS queue** for the *target* and select the Lambda function you would like to send those events to. Click **Next**.

6. In *Step 4 Configure tags*, you can optionally add **tags**. Click **Next**.

7. In *Step 5 Review and create*, review the rule information and click **Create rule**.

The EventBridge rule you created routes S3 event notifications to the Lambda function. When a new file is uploaded to the S3 bucket, EventBridge will send an event to the

Lambda function containing the location of that file in S3. The Lambda function can then use that S3 file location to load and process the contents of the uploaded file.

Event Retry Policy and Dead-Letter Queues

When creating an EventBridge rule, you can optionally specify a dead-letter queue (DLQ) to handle events that fail to be delivered to the rule's targets. Failed event deliveries can happen due to unavailable targets, insufficient permissions, network issues, or other transient errors.

By default, EventBridge will automatically retry failed event deliveries to targets for up to 24 hours, using an *exponential backoff* and *jitter delay* of up to 185 retry attempts. However, some errors like missing permissions or deleted targets will fail continuously.

Note: *Exponential backoff and jitter delay are two related techniques used in computing systems to handle retries for failed operations in a controlled and efficient manner.*

Exponential backoff is a strategy used to gradually increase the delay between retries for a failed operation. Instead of retrying immediately after a failure, the system waits for a short initial delay. If the operation fails again, the delay is increased exponentially (for example, doubled) before the next retry attempt. This process continues, with the delay growing exponentially, until a maximum delay is reached or the operation succeeds.

The rationale behind exponential backoff is to avoid overwhelming the system with rapid retries, which could further exacerbate the problem or cause additional failures. By introducing increasingly longer delays between retries, the system is given time to recover or for the underlying issue to be resolved.

Jitter delay is a technique used in conjunction with exponential backoff to introduce a random variation in the delay time. Instead of using a fixed delay interval, a small random value (jitter) is added or subtracted from the calculated delay.

The purpose of jitter delay is to prevent multiple clients or systems from retrying at the exact same time after a failure. If multiple clients were to retry simultaneously after the same fixed delay, it could lead to a synchronized load on the system, potentially causing further congestion or failures.

By adding a random jitter to the delay, the retry attempts from different clients or systems become slightly out of sync, distributing the load more evenly and reducing the risk of synchronized retries overwhelming the system.

Rather than pointlessly retrying such failed events, EventBridge will send them directly to the DLQ if one is configured. The DLQ is an Amazon SQS queue that retains the events for later reprocessing.

Using a DLQ allows you to avoid losing events after all retries are exhausted. You can then fix the underlying delivery issue, such as updating permissions or recreating deleted targets. Once resolved, you can retrieve and process the failed events from the DLQ so that no events are lost.

Configuring a DLQ provides an automated way of catching and retaining failed events for later reprocessing after transient issues have been fixed. This approach ensures that no data is permanently lost.

Now, we will look at the steps to configure the dead-letter queue on the **OrderCreatedRule** rule that was created previously. Before that, you need to create an SQS queue to use as the DLQ. We covered how to create SQS queues in the previous chapter.

1. From the **Amazon EventBridge** dashboard, on the left sidebar, click **Rules**, select the **OrderingSystemEventBus** event bus, select the **OrderCreatedRule**, and click **Edit**.

2. On the left sidebar, click *Step 3 Select target(s)* and then click **Additional settings** at the bottom of **Target 1**.

3. Select **Matched events** for the Configure target input, select **Select an Amazon SQS queue in the current AWS account to use as the dead-letter queue**, and select the SQS queue you created, as shown in *Figure 4.18*.

Figure 4.18: *Configuring an Amazon SQS queue as dead-letter-queue for an Amazon EventBridge rule*

4.   On the left sidebar, click *Step 5 Review and update* and then click `Update rule`.

If the target Lambda function fails to process an event, that event will now be sent to the Amazon SQS queue, which acts as a dead-letter queue. To retry processing those failed events, you can configure the dead-letter queue as an event source for the same Lambda function that originally failed. This will trigger the Lambda function to receive the messages from the DLQ and attempt to process them again.

Amazon EventBridge Schemas

Another useful feature of Amazon EventBridge is the ability to define schemas that validate the structure of events sent to EventBridge. `EventBridge schemas` are JSON schemas that define the structure and values of events propagated through EventBridge. When you define a schema and associate it with an EventBus, EventBridge will validate that incoming events match the schema before allowing them to be sent through. This allows you to enforce standards and catch issues early on.

Here are some important capabilities of EventBridge schemas:

- **Schema registry**: The schema registry stores and tracks schemas used by applications. It contains AWS, SaaS, and custom schemas, which can be searched, discovered, and added.

- **Schema discovery**: Schema discovery automatically finds and registers event schemas from event buses, creating new versions when schemas change, so you can generate code bindings without manual effort.

- **Code bindings**: You can download code bindings for your schema to represent events as strongly typed objects in Java, Python, or TypeScript. This enables validation and autocomplete in IDEs like IntelliJ and VS Code.

Next, we will learn how to identify the schema for the custom event bus that was developed for this project. We will also download the code bindings generated from the schema that was discovered.

Project Time: Discovering the Schema for Our Custom Event Bus

The initial step is to identify the schema for `OrderingSystemEventBus`, which is the custom event bus we developed previously.

1.   From the `Amazon EventBridge` dashboard, on the left sidebar, click `Event buses`, and select the `OrderingSystemEventBus` event bus.

2.   Click `Start discovery`, as shown in *Figure 4.19*.

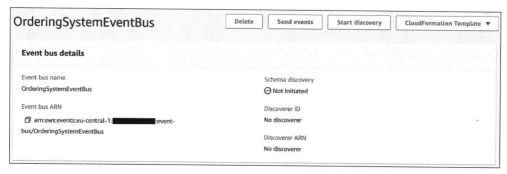

Figure 4.19: *Starting schema discovery for an Amazon EventBridge bus*

Upon initializing event bus discovery, a new EventBridge rule is created to send events to the schema discoverer. To allow schema discovery to occur, you need to publish at least one event to the event bus. After publishing an event, wait a few minutes for the schema to be analyzed. Then, you can view and download the discovered schema along with code bindings.

1. From the **Amazon EventBridge** dashboard, on the left sidebar, click **Schemas**, and select the **Discovered schema registry** tab.

2. Find and click on the schema discovered named **com.example.new-order-service@OrderCreated**, as shown in *Figure 4.20*.

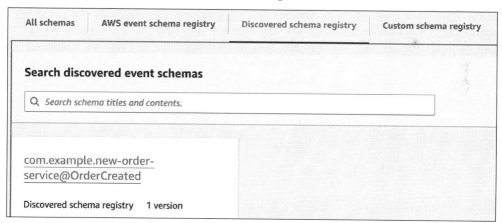

Figure 4.20: *Starting schema discovery for an Amazon EventBridge bus*

3. From the schema dashboard, review the JSON schema of the event that was discovered. The schema contains all the custom detail properties of the **OrderCreated** event that we send to the event bus such as **orderId**, **customerId**, and so on, as shown in *Figure 4.21*.

Figure 4.21: *Viewing the schema discovered for an Amazon EventBridge bus*

4. Finally, click **Download code bindings**. Select **Java 8** and click **Download**.

The Java files that were downloaded contain classes with the same properties that we defined for the **OrderCreated** event in our Lambda functions. These class definitions can be very useful for teams that are creating new rules and want to understand the structure of events sent to the event bus. By examining the event classes, teams can discover the data fields and schemas of events on the bus without having to reverse engineer the raw event data. This enables faster development of new Lambda functions that consume these events.

Conclusion

In summary, Amazon EventBridge provides a flexible and scalable platform for implementing event-driven architectures and choreography patterns. This chapter covered the fundamental concepts of EventBridge including events, event buses, rules, targets, and how to integrate with third-party services. We explored several common choreography design patterns built on EventBridge such as event sourcing, CQRS, scheduler, and claim check patterns. Practical capabilities like archiving events, replaying past events, and using schemas and pipes were also discussed.

By now, you should have a solid understanding of EventBridge's capabilities and how it can be leveraged to create scalable, event-driven serverless architectures. The patterns and best practices covered in this chapter should provide a framework for implementing robust choreography and integration between various application components and services using events. As you build out event-driven systems with EventBridge, always consider the business context, domains, and processes to discover meaningful events and create solutions optimized for observability, traceability, and organizational alignment.

The next chapter in the book provides an in-depth look at Amazon Step Functions, a service on AWS that makes it easy to coordinate the components of distributed applications and microservices using visual workflows. The chapter covers several key design patterns that can be implemented using Step Functions to handle issues like errors and distributed transactions, including the *circuit breaker pattern*, which stops faulty services from overwhelming a system, and the *SAGA pattern*, which manages transactions that span multiple services and provides rollback procedures to maintain data consistency across services.

CHAPTER 5

Orchestration with AWS Step Functions

Introduction

This chapter provides a thorough overview of building orchestration workflows with AWS Step Functions. We first introduce Step Functions and the Amazon States Language, contrasting Standard and Express workflows. Next, you will learn state machine modeling to simulate data flows between states using the Step Functions Data Flow simulator. The chapter then covers visual workflow development with the Step Functions Workflow Studio and orchestration design patterns like SAGA and circuit breaker. Additionally, we discuss error handling, retries, and error management for resilient workflows. Finally, we explore the differences between Step Functions orchestration and Amazon EventBridge choreography. By the end, you will understand how to leverage Step Functions to coordinate event-driven microservices on AWS into scalable and distributed workflows. The core concepts are supplemented with examples and hands-on exercises to apply these new skills.

Structure

In this chapter, we will discuss the following topics:

- Introduction to Orchestration with Step Functions
- Standard versus Express Workflows
- Understanding the Amazon States Language
- Simulating the Data Flow Between States Using the Data Flow Simulator Tool
- Exploring the Step Functions Workflow Studio
- Orchestration Patterns with Step Functions: SAGA, Circuit Breaker
- Error Handling in Step Functions
- Orchestration with Step Functions versus Choreography with EventBridge

Orchestration

In an event-driven architecture, services are designed to be autonomous and loosely coupled. This means that each service is responsible for its own behavior and communication with other services. While this approach provides many benefits, it also introduces a new set of challenges.

One of the biggest challenges is ensuring that events are properly routed and processed. Without proper orchestration, events can be lost or duplicated, leading to inconsistent state and behavior across services. Additionally, without a clear understanding of the event flow, it can be difficult to troubleshoot issues or identify areas for optimization.

Orchestration helps address these challenges by providing a centralized management layer that oversees the event flow. It ensures that events are properly routed and processed, and provides real-time visibility into the system's behavior. It also helps tackle the complexity of event flows and simplifies building business processes spanning across multiple decoupled components.

Orchestration provides several benefits to organizations building event-driven architectures. Here are a few examples:

- **Improved efficiency**: Orchestration helps ensure that events are properly routed and processed, reducing the risk of errors and improving system efficiency.

- **Real-time visibility**: Orchestration provides real-time visibility into the system's behavior, making it easier to identify issues and optimize performance.

- **Flexibility**: Orchestration allows organizations to easily add or remove services from the system, providing greater flexibility and scalability.

- **Resiliency**: Orchestration helps ensure that the system remains operational, even in the event of service failures or other disruptions.

Orchestration is key to taming complexity and unlocking the full potential of event-driven architectures. With robust and scalable orchestration, event-driven systems can deliver intricate business processes, workflows, and decision making: all by reacting to events in a decoupled asynchronous way. The right orchestration platform brings resilience, flexibility, and responsiveness within reach.

AWS Step Functions

AWS Step Functions is a serverless orchestration service that lets you easily coordinate components of distributed applications and microservices using visual workflows. Step Functions allows you to build and run state machines that stitch together services such as AWS Lambda functions, other AWS services, and your own applications into end-to-end workflows.

Step Functions uses state machines as the underlying model for workflows. A state machine is a collection of states that can do work (*Task* states), determine which states to transition to next (*Choice* states), stop an execution (*Fail* states), and so on. The state machine starts with an initial state and transitions through various states until it reaches a terminal state that completes the execution.

Each step in the workflow is represented as a state in the state machine. The transitions between steps are defined by passing output from one step to the input of another step. Step Functions provides visualization, monitoring, and debugging tools, which give visibility into each workflow execution.

Here are some key benefits of using Step Functions for workflow orchestration:

- **Visual workflows**: Step Functions lets you build workflows visually using the AWS Management Console instead of writing code. This makes workflows easy to understand and maintain.

- **Coordination of components**: Step Functions can easily coordinate components and services, including AWS Lambda, Amazon API Gateway, Amazon SNS, and more. This removes the complexity of directly connecting components.

- **Error handling**: Step Functions makes it easier to handle errors through automated retry, catch, and fallback behaviors when exceptions occur. This leads to reliable workflows.

- **Audit history**: Step Functions logs detailed execution history, including execution details, state machine definitions, input and output, and more. This makes it easy to audit and debug workflows.

- **Scalability**: Step Functions can orchestrate massively parallel workflows that involve thousands of distributed components. Workflows automatically scale so you don't have to worry about fleet management.

AWS Step Functions is a serverless orchestration service that helps coordinate connected components at any scale through easy-to-use visual workflows. It provides consistency, visualization, observability, and reliability to workflows involving event-driven services.

Standard versus Express Workflows

When creating a state machine in Step Functions, you have two options for the underlying execution engine: **standard** or **express** workflows. Standard workflows prioritize flexibility and durability, while express workflows optimize for speed and high volume at the lowest cost. When architecting state machines, consider tradeoffs between workflow execution time, durability needs, and budget. Standard workflows suit long-running processes, while express fits transient, high-volume tasks.

Here is an overview of the key differences between standard and express workflows:

Execution Speed

- **Standard workflows**: Provide maximum flexibility for long-running, durable state machines. Standard workflows can run for up to 1 year.

- **Express workflows**: Optimized for high-volume, short-running jobs. Express workflows can run tasks very quickly but are limited to a total execution time of 5 minutes.

Pricing

- **Standard workflows**: Billed for every state transition based on execution time. More cost-effective for long-running workflows.

- **Express workflows**: Billed per execution. More cost-effective for short and high-volume state machines.

Durability

- **Standard workflows**: Fully durable and fault-tolerant. Can resume from failures, making them useful for workflows that cannot afford to restart from scratch.

- **Express workflows**: Not durable. After 5 minutes or machine failure, the execution cannot be resumed and must be re-invoked.

Use Cases

- **Standard workflows**: Long-running, durable, auditable, and mission-critical workflows.

- **Express workflows**: High-volume data processing, IoT applications, and mobile application backends.

Overall, you should choose both workflow types to build resilient applications on AWS. By choosing the right type of workflow, you can create efficient and effective automated processes that help you build and deploy your applications more quickly and reliably.

Understanding the Amazon States Language

AWS Step Functions provides a graphical interface to create state machines and workflows through the Amazon States Language. The **Amazon States Language** defines different types of states that can be used to control the flow of a state machine execution.

Some of the main state types are:

- **Pass**: The Pass state is used to pass the input to the next state in the workflow. It is the default state and is used when no other state is specified.

- **Task**: The Task state is used to perform a specific task, such as invoking a

Lambda function or sending a message to an SQS queue. It takes an action as an input and returns a result.

- **Choice**: The Choice state is used to split the workflow into multiple branches based on a condition. It takes a condition expression as an input and routes the workflow to the corresponding branch.

- **Wait**: The Wait state is used to pause the workflow for a specified amount of time. It takes a time value as an input and waits for that amount of time before proceeding to the next state.

- **Succeed**: The Succeed state is used to indicate that the workflow has completed successfully. It takes a result as an input and ends the workflow.

- **Fail**: The Fail state is used to indicate that the workflow has failed. It takes an error message as an input and ends the workflow.

- **Parallel**: The Parallel state is used to run multiple branches of the workflow simultaneously. It takes a list of branches as an input and runs them in parallel.

- **Map**: The Map state is used to iterate over a list of items and apply a specific action to each item. It takes a list of items as an input and produces a new list of items as output.

Each state has an input and output structure that determines what data can flow through it. By connecting different states together, complex state machine workflows can be created to coordinate various tasks and integrate with backend systems.

Input and Output Between States

In AWS Step Functions, each state in a workflow can have its own input and output. The input is the data that is passed to the state when it is entered, while the output is the data that is produced by the state when it is exited.

For example, consider a simple workflow that consists of two states: a *Start* state and an *End* state. The *Start* state might have an input of a JSON object containing customer data, while the *End* state might have an output of a JSON object containing the customer's order information.

When the workflow is executed, the *Start* state will receive the input JSON object and process it in some way. The output of the *Start* state will then be passed to the *End* state, which will process it further and produce the final output JSON object.

One of the key benefits of using AWS Step Functions is its ability to map inputs and outputs between states. This allows you to create workflows that can process a wide variety of data, and to easily integrate with other systems and services.

For example, consider a workflow that consists of three states: a *Start* state, a *Process* state, and an *End* state. The *Start* state might have an input of a JSON object containing customer data, while the *End* state might have an output of a JSON object containing the customer's order information.

The *Process* state might have an input of a JSON object containing the customer's order details and an output of a JSON object containing the calculated total price. By mapping the input and output of each state, you can create a workflow that can process the customer's order information and produce the final order details.

Here's an example of how the input and output mapping might look for this workflow:

- **Start state:**
    - ○ **Input**: JSON object containing customer data.
    - ○ **Output**: JSON object containing the customer's order details.
- **Process state:**
    - ○ **Input**: JSON object containing the customer's order details.
    - ○ **Output**: JSON object containing the calculated total price.
- **End state:**
    - ○ **Input**: JSON object containing the calculated total price.
    - ○ **Output**: JSON object containing the customer's order information.

By understanding how input and output work between states, you can create workflows that can process a wide variety of data and integrate with other systems and services.

In an upcoming section, we will thoroughly examine the fields that govern the flow of JSON data between states. Specifically, we will look at `InputPath`, `Parameters`, `ResultSelector`, `ResultPath`, and `OutputPath`: the key elements that direct how JSON inputs are transformed into JSON outputs as data passes from one state to the next.

Exploring the Step Functions Workflow Studio

AWS Step Functions provides a graphical interface called the **workflow studio** for authoring and visualizing state machines. The studio can be accessed from the AWS Management console and has three main modes: `Design`, `Code`, and `Config`.

Design Mode

The `Design` mode provides a visual canvas for building state machines using a drag-and-drop interface, as shown in *Figure 5.1*. It enables building a workflow by visual drag and drop of states onto the canvas area and configuring their parameters in the step properties section. Complex workflows can be designed without writing any code.

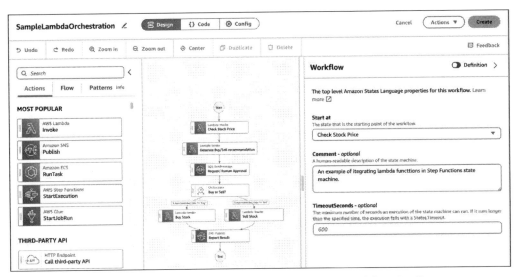

Figure 5.1: *Design mode in AWS Step Functions Workflow Studio*

The design mode is divided into three components. On the left, there is the **States Browser**, in the middle the **Canvas**, and on the right the **Inspector**.

States Browser

The **states browser** is a panel located on the left-hand side of the workflow studio interface. It displays a list of all the states in the workflow and has three tabs: `Actions`, `Flow`, and `Patterns`.

The `Actions` tab contains AWS APIs that can be dragged into the workflow graph canvas and represent *Task* states. The `Flow` tab provides various control flow states that can also be dragged into the workflow, such as the *choice, map, succeed, fail,* and other states that we saw in the previous section. Finally, the `Patterns` tab has reusable templates for common use cases like iteratively processing Amazon S3 data. Together these tabs allow you to visually build state machine workflows by dragging preconfigured states into the canvas.

Canvas

The **canvas** in the middle is where you actually design your workflow by connecting different states. You can drag states from the browser onto the canvas and join them together to build the logic. The canvas provides an easy-to-visualize work surface for building complex state machine workflows using a drag-and-drop approach. You can zoom in/out, pan, align, and distribute states on the canvas.

Inspector

The **inspector** panel on the right allows you to configure the specific state you have selected on the canvas. It displays various configuration fields and options related to the chosen state. For example, if you select a **Task** state, the inspector will show fields to enter the task details. If you select a **Choice** state, it will show rule configuration options. The inspector enables you to easily set up each state without needing to edit raw JSON.

Code Mode

The **Code** mode provides the JSON definition of the state machine created in the **design** mode. The visual workflow design is automatically translated to JSON code, which can be viewed and edited directly in this mode. Developers can write the JSON code definition here directly as well, as shown in *Figure 5.2*.

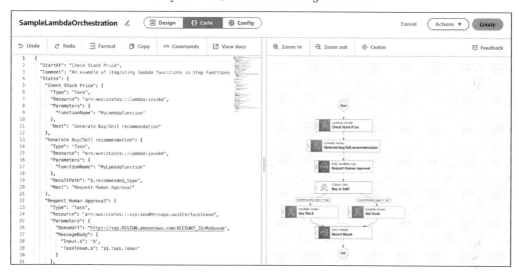

Figure 5.2: *Code mode in AWS Step Functions Workflow Studio*

The code follows the standard *Amazon States Language* specification. Syntax validation warnings are provided while editing to catch issues.

Config Mode

The **Config** mode gives you granular control over defining and managing state machines. Within this interface, you customize key attributes like the state machine's name, permissions, logging, tracing, publishing options, and more during initial creation, as illustrated in *Figure 5.3*.

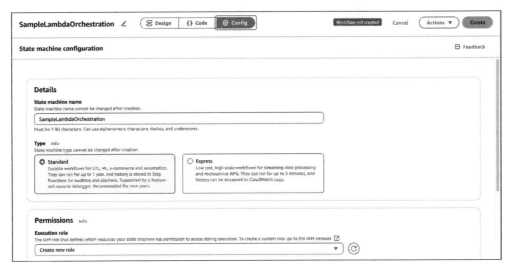

Figure 5.3: *Config mode in AWS Step Functions Workflow Studio*

Specifically, config mode allows you to designate details such as the state machine's identifier and whether it will operate as a **Standard** or **Express** type. You can also leverage AWS IAM to precisely tune permissions to AWS resources. Additionally, config mode empowers you to enable AWS X-Ray tracing for tracking requests as they flow through the state machine.

Note: *AWS X-Ray is a distributed tracing service designed to help you analyze and debug distributed applications, such as microservices architectures. With X-Ray, you can gain insights into the performance of your applications by collecting data about requests as they travel through the different components of the application.*

Creating Your First State Machine

Let's now walk through an example to understand how Step Functions operate. We will create a state machine that calls the *Ordering platform* API we built in *Chapter 3, Messaging with Amazon SQS and Amazon SNS*, and assert that it has been successfully called. The state machine will have the following steps:

1. Invoke the *Ordering platform* API, passing the request body test JSON that we used previously when testing the API.

2. Check that the API returns a 201 HTTP *status code* indicating success.

3. If a 201 status is received, mark the state machine as completed successfully. If not, mark the state machine as failed.

By passing test data to the API and validating the result code, this example will demonstrate the process of chaining together states in Step Functions and conditionally progressing based on API outputs. Let's now open the AWS Management Console and create our state machine:

1. From the list of services, search for *step functions* and click on **Step Functions** to go to the **AWS Step Functions** dashboard.

2. On the left sidebar, click **State machines** and then click the **Create state machine** button.

3. Choose a **Blank** template and click **Select**.

4. On the top, click on the **Config** tab and enter **OrderingAPI-StateMachine** for the name. Note that the name cannot be edited after you create a state machine. Click on the **Design** tab to go back to the editor.

5. On the **States browser** on the left, click on the **Actions** tab, search for *API Gateway*, and drag the **Amazon API Gateway Invoke** state to the empty state labeled **Drag first state here**.

6. Click the **Amazon API Gateway Invoke** state, and on the right, enter **Call the ordering system API** for the *State name* and replace the **API Parameters JSON** with the information of the **ordering-platform-api** we created in the previous chapter. Replace the **ApiEndpoint** with the invoke URL of your API. The **$.NewOrderRequest** is the input JSON that will be sent to the state machine.

```
{
    "ApiEndpoint": "<api id>.execute-api.eu-central-1.amazonaws.
com",
    "Method": "POST",
    "Stage": "prod",
    "Path": "/orders",
    "RequestBody.$": "$.NewOrderRequest"
}
```

7. On the **States browser** on the left, click on the **Flow** tab and drag the **Choice** state below the **Amazon API Gateway Invoke** action on the editor.

8. Enter **API invoked successfully?** for the **State** name, edit **Rule #1** below, and click on the **Add conditions** button.

9. Enter **$.StatusCode** for the **Variable**, **is equal to** for the **Operator**, **Number constant** and **201** for the **Value**, as shown in *Figure 5.4*. Click **Save conditions**.

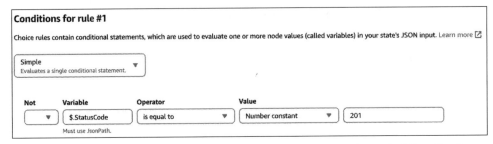

Figure 5.4: *Adding a rule for a Choice state in AWS Step Functions Workflow Studio*

10. From the **Flow** tab, drag the **Success** state below the **$.StatusCode == 201** condition and the **Fail** state below the **Default** condition.

11. *Figure 5.5* shows what your state machine design should look like:

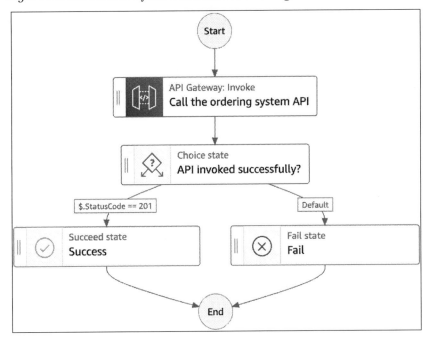

Figure 5.5: *Design of an AWS Step Functions state machine*

12. On the top right, click **Create**, review the permissions of the new role that would be created for the state machine, and click **Confirm**.

13. You will be redirected to a new page. From the **Executions** tab, click **Start execution**.

14. From the popup, enter the **JSON** we have been using for testing new order creation in the previous chapters, as an input inside the **NewOrderRequest** field, as shown in *Figure 5.6*. Click **Start execution**.

Figure 5.6: Starting the execution of an AWS Step Functions state machine

After starting an execution of your AWS Step Functions state machine, a new page opens showing detailed information about that execution. This page includes a graphical view of all the steps that were executed, with specifics on each step and the events that took place. When the state machine finishes executing successfully, all the steps leading up to the final *Success* state will be highlighted in green in the graph, indicating they completed properly. This is depicted in *Figure 5.7*, which shows the graphical workflow with green-colored steps after a successful execution.

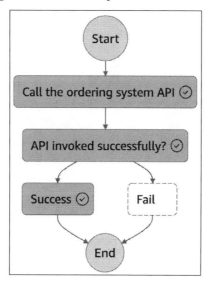

Figure 5.7: Successful execution of an AWS Step Functions state machine

You can click on each step to view the input sent to it, the output it produced, and any error that might have occurred. This debug information about your state machine can help you identify and fix issues.

Step Functions state machines are defined using JSON. The JSON definition for each state machine can be easily deployed to your infrastructure and is available in the **Code** tab when you edit the state machine. For example, the JSON definition for the state machine we just created is as follows:

```json
{
  "Comment": "A description of my state machine",
  "StartAt": "Call the ordering system API",
  "States": {
    "Call the ordering system API": {
      "Type": "Task",
      "Resource": "arn:aws:states:::apigateway:invoke",
      "Parameters": {
        "ApiEndpoint": "<api id>.execute-api.eu-central-1.amazonaws.
com",
        "Method": "POST",
        "Stage": "prod",
        "Path": "/orders",
        "RequestBody.$": "$.NewOrderRequest"
      },
      "Next": "API invoked successfully?"
    },
    "API invoked successfully?": {
      "Type": "Choice",
      "Choices": [
        {
          "Variable": "$.StatusCode",
          "NumericEquals": 201,
          "Next": "Success"
        }
      ],
      "Default": "Fail"
    },
    "Success": {
      "Type": "Succeed"
    },
```

```
    "Fail": {
      "Type": "Fail"
    }
  }
}
```

This JSON can be treated as infrastructure definition code where you manage your infrastructure through machine-readable definition files rather than manual processes. This brings the benefits of version control, testing, and collaboration to infrastructure management.

Note: *AWS Step Functions includes a feature called* **redriving execution** *that allows you to restart failed workflows from the point of failure, rather than forcing you to rerun the entire workflow from the beginning. When an execution fails in Step Functions, you can use redriving execution to pick up where it left off and continue the execution from the unsuccessful step onwards. This recovery mechanism uses the same original input, allowing you to address failures faster without needing to recreate or modify workflow inputs. This feature is available on the executions page. However, it can only be used for Standard workflows that have a failed step, not Express workflows.*

Diving Deep into the Data Flow Between States

As we saw in a previous section, one of the key features of step functions is their ability to process input and output data, which is crucial for integrating with other AWS services and applications. We will now explore the different elements involved in input and output processing in Step Functions, including the **InputPath**, **Parameters**, **ResultSelector**, **ResultPath**, and **OutputPath**, as shown in *Figure 5.8.*

Figure 5.8: Input and output processing in AWS Step Functions

InputPath

The **InputPath** is the location where the input data for a step function is stored. This can be an Amazon S3 bucket, or any data source that can be accessed by the step function. The **InputPath** is specified in the step function's definition, and it's used to retrieve the input data for the step function.

Parameters

Parameters are the input data that is passed to a step function. They are specified in the step function's definition, and they can be either string or integer values. **Parameters** can be used to customize the behavior of the step function, such as specifying the name of an Amazon S3 bucket or the ID of an Amazon DynamoDB table.

ResultSelector

The **ResultSelector** is a powerful feature of step functions that allows you to select the output of a step function. It's used to specify the output data that should be passed to the next step in the workflow. The **ResultSelector** can be a JSONPath expression, which allows you to extract specific data from the output of the previous step.

ResultPath

The **ResultPath** is the location where the output data from a step function is stored. This can be an Amazon S3 bucket, an Amazon DynamoDB table, or any other data source that can be accessed by the step function. The **ResultPath** is specified in the step function's definition, and it's used to store the output data from the step function.

OutputPath

The **OutputPath** is the location where the final output data from a step function workflow is stored. This can be an Amazon S3 bucket, an Amazon DynamoDB table, or any other data source that can be accessed by the step function. The **OutputPath** is specified in the step function's definition, and it's used to store the final output data from the workflow.

Visualizing how data passes through these transitions can be challenging. To aid in this understanding, AWS provides a graphical **Data flow simulator** tool within the Step Functions console. The simulator enables step-by-step debugging of data transitions and helps clarify exactly how input is transformed as it progresses through the steps defined in a state machine. In the next section, we will explore the capabilities of this simulator.

Data Flow Simulator Tool

The **Data flow simulator** is a tool that allows you to simulate the data flow of an AWS Step Functions state machine. It allows you to test and validate the data flow of your state machine without having to deploy it first.

Let's say you have a state machine that processes an order. The state machine has several states, such as **order received**, **order processed**, and **order shipped**. The data flow simulator allows you to simulate the flow of data through the state machine, so you can see how the data would be processed and what the output would be at each state.

To use the data flow simulator, you simply create a new simulation in the AWS Step Functions console. You can then select the state machine you want to simulate and provide some sample input data. The simulator will then run through the state machine and show you the output at each state. You can also see any errors or issues that might occur during the simulation.

It's important to note that the simulator only simulates the data flow and doesn't actually execute any code. This means that the simulation results may not perfectly match the actual behavior of your state machine. Additionally, the simulator only supports a limited number of inputs and outputs, so you may need to simplify your state machine or use sample data to get accurate results.

Let's now see an example of how to use the Data flow simulator from the AWS Management Console using the test JSON that we sent previously to the ordering system API:

1. From the **AWS Step Functions** dashboard, on the left sidebar, click on **Data flow simulator** found under the **Developer resources** section.

2. For the **State Input**, add the test JSON, as shown in *Figure* 5.9. Click **Next**.

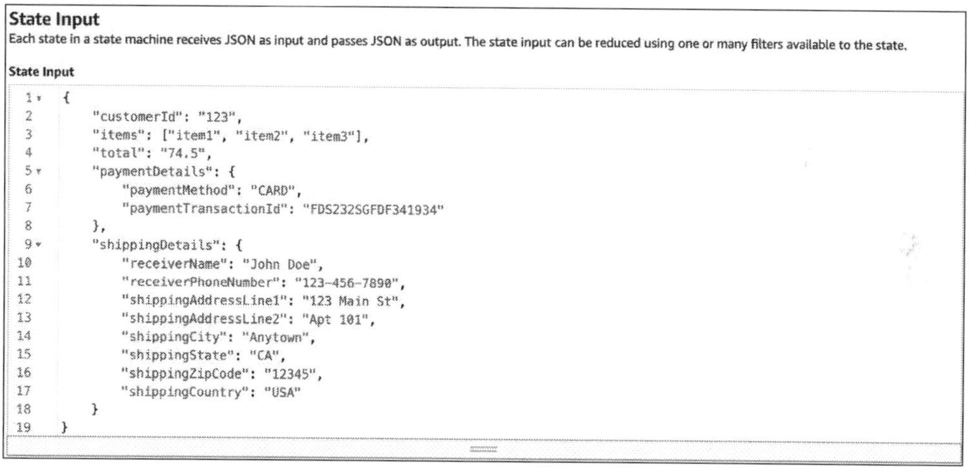

State Input

Each state in a state machine receives JSON as input and passes JSON as output. The state input can be reduced using one or many filters available to the state.

State Input

```
 1 ▾  {
 2         "customerId": "123",
 3         "items": ["item1", "item2", "item3"],
 4         "total": "74.5",
 5 ▾       "paymentDetails": {
 6             "paymentMethod": "CARD",
 7             "paymentTransactionId": "FDS232SGFDF341934"
 8         },
 9 ▾       "shippingDetails": {
10             "receiverName": "John Doe",
11             "receiverPhoneNumber": "123-456-7890",
12             "shippingAddressLine1": "123 Main St",
13             "shippingAddressLine2": "Apt 101",
14             "shippingCity": "Anytown",
15             "shippingState": "CA",
16             "shippingZipCode": "12345",
17             "shippingCountry": "USA"
18         }
19     }
```

***Figure* 5.9:** *Entering the state input in the Data flow simulator tool*

3. For the **Input Path**, do not add anything, as we want the whole JSON to be passed. Click **Next**.

4. For the **Parameters**, add a new field with a unique id, pass only some fields from the original JSON, encode the transaction id, and concatenate the shipping address, as shown in *Figure* 5.10. Click **Next**.

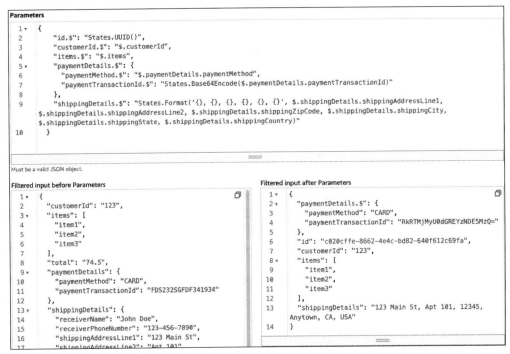

Figure 5.10: *Filtering the input with the Parameters field in the Data flow simulator tool*

5. For the **Task Result**, add a test JSON returned by Amazon API Gateway, which contains the **order id** created, as shown in *Figure* 5.11. Click **Next**.

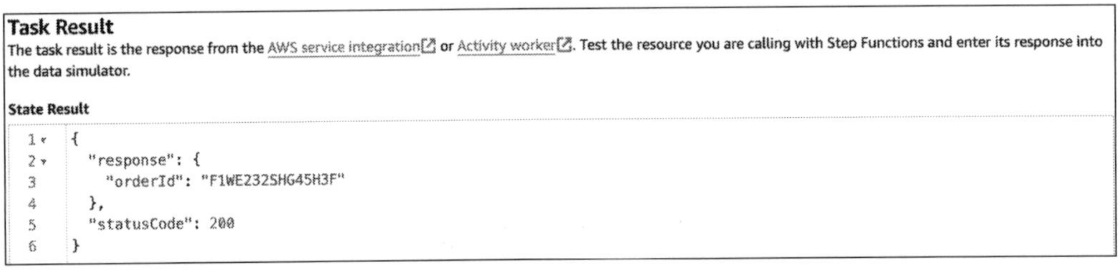

Task Result

The task result is the response from the AWS service integration⧉ or Activity worker⧉. Test the resource you are calling with Step Functions and enter its response into the data simulator.

State Result

```
1 ▾ {
2 ▾   "response": {
3       "orderId": "F1WE232SHG45H3F"
4     },
5     "statusCode": 200
6   }
```

Figure 5.11: *Changing the Task Result response in the Data flow simulator tool*

6. For the **ResultSelector**, select the **order id** from the response, as shown in *Figure* 5.12. Click **Next**.

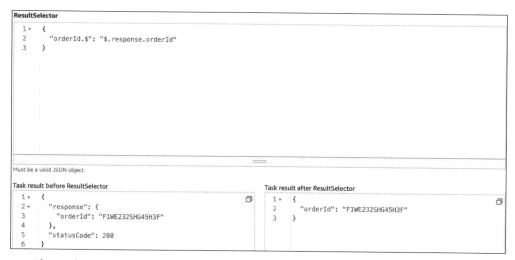

Figure 5.12: *Selecting the result with the ResultSelector in the Data flow simulator tool*

7. For the **ResultPath**, add the **order id** from the response and also the input, as shown in *Figure 5.13*. Click **Next**.

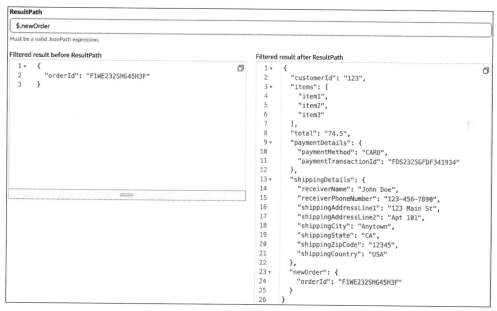

Figure 5.13: *Filtering the result with the ResultPath in the Data flow simulator tool*

8. For the **OutputPath**, do not add anything, as we want the whole JSON to be returned. Click **Next**.

9. Confirm that the **State Output** is your desired final state output.

As we saw from the **Parameters** and **ResultSelector** fields, we used some functions to manipulate the data. Those are called **intrinsic functions**. In the next section, we will explore intrinsic functions in more depth.

Intrinsic Functions

AWS Step Functions allows you to use **intrinsic functions** in your state machine definitions to perform useful computations and data manipulations. The intrinsic functions fall into several categories:

Array Manipulation Functions

- **States.Array**: Returns a JSON array containing the argument values.

  States.Array(1, 2, 3) = [1,2,3]

- **States.ArrayPartition**: Partitions an array into chunks of specified size.

  States.ArrayPartition([1,2,3,4,5], 2) = [[1,2], [3,4], [5]]

- **States.ArrayContains**: Checks if a value exists in an array.

  States.ArrayContains([1,2,3], 2) = true

- **States.ArrayRange**: Creates an array containing a range of elements between the start and end values provided incrementing by the specified step size.

  States.ArrayRange(2, 8, 2) = [2,4,6,8]

- **States.ArrayGetItem**: Gets the element at the specified index in the input array.

  States.ArrayGetItem([1,2,3,4,5], 3) = 4

- **States.ArrayLength**: Returns the length of the input array.

  States.ArrayLength([1,2,3,4,5,6]) = 6

- **States.ArrayUnique**: Returns an array containing only the unique elements from the input array.

  States.ArrayUnique([2,2,5,5,6,7]) = [2,5,6,7]

Data Encoding/Decoding Functions

- **States.Base64Encode**: Encodes a string with Base64.

  States.Base64Encode(input)

- **States.Base64Decode**: Decodes a Base64-encoded string.

  States.Base64Decode(input)

Hash Calculation Function

- **States.Hash**: Calculates a hash digest of a string using the specified algorithm.

  States.Hash(input, 'SHA-256')

JSON Manipulation Functions

- **States.JsonMerge**: Merges two JSON objects.

  ```
  States.JsonMerge(json1, json2, false)
  ```

- **States.StringToJson**: Parses a JSON string into a JSON object.

  ```
  States.StringToJson({\"id\": \"DF34\"}) = {"id": "DF34"}
  ```

- **States.JsonToString**: Converts JSON object to a string.

  ```
  States.JsonToString({"id": "DF34"}) = {\"id\": \"DF34\"}
  ```

Math Functions

- **States.MathRandom**: Generates a random number between provided bounds.

  ```
  States.MathRandom(1, 10) = 4
  ```

- **States.MathAdd**: Sums two numbers.

  ```
  States.MathAdd(1, 2) = 3
  ```

String Manipulation Function

- **States.StringSplit**: Splits string into an array based on delimiter.

  ```
  States.StringSplit('1,2,3', ',') = [1,2,3]
  ```

Unique Identifier Generation Function

- **States.UUID**: Generates a random UUID.

  ```
  States.UUID() = ab78eba0-898a-4c81-aecf-72f4a67efb5e
  ```

Generic Formatting Function

- **States.Format**: Replaces placeholders in template string.

  ```
  States.Format('Hello {}', 'John') = Hello John
  ```

You can find the complete list of intrinsic functions in the official AWS documentation:

https://docs.aws.amazon.com/step-functions/latest/dg/amazon-states-language-intrinsic-functions.html.

Project Time: Orchestrating Multiple Lambda Functions

We are undertaking a complete redesign of the ordering system architecture for our Shopme platform. Rather than using an event bus (SQS, SNS, EventBridge), we will leverage AWS Step Functions for orchestration among the various Lambda functions. This shift from choreography to orchestration will coordinate the flow through key steps: **NewOrder**, **ReserveInventory**, **ProcessPayment**, and the newly introduced **FulfilOrder**.

The Step Functions workflow will provide several advantages. The **Parallel** state will allow the **ReserveInventory** and **ProcessPayment** branches to execute concurrently, independently checking for success before invoking **FulfilOrder**. Previously this was difficult to coordinate with an event bus. Additionally, Step Functions makes it simpler to pass data between components. We will heavily utilize input/output processing with **ResultSelector**, **ResultPath**, and other transformations to customize the workflow.

The goal of this re-architecture is to gain more control and visibility into the ordering process. Step Functions gives us an orchestration layer to sequence Lambda invocations, implement error handling, visualize workflow state, and gain observability into the overall process. By leveraging Step Functions for coordination rather than an event mesh, we aim to improve reliability and traceability.

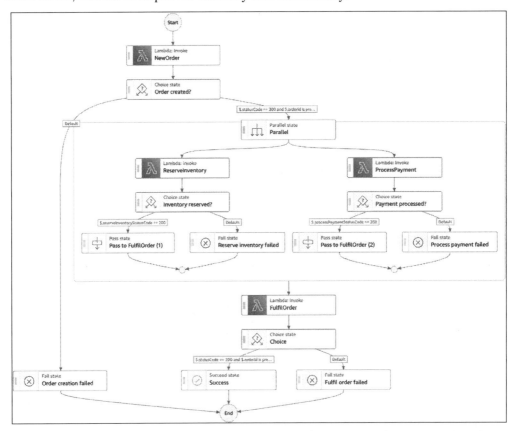

Figure 5.14: *The Ordering system architecture using orchestration with AWS Step Functions*

Next, we will walk through the AWS Step Functions state machine, as shown in *Figure 5.14*. We will explain the purpose and functionality of each state, including the inputs it accepts and the outputs it produces, to understand how the overall workflow is constructed.

State #1: Create a New Order

The state machine is initiated by calling the **NewOrder** service, which creates new orders. The **NewOrder** service accepts input from the state machine, such as the test JSON payload used in previous examples. By passing this test JSON data to the **NewOrder** service, new orders can be created based on the state machine's input:

```
{
    "customerId": "123",
    "items": ["item1", "item2", "item3"],
    "total": "74.5",
    "paymentDetails": {
        "paymentMethod": "CARD",
        "paymentTransactionId": "FDS232SGFDF341934"
    },
    "shippingDetails": {
        "receiverName": "John Doe",
        "receiverPhoneNumber": "123-456-7890",
        "shippingAddressLine1": "123 Main St",
        "shippingAddressLine2": "Apt 101",
        "shippingCity": "Anytown",
        "shippingState": "CA",
        "shippingZipCode": "12345",
        "shippingCountry": "USA"
    }
}
```

When the **NewOrder** service is invoked, Lambda returns an output that contains the response payload with details of the new order creation inside the **Payload** field, as well as a status code inside the **StatusCode** field. If the status code is 200, it means the **NewOrder** service is successfully completed. The response JSON looks like:

```
{
    "ExecutedVersion":"$LATEST",
    "Payload":{
        "orderId":"e1e8d868-eeee-4a6f-9cfc-ab5dc4f33f55",
        "customerId":"123",
```

```
        "orderDate":1706546530431,
        "status":"PLACED",
        "items":[
            "item1",
            "item2",
            "item3"
        ],
        "total":"74.5"
    },
    "SdkHttpMetadata":{
        ...
    },
    "SdkResponseMetadata":{
        "RequestId":"ac79dacd-7c6f-41c7-bfcf-eea70b43e141"
    },
    "StatusCode":200
}
```

The next step is to filter the output using the **OutputPath** field, to extract only the **Payload** field value by specifying **$.Payload**. The filtered **Payload** value will then be passed to the next state in the workflow.

State #2: Verify that the Order Has Been Created

The second state is a **ChoiceState** that checks whether the **NewOrder** service completes successfully. This is done by verifying two conditions - first, checking if the status code of the response was **200**, and second, checking if the **orderId** field was present in the response. The rule for the **ChoiceState** is:

```
$.statusCode == 200 and $.orderId is present
```

The state machine progresses to the next state if the current rule is satisfied; otherwise, the state machine is flagged as a failure.

State #3: Reserve Inventory and Process Payment in Parallel

The **ParallelState** enables concurrent execution of the **ReserveInventory** and **ProcessPayment** services, waiting for responses from both to complete. The input to invoke these services is the payload JSON data that was filtered in a prior state:

```
{
    "orderId": "e1e8d868-eeee-4a6f-9cfc-ab5dc4f33f55",
    "customerId": "123",
    "orderDate": 1706546530431,
    "status": "PLACED",
    "items": [
        "item1",
        "item2",
        "item3"
    ],
    "total": "74.5"
}
```

Using the **ParallelState** allows these two services to run simultaneously rather than sequentially, potentially improving performance. When each of the services completes, they transform the result using the **ResultSelector** property by constructing a new JSON object that only includes the status codes and excludes the service outputs, since those outputs do not need to be passed to subsequent states.

For the **ReserveInventory** service, the response is transformed using the following JSON:

```
{
    "reserveInventoryStatusCode.$": "$.StatusCode"
}
```

Similarly, for the *ProcessPayment* service:

```
{
    "processPaymentStatusCode.$": "$.StatusCode"
}
```

The next step is to confirm that both services in the **ParallelState** complete their execution without errors.

State #4: Verify that Both Services Completed Successfully

The **ReserveInventory** and **ProcessPayment** services are verified to complete successfully using a **ChoiceState**. This **ChoiceState** has a rule that checks if the status code returned by each service is 200, indicating successful completion:

```
$.reserveInventoryStatusCode == 200
$.processPaymentStatusCode == 200
```

Next, we exit the **ParallelState** and proceed to fulfil the order.

State #5: Fulfil the Order

Upon exiting that **ParallelState**, the original input was combined with the outputs of the **ReserveInventory** and **ProcessPayment** services by adding them to a **$.response** field defined in **ResultPath**. The combined input-output data is now passed to the **FulfilOrder** service for further processing:

```
{
  "orderId": "e1e8d868-eeee-4a6f-9cfc-ab5dc4f33f55",
  "customerId": "123",
  "orderDate": 1706546530431,
  "status": "PLACED",
  "items": [
    "item1",
    "item2",
    "item3"
  ],
  "total": "74.5",
  "response": [
    {
      "reserveInventoryStatusCode": 200
    },
    {
      "processPaymentStatusCode": 200
    }
  ]
}
```

When the **FulfilOrder** service is called, we take the response and transform it using **ResultSelector** to construct a new JSON object. This new JSON contains the *order id* and *status code* extracted from the Lambda function's result:

```
{
  "orderId.$": "$.Payload.orderId",
```

```
    "statusCode.$": "$.StatusCode"
}
```

The last step is to confirm that the order has been fulfilled as requested.

State #6: Verify that the Order was Fulfilled

To confirm the order is fulfilled, we check the **FulfilOrder** service response for a **200 statusCode** and verify that the **orderId** field is present:

```
$.statusCode == 200 and $.orderId is present
```

The state machine ends in a **Success** state if this rule is adhered to; otherwise, in a **Fail** state.

Executing the State Machine

Once we begin executing the state machine by inputting the data we saw previously, if everything functions as anticipated, we will see all the steps turn green in the visualization, as depicted in *Figure 5.15*.

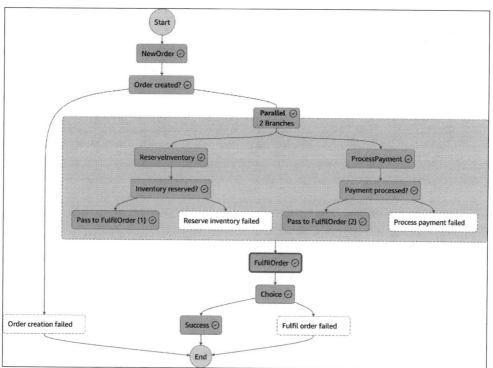

Figure 5.15: *Successful execution of the Ordering system state machine in AWS Step Functions*

Note: *Amazon API Gateway can be integrated with AWS Step Functions, enabling an API Gateway method to invoke a Step Functions state machine. Calling the API method triggers* *the execution of the associated workflow in Step Functions. With this API Gateway proxy integration, Step Functions receives the request body from the API method invocation as direct input to the state machine. This allows a client application to easily kick off a complex, coordinated backend workflow simply through an API call. The client just needs to call the API method without knowledge of the Step Functions workflow.*

Orchestration with AWS Step Functions versus Choreography with Amazon EventBridge

Orchestration and choreography are two different approaches to managing complex workflows in a distributed system. While both AWS Step Functions and Amazon EventBridge offer powerful tools for automating processes, they differ in their underlying philosophy and functionality.

Orchestration is a top-down approach that focuses on managing the overall flow of a process, ensuring that each step is executed in the correct order and that all necessary resources are provisioned and configured. AWS Step Functions is a prime example of an orchestration tool, allowing you to create visual workflows that coordinate multiple AWS services and third-party integrations. With Step Functions, the focus is on the overall workflow, and the tool takes care of managing the individual steps and their dependencies.

On the other hand, choreography is a bottom-up approach that focuses on the individual components of a system and how they communicate with each other. Amazon EventBridge is an example of a choreography tool, allowing you to create event-driven architectures where each component publishes events that other components can subscribe to. With EventBridge, the focus is on the individual components and their interactions, rather than the overall workflow.

Now, let's dive deeper into the advantages and disadvantages of each approach.

Advantages of Orchestration:

- **Easier to manage complex workflows**: Orchestration tools like AWS Step Functions provide a visual interface that makes it easier to manage complex workflows, ensuring that all steps are executed in the correct order and that dependencies are properly handled.

- **Better suited for linear workflows**: Orchestration is ideal for linear workflows where each step follows a predictable pattern. For example, in a content publishing workflow, each step follows a specific order, such as editing, reviewing, and publishing.

- **Centralized management**: Orchestration tools provide a centralized management interface that allows developers to monitor and manage the entire workflow from a single location.

Disadvantages of Orchestration:

- **Inflexibility**: Orchestration tools can be inflexible when it comes to changing the workflow. Making changes to a workflow can be difficult and time-consuming, especially if the changes are significant.

- **Limited scalability**: Orchestration tools can become less efficient as the workflow becomes more complex or as the number of steps increases. This can lead to performance issues and increased latency.

Advantages of Choreography:

- **Flexibility**: Choreography tools like Amazon EventBridge offer more flexibility when it comes to changing the workflow. Developers can add or remove components as needed, and the system can adapt to changing conditions without requiring significant changes to the overall workflow.

- **Scalability**: Choreography tools are designed to handle large volumes of events and can scale horizontally to meet the needs of a growing system. This makes them ideal for real-time data processing and event-driven architectures.

- **Decentralized management**: Choreography tools provide a decentralized management approach, allowing developers to manage individual components independently.

Disadvantages of Choreography:

- **Increased complexity**: Choreography tools can be more complex to set up and manage, especially for developers who are new to event-driven architectures.

- **Higher operational overhead**: Choreography tools require more effort to manage and maintain, as developers need to handle issues such as event versioning, retries, and timeouts.

Both orchestration and choreography have their advantages and disadvantages, and the choice between the two depends on the specific needs of the system. Orchestration is ideal for linear workflows that require centralized management and predictable order, while choreography is better suited for complex, event-driven systems that require flexibility and scalability. AWS Step Functions and Amazon EventBridge offer powerful tools for automating processes, and you can use them in combination to create a hybrid approach that takes advantage of the strengths of both philosophies.

Error Handling in AWS Step Functions

One of the key features of Step Functions is its ability to handle errors and exceptions gracefully, ensuring that your workflows can continue to run smoothly even when things go wrong. Next, we will explore the features **retry on errors** and **catch errors**, and how they can help you handle errors in your Step Functions workflows.

Retry on Errors

The **retry on errors** feature in Step Functions allows you to configure your workflows to retry a step if it fails due to an error. This can be useful in situations where the error is temporary or where the step is likely to succeed on a subsequent attempt. For example, if you are using an AWS Lambda function as a step in your workflow and it fails due to a timeout, you can configure Step Functions to retry the Lambda function after a certain amount of time.

You can also specify the number of retry attempts and the time interval between retries. If the step fails and the retry attempt is successful, Step Functions will continue to the next step in the workflow. If all retry attempts fail, the workflow will fail and you'll receive an error message.

Catch Errors

The **catch errors** feature in Step Functions allows you to handle errors in a more granular way. With catch errors, you can specify a set of error codes or exception types that should be caught and handled by a specific step in your workflow. This can be useful in situations where you want to handle errors differently depending on their severity or nature.

For example, if you are using an Amazon S3 bucket as a step in your workflow and you want to handle errors related to file access or permissions, you can configure Step Functions to catch those errors and handle them in a specific way. You can also use catch errors to handle errors that occur in a specific step, such as a Lambda function or an SQL query.

To use catch errors, you will need to specify the error codes or exception types that you want to catch, as well as the step that should handle the error. You can also specify a `ResultPath` that indicates where the error should be stored in the workflow's output. This can be useful for debugging and troubleshooting purposes.

Best Practices

When using the *retry on errors* and *catch errors* features in Step Functions, it's important to follow some best practices to ensure that your workflows are reliable and efficient. Here are a few tips to keep in mind:

1. **Use retry on errors sparingly**: While the retry on errors feature can be useful, it's important to use it sparingly and only when it makes sense for your

workflow. Retrying a step too many times can lead to unnecessary delays and increased costs.

2. **Use catch errors judiciously**: When using catch errors, make sure you're only catching errors that you can realistically handle in your workflow. Catching too many errors can make your workflow overly complex and difficult to debug.

3. **Test your workflows thoroughly**: Before deploying your workflows to production, make sure you have tested them thoroughly to ensure that they handle errors correctly. Use tools like Amazon CloudWatch and AWS X-Ray to monitor your workflows and identify any issues.

4. **Use error handling in conjunction with other features**: Error handling is just one part of building resilient workflows in Step Functions. Make sure you are also using other features like timeouts, retry policies, and activity timeouts to ensure that your workflows can handle a variety of scenarios.

Error handling is a critical aspect of building scalable and resilient workflows in AWS Step Functions. The *retry on errors* and *catch errors* features provide a powerful way to handle errors and exceptions gracefully, ensuring that your workflows can continue to run smoothly even when things go wrong. By following best practices and using these features judiciously, you can build workflows that are reliable, efficient, and capable of handling a variety of errors and exceptions.

SAGA Pattern with AWS Step Functions

The SAGA pattern is a way to manage distributed transactions and long-running workflows in a microservices architecture. It provides a simple rollback mechanism to maintain data consistency across services without using distributed transactions. AWS Step Functions can be used to effectively implement the SAGA pattern.

The SAGA pattern breaks down a long-running business transaction into a series of independent local transactions. Each local transaction updates the database and publishes a message or event to trigger the next local transaction in the SAGA. If one of the transactions fails, a compensation transaction is triggered to roll back the previous transactions that were already executed.

This *undo* approach provides fault tolerance and data consistency without requiring distributed transactions across microservices. The sequence of local transactions and compensation transactions is coordinated by a SAGA coordinator.

AWS Step Functions enables the implementation of resilient SAGA workflows through configurable retries to handle transient errors and catch blocks to route and recover from expected failure scenarios. This simplifies building distributed applications with coordinated rollback logic using modern microservices.

Project Time: Implementing the SAGA Pattern

In this section, we will incorporate the SAGA pattern into the Ordering system Step Functions workflow constructed earlier. For simplicity, we will remove the flow control states, like Choice and Parallel, and focus solely on applying the SAGA pattern for robust error handling across Lambda functions.

As shown in *Figure 5.16*, the key idea is that each Lambda function will have a corresponding *rollback* Lambda that reverses its state changes on failure. Specifically, if a function throws an error contained in a designated field of its response, its rollback function will trigger to walk back any successful prior state transitions. For example, if the **NewOrder** service fails, the **NewOrder-Rollback** service will activate to cancel any processed order creations. Similarly, a failure in **ProcessPayment** service will recursively invoke the rollback functions for all preceding steps - first **NewOrder-Rollback**, then **ReserveInventory-Rollback**, and finally **ProcessPayment-Rollback**.

In this way, we add reliable failure recovery to the workflow while preserving simplicity by isolating error-handling logic in rollback functions. The SAGA pattern enables precise rollback to a known good state even as we chain together multiple state-mutating steps.

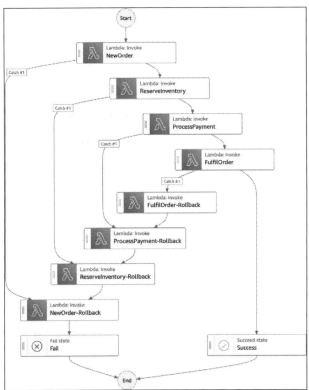

Figure 5.16: *SAGA pattern for the Ordering system using AWS Step Functions*

Error catching for a Lambda function is configured in the **Error Handling** tab of the function's *inspector* panel of the Step Function's *design* mode. As shown in *Figure 5.17*, the **States.ALL** wildcard can be used to match any error name that is thrown by the Lambda function.

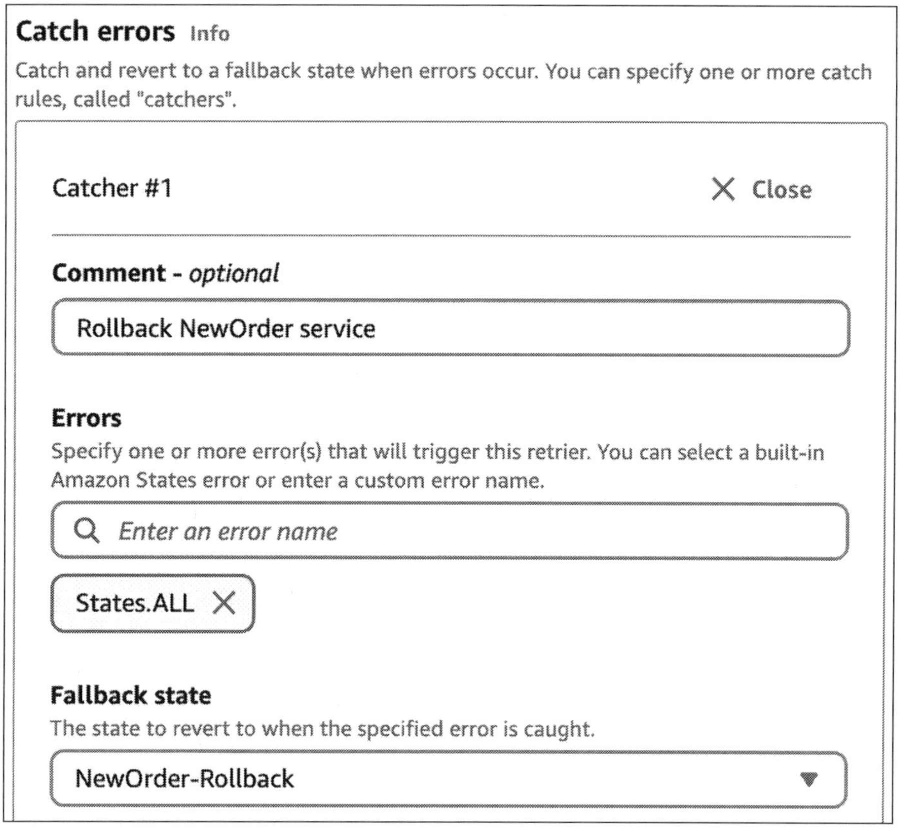

Catch errors Info

Catch and revert to a fallback state when errors occur. You can specify one or more catch rules, called "catchers".

Catcher #1   ✕ Close

Comment - optional

> Rollback NewOrder service

Errors

Specify one or more error(s) that will trigger this retrier. You can select a built-in Amazon States error or enter a custom error name.

> 🔍 *Enter an error name*

> States.ALL ✕

Fallback state

The state to revert to when the specified error is caught.

> NewOrder-Rollback   ▼

Figure 5.17: *Adding a fallback state in the Error Handling tab of the AWS Step Functions Workflow Studio*

The error retries can also be configured in the same tab, as shown in *Figure 5.18*. We can specify the error(s) that will trigger the retrier, the interval in seconds before the first retry attempt, the maximum number of retry attempts, the backoff rate that multiplies the retry interval after each attempt, and the max delay in seconds allowed between retries.

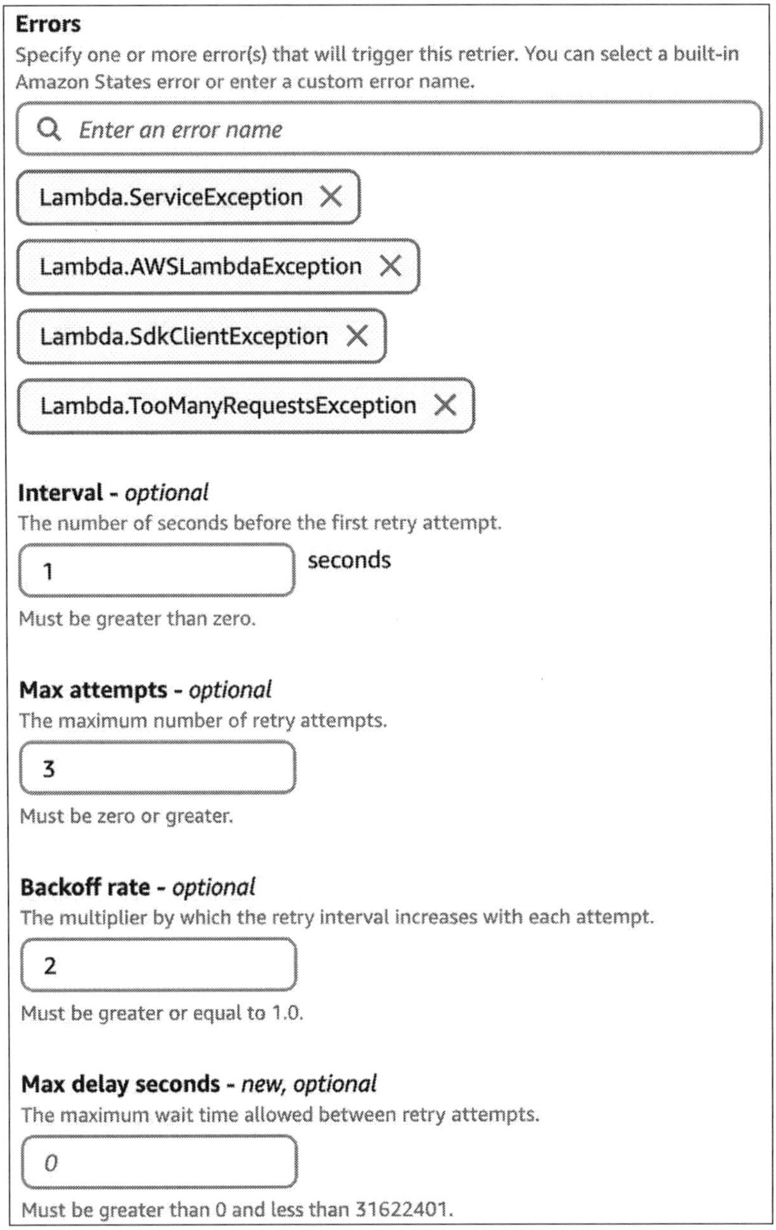

Errors

Specify one or more error(s) that will trigger this retrier. You can select a built-in Amazon States error or enter a custom error name.

> 🔍 *Enter an error name*

> Lambda.ServiceException ✕

> Lambda.AWSLambdaException ✕

> Lambda.SdkClientException ✕

> Lambda.TooManyRequestsException ✕

Interval - *optional*

The number of seconds before the first retry attempt.

> 1   seconds

Must be greater than zero.

Max attempts - *optional*

The maximum number of retry attempts.

> 3

Must be zero or greater.

Backoff rate - *optional*

The multiplier by which the retry interval increases with each attempt.

> 2

Must be greater or equal to 1.0.

Max delay seconds - *new, optional*

The maximum wait time allowed between retry attempts.

> 0

Must be greater than 0 and less than 31622401.

Figure 5.18: *Editing the error retrier properties in the Error Handling tab of the AWS Step Functions Workflow Studio*

Once we implement the state machine and run it successfully, the non-rollback services should change to green status, assuming there are no issues, as shown in *Figure* 5.19.

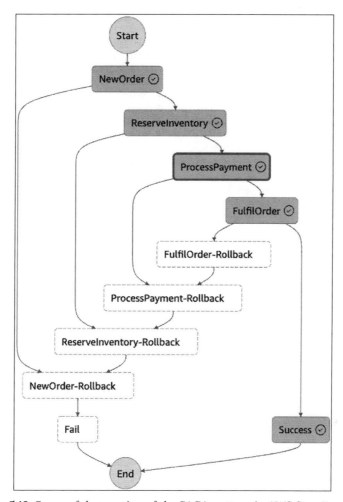

Figure 5.19: *Successful execution of the SAGA pattern in AWS Step Functions*

If a Lambda function throws an error, for example, if invalid input is sent preventing the creation of a new order in DynamoDB, the **NewOrder** state will turn orange to indicate the error was caught. The workflow will then transition to the **NewOrder-Rollback** state, as illustrated in *Figure 5.20*.

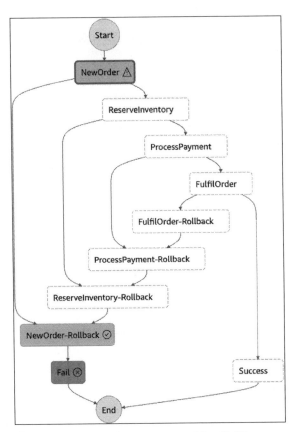

Figure 5.20: *Unsuccessful execution of the SAGA pattern in AWS Step Functions that fallbacks to a rollback state*

The SAGA pattern provides an effective way to rollback state changes if a Lambda function throws an error during execution. However, SAGA does not mitigate the issue of constant failures of a Lambda function. Such failures would trigger frequent re-executions, incurring unnecessary costs. This is where the **circuit breaker** pattern comes in - it acts as a monitoring system that checks if a Lambda function is operating correctly. Next, we take a closer look at the specifics of how the circuit breaker pattern works.

Circuit Breaker Pattern with AWS Step Functions and Amazon DynamoDB

The **circuit breaker** pattern is a resilience design pattern used to detect failures and encapsulate logic for preventing repeated calls to a failed service. The circuit breaker acts like an electrical circuit breaker - when failures reach a threshold, it *trips* the circuit and stops allowing calls to the failing service. This gives the failing service time to recover and prevents a buildup of requests at the same time.

The circuit breaker has three states:

- **Closed**: Allows requests, monitors for failures.
- **Open**: Does not allow requests to the service. Returns an error immediately.
- **Half-open**: Allows some requests to pass through to trial the recovering service. Continues monitoring failures.

If the trial requests are successful, it closes the circuit and resumes normal operation. If requests continue to fail, the breaker reopens the circuit.

Here is how you can implement the circuit breaker pattern on AWS using Step Functions and DynamoDB:

1. Create a DynamoDB table to store the circuit breaker state with attributes like `state` (closed, open, half-open), `failedRequests`, `count`, `timestamps`.

2. Build a Step Functions state machine with two states - *Closed* and *Open*.

3. The Closed state calls the downstream service. On success, it resets the failure counts. On failure, it increments the failure counts in DynamoDB and checks if the threshold is exceeded to transition to the *Open* state.

4. The Open state doesn't call the downstream service to allow it to recover. It starts a timer and periodically checks DynamoDB to see if enough time has elapsed to transition back to the Closed state.

5. Handle the Half-open logic by allowing a single test call to the downstream service to check if it has recovered before fully closing the circuit again.

AWS Step Functions and DynamoDB provide the necessary tools for building resilient applications using the circuit breaker pattern for failure protection and service recovery. The entire state machine workflow and circuit state can be managed and visualized through Step Functions.

Project Time: Implementing the Circuit Breaker Pattern

In this section, we will incorporate the circuit breaker design pattern into the Ordering system's **NewOrder** microservice, which handles the creation of new orders. The purpose of using a circuit breaker is to prevent the **NewOrder** service from being overwhelmed by too many requests when it is having issues.

The circuit breaker status, indicating whether the circuit is closed (allowing requests) or open (blocking requests), will be stored in an Amazon DynamoDB table. Each circuit status entry will contain a timeout specifying when the circuit will toggle state (for example, from open to closed after 10 seconds).

When an order request enters the system, a **GetCircuitStatus** Lambda function will first query DynamoDB to check if the circuit to the **NewOrder** service is closed. If it is open, the order request will immediately fail.

If the circuit is closed, the request will invoke the **NewOrder** service to create the order. If the **NewOrder** service throws any errors due to overload or other issues, a second Lambda function called **UpdateCircuitStatus** will trigger. This will update DynamoDB to flip the circuit state to open and set a timeout for when it will re-enable requests to **NewOrder**.

The state machine diagram in *Figure 5.21* illustrates the workflow we will construct using AWS Step Functions:

1. The **GetCircuitStatus** Lambda function retrieves the circuit status data from DynamoDB.

2. If the circuit is open, the state machine transitions to a fail state.

3. If the circuit is closed, the **NewOrder** service is invoked.

4. If the **NewOrder** service finished successfully, the state machine transitions to a success state.

5. If the **NewOrder** service throws an error, the **UpdateCircuitStatus** Lambda function is triggered, which updates the DynamoDB entry to set the circuit state to open and sets a timeout in DynamoDB.

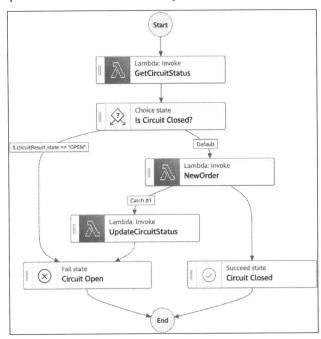

Figure 5.21: *Circuit breaker pattern for the Ordering system using AWS Step Functions*

Now, we will conduct some test executions to observe the system's behavior when the circuit is closed or open. *Figure 5.22* illustrates the happy path scenario - the circuit is closed because the **NewOrder** service successfully completes its execution.

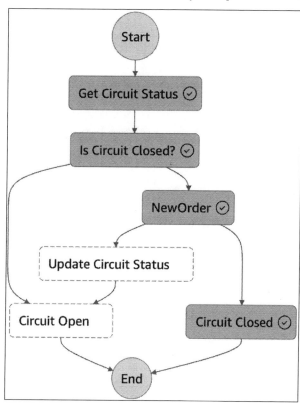

Figure 5.22: *The circuit breaker has closed the circuit because the recent requests have been successfully executed*

However, if the **NewOrder** service throws an error exception, the circuit will transition to an open state and the end-to-end execution will fail, as shown in *Figure 5.23*. The circuit remains in this open state for a configurable timeout period defined in the DynamoDB table.

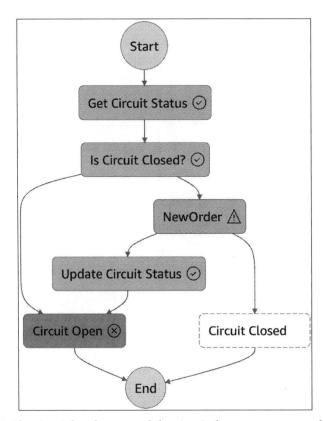

Figure 5.23: *The circuit breaker opened the circuit due to an unsuccessful execution*

The circuit remains in this open state for a configurable timeout period defined in the DynamoDB table. During this timeout period, any subsequent execution attempts before timeout expiration will fail immediately before calling the **NewOrder** service, as shown in *Figure* 5.24. This prevents overwhelming the troubled service with requests and incurring unnecessary costs during a specified cool-down period.

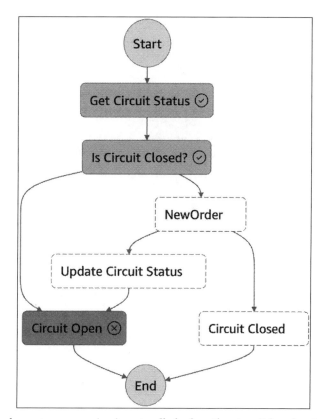

Figure 5.24: *The downstream service is not called when the circuit breaker is in an open state*

After the timeout expires, the next request will check if the circuit is closed again, emulating a half-open state check. This closed state indicates the service has had time to recover and is ready to start handling limited requests to confirm availability.

Implementing circuits enables resilience by preventing cascading failures and allowing services to gracefully degrade during disruptions. Defining timeouts allows balancing availability versus the risk of overloading the recovering subsystem.

Conclusion

In conclusion, this chapter provided a comprehensive introduction to building scalable workflows on AWS using Step Functions. We covered the basics of Step Functions and the Amazon States Language, including contrasts between Standard and Express workflows. You learned how to visually model state machines to simulate data flows. We also discussed orchestration design patterns like SAGA and circuit breaker for resilient workflows. Additionally, we explored error handling and retries to manage failures. Finally, we differentiated between Step Functions orchestration and EventBridge choreography. By now, you should have a strong understanding of how to leverage Step Functions to coordinate event-driven services into robust and distributed workflows on AWS. With the concepts and hands-on exercises covered, you are equipped to start building practical Step Functions orchestrations to automate cloud workflows.

The next chapter delves deeply into Amazon Kinesis, AWS's robust and fully managed real-time streaming service. We will first explain the concept of event streaming and why it is critical for today's data-intensive applications. We will then explore the core components of Amazon Kinesis. This includes Amazon Kinesis Data Streams, which allows for real-time processing of streaming data, as well as Amazon Kinesis Firehose for easily loading streams into AWS data stores and analytics tools.

CHAPTER 6

Event Streaming with Amazon Kinesis

Introduction

This chapter starts by providing an overview of event streaming concepts and benefits, as well as introducing the Amazon Kinesis service. We will then take a deep dive into Amazon Kinesis Data Streams, which enables high-performance data ingestion from various sources and integration with other AWS services. Next, we will explore Amazon Data Firehose (formerly called Amazon Kinesis Data Firehose) for simplifying the transformation and delivery of streaming data to storage targets like Amazon S3. After that, we will cover real-time analytics with Amazon Managed Service for Apache Flink (formerly called Amazon Kinesis Data Analytics) for querying streaming data in real time. By the end of this chapter, you will have a fundamental understanding of stream processing architectures leveraging the various Amazon Kinesis offerings.

Structure

In this chapter, we will discuss the following topics:

- Introduction to Event Streaming with Amazon Kinesis
- Exploring the Amazon Kinesis Services: Amazon Kinesis Data Streams, Amazon Data Firehose, and Amazon Managed Service for Apache Flink
- Streaming Data Ingestion Pattern with Amazon Kinesis Data Streams
- Data Pipeline Pattern with Amazon Data Firehose
- Real-Time Analytics Pattern with Amazon Managed Service for Apache Flink

Event Streaming

Event streaming is a powerful concept in event-driven architectures that allows for the efficient and scalable processing of an extremely high volume of events. Event streaming is the process of streaming events from various sources into a centralized event store. This store can be a database, a data lake, or even a streaming platform.

Event streaming has several benefits, including:

- **Real-time processing**: Events are processed in real-time, allowing for immediate insights and reactions to the events. This can be critical in situations where timely responses are necessary, such as in financial trading or emergency response situations.

- **Scalability**: Event streaming can handle large volumes of events, making it an ideal solution for organizations that generate a high volume of events.

- **Flexibility**: Event streaming allows for the integration of multiple data sources, making it easy to incorporate data from various systems and applications.

- **Cost-effective**: Event streaming can be more cost-effective than traditional data processing methods, as it eliminates the need for batch processing and expensive data storage solutions.

Event streaming works by capturing events from various sources, such as applications, sensors, and databases. These events are then streamed into a centralized event store, where they are processed and analyzed in real time. The processed events can then be used to trigger actions, send notifications, or feed data into analytics systems.

Event-driven architectures are designed to respond to events in real-time, making event streaming a natural fit. In an event-driven architecture, events are generated by various sources, such as user interactions, system events, and external events. These events are then processed by an event processor, which determines the appropriate action to take based on the event.

Event streaming can be used in event-driven architectures to stream events from various sources into a centralized event store. This allows for the efficient and scalable processing of events, enabling the architecture to respond to events in real-time.

One of the most popular streaming services for event-driven architecture is **Amazon Kinesis**, which is a fully managed service provided by AWS that can handle real-time data processing and analytics. In the following sections, we will thoroughly examine Amazon Kinesis and its fundamental services that enable real-time data streaming at scale. Specifically, we will look at **Amazon Kinesis Data Streams** for rapid data intake and processing, **Amazon Data Firehose** (formerly called Amazon Kinesis Data Firehose) for simplified loading into data stores, and **Amazon Managed Service for Apache Flink** (formerly called Amazon Kinesis Data Analytics) for performing queries on streaming data.

Streaming with Amazon Kinesis

Amazon Kinesis makes it easy to collect, process, and analyze real-time, streaming data such as video, audio, application logs, IoT telemetry, and other data streams.

Kinesis provides a number of benefits for event streaming in an event-driven architecture. First, it can handle large volumes of data, scaling to handle tens of thousands of streams and millions of events per second. This means that Kinesis can handle the high volume of events generated by modern applications and services, making it an ideal choice for real-time data processing and analysis.

Second, Kinesis provides low-latency processing of events, which is critical in event-driven architectures where timely responses are essential. Kinesis can process events in real-time, allowing for immediate reaction to changes in the system or environment.

Third, Kinesis provides a fully managed service, which means that AWS handles the underlying infrastructure and maintenance tasks, such as scaling, monitoring, and security. This allows developers to focus on writing code and building applications, rather than managing infrastructure.

Fourth, Kinesis integrates with a wide range of AWS services, such as AWS Lambda, and Amazon S3, making it easy to build end-to-end data pipelines that process and analyze streaming data. This integration also allows for easy scaling and management of data processing tasks.

Finally, Kinesis provides a cost-effective solution for event streaming, with pay-per-use pricing that allows customers to only pay for the resources they use. This makes it an attractive choice for companies that need to process large volumes of data in real-time, without breaking the bank.

Amazon Kinesis Services

Amazon Kinesis consists of three main services: **Amazon Kinesis Data Streams**, **Amazon Data Firehose**, and **Amazon Managed Service for Apache Flink**.

Amazon Kinesis Data Streams is the core service of Amazon Kinesis. It allows users to stream data into AWS for real-time processing and analysis. Data Streams can handle large volumes of data and scale to meet the needs of growing organizations.

Amazon Kinesis Data Streams can be used for:

- **Real-time data processing**: Data Streams can be used to process data in real-time, allowing for immediate insights and reactions to the data.

- **IoT data processing**: Data Streams can handle large volumes of IoT data, making it an ideal solution for organizations that generate a high volume of IoT data.

- **Gaming and financial data processing**: Data Streams can be used to process gaming and financial data in real-time, allowing for immediate insights and reactions to the data.

Amazon Data Firehose is a fully managed service that allows users to collect and compress log data from hundreds of thousands of concurrent applications and streaming data from tens of thousands of concurrent IoT devices. Data Firehose can handle large volumes of data and can deliver data to AWS services such as Amazon S3, Amazon Redshift, and Amazon OpenSearch.

Amazon Data Firehose can be used for:

- **Log data collection**: Data Firehose can collect log data from hundreds of thousands of concurrent applications, making it an ideal solution for organizations that generate a high volume of log data.

- **IoT data ingestion**: Data Firehose can handle large volumes of IoT data, making it an ideal solution for ingesting IoT data from various sources.

- **Data warehousing**: Data Firehose can deliver data to AWS services such as Amazon S3, Amazon Redshift, and Amazon OpenSearch, making it an ideal solution for organizations that need to store and analyze large volumes of data.

Amazon Managed Service for Apache Flink is a fully managed service that allows users to run SQL-like queries on streaming data in real time. It can handle large volumes of data and can be used to process data from a variety of sources, such as IoT devices, application logs, and social media.

Amazon Managed Service for Apache Flink can be for:

- **Real-time analytics**: Managed Service for Apache Flink can be used to run SQL-like queries on streaming data in real time, allowing for immediate insights and reactions to the data.

- **IoT data analysis**: Managed Service for Apache Flink can handle large volumes of IoT data, making it an ideal solution for organizations that generate a high volume of IoT data.

- **Fraud detection**: Managed Service for Apache Flink can be used to detect fraud in real time, allowing for immediate action to be taken to prevent further fraud.

Amazon Kinesis is a powerful streaming service that allows users to process and analyze real-time data streams. With the three main services: Amazon Kinesis Data Streams, Amazon Data Firehose, and Managed Service for Apache Flink, organizations can handle large volumes of data, process data in real-time, and gain immediate insights and reactions to the data. Whether it's for big data processing, IoT data processing, or real-time analytics, Amazon Kinesis has the tools and capabilities to meet the needs of growing organizations.

Next, we will closely examine the three Amazon Kinesis services and then dive deeper into the functionalities of each.

Amazon Kinesis Data Streams

Amazon Kinesis Data Streams is a fully managed streaming service provided by AWS. It allows users to process and analyze real-time data streams, making it an ideal solution for big data processing, IoT data processing, and real-time analytics.

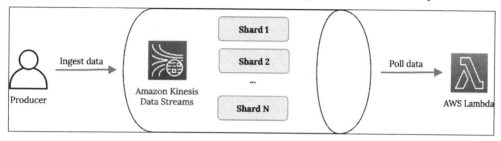

Figure 6.1: *Amazon Kinesis Data Streams consists of shards that are used to process large volumes of data*

The core concepts that allow Kinesis Data Streams to handle real-time streaming workloads at scale include: **streams**, **records**, **shards**, **partition key**, **resharding**, **producers**, and **consumers**.

- **Streams:** A stream is the main entity in Amazon Kinesis Data Streams. It is a sequence of data records that can be processed in real time. Streams can be created and managed using the Amazon Kinesis Data Streams console, the AWS CLI, or SDKs.

- **Records:** A record is a single unit of data that is produced to a stream. Data records can be in various formats, such as JSON, XML, or CSV. Each data record has a unique identifier, called a sequence number, that determines its position in the stream.

- **Shards:** A shard is a subset of a stream that can be processed independently. Shards are used to distribute data across multiple machines, allowing for horizontal scaling and high availability. Each shard can handle a portion of the data, making it easier to process large volumes of data.

- **Partition Key:** A partition key is a unique identifier that determines which shard a data record belongs to. The partition key is used to distribute data across shards, ensuring that data records with the same partition key are processed by the same shard.

- **Resharding:** Resharding is the process of redistributing data across shards. Resharding can be necessary when the volume of data changes, or when the partition key is not evenly distributed.

- **Producers:** Producers are the entities that produce data records to a stream. Producers can be applications, services, or devices that generate data.

- **Consumers:** Consumers are the entities that consume data records from a stream. Consumers can be applications, services, or devices that process or analyze data.

Producers and consumers can interact with streams in various ways, including using the AWS CLI, AWS SDKs, and other methods that we will cover in more detail later.

Choosing the Right Kinesis Data Stream Capacity Mode

Amazon Kinesis Data Streams allows you to choose between two capacity modes that determine how the throughput capacity of a data stream is provisioned and billed: `On-demand` and `Provisioned`.

The **on-demand capacity mode** is a cost-effective option for processing data streams with variable or unpredictable data volumes. With this mode, Kinesis Data Stream automatically scales the resources to match the volume of incoming data. This means that you don't need to worry about provisioning or managing capacity, as Kinesis Data Stream will automatically adjust the resources to handle the data load.

In on-demand capacity mode, you only pay for the resources you use, making it a cost-effective option for workloads with variable data volumes. This mode is preferred if your streaming data volume fluctuates significantly or is unknown. It is ideal for use cases such as IoT sensor data collection, gaming analytics, and real-time personalization.

The **provisioned capacity mode** is a good option for data streams with predictable and consistent data volumes. With this mode, you can provision the desired capacity upfront, and Kinesis Data Stream will guarantee that capacity for you. This means that you can process data at a fixed rate, without any throttling or interruptions.

With provisioned capacity mode, you manually select the number of shards for your Kinesis data stream. Each open shard provides a fixed capacity of 1 MB per second data input and 2 MB per second data output. For example, if you provision 10 shards, it offers 10 MB per second data input capacity. You pay an hourly fee for the provisioned capacity regardless of how much data you actually stream through it.

The provisioned mode is suitable if you know your peak streaming capacities. It guarantees available capacity for your streaming workloads. You may need to periodically rescale shards as your data. This mode is ideal for use cases such as video streaming, audio streaming, and real-time analytics.

Choosing the right capacity mode depends on the specific requirements of your use case. If your data volume is variable or unpredictable, on-demand capacity mode is the best option. It allows you to scale up or down as needed, and you only pay for the resources you use.

On the other hand, if your data volume is predictable and consistent, provisioned capacity mode is the better option. It provides guaranteed capacity and a fixed cost, making it easier to plan and budget for your data processing needs.

Note: *You can transition a Kinesis data stream between on-demand and provisioned capacity modes twice within a 24-hour period. Switching capacity modes does not disrupt applications reading from or writing to the stream. When using on-demand mode, Kinesis auto-scales the number of shards to accommodate your write throughput. If you switch from provisioned to on-demand, the stream keeps the existing shard count initially. Kinesis then adjusts it over time based on usage. In provisioned mode, you manually manage the shard count. If you switch from on-demand to provisioned, the stream keeps the existing shard count initially. You then monitor write throughput and adjust shards as needed to accommodate it.*

Calculating the Number of Shards in Provisioned Mode

When using Amazon Kinesis Data Streams in provisioned mode, you specify the number of shards for your stream instead of relying on auto-scaling. Determining the right number of shards to provision is important for optimizing throughput, costs, and performance.

Here are some tips and best practices to calculate the number of shards in provisioned mode for Amazon Kinesis Data Streams:

- **Determine the desired throughput**: Before calculating the number of shards, determine the desired throughput for your data stream. This will help you to calculate the number of shards required to handle the desired throughput.

- **Analyze the data volume**: Analyze the volume of data that will be streaming into the Kinesis Data Streams. This will help you to determine the number of shards required to handle the data volume.

- **Consider the data compression**: If you are using data compression, it can reduce the amount of data that needs to be processed. This can result in fewer shards being required to handle the data volume.

- **Consider the desired latency**: The desired latency will determine how quickly the data needs to be processed. This can affect the number of shards required, as more shards may be needed to achieve lower latency.

- **Monitor and adjust**: Monitor the performance of your Kinesis Data Streams and adjust the number of shards as needed. This will ensure that your data stream can handle the desired throughput and data volume.

- **Test and validate**: Test and validate your Kinesis Data Streams configuration before deploying it to production. This will ensure that your data stream can handle the desired throughput and data volume.

You can also use the **Amazon Kinesis Data Streams calculator**. Amazon provides a calculator that can help you to determine the number of shards required for your Kinesis Data Streams. This calculator can be accessed on the AWS Management console page where Kinesis data streams are created when selecting the `Provisioned` mode, as depicted in *Figure 6.2*.

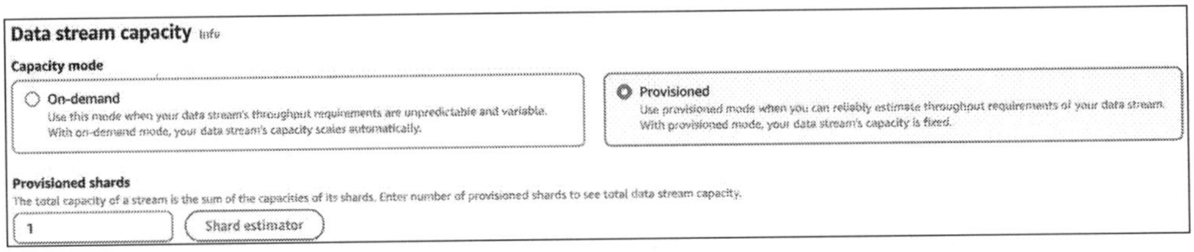

Figure 6.2: *The Shard estimator button to open the Amazon Kinesis Data Streams calculator is located on the page where you create a new Kinesis Data stream in provisioned mode*

Clicking the `Shard estimator` button will open a popup that assists in determining the appropriate number of shards based on your requirements.

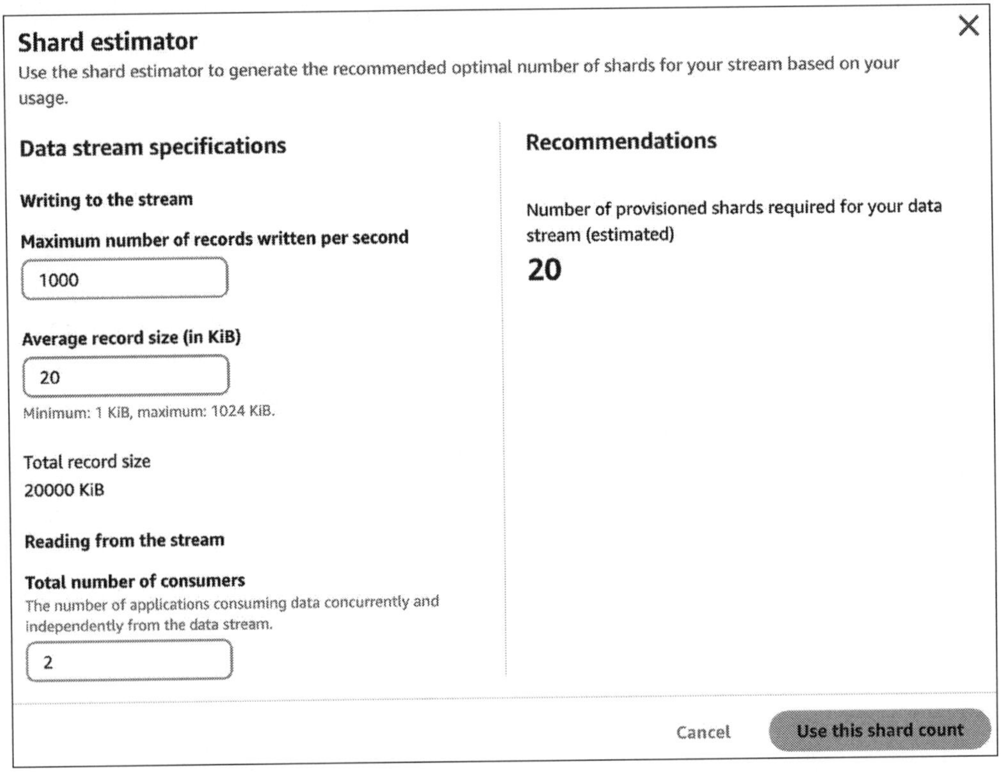

Figure 6.3: *The Shard estimator calculates the recommended number of shards required for your Kinesis data stream*

The shard estimator provides a recommended number of provisioned shards based on the provided metrics. As shown in *Figure 6.3*, inputting a maximum write rate of

1000 records per second, an average record size of 20 KB, and 2 total consumers, the calculator suggests provisioning 20 shards for optimal performance of the Kinesis data stream.

Working with Kinesis Data Streams

Let's now explore the methods that producers and consumers can use to write data to and read data from an Amazon Kinesis data stream.

Producer Applications: Writing to a Data Stream

Kinesis provides great flexibility and several integration options for writing streaming data sources continuously into your data streams for real-time storage and processing. The most commonly used options available to write data to an Amazon Kinesis data stream are as follows:

- **Amazon Kinesis Agent:** Amazon Kinesis Agent is a standalone Java application that offers an easy way to collect and send data to your stream. You can configure the agent to monitor log files, connect to servers or data sources, pre-process the data, and automatically handle sending data records.

- **Amazon Kinesis Producer Library (KPL):** It provides an easy to use and highly configurable library for developers to integrate into their data producer applications. KPL handles partition keys, retry logic, metrics, and so on.

- **AWS SDK:** Amazon Kinesis Data Streams provides SDKs for various programming languages, including Java, Python, and Node.js. These SDKs allow you to write data to a data stream using the programming language of your choice. The SDKs provide a simple and easy-to-use API for writing data to a data stream, and they handle the details of partitioning and serialization for you.

- **Direct PUT Records:** You can make direct REST API calls to write data records in JSON or binary formats into shards within your Kinesis streams. This offers maximum flexibility for any custom integration need.

Consumer Applications: Reading from a Data Stream

There are also a few options available for consuming applications to connect to a Kinesis data stream and process real-time data at scale. The most commonly used options available to read data from an Amazon Kinesis data stream are as follows:

- **Amazon Kinesis Client Library (KCL)**

  To read data from a data stream using Amazon Kinesis Data Streams, you can use the Amazon KCL. The KCL is a library that provides a simple and intuitive way to read data from Amazon Kinesis streams. The KCL supports multiple programming languages, including Java, Python, and Go, and provides a convenient way to build applications that can read and process data from Kinesis streams. With the KCL, you can easily create applications that can handle large volumes of data, scale to meet your needs, and provide low-latency processing of data streams.

- **AWS Lambda**

  AWS Lambda functions can be triggered by Amazon Kinesis Data Streams to process data records from a stream in a serverless way. When Kinesis Data Streams is configured as an event source for Lambda, Lambda will automatically poll the stream and invoke the function to handle each batch of records. This allows stream data to be processed without needing to provision or manage servers.

- **Amazon Data Firehose**

  Amazon Data Firehose is a fully managed service that enables delivering real-time streaming data to destinations like Amazon S3, Amazon Redshift, Amazon OpenSearch Service, and Splunk. It provides an easy way to capture, transform, and load streaming data into data stores and analytics tools. With Firehose, you don't need to write applications for reading and processing streaming data from a Kinesis stream.

- **Amazon Managed Service for Apache Flink**

  Amazon Managed Service for Apache Flink is a fully managed service that enables processing and analyzing streaming data using Apache Flink. It allows you to write SQL, Java, or Scala code to transform and enrich real-time data from Kinesis streams.

Project Time: Streaming Data Ingestion with Amazon Kinesis Data Streams

We will once again revisit the *Shopme* e-commerce platform. We aim to develop a new microservice responsible for ingesting and processing website clickstream data - the trails of clicks users make when browsing a site. For a high-traffic site with potentially hundreds of thousands of simultaneous users, the volume of clickstream data can be massive. Rather than routing this data through Amazon API Gateway, which may not handle such large throughput, we will leverage Amazon Kinesis Data Streams - a scalable streaming service designed for real-time high volume data.

Kinesis Data Streams will buffer the incoming clickstream records into shards - partitions for throughput scaling. Each shard supports up to 1 MB per second write throughput or 1000 records per second. Kinesis will handle the complexity of scaling shards out and ingesting the high volumes of clicks. Once in Kinesis, the stream shards will be read and processed by an AWS Lambda function in a serverless architecture. This polling-based model is similar to Lambda consuming from Amazon SQS queues. Leveraging Kinesis and Lambda provides a scalable, distributed, fault-tolerant clickstream processing pipeline without requiring us to manage infrastructure.

Creating an Amazon Kinesis Data Stream

To begin, we will start by creating an Amazon Kinesis data stream:

1. From the list of services, search for *kinesis* and click `Kinesis` to go to the `Amazon Kinesis` dashboard.

2. On the left sidebar, click `Data streams` and then click the `Create data stream` button.

3. Enter `OrderingSystemClickstream` for the `Data stream name` and choose `On-demand` for the `Capacity mode`, as shown in *Figure 6.4*. Click `Create data stream`.

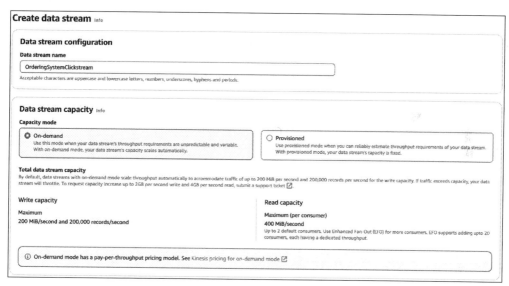

Figure 6.4: Creating an Amazon Kinesis data stream

When creating a new Kinesis data stream, AWS provisions the underlying resources needed to make the stream available. This provisioning process typically takes 10 minutes or less to complete. After it finishes, the Kinesis console will update the stream status from `Creating to Active` to indicate it is ready to receive data records, as shown in *Figure 6.5*. At that point, producers can begin writing records to the stream and consumers pulling from it for processing or analytics, as the full underlying infrastructure has been deployed automatically based on the configured stream properties.

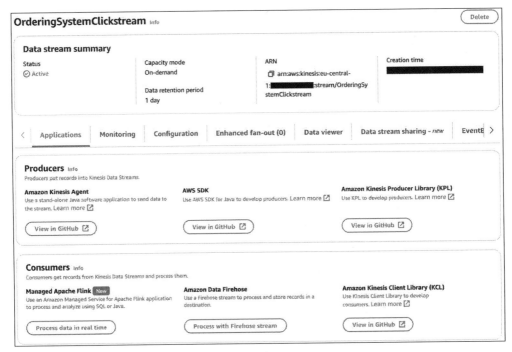

Figure 6.5: *Landing page of an Amazon Kinesis data stream*

Creating a Lambda Function to Read Records from a Data Stream

Our next step will be to create a **Clickstream** Lambda function that ingests and processes the **clickstream** data from the Kinesis stream. This function will then save the processed records to a new DynamoDB table called **clickstreams**, which will contain fields such as **clickstream id, user session, timestamp**, and **page url** to capture key details about the click data. The **LambdaHandler** will be written in Java and utilize the **KinesisEvent** class from the **aws-lambda-java-events** library to access the stream records.

Similar to an SQS-triggered Lambda, Kinesis invokes Lambdas by passing batches of records in the event rather than one record at a time. Processing data in batches allows for more efficient throughput. Let's see how the **LambdaHandler** method for the **Clickstream** service looks like:

```
public class LambdaHandler implements RequestHandler<KinesisEvent, Void>
{


private final Region = Region.EU_CENTRAL_1;
```

```java
    private DynamoDbClient ddb = DynamoDbClient.builder()
        .region(region)
        .build();


    private Gson gson = new Gson();


    private SimpleDateFormat sdf = new SimpleDateFormat("yyyy/MM/dd
hh:mm:ss");


    @Override
    public Void handleRequest(KinesisEvent event, Context context) {
        System.out.println("Received input from Kinesis" + gson.
toJson(event));

        if (event.getRecords().isEmpty()) {
            System.out.println("No Kinesis event received");
        return null;
    }


    for (var record : event.getRecords()) {
        // convert to clickstream event
        var data = new String(record.getKinesis().getData().array());
        var clickstream = gson.fromJson(data, ClickstreamEvent.
class);


        // save Clickstream to DynamoDB
        HashMap<String,AttributeValue> itemValues = new HashMap<>();
        itemValues.put("clickstreamId", AttributeValue.builder()
.s(UUID.randomUUID().toString()).build());
        itemValues.put("session", AttributeValue.builder().s
(clickstream.getSession()).build());
        itemValues.put("timestamp", AttributeValue.builder().s
(sdf.format(new Date())).build());
        itemValues.put("pageUrl", AttributeValue.builder().s
(clickstream.getPageUrl().toString()).build());
```

```
        var request = PutItemRequest.builder()
            .tableName("clickstreams")
            .item(itemValues)
            .build();

        ddb.putItem(request);
    }


    return null;
    }
}
```

The next step is to connect the **Clickstream** Lambda function to the Kinesis data stream to enable real-time data processing. We will set up an event source mapping that automatically triggers the Lambda function each time new data records arrive in the stream.

Adding Kinesis Data Streams as an Event Source for Lambda

To add the **OrderingSystemClickstream** Kinesis data stream as an event source for **Clickstream** Lambda function:

1. From the **Lambda** dashboard of the **Clickstream** function, go to the **Configuration** tab and click **Triggers** from the left sidebar. Click **Add trigger**.

2. Select the **OrderingSystemClickstream** stream, activate the trigger, enter **100** for the **Batch size**, and select **Trim horizon** for the **Starting position**, as shown in *Figure 6.6*. Click **Add**.

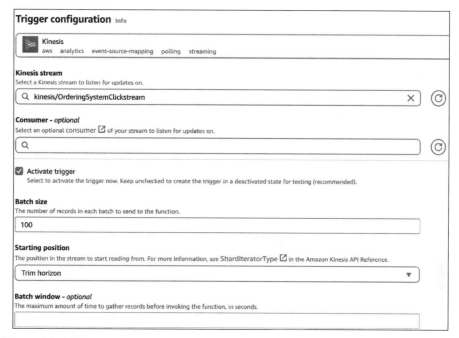

Figure 6.6: *Adding an Amazon Kinesis data stream as an event source for AWS Lambda*

With the event source mapping now established, the Kinesis data stream acts as a trigger for the Lambda function, batching and sending 100 records at a time for processing. The key concepts of **batch size**, **starting position**, and **batch window** are critical to understanding how Kinesis streams integrate with and trigger Lambda functions for stream processing. We will explore these concepts in greater depth in an upcoming section, outlining how each one impacts Lambda performance and scalability when ingesting high volumes of streaming data.

To validate the end-to-end system functionality, the next step is sending test data payloads to the Kinesis stream. As new records get published to the stream, we can observe and verify that those data events invoke the downstream Lambda function correctly for real-time computation on each batch of streaming records.

Writing Data to the Data Stream

To test the end-to-end flow, we will ingest test data to the **OrderingSystemClickstream** Kinesis stream using the AWS CLI **put-record** command. Then, we can validate whether those records trigger the **Clickstream** Lambda function configured via the event source mapping to process each batch of incoming data in real-time. Finally, we can check the **clickstreams** DynamoDB table to verify that the Lambda function successfully saved the computed results from processing those clickstream records.

```
$ aws kinesis put-record \
    --stream-name OrderingSystemClickstream \
    --data  "{\"session\": \"S4321\", \"pageUrl\": \"example.com\"}" \
    --partition-key 123 \
    --cli-binary-format raw-in-base64-out \
    --region eu-central-1
```

Once the test data is published into the Kinesis data stream using the **put-record** command, the AWS CLI will display a confirmation output indicating the data records were successfully transmitted to the stream for intake and processing.

```
{
    "ShardId": "shardId-000000000000",
    "SequenceNumber": "4964931836703494429817543716848463221866597805824
40960002",
    "EncryptionType": "KMS"
}
```

The CLI output contains metadata about the ingestion of the test data into the Kinesis stream, including the **ShardId** indicating which partition the record was stored in, the **SequenceNumber** which uniquely identifies each ingested record, and the **EncryptionType** detailing whether server-side encryption was enabled on the data. The **SequenceNumber** allows processed records to be tracked as they flow through the system. The **EncryptionType** can be set to **NONE** for plaintext data or KMS to leverage AWS Key Management Service for encryption of records at rest, providing an additional layer of security.

The last validation step is to verify that the test data records have been successfully processed and stored by querying the **clickstreams** DynamoDB table. We will execute a CLI command to scan the table contents and confirm that the Lambda function correctly handled the clickstream data it received from Kinesis by saving computed results from the test records into this DynamoDB table.

```
$ aws dynamodb scan --table-name clickstreams --region eu-central-1
```

The query output will display the enriched record that was processed by the Lambda function and then persisted to DynamoDB. This transformed item contains additional fields, such as a unique **clickstreamId** and **timestamp**, which were generated and appended in the Lambda processing layer before storage. These attributes were not originally present when the raw test data was ingested only into Kinesis.

```
{
    "Items": [
        {
```

```
        "clickstreamId": {
            "S": "dad422f1-d8b8-4107-8159-b9a043b011b7"
        },
        "pageUrl": {
            "S": "example.com"
        },
        "session": {
            "S": "S4321"
        },
        "timestamp": {
            "S": "<timestamp>"
        }
    }
],
"Count": 1,
"ScannedCount": 1,
"ConsumedCapacity": null
}
```

Now that we have demonstrated how a Lambda function can ingest and process records from a Kinesis data stream, it is important to dive deeper into some of the key concepts around how Kinesis integrates with and triggers Lambda to handle large volumes of streaming data. Understanding these key learnings can empower optimization of Lambda performance in a Kinesis-Lambda architecture built for scalability.

Understanding How Kinesis Data Streams Trigger Lambda

Amazon Kinesis Data Streams and AWS Lambda provide a powerful combination of services to build scalable data streaming applications. With simple configuration, Kinesis Data Streams can automatically trigger Lambda functions to process data in real-time.

An event source mapping can be created to tie a Kinesis data stream to a Lambda function. This mapping will invoke the Lambda function synchronously whenever a batch of data records is available in the stream. Lambda will process the records in the stream and take action as needed.

As data producers add more records to Kinesis, they are grouped into batches based on size and time frame configurations. When a batch threshold is reached, the Lambda function is triggered with the batch of records passed into the function.

Let's now explain several key concepts to understand how Kinesis triggers Lambda functions. These include configurable properties such as the `batch size`, `batch window`, `starting position`, and `concurrent batches per shard`, some of which were shown in *Figure 6.6* from the previous section.

- **Batch Size:** The batch size determines how many records Kinesis will deliver to Lambda in each invocation. The maximum batch size is 10,000 records. Configuring an appropriate batch size allows you to optimize performance and costs. Too small of a batch will trigger Lambda more often and incur more overhead. Too large of a batch risks hitting Lambda timeouts.

- **Batch Window:** The batch window specifies how long Kinesis will collect records before invoking Lambda. The maximum batch window is 300 seconds. This allows buffering records over a period to reduce the invocation rate of Lambda. Tuning based on your data rate helps prevent too frequent or too infrequent invocations.

- **Starting Position:** When enabling a Kinesis stream as an event source for Lambda, you configure the starting position for consumption. This can be all records in the stream (**Trim horizon**), the latest data arriving (**Latest**), or records starting from a specific time (**At timestamp**). Choose based on your use case needs, like reprocessing historical data or consuming new real-time data only.

- **Concurrent Batches Per Shard:** Kinesis streams consist of shards for throughput scaling. This config sets the number of batches Kinesis will process concurrently per shard. Setting it higher allows faster Lambda scale and higher overall throughput. However, it also incurs more Lambda invocations and costs. Choose based on your data volumes and cost requirements.

Optimizing these configurations allows effective use of Kinesis and Lambda together for serverless stream processing pipelines. Monitor invocation metrics and tuning based on your real workload over time. This helps achieve high performance at scale in a cost-efficient manner.

Resharding a Kinesis Data Stream

As data throughput grows in your Kinesis data stream, you may need to rescale your stream to increase capacity to handle higher workloads. Amazon Kinesis enables resharding your existing stream by splitting or merging shards programmatically to adapt to changes in data flow. This provides flexibility to easily scale stream capacity up or down as demands shift.

There are several reasons why you might need to reshard a Kinesis data stream, including:

- **Scalability**: As the volume of data being processed increases, a single Kinesis stream may become too large to handle. Resharding allows you to split the data into smaller, more manageable streams that can be processed independently, improving overall scalability.

- **Performance**: Resharding can also improve performance by allowing you to distribute the data processing workload across multiple streams. This can be particularly useful if you have a large number of consumers or applications that need to process the data in real time.

- **Data management**: Resharding can help you to better manage your data by allowing you to organize it into different streams based on specific criteria, such as date, time, or event type. This can make it easier to track and analyze the data, as well as to ensure that it is being processed correctly.

Planning ahead is critical when resharding a Kinesis data stream. This can be a complex process with significant implications, so it is important to carefully consider the data volume you need to process, your performance requirements, and the resources at your disposal. You should choose a shard key that is consistent across all streams and evenly distributes data. This promotes proper data processing and prevents individual streams from becoming overloaded.

Resharding a Kinesis data stream involves several steps:

1. **Identify the reason for resharding**: Before you begin, it's important to understand why you need to reshard the data stream. This will help you to determine the best way to split the data and how to configure the new streams.

2. **Choose a shard key**: A shard key is a unique identifier that determines which shard a data record should be written to. Choose a shard key that is evenly distributed and that can handle the volume of data you expect to process.

3. **Split the data stream**: Once you have chosen a shard key, you can use the Kinesis Data Streams API to split the data stream into multiple shards. You can do this by creating a new stream and specifying the shard key and the number of shards you want to create.

4. **Configure the new streams**: Once the new streams have been created, you'll need to configure them to process the data correctly. This may involve setting up different consumers or applications to process the data in each stream, or configuring the streams to write data to different databases or storage systems.

5. **Test the new streams**: Before you start processing data in the new streams, it's important to test them thoroughly to ensure that they are working correctly.

You can do this by simulating data processing scenarios and verifying that the data is being processed correctly in each stream.

Once new streams are created from the resharding process, closely monitor them with tools like Amazon CloudWatch to ensure correct data processing. Track key performance metrics to identify any emerging issues. Thoroughly test the new streams by simulating diverse processing scenarios and confirming the integrity of data flow across each stream testing safeguards against processing problems and data errors prior to launching the resharded streams into production. Careful planning, monitoring, and testing sets up resharding implementations for success.

Amazon Data Firehose

Amazon Data Firehose, formerly called Amazon Kinesis Data Firehose, is a managed service for delivering real-time streaming data to destinations like Amazon S3, Amazon Redshift, Amazon OpenSearch, Splunk, and others. To gain a deeper understanding of how Amazon Data Firehose operates, we will examine some of its core concepts. These include **firehose streams**, **records**, **destinations**, **buffer size**, **buffer interval**, and **data transformation**.

- **Firehose Streams:** A firehose stream is the core entity that transports data. Producers send data to a stream, and consumers read data from it. Streams buffer incoming data before delivering it.

- **Records:** A record is a unit of data sent to a firehose stream. Records can be up to 1 MB in size.

- **Data source:** When creating a firehose stream, you configure the source where it will receive data from. Common source options include AWS services like Amazon CloudWatch Logs, AWS IoT, direct PUTs from your own applications, and Amazon Kinesis Data Streams.

- **Destinations:** Firehose streams can deliver data to various storage and analytics destinations including Amazon S3, Amazon Redshift, Splunk, Amazon OpenSearch, HTTP, and so on.

- **Buffer Size:** Buffer size controls how much data a stream buffers before delivering to destinations. The buffer size ranges from 1 to 128 MB.

- **Buffer Interval:** Buffer interval controls how often buffered data is delivered even if the buffer is not full. The interval ranges from 60 to 900 seconds.

- **Data Transformation:** Data Firehose allows you to optionally specify AWS Lambda functions to transform your data before it is delivered to destinations. Transformations can include converting formats, data masking or filtering, and appending metadata. We will explore this concept in greater detail in the following section.

Data Transformation Using AWS Lambda

Raw data streamed into Firehose is often not ready for analysis. For example, IoT telemetry may be in a binary format. Or clickstream logs might be simple JSON. Analysis requires data to be structured, filtered, and converted into formats such as Parquet, a column-oriented data file format designed for efficient data storage and retrieval. Manually transforming data is time-consuming and hard to scale. AWS Lambda provides a serverless approach to pre-processing Firehose data.

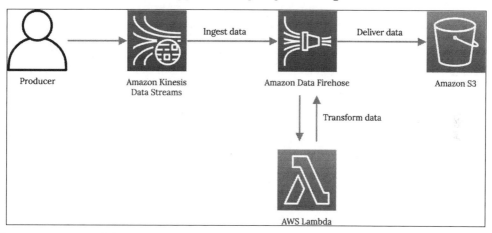

Figure 6.7: *AWS Lambda can be used to transform the data ingested to an Amazon Data Firehose*

As *Figure* 6.7 illustrates, the data transformation flow consists of:

- Raw data is streamed to Firehose in real time
- Firehose invokes the Lambda, passing the records
- Lambda processes and transforms the data
- Transformed record is returned to Firehose
- Firehose delivers the records to destinations

The Firehose stream can be configured with a buffering size that determines how much data to buffer before invoking the Lambda function to transform the batches of data. For example, you could have a 1 MB or 5 MB buffer size. This allows Firehose to optimize cost and throughput by batching records together to send to Lambda.

In addition, a buffering interval can be set that determines the maximum amount of time Firehose will buffer data for, before invoking Lambda, even if the buffer size has not been met. For example, 60 seconds. When either the buffer size or interval is reached, Firehose will invoke the Lambda, passing the batch of records buffered during that period. The Lambda then transforms the records and returns them to Firehose for delivery.

Some common Firehose data transformation use cases include:

- Parsing JSON/CSV into columns
- Filtering PII or unused columns
- Serializing Avro/Protobuf data
- Encrypting sensitive data
- Calling machine learning for enrichment

Firehose with Lambda provides an automated, scalable, and cost-efficient data transformation pipeline for preparation before analysis.

Data Transformation Model for Amazon Kinesis Data Streams

When using Amazon Data Firehose with a Lambda data transformation for Kinesis Data Streams sources, all records output from the Lambda function must contain specific parameters for Amazon Data Firehose to process them. If any required parameters are missing, Amazon Data Firehose will reject the records and count them as data transformation failures.

The Lambda function must return a JSON response containing the following parameters:

```
{
    "recordId": "<recordId from the input>",
    "result": "Ok | Dropped | ProcessingFailed",
    "data": "<Base64 encoded data>"
}
```

The required output parameters are as follows:

- **recordId** (string): The record ID passed from Amazon Data Firehose into the Lambda function. Transformed records must contain the exact same record ID to map back to the original record. Any mismatch will cause a failure.
- **result** (enum): Indicates if the record was transformed successfully. Accepted values are:
  - **Ok** : record transformed successfully
  - **Dropped** : record was intentionally discarded
  - **ProcessingFailed** : transformation unsuccessful.

  Records with **Ok** or **Dropped** are considered successful.

- **data** (string): The payload containing the transformed record data. This must be **base64** encoded.

By requiring these parameters, Amazon Data Firehose is able to maintain consistency and track records flowing through the system. The **recordId** links each output record back to its input for tracing. The *result* parameter gives visibility into failures and drops during processing. And the *data* contains the actual transformed data payload delivered to destinations. Together these allow transparent end-to-end record delivery monitoring.

Project Time: Data Pipeline with Amazon Data Firehose

In this section, we will update our e-commerce platform Shopme by creating a data pipeline to move the clickstream data from the Amazon Kinesis data stream into Amazon S3, which will serve as a **data lake**. A data lake is a centralized repository that allows storing vast amounts of structured and unstructured data in its native format. In contrast to traditional data warehouses that require strict schemas and upfront data modeling, data lakes are designed to handle raw, unlabeled data from diverse sources.

We initially saved new clickstream data in DynamoDB, through a Lambda function, since its high throughput and low latency provide the speed needed to handle a high volume of transactions. However, DynamoDB's non-relational schema makes it difficult to perform flexible analytics.

By piping the raw clickstream data into Amazon S3, our data lake will allow data scientists, analysts, and engineers to explore and process the data using the right tools for their use cases. Multiple teams can access the data lake for machine learning, business intelligence, and other applications. The flexibility of S3 as a data lake removes constraints around how the data must be structured and modelled upfront. As data requirements evolve, we can build pipelines to refine, combine, and structure the raw data from the lake into the optimal format needed by each team.

To enable advanced analysis, we will create an Amazon Data Firehose stream. This stream will source data from Kinesis Data Stream where new clickstream data are sent to. The Firehose stream will buffer the streaming data and transform it as needed, before delivering it to S3.

Teams can then leverage various AWS analytics services to process and extract insights from this detailed clickstream data stored in S3 across desired time horizons. The data lake approach gives us flexibility to refine and analyze the data as needs emerge, without tightly coupling how the data is structured and queried.

Prior to creating a Firehose data stream, some prerequisites must be met. First, an Amazon S3 bucket is required to serve as the destination where the clickstream data will be stored. Additionally, a Lambda function needs to be developed that will transform the incoming data - adding mandatory elements like unique IDs and timestamps. For the data source, we can leverage the **OrderingSystemClickstream** Kinesis stream previously configured in an earlier example.

Note: *A data lake and a data warehouse are two different data storage architectures that serve complementary purposes. The main difference is that a data lake is designed for storing raw, unstructured data in its native formats, while a data warehouse stores structured, processed data that has been cleaned, formatted, and optimized for reporting and analysis.*

A data lake takes a schema on read approach - meaning the schema or structure is defined when data is queried, rather than when it is ingested. This provides more flexibility for storing unstructured and multi-structured data from IoT sensors, social media platforms, mobile devices, and more. The loose structure and vast storage capacity of data lakes make them well-suited for running big data analytics to uncover insights. Data scientists can apply machine learning and AI when querying the data lake to train models.

In contrast, a data warehouse uses a "schema on write" approach. The data structure and model need to be predefined before importing data. This enables faster querying and analysis based on the organized structure. Data warehouses are suited for business reporting and dashboards based on predefined metrics. However, they lack the agility and scalability to store and analyze large volumes of raw and unprocessed data from modern data sources.

Creating an S3 Bucket as the Firehose Destination

The first step is to create an Amazon S3 bucket that will be used as the destination of the Firehose stream:

1. From the list of services, search for **s3** and click **S3** to go to the **Amazon S3** dashboard.

2. On the left sidebar, click **Buckets** and then click the **Create bucket** button.

3. Enter a unique bucket name **new-orders-raw-<unique id>**. Use the default settings for the remaining options and click **Create bucket**.

An **Amazon S3** bucket will be immediately created to ingest and store raw clickstream data in real time as it enters the system. Server-side encryption with S3 managed keys (SSE-S3) will be enabled by default to automatically encrypt all clickstream data at rest. This provides transparent data encryption using keys fully managed by Amazon S3, without requiring any extra steps on your part. The raw clickstream data landing in this S3 bucket will serve as the foundation for further processing and analytics.

Note: *Amazon S3 bucket names have to be globally unique across all existing bucket names in AWS. This means that no two S3 buckets can have the same name, even if they are in different AWS accounts or different AWS regions. The reason for this is that buckets are identified by their name, which forms part of the bucket URL. Since objects are stored in buckets, ensuring unique bucket names allows objects to be unambiguously referenced and retrieved using the combination of the bucket name and object key as a globally unique identifier. If duplicate bucket names were allowed, it could result in situations where a request for an object could resolve to different objects in different buckets with the same name, leading to confusion and unintended data leakage between AWS accounts.*

By enforcing uniqueness of bucket names globally, AWS ensures that each S3 URL precisely identifies a specific bucket and object to maintain correct identity and access control for every object stored in S3. This also simplifies managing permissions and access policies when bucket names define a namespace. The global uniqueness requirement thus provides the necessary semantics to make buckets, objects and their corresponding URLs reliable and unambiguous within AWS S3 architecture and access mechanisms.

The next step is to create an AWS Lambda function that will transform the incoming data from the Firehose stream before it is saved to S3.

Creating a Lambda Function to Transform Data

We will create a Lambda function that will transform data from our Amazon Data Firehose stream before it is loaded into Amazon S3. The **ClickstreamTransformation** service will be a Lambda function responsible for transforming clickstream data sent to our Firehose stream. The raw clickstream JSON events ingested into the Firehose stream will be passed to the **ClickstreamTransformation** Lambda function. This function will parse and transform the data by adding a **clickstreamId** and **timestamp** to the records.

The code of the Lambda function is similar to the **Clickstream** service we saw earlier. The Lambda handler utilizes the **KinesisFirehoseEvent** class from the **aws-lambda-java-events** library to access the firehose stream records.

```
public class LambdaHandler implements RequestHandler<KinesisFireho-
seEvent, TransformedRecords> {

    private Gson gson = new Gson();


    @Override
    public TransformedRecords handleRequest(KinesisFirehoseEvent
```

```java
event, Context context) {
        System.out.println("Received input from Kinesis Firehose"
+ event);

        var response = new TransformedRecords();

    for (var record : event.getRecords()) {
        // convert to clickstream event
        var data = new String(record.getData().array());

        // get clickstream event
        var clickstream = toClickStream(data);

        // create transformed record
        var transformedRecord = new TransformedRecord(
                record.getRecordId(),
                "Ok",
                ByteBuffer.wrap(clickstream.toString().getBytes()));

        response.getRecords().add(transformedRecord);

    }

    return response;
    }

    private Clickstream toClickStream(String event) {
        var request = gson.fromJson(event, ClickstreamEvent.
class);
        var clickstream = new Clickstream();
        clickstream.setClickstreamId(UUID.randomUUID().toString());
        clickstream.setSession(request.getSession());
        clickstream.setTimestamp(new Date());
        clickstream.setPageUrl(request.getPageUrl());
        return clickstream;
    }
}
```

As we previously discussed, the Lambda function transforms the input records and returns a list of the processed records. Each record in the output list contains the **recordId** to identify the record, a **result** field to indicate if the processing succeeded or failed, and a **data** field containing the transformed content for that record.

Now that the S3 bucket and Lambda function for data transformation are configured, we can create the Amazon Data Firehose stream. This Firehose stream will automatically capture data from the Kinesis data stream as the source and handle loading the transformed data into the S3 bucket.

Creating an Amazon Data Firehose Stream

To create an Amazon Data Firehose Stream, follow these steps:

1. From the list of services, search for **firehose** and click **Amazon Data Firehose** to go to the **Amazon Data Firehose** dashboard.

2. On the left sidebar, click **Firehose streams** and then click the **Create Firehose stream** button.

3. In the **Choose source and destination** section, select **Amazon Kinesis Data Streams** for the **Source**, and **Amazon S3** for the **Destination**, as shown in *Figure 6.8*.

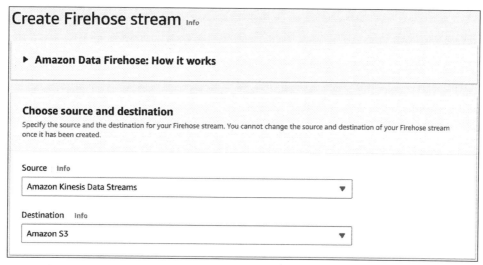

Figure 6.8: *Creating an Amazon Data Firehose stream*

4. In the **Source settings** section, select the **OrderingSystemClickstream** we created earlier for the **Kinesis data stream**. In the **Firehose stream name** section, enter **OrderingSystemClickstream-Firehose** for the **Firehose stream name**, as shown in *Figure 6.9*.

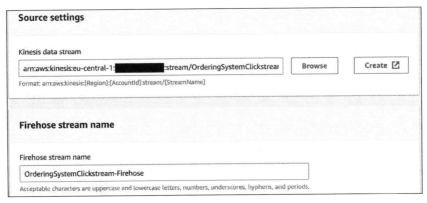

Figure 6.9: *Selecting a Kinesis data stream as the source and entering the name for an Amazon Data Firehose stream*

5. In the `Transform and convert records` section, check the `Turn on data transformation`, and search for the `ClickstreamTransformation` Lambda function, enter `1 MB` for the `Buffer size` and `10 seconds` for the `Buffer interval`, as shown in *Figure 6.10*.

Transform and convert records - *optional*
Configure Amazon Data Firehose to transform and convert your record data.

Transform source records with AWS Lambda Info
To return records from AWS Lambda to Amazon Data Firehose after transformation, the Lambda function you invoke must be compliant with the required record transformation output model. Pricing may vary depending on usage charges.

☑ Turn on data transformation

AWS Lambda function   Version or alias

`clickstream-transformation-service:$LATEST`   Choose a versio... ▾   Browse   Create function

Format: arn:aws:lambda:[Region]:[AccountId]:function:[FunctionName]

Buffer size
The AWS Lambda function has a 6 MB invocation payload quota. Your data can expand in size after it's processed by the AWS Lambda function. A smaller buffer size allows for more room should the data expand after processing.

`1` MB

Minimum: 0.2 MB, maximum: 3 MB.

Buffer interval
The period of time during which Amazon Data Firehose buffers incoming data before invoking the AWS Lambda function. The AWS Lambda function is invoked once the value of the buffer size or the buffer interval is reached.

`10` seconds

Minimum: 0 seconds, maximum: 900 seconds.

Convert record format Info
Data in Apache Parquet or Apache ORC format is typically more efficient to query than JSON. Amazon Data Firehose can convert your JSON-formatted source records using a schema from a table defined in AWS Glue 🔗. For records that aren't in JSON format, create a Lambda function that converts them to JSON in the Transform source records with AWS Lambda section above.

☐ Enable record format conversion

Decompress source records from Amazon CloudWatch Logs - *new* Info
When this feature is turned on, Amazon Data Firehose decompresses Amazon CloudWatch Logs and delivers them to the destination. There will be additional fees for this functionality. Learn more 🔗. To use message extraction, turn on decompression.

☐ Turn on decompression

Figure 6.10: *Using an AWS Lambda function to transform the data ingested to Amazon Data Firehose*

6. In the **Destination settings** section, search for the S3 bucket you created, enter **clickstream-raw/** for the **S3 bucket prefix** and **clickstream-raw-error/** for the **S3 bucket error output prefix**, as shown in *Figure 6.11*. This will save the clickstream data under the **clickstream-raw** prefix and any error that comes from Lambda under the **clickstream-raw-error** prefix.

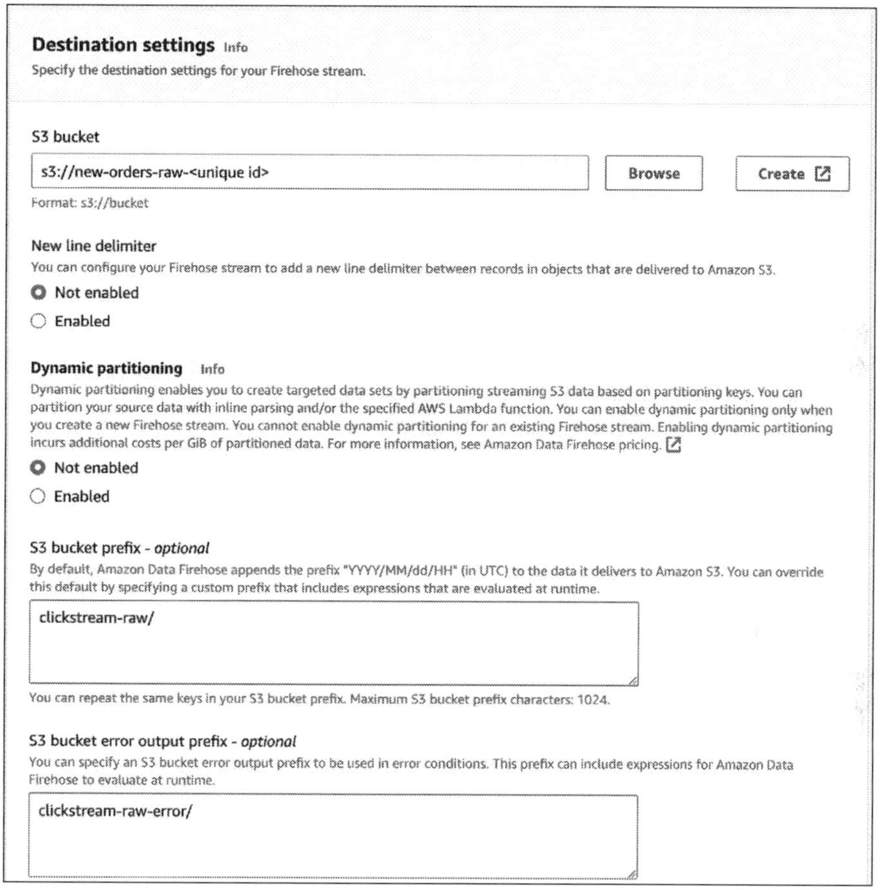

Figure 6.11: *Specifying an Amazon S3 bucket as the destination for an Amazon Data Firehose stream*

7. Scroll to the bottom and click **Create firehose stream**.

You have successfully created a Firehose stream and configured its various properties. Next, we will review what was set up for this Firehose stream to fully understand how it is ingesting from the Kinesis data stream, transforming the records via Lambda, and loading the processed data into S3.

Understanding the Firehose Configuration

We have set up an architecture to ingest new clickstream data into our system.

The flow starts with the **OrderingSystemClickstream** data stream receiving new clickstreams from the ordering system. We then configured a new firehose stream called **OrderingSystemClickstream-Firehose** that picks up the new clickstream data from the stream as its source.

The firehose stream buffers the incoming data every 10 seconds or once 1 MB of data accumulates. It then triggers the **ClickstreamTransformation** Lambda function to enrich and transform each new clickstream record by appending additional attributes. When the Lambda function finishes processing a batch, the transformed records are sent back to the firehose stream which then delivers them to the designated Amazon S3 bucket we set up.

In S3, the clickstream data are stored as JSON files, under the prefix **clickstream-raw**, where each file can contain multiple enriched order records output by the Lambda function. A key capability we can leverage in the future is Firehose's ability to convert the data to columnar formats like Apache Parquet or Apache ORC. Using such formats could improve performance and cost if we query this data using Amazon Athena, a serverless query service that can query data directly from S3.

In summary, the flow orchestrates streaming the new clickstreams -> buffering batches of orders -> transforming each order -> loading the enriched order data into S3 for later analysis. The modular design allows for additional data processing, conversion, analysis, and consumption going forward.

Tip: *Amazon Data Firehose provides a feature to enable **partitioning** of data when using Amazon S3 as the destination, as illustrated in Figure 6.11. Partitioning is important when configuring an Amazon Data Firehose stream with an S3 destination for the following reasons.*

Amazon S3 has limits on the number of reads and writes that can be made per prefix per second. Specifically, S3 supports up to 3,500 read requests per prefix per second, and 5,500 write requests per prefix per second. Without partitioning, a Kinesis Firehose stream would write all data to a single S3 prefix, which could exceed these S3 request rate limits as data throughput increases.

Partitioning in Kinesis Firehose solves this by spreading writes across multiple partitions and S3 prefixes. This avoids hitting any single prefix's request rate limits. For example, a partition key could be set to the delivery stream name and year/month. This would write data across multiple year/month S3 prefixes instead of a single prefix. Even at high data ingest rates, partitions, and prefixes can scale to handle the request throughput while staying under S3 limits per prefix.

Testing the Backend System

We should now validate that the Firehose stream and Lambda function are working as expected to transform and deliver data to S3. To test it out, we first need to send test data to the Kinesis data stream. You can run the following command to stream sample data records that will flow through the architecture:

```
$ aws kinesis put-record \
    --stream-name OrderingSystemClickstream \
    --data  "{\"session\": \"S4321\", \"pageUrl\": \"example.com\"}" \
    --partition-key 123 \
    --cli-binary-format raw-in-base64-out \
    --region eu-central-1
```

After sending test data to the Kinesis stream, you need to wait either 10 seconds or until 1 MB of data has accumulated (if streaming large volumes). Once some time has elapsed, check the S3 bucket where Firehose is loading data. You should see a new **clickstream-raw** prefix created, with nested prefixes for the current year, month, day, and hour. If you open one of the delivered S3 objects, the file will contain the transformed JSON records output by the Lambda function:

```
{
    "clickstreamId":"d08cb598-a924-46cb-8a8a-6142b3bf2e6f",
    "session":"S4321",
    "pageUrl":"example.com",
    "timestamp":"<timestamp>"
}
{
    "clickstreamId":"66dba081-98ca-44ce-a041-a04c7d207238",
    "session":"S4321",
    "pageUrl":"example.com",
    "timestamp":"<timestamp>"
}
```

With data now stored in Amazon S3, the next step is determining how to analyze it. S3 provides a scalable data lake for storage, but to drive insights, we need to process and query that data. Fortunately, AWS offers many services that can integrate directly with S3 to perform analytics.

Next, we will briefly overview some of the AWS options available for analyzing and working with data stored in S3.

Analyzing Data in Amazon S3

Amazon S3 has become a popular place for companies to store large amounts of data, acting as a data lake. With massive amounts of data being loaded into S3, the next step is to analyze this data to gain insights. AWS provides many services that can help analyze and process S3 data.

S3 itself provides basic object storage capabilities, but does not natively support any data analysis or processing functionality. Instead, it is meant to serve as a scalable and resilient repository for data. This can include unstructured data such as web logs, sensor data, text files, and images, as well as structured data like JSON or CSV files. The data lake approach using S3 allows you to store both raw and processed data in an affordable and robust way.

- **Amazon Athena:** Athena enables running SQL queries against data stored in S3 without needing any infrastructure to manage. It works across popular data formats like CSV, JSON, ORC, Avro, and Parquet. By supporting standard SQL syntax and not needing to load data into specialized systems, Athena makes it easy and cost-effective to analyze S3 data on demand. It also integrates with business intelligence tools like Amazon QuickSight for easy reporting and dashboards. The pay-per-query pricing model scales analytics in line with actual usage.

- **AWS Glue:** For preparing messy, complex data for analytics, AWS Glue provides fully managed extract, transform, and load (ETL) functionality. Its data catalog helps automatically profile and index data from S3 for easier querying. Machine learning algorithms identify schema and data types to parse datasets. Glue's auto-generated PySpark and Scala code makes transforming S3 data for target analytics systems like Amazon Redshift simple.

- **Amazon Redshift:** After extracting insights via Athena queries or transforming S3 datasets with Glue, Redshift offers a high-performance data warehouse to centralize analysis. Redshift Spectrum allows efficiently querying exabytes of data in S3 without needing to load it all into Redshift clusters. Redshift makes operational reporting, dashboards, and predictive analytics possible from a petabyte-scale data warehouse synced with S3 storage.

- **Amazon QuickSight:** To visualize insights from your data you can use Amazon QuickSight, a cloud-powered business intelligence service. It seamlessly connects to data stored in Redshift or S3 buckets queried through Athena, automatically prepares the data for analysis, and provides rich visualizations and ad-hoc reporting.

Amazon Managed Service for Apache Flink

Amazon Managed Service for Apache Flink, formerly called Amazon Kinesis Data Analytics, is a fully managed service that makes it easy to perform real-time analytics on streaming data. It is based on the popular open-source **Apache Flink** framework which is designed specifically for stream processing applications.

With Amazon Managed Service for Apache Flink, you can use Java, Scala, Python, or SQL to build and run applications that process and analyze streaming data from sources such as Amazon Kinesis Data Streams.

Some key capabilities enabled by the service include:

- **Time-series analytics**: Perform complex time-series analysis calculations on streaming data to derive insights and metrics. It is useful for monitoring applications.

- **Real-time dashboards**: Process data streams and feed results directly to dashboards to view metrics and analytics in real-time.

- **Managed infrastructure**: The service handles all the underlying resources and infrastructure needed to run Apache Flink, including compute, storage, failover, scaling, and backups.

- **High-level programming interfaces**: You can use the native Apache Flink APIs and libraries to build applications. This includes Flink's DataStream and Table APIs, allowing both stream processing and SQL-based analysis.

- **Flexible runtime options**: Applications can be authored using Java, Scala, Python, or SQL. The service provides an interactive environment for ad-hoc analysis of streams using SQL, Python, and Scala.

The Amazon Managed Service for Apache Flink offers two options for running your Flink jobs:

- **Managed Service for Apache Flink**: Build Flink applications using Java, Scala, or Python (and embedded SQL) with Apache Flink APIs. You develop these applications in an IDE and then run them on the managed Flink service. Use this option if you have programming experience and you want to run a long running job and streaming ETL.

- **Managed Service for Apache Flink Studio**: Interactively query streaming data in real time using standard SQL, Python, and Scala. The Studio allows you to easily build stream processing applications without needing to code against the underlying APIs. Use this option if you want to explore and experiment with data using interactive queries and real-time dashboards.

In this chapter, we will put aside discussing the intricacies of Managed Service for Apache Flink and instead focus our attention on exploring the capabilities of Flink Studio. Flink Studio provides an interactive notebook environment that empowers us to rapidly develop, iterate on, and test Apache Flink jobs that analyze streaming data.

Benefits of Using Apache Flink

Apache Flink is an open-source platform for distributed stream and batch processing. It provides a cost-effective, scalable, and flexible solution for real-time data processing and analytics. In this section, we will explore the main benefits of using Apache Flink and why it's becoming a popular choice for data processing.

- **Scalability:** Apache Flink is designed to scale horizontally, which means it can handle large volumes of data and high data processing rates by adding more nodes to the cluster. This makes it an ideal choice for big data processing and real-time analytics. Flink's scalability allows businesses to process data in real-time, making it easier to make timely decisions and respond to changing market conditions.

- **Low Latency:** Apache Flink is optimized for low-latency processing, making it suitable for real-time data processing and analytics. Flink's low-latency processing capability enables businesses to react to events in real-time, improving their ability to respond to customer needs, detect fraud, and optimize business processes.

- **Stateful Stream Processing:** Apache Flink provides stateful stream processing, which allows it to process streams of data while maintaining the state of the data. This means that Flink can process data in a continuous stream while still retaining information about the data, such as previous values, aggregations, and window functions. Stateful stream processing is particularly useful in use cases like fraud detection, recommendation engines, and real-time analytics.

- **Ease of Use:** Apache Flink provides a simple and easy-to-use API, making it accessible to developers of all skill levels. Flink's API is based on Java and Scala, and it provides a set of pre-defined functions and operators that can be used to build data processing pipelines. This makes it easier for developers to build and deploy data processing applications on Flink.

- **High-Performance:** Apache Flink is designed for high-performance data processing, and it provides several features that make it suitable for large-scale data processing. Flink's performance is optimized for modern hardware, including multi-core CPUs and GPUs. It also provides efficient memory management and data processing algorithms, making it a fast and reliable platform for data processing.

- **Open-Source and Community-Driven:** Apache Flink is an open-source project, which means that it's free to use and community-driven. The Flink community is active and growing, with contributors from various organizations and individuals. This ensures that Flink will continue to evolve and improve, meeting the changing needs of the data processing community.

Working with Managed Service for Apache Flink Studio

Amazon Managed Service for Apache Flink provides an integrated environment for easily building, running, and monitoring Flink jobs. A key capability is the Managed Flink Studio, powered by **Apache Zeppelin** notebooks. Studio notebooks allow you to combine live code, data visualizations, and text narratives into a single interactive interface for stream processing and analysis.

Some key benefits of using Flink Studio notebooks include:

- Rapid development and iteration of streaming pipelines with Flink SQL, Python, and Scala without infrastructure setup.
- Interactive dashboards and real-time data visualizations for analyzing streaming data flows.
- Exploratory analysis and prototyping of streaming machine learning pipelines
- Documentation and sharing of Flink ETL workflows and architectures.

Using Flink SQL in notebooks provides a familiar way to query both batch and real-time streaming data sources registered in the Flink catalog system. This enables unifying access across streams and static tables for analytics.

The key steps when working with streaming data sources like Kinesis Data Streams in Studio notebook are:

1. Ingest streaming data into a Kinesis Data Stream
2. Catalog the stream's schema via an AWS Glue table definition
3. Connect the studio notebook to the Glue table as a Flink SQL source
4. Write SQL queries over the live stream for analytics and visualization

Flink SQL provides powerful capabilities for analyzing data streams and batches using familiar SQL queries. You can perform various relational operations like **SELECT** statements, **JOIN**s across multiple streams and tables, aggregate functions like **SUM** and **COUNT**, **ORDER BY**, and **LIMIT** clauses, and much more.

To dive deeper into the comprehensive SQL support offered by Flink, refer to the Flink SQL documentation on the official Flink website:

https://nightlies.apache.org/flink/flink-docs-release-1.18/docs/dev/table/sql/queries/overview/

Project Time: Real-time Analytics with Amazon Managed Service for Apache Flink

In this section, we will perform real-time analysis on the clickstream data that is ingested into the **OrderingSystemClickstream** Kinesis data stream we set up previously. To enable interactive queries on this streaming data, we will utilize the Apache Flink-powered studio notebook environment in Amazon Managed Service for Apache Flink.

Before running queries in the Studio notebook, we first need to create an external AWS Glue table that will point to the **OrderingSystemClickstream** Kinesis stream as its data source. This Glue table provides a structured view of the schema for the stream's raw clickstream records, allowing Apache Flink SQL queries to be run against the stream.

Creating an AWS Glue Table for the Kinesis Data Stream

To begin, you will need to create an AWS Glue database to contain your Glue table. Once the database is set up, you can create the Glue table that will connect to your Kinesis Data stream.

1. From the list of services, search for **glue** and click **AWS Glue** to go to the **AWS Glue** dashboard.

2. On the left sidebar, expand the **Data Catalog** category, click **Databases,** and then click the **Add database** button.

3. Enter **orderingsystem-database** for the name and click **Create database**.

4. On the left sidebar, click **Tables** and then click the **Add table** button.

5. In the **Table details** section, enter **clickstreams** for the **Name** and select the **orderingsystem-database** for the **Database**, as shown in *Figure 6.12*.

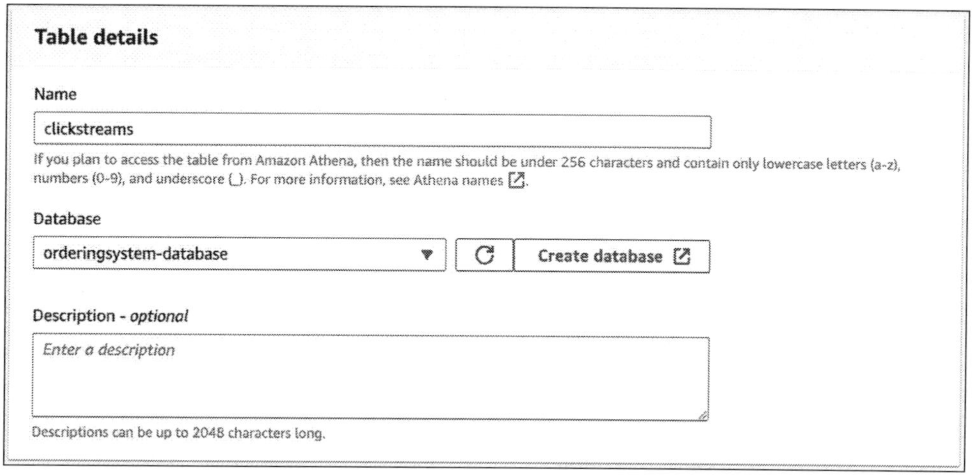

Figure 6.12: *Creating an AWS Glue table that will point to a Kinesis data stream*

6. In the **Data store** section, select **Kinesis** for the **type of source**, select **my account**, and select the **OrderingSystemClickstream** stream for the **Kinesis stream name**, as shown in *Figure 6.13*.

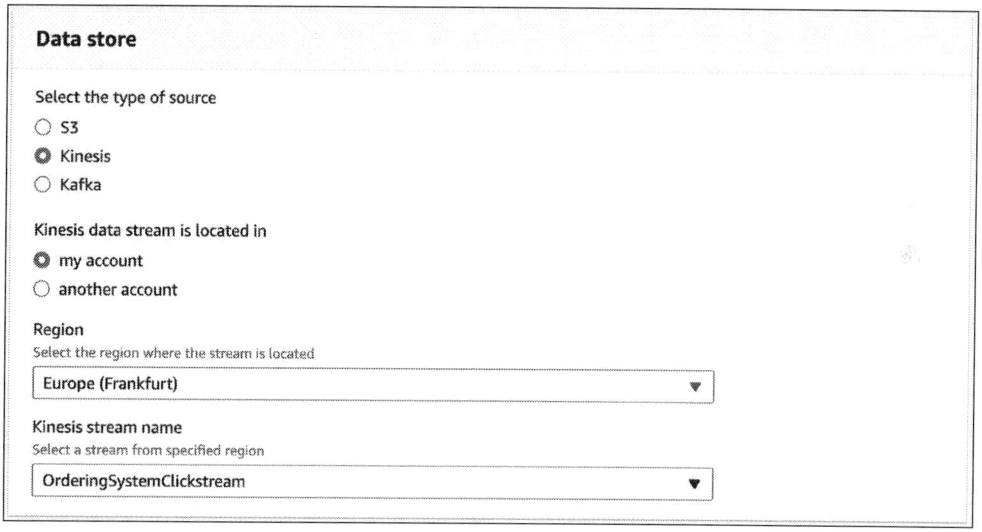

Figure 6.13: *Specifying a Kinesis data stream as the source for an AWS Glue table*

7. In the **Data format** section, select **JSON** for the **Classification** and click **Next**.

8. In the **Schema** section, click **Edit schema as JSON** and enter the following JSON.

```
[
  {
    "Name": "session",
```

```
        "Type": "string"
      },
      {
        "Name": "pageurl",
        "Type": "string"
      }
    ]
```

9. Click **Next**, review the table and click **Create.**

The next step after setting up the Glue table that is linked to the `OrderingSystemClickstream` Kinesis data stream is to create the studio notebook which will process and analyze the streaming data.

Creating a Flink Studio Notebook

Follow these steps to set up a studio notebook environment on Amazon's Managed Service for Apache Flink:

1. From the list of services, search for **flink** and click `Managed Apache Flink` to go to the `Managed Apache Flink` dashboard.

2. On the left sidebar, click `Studio notebooks` and then click the `Create Studio notebook` button.

3. Select the `Quick create with sample code` method, enter `OrderingSystemNotebook` for the `Studio notebook name`, as shown in *Figure 6.14.*

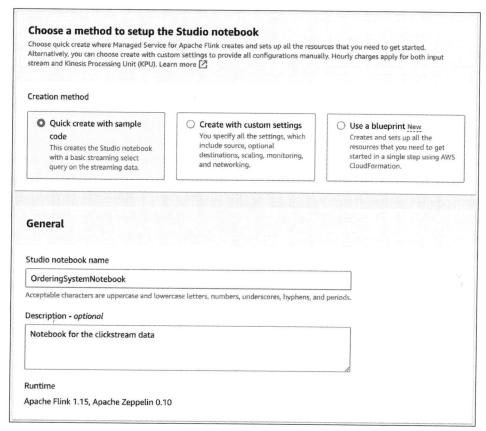

Figure 6.14: *Creating an Amazon Managed Service for Apache Flink Studio notebook*

4. In the **Permissions** section, select the **orderingsystem-database** for the **AWS Glue database**, as shown in *Figure 6.15*.

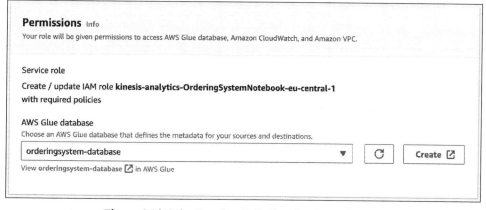

Figure 6.15: *Selecting the AWS Glue database that the Studio notebook will use to access the Glue tables*

5. Scroll down and click `Create Studio notebook`.

To begin using your new studio notebook, first click the **Run** button to initialize it. This may take a few minutes. Once it has finished initializing, click the `Open in Apache Zeppelin` button to launch the notebook in the Zeppelin interface. You can then start using the notebook for data exploration and visualization.

Querying Data with Studio Notebook

Upon opening the studio notebook, the Apache Zeppelin interface will automatically launch in a new tab, as shown in *Figure 6.16*.

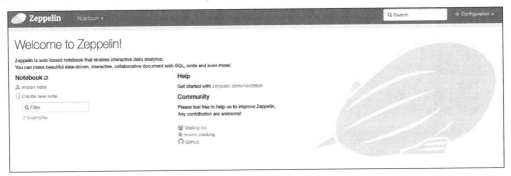

Figure 6.16: *The Apache Zeppelin interface appears when launching the Amazon Managed Service for Apache Flink Studio notebook*

To begin querying data, you first need to create a new note:

1. Click **Create new note** and enter **AnalyzeClickstreamData** for the **Note name**, as shown in *Figure 6.17*. Click **Create**.

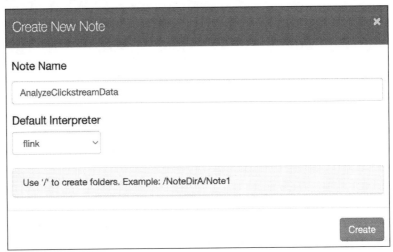

Figure 6.17: *Creating a new note in the Amazon Managed Service for Apache Flink Studio notebook*

2. In the **Zeppelin note** page, enter the following query into a new note:

```
%flink.ssql(type=update)
select * from clickstreams
```

3. Send test data to the kinesis data stream:

```
$ aws kinesis put-record \
    --stream-name OrderingSystemClickstream \
    --data  "{\"session\": \"S4321\", \"pageurl\": \"example.
com\"}" \
    --partition-key 123 \
    --cli-binary-format raw-in-base64-out \
    --region eu-central-1
```

The test data will be displayed in the output of this notebook in a few seconds, as illustrated in *Figure 6.18*.

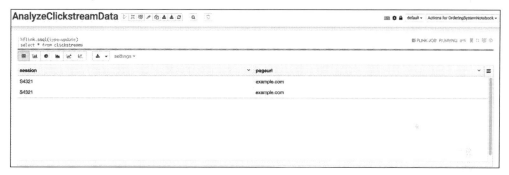

Figure 6.18: *Running an SQL query in the Amazon Managed Service for Apache Flink Studio notebook*

To make the most of the powerful data processing capabilities offered by the Studio notebook environment, we highly recommend to gain proficiency with Apache Flink.

Conclusion

This chapter provided a comprehensive overview of the Amazon Kinesis streaming data solutions. We started with an introduction to key streaming concepts and the benefits of a streaming architecture. We then explored the core Amazon Kinesis services that enable you to build robust real-time data pipelines. First, we looked at Amazon Kinesis Data Streams for high volume and real-time data ingestion from many sources. This acts as the foundational *building block* for streaming architectures in AWS. Next, we covered Amazon Data Firehose which simplifies the process of loading streaming data into AWS data stores and analytics tools. It eliminates much of the complexity around data transformations and delivery. Finally, we discussed how to enable real-time analytics by using Amazon Managed Service for Apache Flink to run SQL queries against data streams.

By leveraging these fully managed services together, you can build scalable stream processing applications that tap into real-time data without having to manage the underlying infrastructure. The services integrate tightly with other AWS offerings for easy access to storage, analytics, machine learning, and more.

After examining messaging through Amazon SQS and Amazon SNS in *Chapter 3, Messaging with Amazon SQS and Amazon SNS*, choreography with Amazon EventBridge in *Chapter 4, Choreography with Amazon EventBridge*, orchestration using Amazon Step Functions in *Chapter 5, Orchestration with AWS Step Functions*, and event streaming via Amazon Kinesis in this chapter, we now turn our attention to the critical task of testing these services and architectural patterns. Proper testing is imperative to ensure these building blocks interoperate correctly and deliver robust, resilient system behavior. In the next chapter, we will explore best practices for unit, integration, and end-to-end testing of distributed applications constructed using these AWS services.

CHAPTER 7

Testing Event-Driven Systems

Introduction

This chapter starts by providing an overview of the AWS Shared Responsibility Model and the importance of understanding it. It then discusses the different layers of software testing, including unit, integration, end-to-end, contract, and performance testing. Unit testing using mock libraries is covered, with examples of how to write effective unit tests and the benefits of using mock libraries for isolating dependencies. Integration testing is explored, with a focus on using emulators like AWS SAM, Step Functions Local, and LocalStack to test AWS services locally before deploying to the cloud. End-to-end testing in AWS is discussed, including strategies for testing complete applications and services in a staging or production-like environment. Contract testing is introduced as a way to ensure that different components of a system can communicate effectively. Performance testing is covered, with guidance on how to load test AWS services and applications to ensure they can handle expected traffic and scale as needed. Finally, manual testing through the AWS Management Console is also discussed. By the end of this chapter, you will have a solid understanding of the various testing strategies and tools available for ensuring the reliability and performance of your AWS applications and services.

Structure

In this chapter, we will discuss the following topics:

- Introduction to AWS Shared Responsibility Model
- Unit Testing Using Mock Libraries
- Integration Testing Using Emulators like AWS SAM, Step Functions Local, and Localstack
- End-to-End Testing in AWS
- Contract Testing

- Performance Testing Using Artillery
- Manual Testing via the AWS Management Console

Introduction to AWS Shared Responsibility Model

The **AWS Shared Responsibility Model** is a fundamental concept that outlines the division of responsibilities between AWS and its customers for ensuring the security and compliance of cloud-based workloads. Understanding this model is crucial to effectively manage your cloud environments and allocate resources for testing and validation.

You should have a clear understanding of what components and aspects of your workloads you need to test, and what aspects are handled by AWS's services and infrastructure. This knowledge helps you focus your testing efforts effectively and avoid redundant or unnecessary testing on areas that AWS has already secured.

What you should test:

- **Business logic and application code**: As a customer, you are responsible for testing and validating the business logic and application code that runs on AWS services. This includes ensuring the correctness of your code, handling edge cases, and verifying that your application behaves as expected under various conditions.

- **Data security and compliance**: You are responsible for securing and protecting your data stored on AWS services. This includes implementing appropriate access controls, encryption mechanisms, and adhering to relevant compliance standards and regulations specific to your industry or region.

- **Identity and access management (IAM)**: You should thoroughly test and validate your IAM policies, roles, and user permissions to ensure that only authorized personnel have access to your AWS resources and that the principle of least privilege is followed.

- **Network configuration and security groups**: If you are using AWS networking services, such as Virtual Private Clouds (VPCs) and security groups, you should test and validate your network configurations to ensure proper isolation, traffic routing, and access controls.

- **Operational processes and monitoring**: You are responsible for implementing and testing operational processes, such as backup and recovery procedures, monitoring and logging mechanisms, and incident response plans.

What you should not test:

- **High availability and scalability of serverless services**: AWS serverless services, such as AWS Lambda and API Gateway, are designed to be highly available and scalable by default. As a customer, you do not need to test or validate these aspects, as AWS is responsible for ensuring the underlying infrastructure meets these requirements.

- **Physical infrastructure security**: AWS is responsible for the security of its physical infrastructure, including data centers, hardware, and networking equipment. You do not need to test or validate these aspects, as they fall under AWS's responsibility.

- **Underlying cloud infrastructure**: AWS manages and maintains the underlying cloud infrastructure, including compute, storage, and networking resources. You do not need to test or validate the availability, scalability, or security of these core infrastructure components, as AWS is responsible for these aspects.

By adhering to the Shared Responsibility Model, you can focus your testing efforts on the areas that are within your control and responsibilities, while relying on AWS to ensure the security, availability, and scalability of the underlying cloud infrastructure and services.

Remember, the Shared Responsibility Model is a continuous process, and it's essential to regularly review and update your testing strategies to align with any changes in your workloads, compliance requirements, or AWS service updates.

Layers of Software Testing

Testing is a crucial aspect of software development, ensuring that the application or system meets the required specifications, functions correctly, and delivers a seamless user experience. There are various layers of testing, each serving a distinct purpose and addressing different aspects of the software. The layers of testing that we will focus on are **unit testing**, **integration testing**, **end-to-end testing**, **contract testing**, **performance testing**, and **manual testing**.

The pyramid depicted in *Figure 7.1* illustrates that different layers of testing have varying speeds, levels of integration or isolation, and associated costs. Specifically, the higher layers of testing, such as end-to-end testing, are slower, involve more integration, and are more expensive. Conversely, the lower layers of testing, such as unit testing, are faster, provide more isolation, and are generally less expensive.

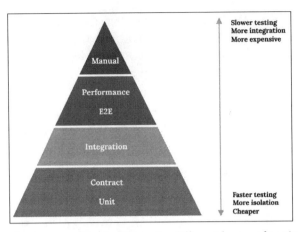

Figure 7.1: *A visual representation depicting the different layers of testing, arranged in a pyramidal structure, illustrating the trade-offs between speed, integration/isolation, and associated costs for each layer*

Unit Testing

Unit testing is the foundation of software testing, focusing on the smallest testable units or components of an application. These units can be individual functions, methods, or classes. The primary goal of unit testing is to verify the correctness of these isolated units by checking their inputs, outputs, and internal behavior. It helps identify and fix defects early in the development process, reducing the overall cost of fixing issues later on. Unit tests are typically written and executed by developers as they write the code. Unit testing is particularly relevant in event-driven systems, such as those built on AWS Lambda, where individual functions or components respond to specific events or triggers.

Integration Testing

Once the individual units have been thoroughly tested, integration testing comes into play. This level of testing verifies the interaction and communication between different components or modules within the application. Integration testing aims to uncover any defects or issues that may arise when these units are integrated and expected to work together seamlessly. It helps identify interface mismatches, data corruption, and other integration-related problems that may not have been detected during unit testing. Integration testing applies to many event-driven services in AWS, including API Gateway, Lambda, EventBridge, SQS, SNS, Kinesis, and so on.

End-to-End Testing

End-to-end testing (E2E) is a comprehensive approach that simulates real-world scenarios and validates the entire software system from start to finish. It involves testing the application as a whole, including all components, interfaces, and external dependencies. E2E testing ensures that the application meets the specified requirements, functions as expected, and provides a satisfactory user experience across different environments and platforms. E2E testing can be applied to the entire infrastructure on AWS.

Contract Testing

Contract testing is a software testing approach that focuses on ensuring the correct behavior of an application or service by validating the communication between different components or services. In the AWS ecosystem, contract testing can be applied to various services to verify that they are functioning as expected and adhering to the defined contracts or agreements.

One service where contract testing can be particularly useful in AWS is Lambda. Lambda functions often interact with other AWS services, such as SQS for asynchronous message processing or EventBridge for event-driven architectures. By using contract testing, you can validate that Lambda functions correctly handle different input scenarios, produce the expected output, and integrate seamlessly with other services.

Performance Testing

Performance testing evaluates the application's behavior under various load conditions, including normal, peak, and stress situations. It measures metrics such as response times, throughput, resource utilization, and scalability. Performance testing helps identify bottlenecks, optimize application performance, and ensure that the system can handle the expected load without compromising its functionality or user experience. Performance testing in AWS can be done by generating high traffic to front-door systems like Amazon API Gateway.

Manual Testing

Manually testing serverless services via the AWS Management Console can be a valuable technique to validate their functionality and behavior. By utilizing the user-friendly interface provided by the console, you can simulate various scenarios, input data, and observe the real-time responses from the serverless services. Furthermore, the console provides access to detailed logs and monitoring tools, enabling you to analyze and troubleshoot any issues that may arise during the testing process.

These different layers of testing complement each other and collectively contribute to the overall quality and reliability of the software. While each layer has its specific focus and objectives, they work together to identify and mitigate potential issues throughout the development lifecycle.

It's important to note that testing should be an integral part of the software development process, not an afterthought. By incorporating testing practices early and consistently, you can catch and fix defects more efficiently, reduce technical debt, and deliver high-quality software that meets customer expectations. In the following section, we will delve deeper into the various testing layers and explore how we can test them on AWS, starting with unit testing.

Unit Testing Using Mocks

Unit testing is a vital part of software development which helps to validate that code components function properly and meet requirements. While unit testing applies mainly to code containing business logic rather than cloud services, it can still be leveraged for AWS Lambda functions. In this section, we will concentrate on unit testing AWS Lambda functions using mock libraries specifically.

In unit testing, mock libraries (or mocking frameworks) are tools that allow you to create mock objects or simulate the behavior of external dependencies used by the code under test. These mock objects are used as substitutes for real objects or services that the code interacts with, such as databases, APIs, or other external systems.

In the context of Lambda functions, unit testing is crucial because it allows you to verify that your code works correctly without relying on external services. This is particularly important because Lambda functions are often triggered by events from these services, and it can be challenging to simulate these events in a testing environment.

To unit test Lambda functions effectively, you need to mock the requests that trigger the functions. This involves simulating the requests from AWS services such as API Gateway, Amazon SQS, Amazon SNS, Amazon EventBridge, and so on.

Major Lambda languages have mocking libraries that facilitate this. **Mockito** is a mocking framework for Java, while **EasyMock** serves the same purpose for the .NET ecosystem. In the Python world, `moto` is a library that enables mocking the boto AWS SDK. Similarly, the `aws-sdk-mock` library provides mocking capabilities for the AWS SDK for JavaScript.

We will primarily concentrate on unit testing Lambda functions developed in Java, as all the examples in this book are written in Java. However, the same techniques are applicable to all programming languages. More specifically, we will explore how `Mockito` and `aws-lambda-java-tests`, a library that simplifies testing, work.

Mockito

When writing unit tests for AWS Lambda functions in Java, you can utilize Mockito, a widely adopted mocking library. Mockito enables you to create mock objects that simulate the behavior of the events passed to the Lambda handler function. To incorporate Mockito into your project, you need to add the following dependency to your project's build file, **pom.xml**.

```
<dependency>
        <groupId>org.mockito</groupId>
        <artifactId>mockito-junit-jupiter</artifactId>
        <version>5.11.0</version>
        <scope>test</scope>
</dependency>
```

To test the Lambda handler method, we should leverage the useful annotations provided by Mockito to mock the event payload. For instance, if we want to test the **NewOrder** service created in *Chapter 3, Messaging with Amazon SQS and Amazon SNS*, by supplying a test event, we need to mock the **APIGatewayV2HTTPEvent** object representing the event.

```java
@ExtendWith(MockitoExtension.class)
public class LambdaHandlerMockito {


    @Mock
    private APIGatewayV2HTTPEvent event;


    private String body = "{\"customerId\":\"123\",\"items\":
[\"item1\",\"item2\",\"item3\"],\"total\":\"74.5\",\"paymentDe-
tails\":{\"paymentMethod\":\"CARD\",\"paymentTransactionId\":\"FDS232S-
GFDF341934\"},\"shippingDetails\":{\"receiverName\":\"John Doe\",\"re-
ceiverPhoneNumber\":\"123-456-7890\",\"shippingAddressLine1\":\"123
Main St\",\"shippingAddressLine2\":\"Apt 101\",\"shipping-
City\":\"Anytown\",\"shippingState\":\"CA\",\"shippingZip-
Code\":\"12345\",\"shippingCountry\":\"USA\"}}";


    @Test
    public void testLoadApiGatewayRestEvent() throws IOException {
        Mockito.when(event.getBody()).thenReturn(body);
```

```
        assertThat(event).isNotNull();

        var response = new LambdaHandler().handleRequest(event,
null);

        assertThat(response).isNotNull();
        assertThat(response.getBody()).isNotNull();
    }
}
```

In the test class **LambdaHandlerMockito**, the **@ExtendWith(MockitoExtension. class)** annotation from Mockito is employed to set up the mocking environment. The **APIGatewayV2HTTPEvent** object, named *event*, is marked with the **@Mock** annotation, indicating that it will be a mock object during the tests. The Lambda handler under test accepts this mocked *event* object. Through Mockito's mocking capabilities, specifically the **Mockito.when(event.getBody()).thenReturn(body)** statement, the behavior of the **event.getBody()** method is stubbed to return a predefined value (*body*) whenever called during the test execution. This allows the test to simulate scenarios with specific event body contents without relying on actual API Gateway events.

aws-lambda-java-tests

The **aws-lambda-java-tests** library simplifies the process of testing Java-based AWS Lambda functions by providing out-of-the-box capabilities for Lambda event serialization and injection. This library helps you to more effectively validate your Lambda functions in isolation by streamlining the mocking and testing processes.

To incorporate the **aws-lambda-java-tests** library into your Maven project, you need to include the following dependency in your project's build file, **pom.xml**:

```xml
<dependency>
    <groupId>com.amazonaws</groupId>
    <artifactId>aws-lambda-java-tests</artifactId>
    <version>1.1.1</version>
    <scope>test</scope>
</dependency>
```

In the unit tests, you can utilize the **aws-lambda-java-tests** library to inject an API Gateway event payload directly into the handler method of a Lambda function. This library provides annotations that simplify the process of testing, eliminating the need to manually create mock objects for the **APIGatewayV2HTTPEvent** event.

```
@ParameterizedTest
@Event(value="src/test/resources/apigw_rest_event.json", type=APIGate-
wayV2HTTPEvent.class)
public void testLoadApiGatewayRestEvent(APIGatewayV2HTTPEvent event) {
    assertThat(event).isNotNull();


    var response = new LambdaHandler().handleRequest(event, null);


    assertThat(response).isNotNull();
    assertThat(response.getBody()).isNotNull();
}
```

The **@ParameterizedTest** annotation, when applied to a method in the test class, indicates that the method is a parameterized test method. This means that the test method will be executed multiple times with different sets of input parameters. On the other hand, the **@Event** annotation allows you to inject an **APIGatewayV2HTTPEvent** object into the Lambda handler method. This event object is loaded from a JSON file and represents an HTTP request that would be received by the API Gateway and forwarded to the Lambda function.

Until now, we have focused on unit testing, the core business logic of our system, primarily targeting AWS Lambda functions. In the upcoming section, we will look more closely at testing other AWS services and explore techniques for conducting integration testing within the AWS ecosystem.

Integration Testing Using Emulators

In the world of modern software development, integration testing plays a crucial role in ensuring that different components of an application work seamlessly together. However, setting up and maintaining the required infrastructure and services for integration testing can be time-consuming and costly. This is where emulators come into play, providing you with a lightweight and cost-effective way to simulate various services and environments locally. Three useful emulators for testing event-driven microservices on AWS are **AWS Serverless Application Model**, **AWS Step Functions Local**, and **LocalStack**.

- **AWS Serverless Application Model (AWS SAM):** A useful tool for integration testing is AWS SAM. SAM is a framework that simplifies the development, testing, and deployment of serverless applications on AWS. It provides a local environment for running and testing Lambda functions, API Gateway endpoints, using Docker containers. With SAM, you can quickly iterate and test your serverless applications locally before deploying them to the cloud.

- **AWS Step Functions Local:** AWS Step Functions Local is another valuable tool for integration testing, specifically for serverless applications that involve orchestrating multiple AWS services. Step Functions Local allows you to simulate AWS Step Functions locally, enabling you to test and debug your state machines without the need for a real AWS account. This tool is particularly useful when testing complex workflows that involve multiple Lambda functions, service integrations, and error handling scenarios.

- **LocalStack:** Another popular emulator is LocalStack, an open-source tool that emulates AWS cloud services on your local machine. With LocalStack, you can test your application's integration with services like AWS Lambda, API Gateway, DynamoDB, EventBridge, SQS, SNS, S3, and more, without the need for an actual AWS account or incurring cloud costs. LocalStack simplifies the testing process by allowing you to spin up entire environments locally, enabling faster feedback loops and easier debugging.

The combination of these emulators and tools provides you with a powerful arsenal for integration testing. For example, you could use LocalStack to emulate services like DynamoDB and EventBridge, AWS SAM to test and debug your Lambda functions, and AWS Step Functions Local to orchestrate and test the entire workflow locally. This approach not only saves time and resources but also helps catch integration issues early in the development cycle, reducing the risk of production issues and improving overall application quality.

Testing Lambda and API Gateway with AWS SAM

AWS SAM is a powerful tool that simplifies the process of building, testing, and deploying serverless applications on AWS. It provides a convenient way to locally test your Lambda functions and API Gateway endpoints before deploying them to the cloud. This section will guide you through the process of setting up SAM, installing Docker, which is a necessary prerequisite, and leveraging the `sam local` commands to test your Lambda functions and API Gateway locally.

Setting Up AWS SAM

AWS SAM CLI is a command-line tool that facilitates working with serverless applications. It supports Windows, Linux and macOS operating systems. You can install it using a package manager like **Homebrew** (for macOS) or by downloading the installer from the AWS SAM website:

https://docs.aws.amazon.com/serverless-application-model/latest/developerguide/install-sam-cli.html

AWS SAM leverages *Docker* to create a local environment for testing your serverless applications. Docker is an open-source platform that allows you to build, deploy, and run applications inside containers. You can download and install Docker from the official website:

https://www.docker.com/get-started

Once you have both AWS SAM CLI and Docker installed, you're ready to start testing your Lambda functions and API Gateway locally.

Testing Lambda Functions with AWS SAM

AWS SAM allows you to test Lambda functions locally using the `sam local invoke` command. This command simulates an actual Lambda invocation, enabling you to validate your function's logic, test different input payloads, and inspect the output and logs.

To test a Lambda function locally, follow these steps:

1. Navigate to your project directory containing your template file **template.yml** or **template.json**. If you use AWS CDK to create your infrastructure you will find the template file inside the **cdk.out** folder.

2. Use the `sam local generate-event` command to generate an event payload for your **Lambda** function. To generate an API Gateway proxy event payload for a specific body:

   ```
   $ sam local generate-event apigateway aws-proxy
   ```

3. Use the `sam local invoke` command to invoke your **Lambda** function locally:

   ```
   $ sam local invoke LogicalIdOfYourLambdaFunction --event event.json
   ```

   Replace **LogicalIdOfYourLambdaFunction** with the logical ID of your **Lambda** function defined in the template file, and **event.json** with the path to your event payload file. This command will execute your **Lambda** function locally using the provided event payload, and you'll see the function's output printed in the terminal.

Next, we will explore a practical demonstration of testing the **NewOrder** Lambda function, which we developed in *Chapter 3, Messaging with Amazon SQS and Amazon SNS*.

Testing the NewOrder Lambda Function

We will now test the **NewOrder** Lambda function with AWS SAM. The logical ID of the Lambda function was **Lambda_NewOrderService** and accepted as input an API Gateway request.

To begin, we must create a simulated API Gateway event payload by using the test request for a new order, which we previously sent to API Gateway, and embed it within the body of an HTTP request.

```
$ sam local generate-event apigateway aws-proxy \
  --body '{
    "customerId": "123",
    "items": ["item1", "item2", "item3"],
    "total": "74.5",
    "paymentDetails": {
        "paymentMethod": "CARD",
        "paymentTransactionId": "FDS232SGFDF341934"
    },
    "shippingDetails": {
        "receiverName": "John Doe",
        "receiverPhoneNumber": "123-456-7890",
        "shippingAddressLine1": "123 Main St",
        "shippingAddressLine2": "Apt 101",
        "shippingCity": "Anytown",
        "shippingState": "CA",
        "shippingZipCode": "12345",
        "shippingCountry": "USA"
    }
}' > event.json
```

The execution of this command has resulted in storing the **APIGateway** event payload in a file named **event.json**. Upon inspecting the contents of this file, you will observe that the **body** field within the data has been encrypted, rendering its content unreadable in plain text.

We can then validate the functionality of the **NewOrder** Lambda function by providing the **event.json** file as input and specifying the template file associated with our project.

```
$ sam local invoke Lambda_NewOrderService -t CdkExampleStack.template.
json -e event.json
```

This command may require some time during the initial run as it needs to download the Docker image required for the Lambda function to execute. Then, it will invoke the Lambda function and provide the output, which is a new order ID.

Testing API Gateway with AWS SAM

API Gateway plays a crucial role in exposing Lambda functions as HTTP APIs, making it essential to test the integration between Lambda and API Gateway during development. AWS SAM provides the **sam local start-api** command to spin up a local API Gateway instance, allowing you to test your API endpoints without deploying to the cloud.

To test an API Gateway locally, follow these steps:

1. Navigate to your project directory containing your template file **template.yml** or **template.json**. If you use AWS CDK to create your infrastructure you will find the template file inside the **cdk.out** folder.

2. Use the **sam local start-api** command to start a local API Gateway instance:

   ```
   $ sam local start-api
   ```

   This command will start a local API Gateway instance and expose it at *http://127.0.0.1:3000*.

3. You can then use tools like **curl**, **Postman**, or a web browser to send *HTTP* requests to the local API Gateway and test your API endpoints. For example, if you have a *GET* endpoint **/hello** mapped to a Lambda function, you can test it by sending a *GET* request to **http://127.0.0.1:3000/hello**.

Next, we will look at a practical demonstration of testing the API for the *Ordering Platform*, which we created in *Chapter 3, Messaging with Amazon SQS and Amazon SNS*.

Testing the Ordering Platform API

We will now test the *Ordering Platform* API, which was a RESTful API developed using Amazon API Gateway, providing an endpoint for creating new orders. To begin, we will execute the **sam local start-api** command which will launch a local instance of the API Gateway service by providing the template file associated with our project.

```
$ sam local start-api -t CdkExampleStack.template.json
```

When you start the local instance of API Gateway, it creates a new POST endpoint that accepts new orders at the following URL: **http://127.0.0.1:3000/orders**. To test this endpoint, we will use a **curl** command from a terminal to send a request to this URL, passing the necessary data to API Gateway.

```
$ curl -X POST http://127.0.0.1:3000/orders \
  --header 'Content-Type: application/json' \
  --data-raw '{
    "customerId": "123",
    "items": ["item1", "item2", "item3"],
    "total": "74.5",
    "paymentDetails": {
        "paymentMethod": "CARD",
        "paymentTransactionId": "FDS232SGFDF341934"
    },
    "shippingDetails": {
        "receiverName": "John Doe",
        "receiverPhoneNumber": "123-456-7890",
        "shippingAddressLine1": "123 Main St",
        "shippingAddressLine2": "Apt 101",
        "shippingCity": "Anytown",
        "shippingState": "CA",
        "shippingZipCode": "12345",
        "shippingCountry": "USA"
    }
}'
```

The **curl** command resembles the ones we previously executed against live API Gateway environments hosted on AWS. However, in this case, we are utilizing a local environment, which simplifies the testing process for our API without the need for deployment to AWS, thereby avoiding any associated costs.

Testing Step Functions with Step Functions Local

As with any software application, testing is crucial to ensure the correctness and reliability of your Step Functions workflows. However, testing Step Functions directly in the AWS environment can be time-consuming and costly. This is where Step Functions Local comes into play.

Step Functions Local is a tool provided by AWS that allows you to run and test your state machines locally on your development machine. It helps streamline the development and testing process by providing a lightweight and cost-effective environment for iterating on your Step Functions workflows.

In the following section, we will explore the necessary steps to execute a state machine on your local machine utilizing the Step Functions Local tool.

Setting Up Step Functions Local

Setting up AWS Step Functions locally can be useful for testing and debugging your state machines before deploying them to the AWS Cloud. You can use either Docker or the Java downloadable version, depending on your preference and setup.

Using Docker

1. Install Docker on your machine if you haven't already.

2. Pull the AWS Step Functions Local Docker image from the AWS public repository:

   ```
   $ docker pull amazon/aws-stepfunctions-local
   ```

3. Run the Docker container with the necessary port mapping:

   ```
   $ docker run -p 8083:8083 amazon/aws-stepfunctions-local
   ```

   This command starts the Step Functions Local container and maps the container's port 8083 to the host's port 8083.

4. You can now interact with the Step Functions Local server using the AWS CLI or an SDK by specifying the endpoint URL **http://localhost:8083**.

Using the Java downloadable version

1. Download the latest version of the AWS Step Functions Local Java package from the AWS Step Functions developer guide:

   https://docs.aws.amazon.com/step-functions/latest/dg/sfn-local-jar.html

2. Extract the downloaded ZIP file.

3. Open a terminal or command prompt and navigate to the extracted directory.

4. Start the Step Functions Local server:

   ```
   $ java -jar StepFunctionsLocal.jar
   ```

This command starts the Step Functions Local server on the default port 8083.

5. You can now interact with the Step Functions Local API using the endpoint `http://localhost:8083`. You can use the AWS CLI or the AWS SDKs to create, update, and execute state machines locally.

Both the Docker and Java downloadable versions provide a local environment for testing and debugging AWS Step Functions state machines without the need to deploy them to the AWS Cloud. The Docker version is easier to set up and manage, while the Java downloadable version provides more flexibility in terms of configuration and customization.

Note that Step Functions Local is designed for testing and development purposes only, and should not be used in production environments. When you're ready to deploy your state machines, you'll need to create them in the AWS Step Functions service in the AWS Cloud.

Testing Step Functions

We will now use a very simple state machine definition we created in *Chapter 5, Orchestration with AWS StepFunctions*, in Step Functions Local and test the *Ordering Platform* API.

In a new terminal, navigate to the directory the state machine definition resides and run the following command to create a new state machine.

```
$ aws stepfunctions --endpoint http://127.0.0.1:8083 create-state-ma-
chine \
    --definition file://stepfunctions_state_machine.json \
    --name OrderingAPI-StateMachine \
    --role-arn arn:aws:iam::012345678901:role/DummyRole
```

This command will create a new state machine locally using the provided state machine definition and output a state machine ARN.

```
{
    "stateMachineArn": "arn:aws:states:us-east-1:123456789012:stateMa-
chine:OrderingAPI-StateMachine",
    "creationDate": "<datetime>"
}
```

Use the state machine ARN to start a new execution by passing a test input to the state machine.

```
$ aws stepfunctions --endpoint http://127.0.0.1:8083 start-execution \
    --state-machine-arn <STATE_MACHINE_ARN> \
```

```
    --input '{
     "NewOrderRequest":{
        "customerId":"123",
        "items":[
            "item1",
            "item2",
            "item3"
        ],
        "total":"74.5",
        "paymentDetails":{
            "paymentMethod":"CARD",
            "paymentTransactionId":"FDS232SGFDF341934"
        },
        "shippingDetails":{
            "receiverName":"John Doe",
            "receiverPhoneNumber":"123-456-7890",
            "shippingAddressLine1":"123 Main St",
            "shippingAddressLine2":"Apt 101",
            "shippingCity":"Anytown",
            "shippingState":"CA",
            "shippingZipCode":"12345",
            "shippingCountry":"USA"
        }
    }
}'
```

Replace **<STATE_MACHINE_ARN>** with the **ARN** returned from the previous step.

This command will create a new execution and output an execution ARN.

```
{
    "executionArn": "arn:aws:states:us-east-1:123456789012:execu-
tion:OrderingAPI-StateMachine:32bfbfe1-6f82-4dfc-9ad9-d416683e558d",
    "startDate": "<datetime>"
}
```

You can now describe the execution to see its status and output.

```
$ aws stepfunctions --endpoint http://127.0.0.1:8083 describe-execution
\
  --execution-arn <EXECUTION_ARN>
```

Replace **<EXECUTION_ARN>** with the **ARN** returned from the previous step.

This will show you the current status of the execution, as well as any output or errors that occurred during the execution.

By following these steps, you can test and debug your state machine locally using the AWS CLI and Step Functions Local without deploying it to AWS or using AWS SAM.

Testing AWS Services with LocalStack

LocalStack provides local emulations of many AWS services, allowing you to test your applications and infrastructure without connecting to the actual AWS cloud. This is useful for faster development iterations, integration testing, and avoiding charges for AWS usage. Next, we will see how to install and test our AWS infrastructure with **LocalStack**.

Installing LocalStack

LocalStack is available as a Docker container, making it easy to set up and run on any system with Docker installed. To install LocalStack, follow these steps:

1. Install Docker on your system if you haven't already done so.

2. Pull the LocalStack Docker image by running the following command:

    ```
    $ docker pull localstack/localstack
    ```

3. Start the LocalStack container by running:

    ```
    $ docker run -dp 4566:4566 --name localstack localstack/lo-
    calstack
    ```

    This command starts the LocalStack container and maps the default LocalStack service endpoint **http://localhost:4566** to your local machine.

With LocalStack operational, we will proceed to explore the process of testing the *Ordering Platform* API.

Testing with LocalStack

To test *Ordering Platform* API using LocalStack, we first need to make sure that

LocalStack is installed and running with the required services. You can verify this by sending a health check request.

```
$ curl http://localhost:4566/_localstack/health
```

If LocalStack is functioning properly, the response you receive should display the operational condition of every service it supports.

```
{"services": {"acm": "available", "apigateway": "running", "cloudfor-
mation": "running", "cloudwatch": "running", "config": "available",
"dynamodb": "running", "dynamodbstreams": "available", "ec2": "avail-
able", "es": "available", "events": "running", "firehose": "available",
"iam": "running", "kinesis": "available", "kms": "available", "lambda":
"running", "logs": "available", "opensearch": "available", "redshift":
"available", "resource-groups": "available", "resourcegroupstaggingapi":
"available", "route53": "available", "route53resolver": "available",
"s3": "running", "s3control": "available", "scheduler": "available",
"secretsmanager": "available", "ses": "available", "sns": "running",
"sqs": "running", "ssm": "running", "stepfunctions": "available", "sts":
"running", "support": "available", "swf": "available", "transcribe":
"available"}, "edition": "community", "version": "3.2.1.dev"}
```

Then we would need to install the **aws-cdk-local** package which is a robust library that mimics the behavior of AWS CDK but operates within a local environment.

```
$ npm install -g aws-cdk-local
```

This command will install the **aws-cdk-local** package globally on your system.

Next, navigate to your project root directory and bootstrap the LocalStack environment using the **cdklocal** command:

```
$ cdklocal bootstrap
```

This command creates the necessary AWS CloudFormation resources and prepares the environment for deploying your application.

With the environment set up, we can now deploy the sample ordering system application using the **cdklocal deploy** command:

```
$ cdklocal deploy
```

This command will deploy the resources to the LocalStack environment.

During the deployment process, you'll be prompted to confirm the changes and provide any required input parameters. Once the deployment is complete, the *Ordering Platform* API will be up and running in the LocalStack environment.

Now that the application is deployed, you can start testing the *Ordering Platform* API using LocalStack. You can interact with the application's endpoints, simulate user orders, and verify the expected behavior.

```
curl -X POST http://127.0.0.1:4566/orders \
  --header 'Content-Type: application/json' \
  --data-raw '{
    "customerId": "123",
    "items": ["item1", "item2", "item3"],
    "total": "74.5",
    "paymentDetails": {
        "paymentMethod": "CARD",
        "paymentTransactionId": "FDS232SGFDF341934"
    },
    "shippingDetails": {
        "receiverName": "John Doe",
        "receiverPhoneNumber": "123-456-7890",
        "shippingAddressLine1": "123 Main St",
        "shippingAddressLine2": "Apt 101",
        "shippingCity": "Anytown",
        "shippingState": "CA",
        "shippingZipCode": "12345",
        "shippingCountry": "USA"
    }
}'
```

One advantage of using LocalStack is that you can easily inspect and debug the application's interactions with various AWS services. You can explore the contents of DynamoDB tables, view logs in CloudWatch, or check the state of Lambda functions, all within the LocalStack environment. The preceding patterns can be used to test other services like EventBridge, Kinesis, and so on.

The LocalStack documentation offers practical examples that assist you in applying real-world scenarios to swiftly and easily create, set up, and deploy applications on your local machines:

https://docs.localstack.cloud/applications/

E2E Testing in the AWS Cloud

End-to-end testing is a crucial aspect of validating the functionality and integration of microservices in an event-driven architecture. It involves testing the entire application flow, from the initial event trigger to the final output or side effect, ensuring that all components work together seamlessly. In the context of the AWS cloud, there are several tools and services that can facilitate effective end-to-end testing for event-driven microservices.

End-to-end testing in AWS is often done with front-door systems like Amazon API Gateway, which serves as the entry point for your applications and can be used to invoke and test the entire application flow. API Gateway integrates with other AWS services, allowing you to trigger events and test the subsequent actions and responses across your microservices architecture.

When implementing end-to-end testing for event-driven microservices in AWS, it's essential to follow best practices and adopt a comprehensive testing strategy. This includes creating realistic test scenarios that mimic real-world usage, incorporating edge cases and failure scenarios, and automating the testing process as much as possible.

By leveraging the powerful services and tools provided by AWS, such as API Gateway, Lambda functions, Step Functions, and various testing frameworks, you can effectively test and validate your event-driven microservices architectures, ensuring reliability, scalability, and a seamless user experience.

Next, you will find a practical guide on how to conduct end-to-end testing in AWS for event-driven microservices.

Setting Up a Separate Testing Account

Start by creating a separate testing account in AWS that mirrors your production account as closely as possible. This will help you catch any issues that may arise due to differences in configuration or resources.

Using separate AWS accounts to isolate test environments from production and other critical environments is a security best practice. Here are some reasons you should use dedicated test accounts and tips for setting them up securely:

Some key benefits of separate test accounts include:

- **Prevent accidental changes or deletions**: Having a separate test account ensures you cannot accidentally modify resources in your production account while testing. Changes made in the test account will only impact test resources.

- **Limit blast radius**: Any failures, configuration errors, or security incidents that happen in the test environment are contained within the test account and do not put other environments at risk.

- **Simulate real-world conditions**: With a separate account, you can replicate the policies, user permissions, and resources of your production environment for more realistic testing.

- **Separate billing**: You can track spending and usage on test activities independently from your production infrastructure costs.

When creating a secure test account in AWS, it's advisable to follow these guidelines:

- **Start with an organizational account**: Use AWS Organizations to create a separate test account under your master account. You maintain administrative control through the organization while keeping the account self-contained.

- **Implement least privilege access**: Give testers only the permissions they need through IAM policies. Revoke unnecessary privileges to limit what testers can access.

- **Mirror production security controls**: Apply the same baseline of security groups, VPC settings, encryption standards, audit logging, and more that you enforce in your production environment.

- **Automate cleanup**: Schedule automated shutdown and deletion of test resources that are not in use to prevent lingering insecure configurations.

- **Rotate credentials**: Require IAM users in the test account to periodically rotate access keys and passwords.

Following these best practices will allow your team to experiment freely and securely using your test AWS account while minimizing risk to your production environments.

API Testing for API Gateway

Effective end-to-end testing for Amazon API Gateway functions is crucial for ensuring the reliability, scalability, and maintainability of your serverless applications. This comprehensive approach starts with defining comprehensive test scenarios that cover various request paths, request bodies, headers, and expected responses. These test cases should encompass happy paths, edge cases, and error scenarios, ensuring that the application behaves as expected under a wide range of conditions.

To execute end-to-end tests, you can leverage several options, including:

- **AWS SDK**: Utilize the AWS SDK for your preferred language (for example, Node.js, Python, Java) to make HTTP requests to your API Gateway endpoints and invoke Lambda functions directly, allowing you to programmatically interact with your serverless components.

- **API Testing Tools**: Leverage powerful tools like *Postman*, to send requests to your API Gateway endpoints and inspect the responses, facilitating manual or automated testing workflows.

- **Serverless Testing Frameworks**: Employ frameworks like Serverless Framework's built-in testing capabilities or serverless-bundle to streamline the deployment of your functions and run tests against them, ensuring end-to-end validation.

Once you have established a mechanism for executing tests, it's crucial to implement robust assertions that validate the expected behavior of your API Gateway. These assertions may include verifying HTTP response codes, response bodies, logs, and any side effects (for example, updates to a database or third-party services).

Additionally, leveraging code coverage tools can provide valuable insights into the effectiveness of your test suite by measuring the percentage of your code covered by tests. By identifying untested areas, you can enhance your test suite and ensure comprehensive coverage, reducing the risk of undetected bugs or regressions.

There are many widely used tools available for API testing that can simplify the process of end-to-end testing for AWS Lambda and API Gateway, including:

- **Postman**: Postman is a popular API testing tool that supports various programming languages and platforms. It allows you to create test suites, automate API testing, and integrate with CI/CD pipelines.

- **Katalon Studio**: Katalon Studio is a comprehensive testing solution that includes API testing capabilities. It supports multiple programming languages and provides features like data-driven testing, test case management, and reporting.

- **SoapUI**: SoapUI is an open-source API testing tool primarily focused on SOAP and REST APIs. It is written in Java and provides features like data-driven testing, assertions, and load testing.

- **Cypress**: Cypress is a popular end-to-end testing framework primarily used for web applications, but it also supports API testing through its dedicated API testing module.

- **Jmeter**: JMeter is an open-source load testing tool that can also be used for API testing. It supports various protocols and provides features like assertions, data parameterization, and reporting.

- **REST Assured**: REST Assured is a Java-based library that simplifies testing for RESTful APIs. It provides a domain-specific language (DSL) for writing tests and supports various assertions and data-driven testing.

- **Apigee**: Apigee is a comprehensive API management platform that includes API testing capabilities. It provides features like API monitoring, load testing, and integration with popular CI/CD tools.

By embracing end-to-end testing practices for Amazon API Gateway, you can enhance the reliability, scalability, and maintainability of your serverless applications, delivering a superior user experience and minimizing the risk of undetected issues.

Automate Testing with CI/CD Pipelines

AWS CodePipeline and **AWS CodeBuild** offer powerful tools to streamline the continuous integration and continuous delivery (CI/CD) process, enabling seamless integration of end-to-end tests into your software development lifecycle.

With AWS CodePipeline, you can orchestrate the entire software release process, from code commits to deployment. By incorporating end-to-end tests into your pipeline, you can automatically validate the functionality and integration of your microservices with every code change or deployment. This proactive approach helps catch issues early in the development cycle, reducing the risk of introducing bugs or regressions into your production environment.

AWS CodeBuild, on the other hand, provides a fully managed build service that can be seamlessly integrated with CodePipeline. This service allows you to define custom build specifications, including the execution of end-to-end tests. By leveraging CodeBuild, you can ensure that your end-to-end tests are executed consistently across different environments, minimizing the risk of environment-specific issues.

The integration of end-to-end tests into your CI/CD pipeline can take various forms, depending on your application's architecture and testing requirements. For example, you can implement tests that simulate real-world scenarios by invoking multiple microservices and validating their interactions.

Furthermore, AWS CodePipeline and CodeBuild offer extensive integration with other AWS services, such as AWS Lambda, enabling end-to-end testing of serverless applications. This flexibility allows you to tailor your testing approach to meet the specific needs of your application architecture.

By embracing end-to-end testing as an integral part of your CI/CD pipeline, you gain confidence in the quality and reliability of your microservices-based applications. With every code change or deployment, you can ensure that your application components are functioning as expected, both individually and as an integrated system, ultimately delivering a superior user experience and minimizing the risk of production issues.

Using Infrastructure as Code (IaC)

AWS CloudFormation plays a vital role in streamlining and automating the provisioning of the required infrastructure and resources for comprehensive end-to-end testing.

With CloudFormation, you can define and manage the entire infrastructure stack using declarative templates. These templates act as blueprints, specifying the desired state of your resources, including compute instances, networking components, storage, databases, and more. By leveraging CloudFormation, you can provision and configure the necessary testing environment consistently and reliably across different stages of the development lifecycle, such as development, staging, and production.

Furthermore, CloudFormation templates enable version control and collaboration, allowing teams to review, track, and manage changes to the infrastructure configuration over time. This promotes transparency, reproducibility, and ensures that the testing environment remains consistent and aligned with the codebase, enabling effective end-to-end testing.

CloudFormation also supports rollback mechanisms, which can automatically revert changes to the infrastructure if any issues arise during the provisioning process. This feature helps maintain a stable testing environment and minimizes the risk of disruptions or inconsistencies that could impact the reliability of end-to-end tests.

By embracing the IaC with AWS CloudFormation, organizations can streamline their end-to-end testing processes, ensuring consistent and reliable testing environments across different stages of the software development lifecycle. This approach not only improves the quality and reliability of applications but also fosters collaboration, transparency, and efficient resource management within teams.

Monitoring and Analyzing Test Results

In the realm of end-to-end testing for microservices, leveraging the power of AWS services such as **Amazon CloudWatch**, **Amazon CloudTrail**, and **AWS X-Ray** can prove to be invaluable. These tools offer comprehensive monitoring and analysis capabilities, enabling you to gain deep insights into the performance and behavior of your microservices during the testing phase.

Amazon CloudWatch, a robust monitoring service, empowers you to collect and track metrics, logs, and events from your microservices in real-time. By setting up custom dashboards and alarms, you can proactively identify potential bottlenecks, latency issues, or other performance-related problems that may arise during end-to-end testing. This proactive approach allows you to address issues before they escalate, ensuring a seamless testing experience.

Complementing CloudWatch, Amazon CloudTrail provides a comprehensive audit trail of all actions and events occurring within your AWS environment. By analyzing CloudTrail logs, you can gain valuable insights into the interactions between your microservices, enabling you to pinpoint potential integration or communication issues that may surface during end-to-end testing scenarios.

Furthermore, AWS X-Ray offers a powerful distributed tracing capability, allowing you to analyze and debug performance issues across your entire microservices architecture. By tracing requests as they navigate through different components, you can identify bottlenecks, latencies, and potential points of failure, facilitating a more efficient and effective end-to-end testing process.

It is important to note that while monitoring and troubleshooting are crucial aspects of end-to-end testing, they will be explored in greater depth in *Chapter 8, Monitoring and Troubleshooting*. This dedicated chapter will delve into advanced monitoring techniques, troubleshooting strategies, and best practices to ensure a robust and reliable microservices ecosystem.

Contract Testing

Contract testing is a technique used in software development to ensure that different components or services within a distributed system can communicate with each other correctly. It involves testing the integration points between these components or services based on a pre-defined contract.

The main idea behind contract testing is to create a contract that defines the expectations for the communication between two parties (for example, a client and a server, a consumer and a provider, or two microservices). This contract typically specifies the request/response format, data structures, and the behavior expected from each party.

While contract testing offers substantial benefits, its adoption among developers has been relatively slow due to the time and effort required to create and maintain these types of tests.

Contract testing in event-driven systems on AWS can be achieved using various tools and techniques. Here's a general approach you can follow:

- **Define contract specifications**: Start by defining the contract specifications for your events. These specifications should include the event structure, payload format, and any other relevant details that producers and consumers need to adhere to. You can use formats like JSON Schema, Apache Avro, or Protocol Buffers to define these contracts.

- **Use contract testing libraries**: Leverage contract testing libraries like Pact or Spring Cloud Contract to set up contract tests. These libraries allow you to define the expected behavior of your event producers and consumers based on the contract specifications.

- **Set up consumer-driven contract testing**: In consumer-driven contract testing, the consumer team defines the contract expectations, and the producer team uses these expectations to create a mock service that serves the contracts during testing. Tools like Pact facilitate this approach by providing a mock server and a contract verification process.

- **Integrate with CI/CD pipeline**: Integrate your contract tests into your CI/CD pipeline. This ensures that any changes to the event contracts or the producer/consumer implementations are automatically validated through the contract tests.

- **Monitor and maintain contracts**: Regularly monitor and maintain your event contracts. As your system evolves, ensure that all parties (producers and consumers) adhere to the agreed-upon contracts. Consider versioning your contracts and establishing a process for introducing breaking changes.

- **Use AWS services for testing and deployment:**
  - **AWS CodePipeline**: Use AWS CodePipeline to orchestrate your CI/CD pipeline, including running contract tests and deploying your event-driven components.

  - **AWS CodeBuild**: Use AWS CodeBuild to run your contract tests as part of your CI/CD pipeline.

  - **AWS Lambda**: If you're using AWS Lambda functions as event producers or consumers, you can invoke them locally during contract testing using the AWS SAM CLI.

  - **AWS EventBridge**: If you're using AWS EventBridge for event routing and processing, you can create test events and replay them during contract testing.

  - **AWS Step Functions**: If you're using AWS Step Functions for orchestrating event-driven workflows, you can create test cases and invoke them during contract testing.

- **Leverage AWS CDK or AWS CloudFormation**: Use AWS CDK or AWS CloudFormation to define and provision your event-driven infrastructure as code, including resources like AWS Lambda functions, AWS EventBridge rules, AWS Step Functions state machines, and AWS CodePipeline pipelines.

By following these steps, you can establish a robust contract testing practice for your event-driven systems on AWS, ensuring that producers and consumers remain compatible and reducing the risk of integration issues.

Performance Testing

Performance testing, also known as load testing, is the process of evaluating the behavior of a system or application under different loads, simulating real-world scenarios, and identifying potential bottlenecks or performance issues. In the context of AWS, performance testing is essential for ensuring that your applications and services can handle the expected traffic load while maintaining acceptable response times and resource utilization.

One popular tool for load testing is Artillery. **Artillery** is an open-source, modern, and powerful load testing toolkit that can be used to test a wide range of systems, including APIs, web applications, and microservices. It is designed to be highly scalable, easy to use, and capable of simulating realistic user traffic patterns.

In load testing, percentiles like **p95** and **p99** are used to measure the response times or latencies of requests. These percentiles provide insights into the performance characteristics of the system under test and help identify potential bottlenecks or performance issues.

The **p95** represents the response time at which 95% of the requests are served within that time or faster. In other words, only 5% of the requests have a response time greater than the **p95** value. This metric helps identify potential performance issues that affect a small percentage of requests.

For example, if the **p95** value for a particular test is 500 milliseconds, it means that 95% of the requests were served within 500 milliseconds, while the remaining 5% took longer than that. If the **p99** value is 1000 milliseconds, it indicates that 99% of the requests were served within 1 second, and only 1% of the requests took longer than that.

Load Testing Amazon API Gateway with Artillery

In this section, we will focus on conducting load testing on Amazon API Gateway, which serves as an entry point for applications to access data, business logic, or functionality from backend services.

When you perform load testing on Amazon API Gateway, you're not just testing the API Gateway service itself, but also the entire backend system that it's connected to. API Gateway acts as a front door to your backend services, which could include AWS Lambda functions, Amazon EventBridge event buses, Amazon DynamoDB tables, and other AWS services or custom-built applications.

By simulating a high volume of requests through API Gateway, you are essentially stress-testing the entire architecture of your backend system. This allows you to identify potential bottlenecks, performance issues, or scaling limitations that may arise when your application is under heavy load. The load testing process ensures that your backend services can handle the anticipated traffic and respond within acceptable latency thresholds, even during peak demand periods.

Additionally, load testing API Gateway provides insights into the overall resilience and scalability of your system. It helps you understand how your backend services behave when faced with spikes in traffic, and whether they can automatically scale up or down as needed to meet the changing demand. By simulating real-world scenarios, you can proactively identify and address any weaknesses in your system before they impact your end-users.

To load test Amazon API Gateway using Artillery, you need to first install Artillery, then create a test script and finally run and analyze the results of the load test. Let's look at those steps one by one.

Installing Artillery

You can install Artillery globally using *npm* by running the following command in a new terminal window:

```
$ npm install -g artillery
```

This command will install the latest version of Artillery globally on your system, making it accessible from anywhere in your terminal.

Creating a Test Script

Artillery uses a YAML or JSON file to define the test scenarios. Here's an example of a YAML script to perform load testing on the Ordering Platform API by passing a new order request within the request body.

```
config:
  target: "<api id>.execute-api.eu-central-1.amazonaws.com"
  phases:
    - duration: 60
      arrivalRate: 30
  http:
    timeout: 29
scenarios:
  - flow:
      - post:
          url: "/orders"
          json:
            customerId: "123"
            items:
              - item1
              - item2
              - item3
            total: "74.5"
            paymentDetails:
              paymentMethod: CARD
              paymentTransactionId: FDS232SGFDF341934
            shippingDetails:
```

```
        receiverName: John Doe

        receiverPhoneNumber: 123-456-7890

        shippingAddressLine1: 123 Main St

        shippingAddressLine2: Apt 101

        shippingCity: Anytown

        shippingState: CA

        shippingZipCode: "12345"

        shippingCountry: USA
```

In this example, the **artillery.yml** file is configured to load test the POST API endpoint **orders** with the provided JSON request body. The load testing duration is set to **60** seconds, and **30** virtual users will arrive per second.

Run the Test

To run the load test, navigate to the directory containing your YAML test script and execute the following command:

```
$ artillery run artillery.yml
```

Artillery will start sending requests to the specified API Gateway endpoint according to the defined load scenario. During the test, Artillery will report various metrics, such as the number of successful and failed requests, response times, and throughput.

Analyze the Results

After the test completes, Artillery will generate a report in the console, providing detailed statistics and metrics about the test. You can analyze these results to identify potential performance bottlenecks, optimize your API Gateway configuration, or adjust your backend services to handle the expected load.

```
http.codes.201: ...................................... 1800

http.downloaded_bytes: ............................... 64800

http.request_rate: ................................... 30/sec

http.requests: ....................................... 1800

http.response_time:

    min: ............................................. 66

    max: ............................................. 278

    mean: ............................................ 100.1
```

```
   median: .................................................. 77.5

   p95: ...................................................... 183.1

   p99: ...................................................... 219.2

http.responses: .............................................. 1800

vusers.completed: ............................................ 1800

vusers.created: .............................................. 1800

vusers.created_by_name.0: .................................... 1800

vusers.failed: ................................................. 0

vusers.session_length:

   min: ...................................................... 79.6

   max: ...................................................... 293.9

   mean: ..................................................... 117.5

   median: ................................................... 94.6

   p95: ...................................................... 202.4

   p99: ...................................................... 237.5
```

The results show that out of the 1800 requests sent, all were successfully processed, and the API Gateway returned an HTTP status response of 201 (Created) for each request. Additionally, the 99th percentile (**p99**) response time, which means that 99% of the requests were processed within this duration, was 219.2 milliseconds.

Note: *Performing load testing on AWS services like Amazon API Gateway is a crucial step in ensuring the performance and scalability of your application. However, it's essential to approach this process with caution and proper planning. Load testing can potentially result in increased resource usage and data transfers, leading to higher costs on your AWS bill. To mitigate this risk, it's advisable to conduct your load testing in a dedicated, non-production environment that closely mirrors your production setup.*

By creating a separate testing environment, you can simulate real-world scenarios without affecting your live systems and end-users. This approach allows you to safely push the boundaries of your infrastructure, identify potential bottlenecks, and fine-tune your configurations before deploying changes to your production environment.

Furthermore, it's recommended to closely monitor resource utilization and data transfer during load testing. AWS provides various monitoring tools, such as Amazon CloudWatch and AWS Cost Explorer, that can help you track and analyze your resource consumption and associated costs. This visibility enables you to make informed decisions about optimizing your infrastructure and managing costs effectively.

Manual Testing via the AWS Management Console

Manual testing of AWS serverless services through the AWS Management Console can be a valuable approach to validate their functionality and behavior. By leveraging the intuitive user interface provided by the console, you can simulate various scenarios, input data, and observe the responses from the serverless services in real time. This hands-on testing method allows for a thorough understanding of the service's capabilities, ensuring that it meets your specific requirements and behaves as expected before integrating it into your application or production environment. Additionally, the console provides access to detailed logs and monitoring tools, enabling you to analyze and troubleshoot any issues that may arise during the testing process.

Invoke APIs for API Gateway

API Gateway has a test invocation feature in the AWS Management Console where you can send test requests and test various responses. Navigate to the API Gateway dashboard of your API, for example the *Ordering Platform* API, select the **POST** method of the **/orders** resource **Test** tab, and add a test request body, as shown in *Figure* 7.2.

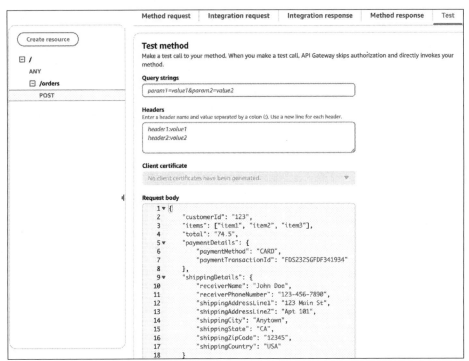

***Figure* 7.2:** *Sending a test request from the Amazon API Gateway dashboard*

After clicking the **Test** button, you can observe the API call's latency, status, and response body, as shown in *Figure 7.3*.

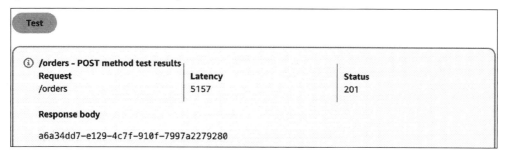

Figure 7.3: *The API response obtained through the test functionality in the Amazon API Gateway dashboard*

Execute AWS Lambda Functions

To use the test functionality of Lambda, navigate to the Lambda dashboard of your Lambda function, for example the **NewOrder** service, select the **Test** tab, enter a name, select the **apigateway-aws-proxy** template, and embed a test new order in the body field, as shown in *Figure 7.4*.

Figure 7.4: *Sending a test request from the AWS Lambda dashboard*

Start the testing process by clicking the **Test** button. Once the Lambda function execution is complete, examine the response data, which is illustrated in *Figure 7.5*.

⊘ **Executing function: succeeded** (logs ⬚)

▼ Details

The area below shows the last 4 KB of the execution log.

```
{
    "statusCode": 201,
    "body": "f1815210-0390-4aec-8015-aa4b31deea53",
    "isBase64Encoded": false
}
```

Summary

Code SHA-256
X2ik/hOUZg3u1xV1ckFn2UkPWk8daO1z3uA3JLvLwjl=

Execution time
2 minutes ago (▓▓▓▓▓▓▓▓▓▓▓▓▓▓▓)

Request ID
ec39b1df-4e65-4453-aef7-cd65af14fdea

Function version
$LATEST

Init duration
2126.16 ms

Duration
2933.01 ms

Billed duration
2934 ms

Resources configured
512 MB

Max memory used
163 MB

Log output

The section below shows the logging calls in your code. Click here ⬚ to view the corresponding CloudWatch log group.

```
SLF4J: Failed to load class "org.slf4j.impl.StaticLoggerBinder".
SLF4J: Defaulting to no-operation (NOP) logger implementation
SLF4J: See http://www.slf4j.org/codes.html#StaticLoggerBinder for further details.
START RequestId: ec39b1df-4e65-4453-aef7-cd65af14fdea Version: $LATEST
Received order request from API GatewayAPIGatewayV2HTTPEvent(version=null, routeKey=null, rawPath=null, rawQueryString=null,
cookies=null, headers={Accept=text/html,application/xhtml+xml,application/xml;q=0.9,image/webp,*/*;q=0.8, Accept-Encoding=gzip,
deflate, sdch, Accept-Language=en-US,en;q=0.8, Cache-Control=max-age=0, CloudFront-Forwarded-Proto=https, CloudFront-Is-Desktop-
Viewer=true, CloudFront-Is-Mobile-Viewer=false, CloudFront-Is-SmartTV-Viewer=false, CloudFront-Is-Tablet-Viewer=false, CloudFront-
Viewer-Country=US, Host=1234567890.execute-api.us-east-1.amazonaws.com, Upgrade-Insecure-Requests=1, User-Agent=Custom User Agent
String, Via=1.1 08f323deadbeefa7af34d5feb414ce27.cloudfront.net (CloudFront), X-Amz-Cf-Id=cDehVQoZnx43VYQb9j2-nvCh-
```

Figure 7.5: *The response obtained through the test functionality in the AWS Lambda dashboard*

The output displays the response body generated by the Lambda function, along with additional details about the function's execution, such as the duration and memory consumption. We will delve deeper into monitoring and troubleshooting Lambda functions in the next chapter, where these performance metrics will be explored in greater depth.

Test Asynchronous Communication with Amazon SQS and Amazon SNS

If your microservices communicate asynchronously using Amazon SQS or Amazon SNS, you can leverage your testing capabilities. For SQS, you can send test messages to queues and verify that your microservices process them correctly. For SNS, you can publish test messages to topics and verify that subscribed microservices receive and handle them as expected.

To send a test message to an SQS queue, navigate to the SQS dashboard, select your SQS queue, for example the **OrderCreatedQueue** queue we created in *Chapter 3, Messaging with Amazon SQS and Amazon SNS*, and click the **Send and receive**

messages button. From the **Send and receive messages** dashboard, enter a test message and click **Send message**, as shown in *Figure* 7.6.

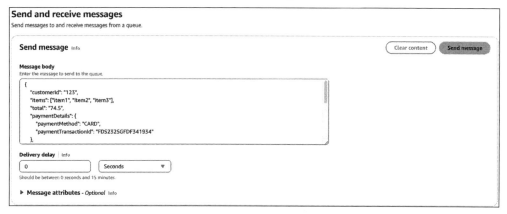

Figure 7.6: *Sending a test message from the Amazon SQS dashboard*

In the **Receive messages** section, you can click **Poll for messages** to get the message, unless the Lambda function has already processed it, as shown in *Figure* 7.7.

Figure 7.7: *Polling for messages from the Amazon SQS dashboard*

Then you can click the message and view its details.

To publish a message to SNS, you can follow the same steps. Navigate to the SNS dashboard, select your SNS topic, for example the **OrderCreatedTopic** topic we created in *Chapter* 3, and click the **Publish message** button. From the **Publish message to topic** dashboard, enter a test message in the message body and click **Publish message**.

Test Integration with Amazon EventBridge

You can use EventBridge to simulate real-world events and test how your microservices respond to them. Create test events and configure EventBridge rules to route them to your Lambda functions or other targets.

EventBridge also allows you to send test events from the AWS Management Console. To use the test functionality of EventBridge, navigate to the **EventBridge** dashboard, select **Event buses** from the left pane, and click the **Send events** button. From the **Send events** dashboard, select the event bus you want to send events to, for example, the **OrderingSystemEventBus** we created in *Chapter 4, Choreography with Amazon EventBridge*, enter **com.example.new-order-service** for the *Event source*, enter **OrderCreated** for the **Detail type**, and enter the test order request in the **Event detail**, as shown in *Figure 7.8*.

Figure 7.8: *Sending a test event from the Amazon EventBridge dashboard*

Click the **Send** button below and the event will now be routed to the Lambda function for processing.

Simulate Streaming Data with Amazon Kinesis

In cases where your microservices consume or produce streaming data, you can use Amazon Kinesis to simulate real-time data streams. Create test data streams and configure your microservices to consume or produce data from/to these streams. You can then verify the correct handling of the data by your microservices.

To send test streaming data to Amazon Kinesis, you can use the **Amazon Kinesis Data Generator** tool. This tool allows you to generate test data streams and send them to your Kinesis data streams or Data Firehose streams. However, an Amazon Cognito user pool in your account and a user in that pool are also required. A CloudFormation stack is provided to create the AWS infrastructure for the Cognito user pool.

As shown in *Figure 7.9*, once you're in the Kinesis Data Generator, you'll need to provide some configuration details. Select the AWS region where your Kinesis data stream or Firehose delivery stream is located. Then, choose the Kinesis service, for example the **OrderingSystemClickstream** data stream we created in *Chapter 6, Event Streaming with Amazon Kinesis*, and specify the name of your target stream. You can also configure the record template, which defines the structure and content of the test data records. The template supports various data types and can include static values or random data generators. After configuring the record template, set the desired data rate (records per second) to be sent.

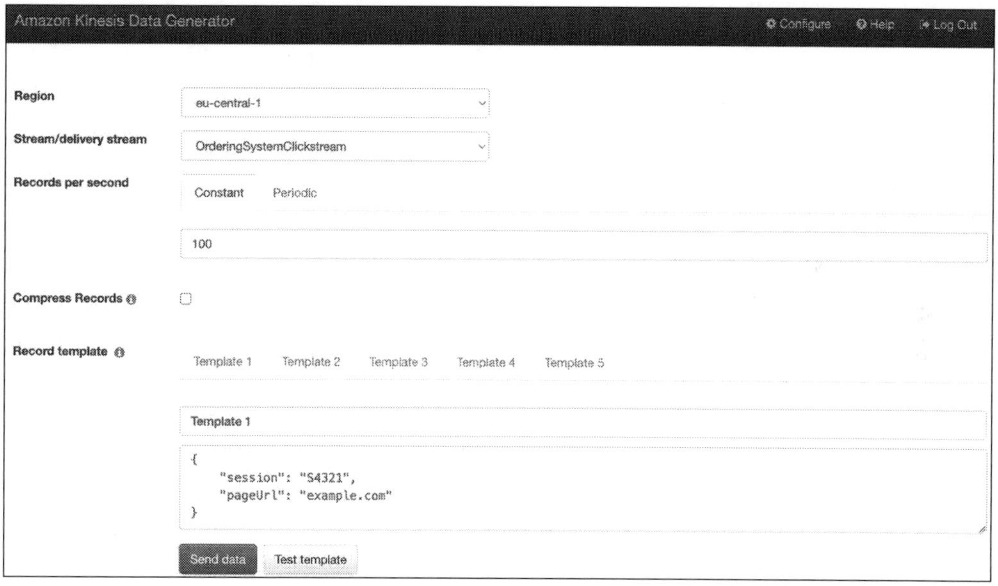

Figure 7.9: *Sending test streaming data from the Amazon Kinesis Data Generator tool*

Finally, review your settings and start the data generation process. The Kinesis Data Generator will send the test data to your specified Kinesis stream, allowing you to simulate and test your data ingestion and processing pipelines.

For detailed instructions and guidance on utilizing this tool effectively, refer to the comprehensive documentation available on the official GitHub repository:

https://github.com/awslabs/amazon-kinesis-data-generator

Orchestrate Complex Workflows with AWS Step Functions

When dealing with event-driven microservices orchestrated using AWS Step Functions, you have the ability to create test state machines and execute them to validate the correct sequence of events and data flow between your microservices. This powerful feature offered by Step Functions allows you to thoroughly test and debug your workflows before deploying them to production environments.

In *Chapter 5, Orchestration with AWS StepFunctions*, we explored numerous examples that demonstrated how to test an execution within Step Functions effectively. These examples showcased the various techniques for simulating real-world scenarios, injecting test data, and validating the expected outcomes. By following these examples, you can build robust test cases tailored to your specific microservices architecture, ensuring that your event-driven workflows are thoroughly tested and ready for production deployment.

Conclusion

In this chapter, we explored the crucial aspects of software testing in the context of AWS applications and services. We began by emphasizing the importance of the AWS Shared Responsibility Model, which outlines the division of responsibilities between AWS and its customers for securing and maintaining cloud resources.

We then delved into the different layers of software testing, including unit testing, integration testing, end-to-end testing, contract testing, and performance testing. Unit testing using mock libraries was covered, highlighting the benefits of isolating dependencies and ensuring efficient testing of individual components. Integration testing was discussed, with a focus on leveraging emulators and local testing tools like AWS SAM, Step Functions Local, and LocalStack to streamline the development and testing process.

End-to-end testing in AWS environments was explored, providing strategies for testing complete applications and services in staging or production-like environments. This approach helps ensure that all components work together seamlessly and identify potential issues before deploying to production.

We also introduced contract testing as a way to ensure that different components of a system can communicate effectively, adhering to predefined contracts or interfaces. This approach promotes modular development and facilitates the integration of services from different teams or organizations.

We covered performance testing, which is crucial for ensuring that AWS applications and services can handle expected traffic loads and scale as needed. By load testing and monitoring performance metrics, you can identify and address potential bottlenecks, optimize resource utilization, and ensure a seamless user experience.

Finally, while automated testing is crucial for ensuring the reliability and scalability of AWS applications and services, we explored how manual testing through the AWS Management Console can also serve a valuable purpose. The AWS Management Console provides a user-friendly interface for interacting with various AWS services, enabling you to manually validate functionality, explore configurations, and verify expected behaviors.

Throughout this chapter, we emphasized the importance of following best practices and leveraging the tools and services provided by AWS to streamline the testing process. By implementing a comprehensive testing strategy that spans all layers, you can ensure the reliability, scalability, and performance of your AWS applications and services, ultimately delivering a high-quality user experience.

In the upcoming chapter, we will delve into the intricate aspects of monitoring and troubleshooting event-driven systems. We will explore how to utilize Amazon CloudWatch, a robust monitoring service that offers comprehensive metrics and log viewing capabilities, enabling you to gain valuable insights into the performance and health of your event-driven architectures. We will also discuss AWS CloudTrail, a service that records API calls made within your AWS account, providing an audit trail for security analysis and operational troubleshooting. Additionally, we will examine AWS X-Ray, a powerful troubleshooting tool designed for tracing and analyzing distributed applications.

CHAPTER 8

Monitoring and Troubleshooting

Introduction

This chapter starts by providing an introduction to monitoring and troubleshooting in AWS, including logs, metrics, and traces. It will then delve into logging with Amazon CloudWatch Logs, covering how to collect, store, and analyze log data from various AWS services and applications. We will explore Monitoring with Amazon CloudWatch Metrics, discussing how to collect and visualize metrics from AWS resources and applications. We will also cover Proactive monitoring with Amazon CloudWatch Alarms, explaining how to set up alarms and receive notifications based on predefined thresholds. The chapter will also discuss how to track account activity with AWS CloudTrail, a service that records API calls and related events for auditing and compliance purposes. Next, we will be introduced to Visualizing cloud resources with Amazon CloudWatch Dashboards, allowing us to create customized dashboards to monitor our AWS environment. The chapter also covers Distributed tracing with AWS X-Ray, enabling you to analyze and debug distributed applications by reviewing requests as they travel through your application components. Finally, the chapter will touch on third-party observability partners, highlighting how you can integrate external monitoring and observability tools with your AWS environment. By the end of this chapter, you will have a solid understanding of the various monitoring and troubleshooting tools available in AWS, enabling you to effectively monitor, troubleshoot, and maintain your applications and services.

Structure

In this chapter, we will discuss the following topics:

- Introduction to Monitoring and Troubleshooting: Logs, Metrics, Traces
- Logging with Amazon CloudWatch Logs
- Monitoring with Amazon CloudWatch Metrics
- Proactive Monitoring with Amazon CloudWatch Alarms

- Tracking Account Activity with AWS CloudTrail
- Visualizing Cloud Resources with Amazon CloudWatch Dashboards
- Distributed Tracing with AWS X-Ray
- Third-Party Observability Partners

Introduction to Monitoring and Troubleshooting

In today's complex and distributed systems, effective monitoring and troubleshooting are crucial for ensuring the smooth operation and performance of applications and infrastructure. Monitoring and troubleshooting event-driven systems require a comprehensive approach that combines observability, robust logging and monitoring, distributed tracing, and effective incident response procedures. Let us discuss it in more detail here:

- **Embrace observability**: Observability is the ability to understand the internal state of a system based on its external outputs. In event-driven systems, observability is key to gaining insights into the flow of events, the performance of services, and the overall system health.

- **Implement robust logging and monitoring**: Effective logging and monitoring strategies are essential for identifying and diagnosing issues in event-driven systems.

- **Embrace distributed tracing**: Event-driven systems often involve multiple services and components interacting with each other. Distributed tracing helps in understanding the end-to-end flow of requests and pinpointing bottlenecks or failures across the system.

- **Implement alerting and incident response**: Timely detection and effective response to incidents is crucial for maintaining system availability and minimizing downtime.

The three pillars that form the foundation of modern monitoring and troubleshooting practices are **logs**, **metrics**, and **traces**. Effective monitoring and troubleshooting require a holistic approach that combines all those pillars. Logs provide detailed context and insight into specific events, metrics measure system performance and health, and traces connect the dots by following requests across distributed components. Let's examine those pillars more closely.

Logs

Logs are textual records that capture events, errors, warnings, and other relevant information generated by applications, services, and systems. They provide valuable insights into the behavior and state of a system at a particular point in time. Logs are essential for:

- **Debugging**: Logs help identify and diagnose issues by providing detailed information about what went wrong and when.

- **Auditing**: Logs can be used to track user activity, security events, and compliance requirements.

- **Troubleshooting**: Logs offer a historical perspective, allowing you to trace back and understand the sequence of events that led to an issue.

Metrics

Metrics are numerical measurements that quantify various aspects of a system's performance, health, and resource utilization. Metrics are typically collected and aggregated over time, enabling the tracking and analysis of trends and patterns. Common examples of metrics include CPU usage, memory utilization, network throughput, and request latency. Metrics are invaluable for:

- **Performance monitoring**: Metrics provide real-time visibility into the performance of applications and infrastructure, enabling proactive identification of bottlenecks and optimization opportunities.

- **Capacity planning**: By analyzing historical metrics, you can forecast future resource requirements and plan for scalability.

- **Alerting and incident response**: Metrics can be used to set thresholds and trigger alerts when certain conditions are met, enabling prompt action to address issues.

Traces

Traces, also known as distributed tracing, provide a comprehensive view of a single request or transaction as it propagates through multiple services and components in a distributed system. Traces enable you to follow the path of a request, capturing timing information, metadata, and any errors or exceptions that occurred along the way. Traces are essential for:

- **Latency analysis**: Traces help identify performance bottlenecks by breaking down the end-to-end latency of a request into its constituent parts, allowing you to pinpoint the root cause.

- **Root cause analysis**: By following the trace of a request, you can identify the specific component or service responsible for an issue, streamlining the troubleshooting process.

- **Dependency mapping**: Traces reveal the intricate dependencies between services, aiding in understanding the overall system architecture and potential failure points.

By leveraging these three pillars, you can gain visibility into your systems, detect and diagnose issues promptly, and ensure optimal performance and reliability. As modern systems continue to grow in complexity, the ability to monitor, analyze, and troubleshoot effectively becomes increasingly crucial for successful operations and delivering high-quality user experiences.

Monitoring and Troubleshooting on AWS

AWS provides a robust set of monitoring and troubleshooting tools to help maintain high performance, security, and operational efficiency by analyzing logs, metrics, and traces. The three core services in this domain are:

- **Amazon CloudWatch**: This is a monitoring and observability service that collects and tracks metrics, logs, and events from various AWS resources and applications. It allows you to set alarms, visualize data, and gain system-wide visibility into resource utilization, application performance, and operational health.

- **AWS CloudTrail**: CloudTrail is a service that records API calls made within your AWS account. It captures information about the identity of the API caller, the time of the call, the source IP address, and more. This helps with auditing, security analysis, and troubleshooting by providing a comprehensive log of activities and changes made to your AWS resources.

- **AWS X-Ray**: X-Ray is a distributed tracing service that helps you analyze and debug distributed applications, such as those built using a microservices architecture. It collects data about requests as they travel through your application and provides end-to-end visibility into application performance and potential issues.

By leveraging these three core monitoring and troubleshooting services, AWS empowers you to maintain a high level of operational excellence, ensure application reliability, and rapidly identify and resolve issues.

The following sections will provide a more in-depth examination of those services and how monitoring and troubleshooting work for the AWS services we covered in this book including AWS Lambda, Amazon API Gateway, Amazon SQS, Amazon SNS, Amazon EventBridge, AWS Step Functions, and Amazon Kinesis.

Monitoring with Amazon CloudWatch

Amazon CloudWatch is a powerful monitoring service that enables you to collect, analyze, and take action on metrics and logs from your AWS resources, applications, and services. It provides a comprehensive view of your cloud environment, allowing you to monitor your resources' performance, detect anomalies, and gain insights into their overall health.

CloudWatch is designed to work seamlessly with other AWS services, making it easy to integrate monitoring capabilities into your existing infrastructure. Here's an overview of its key features:

- **Log monitoring**: CloudWatch Logs allows you to collect, monitor, and store log files from your Lambda functions, Step Function state machines and other sources. This feature provides valuable insights into application and system behavior, making it easier to troubleshoot issues and identify potential problems.

- **Metric monitoring**: CloudWatch collects and tracks metrics from various AWS services that provide insights into resource utilization, operational performance, and overall system health.

- **Alarms and notifications**: CloudWatch enables you to set alarms based on predefined thresholds for your metrics or log events. When an alarm is triggered, you can receive notifications via email or SMS, or integrate with other AWS services like Amazon SNS to take automated actions.

- **Dashboards and visualization**: CloudWatch offers customizable dashboards that provide a centralized view of your monitored resources. You can create and customize dashboards with various widgets, including line graphs, stacked area charts, and heat maps, to visualize your metrics and logs in a meaningful way.

By leveraging Amazon CloudWatch, you can gain valuable insights into your AWS resources, applications, and services, enabling you to proactively identify and resolve issues, optimize performance, and ensure the overall health and reliability of your cloud infrastructure.

Logging with CloudWatch Logs

Amazon CloudWatch Logs allows you to monitor, store, and access log files from various AWS resources and applications. It provides a centralized and scalable platform for log management, making it easier to collect and analyze log data from your applications, systems, and services running on AWS.

With CloudWatch Logs, you can ingest log data from various sources, such as API Gateway APIs, AWS Lambda functions, and more. This log data can be used for debugging, troubleshooting, auditing, and gaining insights into the performance and behavior of your applications and infrastructure.

In CloudWatch Logs, there are two main concepts: **log groups** and **log streams**:

- **Log group**: A log group is a logical grouping of log streams that share the same retention, monitoring, and access control settings. Each log group represents a collection of log data from one or more sources, such as an application or service. For example, you might create a separate log group for each application or environment.

- **Log stream**: A log stream is a sequence of log events that share the same source. Each log stream belongs to a log group, and it represents the log data generated by a specific instance or component of your application or service.

By organizing log data into log groups and log streams, CloudWatch Logs provides a structured way to manage and access your log data. You can define retention policies for log groups, set up metric filters to monitor specific log patterns, and integrate with other AWS services like Amazon Kinesis or AWS Lambda for real-time log processing and analysis.

AWS Lambda is the only service that we covered, where you can write code and can directly send custom logs to CloudWatch Logs. Other AWS services that can integrate with CloudWatch Logs include Amazon API Gateway, Amazon EventBridge, AWS Step Functions, and Amazon Kinesis. However, Amazon SQS and SNS do not directly integrate with CloudWatch Logs. In the following sections, we will explore practical examples demonstrating how to send log data from code executed within AWS Lambda functions, as well as methods to enable logging capabilities for Amazon API Gateway.

Tip: *CloudWatch logs also provide a feature called **log tailing**, which allows you to view and monitor the logs in real-time as they are being generated. This can be particularly useful during the development and debugging phases, as it enables you to observe the execution of your Lambda function and identify any issues or unexpected behavior immediately.*

Logging in AWS Lambda

CloudWatch Logs is enabled by default in Lambda functions, which means that any standard output generated by the Lambda function's code, such as print statements or log messages, is automatically captured and sent to CloudWatch Logs. This provides a convenient way to monitor and troubleshoot the execution of your Lambda functions.

In the case of Java code running in a Lambda function, any output written to `System.out` or `System.err` will be captured and sent to CloudWatch Logs. For example, if you have a line like `System.out.println("Hello, Lambda!")` in your Java code, the output `Hello, Lambda!` will be logged in CloudWatch Logs.

Each Lambda function has its own dedicated CloudWatch log group, which acts as a container for the log streams associated with that function. A log stream is created for each invocation of the Lambda function, and it contains the log entries generated during that specific execution. This separation of logs into streams helps to organize and manage the log data more effectively.

Let's explore the CloudWatch Logs generated by the **NewOrder** service we created in *Chapter 3, Messaging with Amazon SQS and Amazon SNS*. Head over to the Lambda dashboard for the **NewOrder** service, then navigate to the **Monitor** tab. You can view the recent logs if you scroll down or click on the **View CloudWatch logs** button. This action will open the CloudWatch logs in a new tab. Once there, switch to the **Log streams** tab and select the most recent log stream. You should then be able to view the output generated by the service.

```
START RequestId: 0665ef7e-e0c6-475e-857d-d2c6affd2c2e Version: $LATEST
```

Received order request from API Gateway: APIGatewayV2HTTPEvent(version=null, routeKey=null, rawPath=null, rawQueryString=null, cookies=null, headers=null, queryStringParameters=null, pathParameters=null, stageVariables=null, body={"customerId":"123","items":["item1","item2", "item3"],"total":"74.5","paymentDetails":{"paymentMethod":"CARD","paymentTransactionId":"FDS232SGFDF341934"},"shippingDetails":{"receiverName":"JohnDoe","receiverPhoneNumber":"123-456-7890","shippingAddressLine1":"123MainSt","shippingAddressLine2":"Apt101","shippingCity":"Anytown","shippingState":"CA","shippingZipCode":"12345","shippingCountry":"USA"}}, isBase64Encoded=false, requestContext=null)

```
END RequestId: 0665ef7e-e0c6-475e-857d-d2c6affd2c2e
```

REPORT RequestId: 0665ef7e-e0c6-475e-857d-d2c6affd2c2e Duration: 2742.62 ms Billed Duration: 2743 ms Memory Size: 512 MB Max Memory Used: 163 MB Init Duration: 1773.77 ms

You will observe that the following standard output from the Lambda function automatically gets logged in CloudWatch logs without the need to include any additional libraries or code.

```
System.out.println("Received order request from API Gateway: " + event);
```

Furthermore, when a Lambda function is invoked, Amazon CloudWatch captures various metrics related to its execution, as shown in the last line displaying the execution report. These metrics offer valuable insights into the function's performance and resource utilization. The information logged to CloudWatch includes:

- **Duration**: This metric represents the total execution time of the Lambda function, measured in milliseconds. It encompasses the time required for the function to complete its task, including any initialization, processing, and clean-up operations.

- **Billed Duration**: Lambda functions are billed based on their execution time, rounded up to the nearest multiple of 100 milliseconds. The billed duration metric reflects the actual time for which you will be charged, taking into account this rounding behavior.

- **Memory Size**: Each Lambda function is configured with a specific amount of memory allocated to it. The memory size metric represents the amount of memory (in MB) that was allocated to the function during its execution.

- **Max Memory Used**: This metric indicates the maximum amount of memory (in MB) that the Lambda function actually utilized during its execution. It helps identify potential memory bottlenecks or opportunities for optimization.

- **Init Duration**: When a Lambda function is invoked for the first time or after a certain period of inactivity, it goes through an initialization phase. The `init` duration metric measures the time taken for this initialization process, which includes actions like importing dependencies, loading code, and setting up the execution environment.

CloudWatch does more than just capturing logs from Lambda functions; it also collects metrics related to the performance and health of the system, which we will explore in an upcoming section.

Logging in to Amazon API Gateway

Amazon API Gateway is a managed service, which means you cannot directly add logs from your code. However, it provides two types of logs through Amazon CloudWatch: **execution logs** and **access logs**.

Execution logs capture detailed information about requests and responses that pass through API Gateway, including the integration requests sent to the backend and the corresponding responses received from the backend. These logs can provide valuable insights into the performance and behavior of your backend services, making them an essential tool for troubleshooting issues with your API.

Access logs capture information about requests and responses that pass through API Gateway, similar to an access log from a web server. These logs provide details about who has accessed your API, how they accessed it, and the response status. Access logs can help you analyze traffic patterns, identify potential security issues, and monitor API usage. Access logs include data such as the request and response metadata, client IP address, latency, response length, and HTTP status codes.

Both execution logs and access logs are stored in Amazon CloudWatch logs. By default, these logs are not enabled for your API Gateway API. To enable CloudWatch logs for your **OrderingPlatform API** in the Amazon API Gateway dashboard, follow these steps:

1. From the **API Gateway** dashboard of the **OrderingPlatform API**, click on **Stages** from the left sidebar.

2. Select the **prod** stage and click on **Edit** next to the **Logs and tracing** section.

3. Select the **Full request and response logs** for the **CloudWatch logs** and select the **Detailed metrics**. Click **Save changes**.

API Gateway is now configured to record requests made to your API. You won't need to redeploy the API when you modify the logging configuration.

The log group created in CloudWatch logs includes the API Gateway ID and the stage which is prod in our case:

```
API-Gateway-Execution-Logs_<API Gateway ID>/prod
```

If we open a log trace, we will find logging details including the request body, Lambda request, integration latency with Lambda and the response body:

Method request body before transformations:

```
{
    "customerId": "123",
    "items": [
        "item1",
        "item2",
        "item3"
    ],
    "total": "74.5",
    "paymentDetails": {
        "paymentMethod": "CARD",
        "paymentTransactionId": "FDS232SGFDF341934"
    },
    "shippingDetails": {
        "receiverName": "John Doe",
        "receiverPhoneNumber": "123-456-7890",
        "shippingAddressLine1": "123 Main St",
        "shippingAddressLine2": "Apt 101",
        "shippingCity": "Anytown",
        "shippingState": "CA",
        "shippingZipCode": "12345",
        "shippingCountry": "USA"
    }
}
```

Endpoint request URI: https://lambda.eu-central-1.amazonaws.com/2015-03-31/functions/arn:aws:lambda:eu-central-1:<account id>:function:new-order-service/invocations

Received response. Status: 200, Integration latency: 5149 ms

Endpoint response body before transformations:

```
{
    "statusCode": 201,
    "body": "25490f63-1764-4fd5-a406-fd930833a33b",
    "isBase64Encoded": false
}
```

These logs can provide valuable insights into the operation and performance of your APIs, helping you to diagnose issues, optimize performance, and monitor usage patterns.

Amazon CloudWatch Logs Insights

Amazon CloudWatch Logs Insights is a feature that enables you to interactively search, analyze, and visualize log data stored in Amazon CloudWatch Logs. With its advanced querying capabilities, you can quickly and easily explore your logs, identify patterns, and uncover valuable insights that can help you improve application performance, enhance security, and streamline operational efficiency.

One of the key advantages of CloudWatch **Logs Insights** is its user-friendly query language, which is based on SQL. This familiar syntax allows developers, administrators, and operations teams to leverage their existing SQL skills to query and analyze log data effectively. The service supports a wide range of SQL commands, including filters, aggregations, joins, and nested queries, making it easy to extract meaningful information from complex log data.

CloudWatch Logs Insights also provides powerful visualization capabilities, allowing you to present your log data in a clear and concise manner. You can create customizable charts and graphs to visualize trends, anomalies, and patterns in your log data, enabling you to quickly identify and respond to potential issues or opportunities.

Another significant benefit of CloudWatch Logs Insights is its seamless integration with other AWS services. By leveraging CloudWatch Logs Insights, you can analyze logs from various AWS services, such as AWS Lambda, Amazon API Gateway, AWS Step Functions and more. This integration simplifies the log management process and provides a centralized view of your entire AWS environment.

The CloudWatch **Logs Insights** can be found on the left sidebar of the CloudWatch dashboard in the AWS Management console. *Figure 8.1* showcases a sample query that retrieves valuable insights into the performance of the **NewOrder** Lambda function. Specifically, this query calculates the average, maximum, and minimum durations for executions of the **NewOrder** Lambda function. These duration metrics are derived from the logs that the Lambda function automatically sends to CloudWatch Logs, providing a comprehensive view of the function's performance.

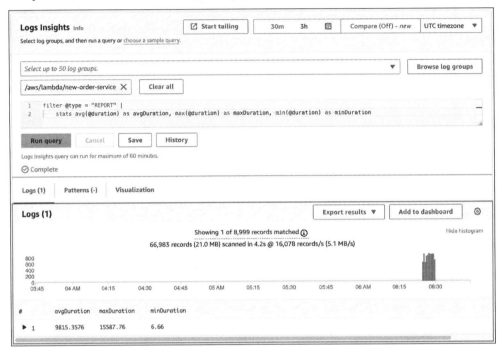

Figure 8.1: *Running a query in Amazon CloudWatch Logs Insights to find the average, maximum, and minimum durations of a Lambda function*

By leveraging Logs Insights, you can gain deeper insights into the behavior and performance of your AWS services, enabling you to identify potential bottlenecks, optimize resource utilization, and ensure efficient execution. Additionally, you can create custom queries tailored to your specific use case, enabling you to extract valuable information from the log data and make data-driven decisions for your AWS applications.

Amazon CloudWatch Metrics

Amazon CloudWatch Metrics provide valuable insights into the operational behavior and performance of your AWS resources, allowing you to monitor and analyze their activities. These metrics can help you identify and troubleshoot issues, optimize resource utilization, and make informed decisions about capacity planning and scaling.

The CloudWatch Metrics dashboard offers a powerful and intuitive interface to monitor and analyze the performance metrics of your AWS services. It provides a comprehensive view of key operational data, enabling you to identify trends, detect anomalies, and gain valuable insights into your services' behavior. With its advanced filtering capabilities, you can slice and dice the metrics based on various criteria, such as time range, resource tags, or specific dimensions, allowing you to drill down and isolate specific areas of interest. This level of granular visibility empowers you to proactively address issues, optimize resource utilization, and ensure your AWS services are operating efficiently and effectively.

The AWS services discussed in this book have various metrics that need to be monitored to ensure optimal performance and efficiency. Here's an overview of the monitoring capabilities that CloudWatch offers for each service:

AWS Lambda

- **Invocation metrics**: CloudWatch collects metrics like invocation count, duration, errors, throttles, and concurrent executions for Lambda functions.
- **Asynchronous invocation metrics**: For asynchronous invocations, CloudWatch tracks metrics like queue age, record age, and destination delivery failures.

Amazon API Gateway

- **API call metrics**: CloudWatch captures metrics like API call count, latency, integration latency, cache hit count, and cache miss count for API Gateway APIs.
- **Stage-level metrics**: Metrics like data latency, data processed, and data received/sent are available at the stage level.

Amazon SQS

- **Queue metrics**: CloudWatch monitors metrics like approximate number of messages, message sent/received counts, message age, and queue age for SQS queues.
- **Queue delay metrics**: Metrics like oldest message age, number of delayed messages, and queue delay health are available.

Amazon SNS

- **Topic metrics**: CloudWatch collects metrics like the number of notifications published, delivered, failed, and filtered for SNS topics.
- **Subscription metrics**: Metrics like number of confirmation failures, deliveries, and notification failures are available at the subscription level.

Amazon EventBridge

- **Event bus metrics**: CloudWatch monitors metrics like the number of events matched, rules triggered, deliveries failed, and retry attempts for EventBridge event buses.

- **Rule metrics**: Metrics like the number of events matched, deliveries failed, and retry attempts are available at the rule level.

AWS Step Functions

- **State machine metrics**: CloudWatch tracks metrics like execution time, billed duration, throttled/failed executions, and consumed provisioned concurrency for Step Functions state machines.
- **Activity metrics**: Metrics like activity schedule/start/succeed/fail counts and activity duration are available.

Amazon Kinesis

- **Kinesis Data Streams metrics**: CloudWatch monitors metrics like incoming/outgoing byte/record counts, iterator age, data age, and shard-level metrics for Kinesis Data Streams.
- **Data Firehose metrics**: Metrics like incoming/outgoing byte/record counts, delivery failures, and transform failures are available for Data Firehose.

In addition to these service-specific metrics, CloudWatch also provides the ability to set alarms, create custom metrics, and visualize the data using CloudWatch Logs and CloudWatch Dashboards. This allows for comprehensive monitoring and alerting across your AWS resources and services.

While we won't delve into all the metrics for every service, it's crucial to monitor all the services within your systems for optimal performance. In the upcoming section, we'll explore how to leverage CloudWatch Metrics to monitor Lambda functions effectively.

Exploring the CloudWatch Metrics for Lambda

With CloudWatch Metrics, you can monitor key aspects of your Lambda functions, such as invocation counts, duration, errors, throttles, and concurrent executions. These metrics help you understand the load on your functions, identify performance bottlenecks, and detect potential issues before they escalate. Additionally, CloudWatch Metrics can be used to set up alarms and trigger notifications when specific thresholds are breached, allowing you to proactively respond to potential issues. By leveraging CloudWatch Metrics, you can gain visibility into your Lambda functions, optimize their performance, and ensure they are running smoothly and efficiently.

To effectively monitor and optimize Lambda functions, Lambda provides a set of essential metrics. Among these, some of the most commonly used are **invocations**, **duration**, **error count** and **success rate**, **throttles**, and **total concurrent executions**. Let's delve into each of these metrics and understand their significance.

- **Invocations**: This metric represents the total number of times a Lambda function has been triggered or invoked. It is a fundamental measure that provides insights into the overall usage and load on a particular function.

- **Duration**: The duration metric measures the execution time of a Lambda function, typically measured in milliseconds. It tracks the time elapsed from when the function starts executing until it completes or times out

- **Error count and success rate**: These two metrics go hand-in-hand. Error count represents the number of times a Lambda function failed to execute successfully due to various reasons, such as coding errors, resource limitations, or external dependencies. Success rate, on the other hand, indicates the percentage of successful invocations out of the total invocations.

- **Throttles**: Throttles occur when a Lambda function exceeds the configured concurrency limit or the account-level concurrent execution limit. When a function is throttled, subsequent invocations are temporarily rejected until resources become available.

- **Total concurrent executions**: This metric represents the number of Lambda function instances that are currently running concurrently. It is a valuable indicator of the overall load on your Lambda functions and can help you optimize resource allocation and cost management.

These metrics provide valuable insights into the performance, reliability, and scalability of your AWS Lambda functions. By consistently monitoring and analyzing these metrics, you can proactively identify and address issues, optimize resource utilization, and ensure that your serverless applications are running efficiently and cost-effectively.

Viewing the CloudWatch Metrics from the CloudWatch Dashboard

In this section, we will explore how to view the CloudWatch Metrics for the **NewOrder** service, which is a Lambda function we created for the *Ordering Platform* in *Chapter 3, Messaging with Amazon SQS and Amazon SNS*. To be able to analyze some metrics, a load test was performed by sending 30 concurrent requests to the *Ordering Platform* API over a 5-minute period, utilizing *Artillery*, a load testing tool covered in *Chapter 7, Testing Event-Driven Systems*.

To monitor the **NewOrder** Lambda function during this 5-minute duration:

1. From the list of services, search for **cloudwatch** and go to the **CloudWatch** dashboard.

2. From the **CloudWatch** dashboard, on the left sidebar click **All metrics** under the **Metrics** category.

3. From the *Browse* tab, select `Lambda` and then click on `By Function Name`.

4. Search for the `new-order-service`, select all the metrics and then select the `Graphed metrics` tab.

5. Change the period for all the metrics to 1 minute and the statistic to `sum` or `average` depending on the metrics, as shown in *Figure 8.2*.

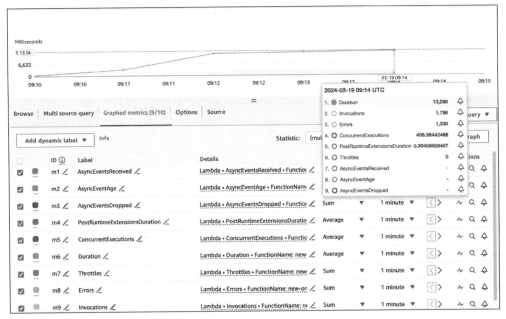

Figure 8.2: *Viewing the metrics of a Lambda function from the CloudWatch metrics dashboard*

The `CloudWatch` dashboard provides a comprehensive view of all metrics in a single, unified graph, offering a more holistic perspective compared to the Lambda dashboard's specialized focus, which we will cover in the next section. With CloudWatch, you have the flexibility to filter metrics based on various statistical parameters, such as sum, average, minimum, maximum, and more. Additionally, you can define the interval period for data aggregation, ranging from a granular 1-second resolution up to a broad 30-day window. This level of customization allows you to tailor the data visualization to your specific monitoring needs, enabling you to gain deeper insights into your application's performance and operational health.

Viewing the CloudWatch Metrics from Lambda Dashboard

The `Lambda` dashboard offers a user-friendly interface to monitor the performance metrics of your Lambda functions. However, its filtering capabilities are somewhat limited. To access the metrics for the **NewOrder** service, navigate to the **Lambda** dashboard specific to the **NewOrder** service, and then select the **Monitor** tab.

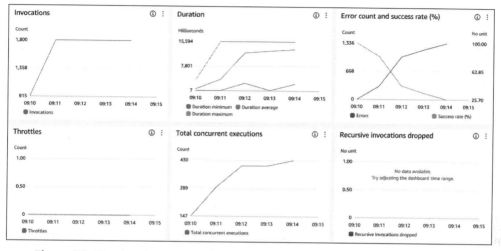

Figure 8.3: *Viewing the metrics of a Lambda function from the Lambda dashboard*

The **Lambda** dashboard presents separate graphs for various metrics, such as **invocations**, **duration**, and others, as illustrated in *Figure 8.3*. However, if you need to monitor all the functions of your system on a single dashboard, the **Lambda** dashboard may not be the ideal solution, as it only displays the dashboard for a specific function. Nevertheless, it offers a convenient way to quickly glance at the metrics of an individual Lambda function.

Advanced Filtering with CloudWatch Metrics

Amazon CloudWatch Metrics dashboard provides several filtering options for metrics. You can filter metrics based on various criteria, including:

- **Metric name**: You can filter metrics by their name, which can be useful when you have multiple metrics associated with a specific AWS resource or service.

- **Namespace**: CloudWatch organizes metrics into namespaces, which are typically related to specific AWS services (Lambda, ApiGateway, SQS, SNS, and more). You can filter metrics by their namespace.

- **Dimensions**: Dimensions are name-value pairs that provide additional context for metrics. For example, for Lambda metrics, the dimensions include **Function Name** and **Resource (ARN)**. You can filter metrics by specifying values for specific dimensions.

- **Metric value**: You can filter metrics based on their numeric values, allowing you to focus on metrics that exceed or fall below certain thresholds.

- **Metric statistic**: CloudWatch calculates statistical values (average, maximum, minimum, sum, and more) for metrics over specified periods. You can filter metrics based on these statistics.

- **Period**: Metrics are reported at specific periods, such as every minute or every five minutes. You can filter metrics based on the reporting period.

- **Time range**: You can specify a time range to filter metrics for a specific period, allowing you to analyze historical data or focus on recent metrics.

- **Resource**: Many AWS services allow you to filter metrics by the specific resource (for example, Lambda function, SQS queue, and more) associated with the metric.

These filtering options can be combined to narrow down the metrics you want to analyze or visualize in CloudWatch Dashboards, which we will explore in an upcoming section, or used for setting up alarms and triggers for automated actions.

Detailed Monitoring with Lambda Insights

AWS offers an advanced monitoring feature called **Insights**, which enhances the capabilities of CloudWatch Metrics for some AWS services. One such service is Lambda which provides `Lambda Insights`. With Lambda Insights, you get a comprehensive view of your Lambda function's performance, enabling you to identify and resolve issues more efficiently.

While CloudWatch Metrics for Lambda provides basic metrics such as execution time, invocations, and errors, Lambda Insights takes monitoring to a whole new level. It provides a wealth of additional metrics and insights. With `Lambda Insights`, you gain access to detailed metrics such as CPU time, memory utilization, and disk and network usage, enabling you to proactively identify and address potential bottlenecks or resource constraints. Additionally, it captures and aggregates diagnostic information like cold starts, equipping you with the necessary data to isolate and resolve issues swiftly.

To harness the full potential of `Lambda Insights`, you need to enable it through the Lambda Insights enhanced monitoring configuration. This process can be completed in a few simple steps:

1. From the `Lambda` dashboard of your Lambda function, go to the `Configuration` tab and click on `Monitoring and operations tools` from the left sidebar.

2. In the `Monitoring and operations tools` section, click on `Edit` next to `Additional monitoring tools`.

3. Enable the `Enhanced monitoring` option under the `CloudWatch Lambda Insights` section and click `Save` to apply the changes.

Once enabled, you will notice that a new Lambda layer with version ARN

`arn:aws:lambda:eu-central-1:580247275435:layer:LambdaInsightsExtensi`
`on:49` is added to your Lambda function which is responsible for sending the new metrics to CloudWatch, as shown in *Figure 8.4*.

Figure 8.4: *Lambda Insights adds a new layer to a Lambda function*

A **Lambda layer** is a way to package libraries, custom runtimes, data, or configuration files that can be used by multiple Lambda functions. It allows you to centralize and share code and data across different functions, reducing code duplication and making it easier to manage and update dependencies. Lambda layers are zip archives that contain libraries or other dependencies, and they can be versioned and shared between functions within the same AWS account or across different accounts.

Lambda Insights will start gathering and displaying advanced monitoring information, enabling you to gain a deeper understanding of your Lambda functions' performance. *Figure 8.5* illustrates the Lambda Insights view accessible from the **Lambda** dashboard.

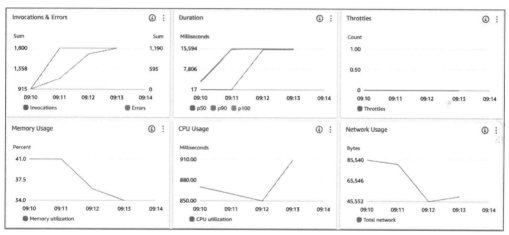

Figure 8.5: *Viewing the Lambda Insights metrics from the Lambda dashboard*

Alternatively, you can access the same metrics through the CloudWatch Metrics dashboard, similar to the previous example, but under a dedicated namespace called **Lambda Insights**.

Proactive Monitoring with Amazon CloudWatch Alarms

CloudWatch Alarms is a powerful tool that allows you to define thresholds for specific metrics associated with your AWS resources. These alarms continuously monitor the metrics and trigger actions when the defined thresholds are breached. By setting up appropriate alarms, you can stay informed about potential issues, mitigate risks, and take corrective actions before they escalate into more significant problems.

Here are some key benefits of using CloudWatch Alarms:

- **Proactive monitoring**: CloudWatch Alarms provide real-time visibility into the health and performance of your AWS resources. By monitoring critical metrics, such as CPU utilization, network traffic, and disk space, you can detect anomalies or potential issues before they impact your applications or services.

- **Automated responses**: CloudWatch Alarms can be configured to automatically trigger actions when specific thresholds are met. These actions can include sending notifications to designated recipients (e.g., via email, or SMS), or executing custom remediation workflows using AWS Lambda functions.

- **Cost optimization**: By monitoring resource utilization and setting appropriate alarms, you can identify underutilized or overprovisioned resources. This information can help you optimize your resource allocation and potentially reduce costs by scaling down or terminating unnecessary resources.

- **Compliance and auditing**: CloudWatch Alarms can assist in meeting compliance requirements by providing visibility into resource performance and alerting you when specific metrics deviate from expected ranges or thresholds.

Setting up CloudWatch Alarms is straightforward and can be done through the AWS Management console, AWS Command Line Interface (CLI), or programmatically using AWS SDKs. You can create alarms based on a wide range of metrics, including those provided by AWS services or custom metrics that you define.

To get started with CloudWatch Alarms, you need to identify the relevant metrics and resources you want to monitor. Then, you can define thresholds and configure actions to be taken when those thresholds are breached. CloudWatch Alarms support various statistic types, such as minimum, maximum, average, and sum, allowing you to tailor the alarm conditions to your specific monitoring requirements.

Note: *You don't have to set up CloudWatch Alarms for all metrics for the serverless services that we covered in the book. Setting CloudWatch Alarms is optional and depends on your specific monitoring requirements and the importance of certain metrics for your application. Here are some general guidelines:*

- **AWS Lambda**: *Consider setting alarms for metrics like **Errors**, **Throttles**, and **ConcurrentExecutions** if you want to monitor for issues like function errors, throttling, and concurrency limits.*

- **Amazon API Gateway**: *Alarms for metrics like **4XXError**, **5XXError**, **IntegrationLatency**, and **CacheHitCount** can be useful to monitor for client errors, server errors, backend integration latency, and caching effectiveness.*

- **Amazon SQS**: *ApproximateAgeOfOldestMessage*, *ApproximateNumberOf MessagesVisible*, and *ApproximateNumberOfMessagesNotVisible* can help monitor for message backlogs and queue health.

- **Amazon SNS**: Alarms for *NumberOfNotificationsFailed* and *NumberOfNotificationsSuccessful* can be useful to monitor for delivery failures and successes.

- **Amazon EventBridge**: Alarms for *FailedInvocations* and *MatchedEvents* can help monitor delivery failures and event matching issues.

- **AWS Step Functions**: Alarms for *ExecutionThrottled*, *ExecutionsTimedOut*, and *ExecutionsFailed* can help monitor for throttling issues, timeouts, and execution failures.

- **Amazon Kinesis**: Alarms for *GetRecords.IteratorAgeMilliseconds*, *PutRecord.Success*, and *GetRecords.Success* can help monitor for data processing delays, successful record puts, and successful record gets.

The specific metrics and thresholds to set alarms for depend on your application's requirements, performance expectations, and the criticality of the services involved. It's generally a good practice to start with monitoring the most critical metrics and then expand as needed based on your observations and monitoring needs.

Configuring a CloudWatch Alarm

In this section, we will explore the process of configuring a CloudWatch alarm that will trigger when the **Ordering Platform** API encounters server errors (**HTTP status 5XX**):

1. From the CloudWatch dashboard, on the left sidebar click **All alarms** under the **Alarms** category and then click on the **Create alarm** button.

2. In *Step 1 Specify metric and conditions*, click **Select metric**. From the **Browse** tab, select **APIGateway** and then click on **By Api Name**. Search for the **ordering-platform-api**, select the **5XXError** and click **Select metric**. Select **Sum** for the **Statistic**, **5 minutes** for the **Period** and **Greater than 10** for the **Condition**, as shown in *Figure 8.6*. Click **Next**.

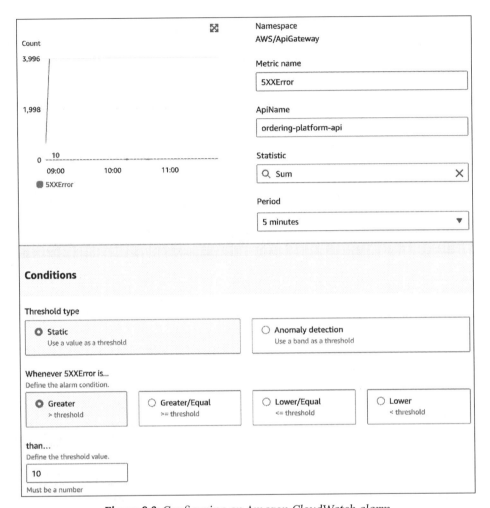

Figure 8.6: *Configuring an Amazon CloudWatch alarm*

3. In *Step 2 Configure actions*, select **In alarm**, select **Create new topic** and enter your email to the **Email endpoints that will receive the notification**. Click **Create topic** and click **Next**.

4. In *Step 3 Add name and description*, enter **Ordering Platform API 5XX errors** for the **Alarm name**. Click **Next**.

5. In *Step 4 Preview and create*, review your alarm and click **Create alarm**.

Upon creating the alarm, you will initially encounter an **Insufficient data** state. This indicates that the alarm has not yet gathered the required data to trigger alerts for potential errors. The configured alarm is designed to notify you via email if the **Ordering Platform API** generates more than 10 5XX errors within a 5-minute window.

Visualizing Cloud Resources with Amazon CloudWatch Dashboards

Amazon CloudWatch Dashboards provide a powerful solution for AWS users to gain real-time insights into their cloud infrastructure and applications. Next, we will explore the benefits and features of CloudWatch dashboards, offering a comprehensive overview of this essential monitoring tool.

- **Centralized monitoring hub**: CloudWatch Dashboards act as a centralized hub for monitoring various AWS resources and services. With a single dashboard, you can consolidate metrics, logs, and alarms from multiple sources, including Amazon S3 buckets, AWS Lambda functions, and more. This consolidated view enables you to quickly identify issues, track performance, and make informed decisions based on comprehensive data.

- **Customizable visualization**: One of the key strengths of CloudWatch Dashboards is their flexibility and customization capabilities. You can create personalized dashboards tailored to your specific monitoring needs by selecting from a wide range of widgets and visualizations. These include line graphs, stacked area charts, pie charts, and more. Additionally, you can configure metrics, thresholds, and alarms to receive timely notifications and alerts when predefined conditions are met.

- **Collaboration and sharing**: CloudWatch Dashboards facilitate collaboration and knowledge sharing within teams and organizations. You can easily share dashboards with specific users or groups, enabling seamless communication and streamlining troubleshooting processes. This feature is particularly useful for DevOps teams, ensuring everyone has access to the same monitoring data and insights.

- **Cost optimization**: By monitoring resource utilization and performance metrics through CloudWatch Dashboards, you can identify potential areas for cost optimization. For instance, you can track underutilized resources, detect performance bottlenecks, and make informed decisions about scaling resources up or down based on real-time data. This ultimately helps you manage costs more effectively while maintaining optimal performance.

In the next section, we will explore the process of setting up a CloudWatch Dashboard, which enables you to monitor various AWS services and their associated metrics.

Creating a CloudWatch Dashboard

Creating a comprehensive CloudWatch dashboard that provides insightful visualizations and real-time monitoring of your AWS resources is a relatively straightforward process. The CloudWatch console offers an intuitive interface that empowers you to seamlessly configure and customize dashboards tailored to your specific requirements. With a few clicks, you can effortlessly add widgets that display metrics, logs, and alarms, enabling you to gain valuable insights into the performance, health, and operational status of your AWS services. Additionally, CloudWatch's flexible dashboard design allows you to organize and arrange these widgets in a manner that facilitates efficient monitoring and troubleshooting, ensuring you have a centralized and informative view of your entire AWS ecosystem.

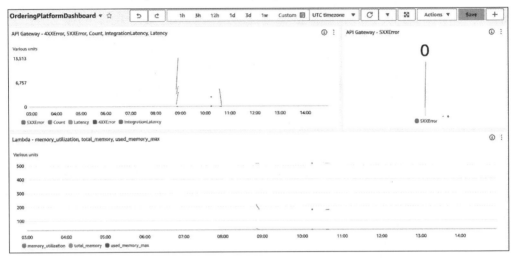

Figure 8.7: *Viewing several widgets in Amazon CloudWatch Dashboard*

The CloudWatch dashboard named **OrderingPlatformDashboard** displayed in *Figure 8.7* consists of three widgets. The top-left widget presents various metrics related to the *Ordering Platform* API, including **4XXError**, **5XXError**, **Count**, **IntegrationLatency**, and **Latency**. The top-right widget illustrates the total number of 5XX*Errors* that occurred within the last 12 hours. Lastly, the bottom widget depicts the *Lambda Insights* metrics for the **NewOrder** Lambda function.

Tracking Account Activity with AWS CloudTrail

AWS CloudTrail is a logging service that captures and records all API calls made within your AWS account. This includes calls made through the AWS Management console, AWS Command Line Interface (CLI), AWS SDKs, and higher-level AWS services.

CloudTrail captures information such as the identity of the API caller, the time of the API call, the source IP address, the request parameters, and the response elements returned by the AWS service. This valuable data can be used for various purposes, including security analysis, operational troubleshooting, and compliance auditing.

CloudTrail captures three main types of events:

- **Management events**: Management events are actions performed by users, services, or applications within the AWS Management Console, AWS Command Line Interface (CLI), or AWS SDKs. These events include operations such as creating or modifying AWS Lambda functions or Amazon S3 buckets and configuring AWS Identity and Access Management (IAM) roles and policies.

- **Data events**: Data events capture activity related to data resources within your AWS environment. These events include operations such as accessing or modifying objects in Amazon S3 buckets, inserting or modifying data in Amazon DynamoDB tables, and executing AWS Lambda functions.

- **Insight events**: Insight events are automatically detected by AWS CloudTrail and provide insights into potential security or operational issues within your AWS environment. These events include activities such as failed API calls due to unauthorized access attempts, unauthorized changes to resources, or potential data leaks.

CloudTrail plays a crucial role in monitoring and auditing your AWS environment. Here are some key benefits of using CloudTrail:

- **Security and compliance**: CloudTrail provides a detailed audit trail of all API activities, allowing you to monitor and investigate any unauthorized or suspicious activity within your AWS account. This is essential for meeting compliance requirements and ensuring the security of your cloud resources.

- **Operational troubleshooting**: With CloudTrail, you can easily track and review API calls made by your applications, services, or users. This information can be invaluable when troubleshooting issues or tracing the root cause of operational problems.

- **Resource change monitoring**: CloudTrail tracks changes made to your AWS resources, such as launching or terminating instances, modifying security groups, or creating new IAM users. This visibility helps you monitor and understand changes to your infrastructure, ensuring consistency and preventing unauthorized modifications.

CloudTrail offers two types of trails to cater to different logging and monitoring requirements:

- **CloudTrail Trail:** A trail captures events and activities across all AWS services, including serverless services like Lambda, API Gateway, and Step Functions. The logs are stored in an Amazon S3 bucket that you specify, and you can optionally configure CloudTrail to send log files to Amazon CloudWatch Logs for real-time analysis.

- **CloudTrail Lake Event Data Store**: CloudTrail Lake is a fully managed service that provides a modern and cost-effective way to store, analyze, and query your CloudTrail event data with SQL-based queries on your events.

In the following section, we will explore how to configure a CloudTrail Lake Event Data Store, which offers a user-friendly and convenient approach to analyzing data from the CloudTrail dashboard. To fully harness the capabilities of CloudTrail Trail, it is essential to leverage powerful analytical tools such as Amazon Athena and Amazon QuickSight.

Analyzing a CloudTrail Lake Event Data Store

To get started with CloudTrail Lake Event Data Store, you need to create an event data store:

1. From the list of services, search for **cloudtrail** and go to the **CloudTrail** dashboard.

2. From the CloudTrail dashboard, on the left sidebar click **Event data stores** under the **Lake** category and then click on the **Create event data store** button.

3. In *Step 1 Configure event data store*, enter **ordering-platform-event-data-store** for the **Event data store name** and use the default settings for the remaining options. Click **Next**.

4. In *Step 2 Choose events*, select the **Management events** for the **CloudTrail** *Events* and click **Next**.

5. In *Step 3 Review and create*, review the event data store and click **Create event data store**.

The process of creating an event data store takes a while to complete. However, once the event data store is successfully enabled, you can start your data analysis journey. On the CloudTrail dashboard, you will find the **Query** option in the left sidebar, enabling you to explore the wealth of collected data.

Within the **Query** section, you'll discover a set of pre-written sample queries that can serve as a starting point for your exploration. Alternatively, if you prefer a more customized approach, you have the flexibility to craft your own queries tailored to your specific needs.

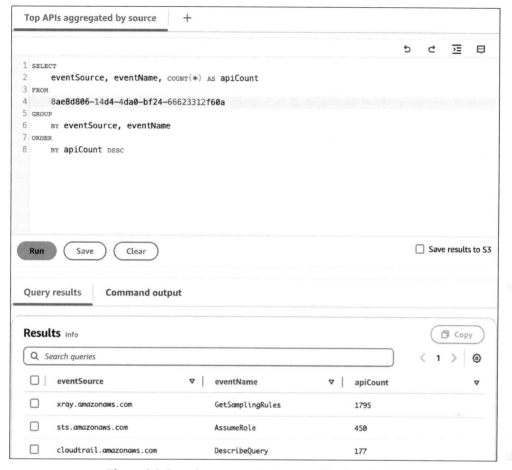

Figure 8.8: Running a query in Amazon CloudTrail Lake

Figure 8.8 depicts the top APIs aggregated by source sample query, showcasing the most frequently used services. Among them, you'll find X-Ray, which retrieves all sampling rules, STS used for assuming roles, and CloudTrail, which allows you to describe and query CloudTrail events.

While these sample queries provide a solid foundation, the true power lies in your ability to construct more advanced and sophisticated queries. By leveraging the rich data available in the event data store, you can conduct comprehensive audits of CloudTrail events, uncovering valuable insights and ensuring compliance with your organization's policies and best practices.

Distributed Tracing with AWS X-Ray

AWS X-Ray is a powerful distributed tracing service that helps you analyze and debug production applications, especially those built on a microservices architecture. With the rise of serverless computing, X-Ray has become an invaluable tool for monitoring and troubleshooting serverless applications.

Serverless services, such as AWS Lambda, remove the need to provision and manage servers, allowing you to focus on writing code. However, this paradigm shift introduces new challenges when it comes to monitoring and debugging applications that span multiple services and resources.

X-Ray addresses these challenges by providing end-to-end tracing capabilities for serverless applications. It collects data about requests as they travel through your application, allowing you to visualize the application's components, identify performance bottlenecks, and trace the root cause of errors and exceptions.

Here's how X-Ray works for serverless services:

1. **Instrumentation**: AWS X-Ray integrates with various AWS services, including Lambda, API Gateway, and AWS Step Functions. This integration enables X-Ray to automatically capture and record data about requests and responses as they pass through these services.

2. **Tracing data**: X-Ray collects and records data such as timing information, and metadata about each request. This data is organized into segments and subsegments, which represent the different components and operations involved in processing a request.

3. **Service map**: The tracing data collected by X-Ray is used to generate a service map, which is a visual representation of your application's architecture. The service map shows the relationships between the various components of your application and the flow of requests between them.

4. **Trace analysis**: X-Ray provides a detailed trace view that allows you to analyze the behavior of individual requests as they move through your application. This view includes timing information, and error messages, enabling you to quickly identify and troubleshoot issues.

5. **Filtering and searching**: X-Ray supports advanced filtering and searching capabilities, allowing you to find specific traces based on criteria such as service name, error code, or response time. This makes it easier to investigate and resolve issues in complex applications.

6. **Integration with other AWS services**: X-Ray integrates with other AWS services, such as AWS CloudWatch and AWS CloudTrail, providing a comprehensive monitoring and logging solution for your serverless applications.

Among the serverless services that we covered throughout the book, AWS Lambda, Amazon API Gateway, and AWS Step Functions support AWS X-Ray for distributed tracing and monitoring. In the upcoming section, we will explore how to enable and view X-Ray traces specifically for API Gateway and Lambda.

X-Ray Traces in API Gateway and Lambda

AWS X-Ray seamlessly integrates with AWS services like API Gateway and Lambda, allowing you to trace requests as they flow through your application's components.

With API Gateway integration, X-Ray captures detailed metrics for each API call, such as latency, integration latency, and any errors that may occur. When you enable X-Ray tracing, API Gateway generates segments for each method execution, containing comprehensive information like start and end times, request and response data, triggered Lambda functions, and other relevant metadata. These traces are conveniently accessible through the AWS X-Ray console, providing a holistic view of your API's performance.

Lambda also natively integrates with X-Ray, offering invaluable insights into function executions. By enabling active tracing for your Lambda functions, X-Ray captures granular data about each invocation, including the invocation source, start and end times, log entries, errors, and downstream calls to other AWS services. You can examine traces for completed executions and even dive into subsegments representing specific parts of your function code, facilitating easy identification and troubleshooting of performance bottlenecks or issues.

Note: *In the context of AWS X-Ray, a segment represents a logical unit of work that is executed within a component or service. It typically corresponds to a single request or operation. Examples of segments include an API Gateway method execution, a Lambda function invocation or a database query execution.*

A subsegment, on the other hand, is a smaller unit of work within a segment. It represents a specific part or step within the overall execution of the segment. Subsegments can be used to break down a segment into more granular components, providing additional visibility and insights. Examples of subsegments include a specific part of a Lambda function's code execution, a downstream service call made by a Lambda function or API Gateway integration, a database query within a larger database transaction.

Viewing the X-Ray Traces for API Gateway and Lambda

In this section, we will examine the X-Ray traces sent to the `Ordering Platform` we developed in *Chapter 3, Messaging with Amazon SQS and Amazon SNS*. We will observe the complete trace from the *Ordering Platform API* to the `NewOrder` Lambda function.

X-Ray is not activated by default in API Gateway and Lambda. To enable it for API Gateway, you need to activate it for a stage. Let's go through the steps to enable it for the production stage of the *Ordering Platform API*:

1. From the **API Gateway** dashboard of the **OrderingPlatform API**, click on **Stages** from the left sidebar.

2. Select the **prod** stage and click on **Edit** next to the **Logs and tracing** section.

3. Select the **X-Ray tracing** option and click **Save changes**.

Just like configuring CloudWatch logs, you don't need to redeploy your API when enabling X-Ray. Enabling X-Ray for Lambda functions is also a fairly straightforward process:

1. From the **Lambda** dashboard of the **NewOrder** service, go to the **Configuration** tab and click on **Monitoring and operations tools** from the left sidebar.

2. In the **Monitoring and operations tools** section, click on **Edit** next to **Additional monitoring tools**.

3. Enable the **AWS X-Ray Active tracing** option and click **Save** to apply the changes.

It's time to send requests to the **Ordering Platform API** and examine the X-Ray traces. Navigate to the **X-Ray dashboard** within the AWS Management console, which is accessible through the CloudWatch dashboard.

In the X-Ray dashboard, you will notice two nodes representing the **NewOrder** Lambda function and one node for the **Ordering Platform API**, as illustrated in *Figure* 8.9. The two nodes for Lambda represent the Lambda context, which provides runtime information about the Lambda function's execution environment, and the actual Lambda function itself.

Figure 8.9: *Viewing a trace from Amazon API Gateway and AWS Lambda in AWS X-Ray*

As you scroll further down, you'll notice individual traces corresponding to each request, as shown in *Figure 8.10*.

ID	Trace status	Timestamp	Response code	Response Time	Duration
...53cc02d95a60b1524036d8a1	⊗ Fault (5xx)	21.1min (2024-03-29 10:57:10)	502	15.573s	15.573s
...18fe34ac771b0481536d6de1	⊗ Fault (5xx)	21.1min (2024-03-29 10:57:09)	502	15.566s	15.566s
...774b9b61595cfa0041e95c22	⊘ OK	21.1min (2024-03-29 10:57:09)	201	4.645s	4.645s
...10eb17614196255d491e8d20	⊘ OK	21.1min (2024-03-29 10:57:08)	201	8.958s	8.976s

Figure 8.10: *Showing detailed information of all the AWS X-Ray traces*

Some of the traces have failed, and we need to understand the reasons behind those failures. To gain insights, it would be beneficial to start by examining a successful trace and studying its details. By doing so, we can establish a baseline understanding of what constitutes a successful execution and identify any potential deviations or anomalies in the failed traces.

Figure 8.11: *Showing the segments timeline of a successful AWS X-Ray trace*

The request flow, which was successfully completed, is illustrated in *Figure 8.11*. A client initiated the request by calling the API Gateway, which was then integrated with Lambda. The overall response time for the request was 4.64 seconds. Within this duration, Lambda took 1.73 seconds for initialization, 2.91 seconds for invocation, and no time (0 seconds) for overhead operations.

Let's delve deeper into the significance of those metrics in the context of Lambda:

- **Initialization**: This represents the time it takes for AWS Lambda to initialize and prepare the execution environment for running your Lambda function. It includes tasks like provisioning the necessary resources, loading the function code, and setting up the runtime environment.

- **Invocation**: This is the time it takes for AWS Lambda to execute your function code, starting from when the function handler is invoked until the function completes its execution. It measures the actual runtime of your Lambda function, excluding the initialization time.

- **Overhead**: This time represents the additional overhead incurred by AWS Lambda for executing your function beyond the initialization and invocation times. It includes tasks like setting up the execution environment, loading input event data, preparing the response, and any other internal operations performed by the Lambda service. The overhead time is typically small compared to the initialization and invocation times but can vary depending on the size and complexity of your function.

Let's see an example of a failed trace now. If at least one error occurs, the trace will be flagged as failed, as illustrated in *Figure 8.12*.

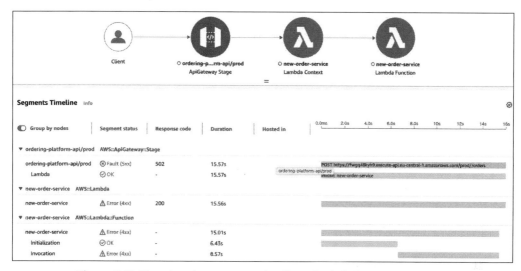

Figure 8.12: *Showing the segments timeline of a failed AWS X-Ray trace*

X-Ray seamlessly integrates with CloudWatch, enabling you to delve into the logs section, if you scroll further down, and pinpoint the root cause of any errors. In our particular scenario, the error was attributed to the 15-second timeout constraint we had imposed on the Lambda function:

```
Task timed out after 15.53 seconds
```

The X-Ray trace's logs section displays not only the logs generated by the Lambda function but also the execution logs for API Gateway, which were covered in a previous section.

Third-Party Observability Partners

While AWS offers a suite of cloud-native observability solutions, as we saw in this chapter, it's important to recognize that there are additional options available for organizations seeking another more comprehensive approach. One such option is the combination of Amazon Kinesis Data Streams and Amazon Data Firehose, which provide a powerful and flexible way to stream logs and data to various third-party observability partners.

As we saw in *Chapter 6, Event Streaming with Amazon Kinesis*, Amazon Kinesis Data Streams is a scalable and durable real-time data streaming service that can continuously capture and store data from hundreds of thousands of sources, such as website clickstreams, IoT sensors, and application logs. With its ability to handle high-throughput data streams, Kinesis Data Streams ensures that your data is ingested and processed efficiently, even during periods of high traffic or bursts.

Amazon Data Firehose, on the other hand, is a fully managed service that reliably captures, transforms, and loads streaming data into compatible destinations. By integrating with Kinesis Data Streams, Data Firehose can seamlessly route your log and event data to a variety of AWS observability partners, including Amazon OpenSearch, Datadog, Elastic, and other observability services.

This integration opens up a world of possibilities for organizations seeking advanced observability capabilities. For instance, *Amazon OpenSearch*, a secure, open-source log analytics service, provides powerful search and analytics capabilities, enabling you to gain deep insights into your application and infrastructure logs. *Datadog*, another popular observability partner, offers a comprehensive monitoring platform that combines metrics, traces, and logs, providing a unified view of your entire stack.

Similarly, *Elastic* provides a powerful and flexible solution for log management, search, and analysis. By leveraging these observability partners, organizations can benefit from their advanced features, such as customizable dashboards, alerting capabilities, anomaly detection, and more.

The beauty of this approach lies in its flexibility and scalability. You can choose the observability partner that best suits their needs, whether it's seamless integration with their existing tools, advanced analytics capabilities, or specific industry-tailored features. Additionally, by leveraging Kinesis Data Streams and Data Firehose, you can easily scale their observability efforts as their data volumes and requirements grow.

Conclusion

This chapter provided a comprehensive overview of monitoring and troubleshooting in AWS. It covered the essential tools and services that AWS offers for logging, monitoring, alerting, auditing, and tracing. By leveraging these powerful capabilities, you can gain deep insights into your AWS resources, applications, and services, enabling you to proactively identify and resolve issues, ensure compliance, and optimize performance.

With Amazon CloudWatch Logs, you can centralize and analyze log data from various sources, while CloudWatch Metrics allows you to collect and visualize metrics for real-time monitoring. CloudWatch Alarms help you stay ahead of potential issues by triggering notifications based on predefined thresholds. AWS CloudTrail provides valuable auditing capabilities by recording API calls and events, ensuring compliance and security.

Additionally, this chapter explored how to create customized dashboards with CloudWatch Dashboards, enabling you to visualize and monitor your AWS environment in a unified view. For distributed applications, AWS X-Ray offers powerful tracing capabilities, allowing you to analyze and debug requests as they travel through your application components.

Finally, the chapter   highlighted the integration possibilities with third-party observability partners, enabling you to leverage external monitoring and observability tools alongside AWS services.

By mastering the concepts and tools covered in this chapter, you will be well-equipped to effectively monitor, troubleshoot, and maintain your AWS-based applications and services, ensuring optimal performance, reliability, and compliance with industry standards.

In the upcoming chapter, we will explore various optimization techniques and best practices tailored for event-driven microservices within the AWS environment. We will cover how to optimize and reduce the cold starts of our Lambda functions, how to maximize the requests our microservices can handle through API Gateway, long polling versus short polling for Amazon SQS, and more. Furthermore, we will delve into strategies to optimize the cost-effectiveness of our architectures and address best practices regarding the security of our services, ensuring robust safeguards and adherence to industry standards.

CHAPTER 9

Optimizations and Best Practices for Production

Introduction

This chapter starts by providing an overview of AWS Service Quotas and the importance of understanding the limits imposed on various AWS services to ensure optimal resource utilization and prevent throttling. It will then delve into the world of AWS Serverless Services, exploring the benefits of event-driven architectures and the seamless scaling capabilities offered by services such as AWS Lambda. Optimizing AWS Lambda is covered in-depth, with techniques for reducing cold starts, optimizing memory allocation, and leveraging concurrent executions. We will explore Asynchronous Invocation and Batching, showcasing strategies for improving performance and cost-effectiveness by decoupling tasks and processing them in batches. Fault Tolerance and Reliability are discussed, emphasizing the importance of designing resilient systems that can withstand failures and recover gracefully. The concept of Idempotency will be introduced, highlighting its significance in ensuring consistent and predictable outcomes, especially in distributed systems. Caching, Data Partitioning, and Parallel Processing are explored as techniques for enhancing performance and scalability, enabling efficient data access and enabling concurrent processing of large workloads. We will also cover Security and Access Control, emphasizing the need for robust access management, encryption, and compliance with industry standards and best practices. Finally, the chapter emphasizes the importance of Infrastructure as Code (IaC), discussing how it streamlines provisioning, configuration management, and promotes consistency across environments. By the end of this chapter, you will have a comprehensive understanding of key architectural patterns, optimization techniques, and best practices for building scalable, resilient, and secure event-driven microservices in AWS.

Structure

In this chapter, we will discuss the following topics:

- Introduction to Optimizations
- Understanding AWS Service Quotas
- Leverage AWS Serverless Services
- Optimizing AWS Lambda
- Implement Asynchronous Invocation and Batching
- Fault Tolerance and Reliability
- Design for Idempotency
- Caching, Data Partitioning, and Parallel Processing
- Security and Access Control
- Use Infrastructure as Code (IaC)

Introduction to Optimizations

Ensuring optimal performance and cost-effectiveness for your event-driven services is crucial before deploying them into a production environment. By optimizing your architectures, you can achieve improved performance and reduced operational costs for your AWS infrastructure. This chapter will explore various techniques to streamline your architectures, empowering you to unlock their full potential.

Optimizing your architecture is an ongoing journey, requiring continuous evaluation and refinement. As your business evolves and new technologies emerge, it's essential to proactively seek opportunities for optimization. Embracing this mindset will enable you to consistently deliver superior performance, scalability, and cost-efficiency, ensuring your event-driven services remain aligned with your ever-changing business requirements.

Through this chapter, you will gain insights into proven strategies and best practices that will equip you with the knowledge and tools necessary to optimize your architectures effectively. Whether it's leveraging advanced AWS serverless services, implementing caching mechanisms, or employing asynchronous invocation and batching, you will discover a wealth of techniques tailored to enhance the performance, resilience, and cost-effectiveness of your event-driven services.

Understanding AWS Service Quotas

AWS offers various services with predefined resource consumption limits, known as **quotas**. These quotas are designed to protect the shared infrastructure and ensure fair usage across all customers. Understanding and effectively managing these quotas is crucial to avoid potential service disruptions or performance issues.

The quotas vary based on the specific AWS service and the region where you operate. For example, the default quota for the request rate in API Gateway is 10,000 requests per second across all APIs within a single AWS account and region. If your application requires a higher request rate, you can submit a quota increase request through the AWS Support Center. AWS evaluates these requests based on your usage patterns and other factors to determine if an increase is warranted. Monitoring your service usage against the applicable quotas and requesting timely increases when your workload demands exceed the current limits is essential.

In addition to service-specific quotas, AWS also enforces account-level quotas that apply across all services within a single AWS account. These account-level quotas include limits on the number of AWS resources you can create and the amount of data transfer you can utilize. Managing these account-level quotas is crucial for maintaining the overall health and performance of your AWS environment.

It is important to note that quotas are not intended to permanently limit your usage. AWS provides mechanisms to request quota increases, which are typically granted based on your usage patterns and requirements. By proactively monitoring and managing your AWS quotas, you can ensure that your applications and services run smoothly without encountering unexpected limitations or service disruptions.

Leverage AWS Serverless Services

AWS serverless services such as AWS Lambda, Amazon API Gateway, Amazon SQS, Amazon EventBridge, and so on, offer numerous benefits for building event-driven microservices. These services help reduce operational overhead and automatically scale based on demand, making them an attractive choice for modern application development.

With serverless services like AWS Lambda, you don't have to provision or manage any servers. AWS handles the underlying infrastructure, operating system, and runtime environment, allowing you to focus solely on writing and deploying your code. Serverless services automatically scale based on incoming traffic or events. You don't need to worry about capacity planning, load balancing, or scaling infrastructure manually. AWS handles the scaling seamlessly, ensuring your application can handle bursts of traffic or high concurrency without any manual intervention.

Serverless services follow a pay-per-use pricing model, meaning you only pay for the actual compute time or resources consumed by your functions or APIs. This can lead to significant cost savings compared to traditional server-based architectures, especially for applications with unpredictable or bursty traffic patterns. AWS Lambda is designed to run in response to events or triggers, making it well-suited for building event-driven microservices. It can be triggered by various AWS services like Amazon API Gateway, Amazon S3, Amazon DynamoDB, Amazon Kinesis, and more, enabling you to build loosely coupled, highly scalable, and reactive systems.

With serverless services, you don't have to worry about tasks like server provisioning, patching, operating system updates, or capacity planning. AWS handles all the underlying infrastructure and operational tasks, allowing you to focus on writing and deploying your application code. AWS Lambda and API Gateway support rapid deployment and iteration cycles. You can deploy new versions of your functions or update your APIs with minimal effort, enabling faster time-to-market and easier experimentation.

AWS serverless services are designed to be highly available and fault-tolerant. For example, AWS Lambda automatically distributes your functions across multiple Availability Zones within a region, ensuring high availability and fault tolerance.

While serverless services offer numerous benefits, they may not be suitable for all workloads, such as long-running tasks or those requiring persistent connections. Long-running tasks refer to processes that take an extended period of time to complete, often longer than the maximum execution time allowed by serverless services. In the case of AWS Lambda, functions have a maximum execution time of 15 minutes. If your task exceeds this limit, it will be terminated. Long-running tasks may include data processing pipelines, machine learning model training, or any other compute-intensive operation that requires a significant amount of time to finish.

Persistent connections, on the other hand, are necessary for scenarios like real-time communication, live streaming, or long-lived connections with clients or other services. AWS Lambda, by itself, is not designed to handle persistent connections because it follows a request-response model, where the function is invoked, processes the request, and returns a response before terminating. To enable persistent connections in a serverless architecture, you need to use Amazon API Gateway with its WebSocket support.

Optimizing AWS Lambda

While Lambda provides a convenient and scalable way to run your applications, optimizing its performance and cost efficiency is crucial, especially for applications with high traffic or complex workloads. Before we explore how to optimize Lambda functions let's first understand how Lambda works under the hood and how it scales.

Here's a high-level overview of how AWS Lambda execution context works under the hood:

1. **Code upload**: Start by uploading your code to AWS Lambda through the AWS Management Console, AWS CLI, or AWS SDKs.

2. **Container initialization**: When you trigger your Lambda function for the first time, AWS creates a lightweight container and initializes it with your code and the necessary runtime environment. The time taken for this initialization process is known as the *cold start*, and it is one of the areas that requires optimization.

3. **Execution context**: Each Lambda function execution has its own execution context, which includes the function code, runtime environment, and temporary storage for the function execution. This execution context is isolated from other functions' executions.

4. **Concurrent executions**: AWS Lambda automatically scales the number of concurrent executions based on the incoming requests and configured concurrency settings. Each concurrent execution gets its own execution context.

5. **Function execution**: Whenever your Lambda function is triggered, AWS executes your code within a containerized execution environment through the Lambda handler method. The duration it takes for the function to complete its execution is referred to as the *warm start* time which can also be optimized.

6. **Reuse of execution context**: If a new invocation of the same function occurs while the previous execution context is still active (within a certain time period), AWS may reuse the existing execution context instead of creating a new one. This helps improve performance by reducing the overhead of creating new containers and eliminating the need to worry about cold starts.

7. **Frozen state**: AWS freezes the execution context after a function completes its execution. This frozen state is maintained for some time in case another invocation occurs, allowing AWS to reuse the existing execution context.

8. **Cleanup**: If no new invocations occur within a certain period, AWS will terminate the execution context container and reclaim the resources.

It's important to note that AWS Lambda is a managed service, so you don't have direct access to the underlying infrastructure or containers. AWS handles the provisioning, scaling, and management of the execution environment transparently. Next, we will explain how concurrency works within the Lambda service.

Explaining Lambda Concurrency

Concurrency in AWS Lambda refers to the ability to handle multiple requests simultaneously for a given function. When your Lambda function receives a request, Lambda provisions a separate execution environment, essentially spinning up a new instance of your function's code, to process that request concurrently with other incoming requests.

As the number of incoming requests increases, Lambda automatically scales the number of execution environments by allocating additional resources to handle the increased workload, as shown in *Figure 9.1*. This scaling process is seamless and transparent to the developer, ensuring that your function can effectively manage high volumes of concurrent requests.

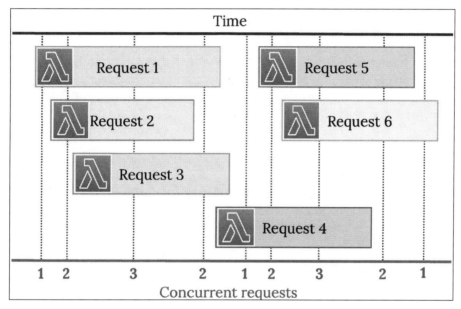

Figure 9.1: *Visualizing how concurrency works for AWS Lambda*

However, it's important to note that AWS Lambda imposes a default concurrency limit of 1,000 *concurrent executions* across all functions within a specific AWS Region for your account. This limit is in place to ensure fair resource allocation and prevent any single account from monopolizing the available compute capacity.

The number of concurrent requests that AWS Lambda can handle is determined by the incoming request rate and the average duration of each request. The formula to calculate concurrency is:

```
Concurrency = (average requests per second) * (average request duration
in seconds)
```

For instance, if you have 300 requests per second, and each request takes an average of 200 milliseconds to complete, then the maximum concurrent requests supported by Lambda would be 60:

```
Concurrency = 300 * 0.2 (seconds) = 60
```

Similarly, if you have 150 requests per second, and each request takes an average of 400 milliseconds to complete, the concurrency would still be 60:

```
Concurrency = 150 * 0.4 (seconds) = 60
```

This implies that by optimizing the request duration of our Lambda function, you can effectively increase the scaling capacity. In other words, if you can reduce the average execution time of our Lambda function, it will allow Lambda to handle a higher number of concurrent requests for the same incoming request rate. Next, we will explore some best practices and techniques for optimizing AWS Lambda.

Lambda Performance and Cost Optimizations

When you optimize AWS Lambda functions, you enhance the overall performance by reducing the latency associated with *cold starts* and *warm starts*. This optimization allows the functions to handle a higher volume of concurrent executions per second, leading to improved scalability and responsiveness.

AWS Lambda's pricing model is primarily based on two factors: the duration of each function invocation and the allocated memory size. By optimizing these aspects, you can effectively minimize the operational costs while ensuring efficient resource utilization. Minimizing the execution time and memory footprint of Lambda functions is crucial for achieving cost-effective and high-performing serverless applications.

Choosing the Right Runtime and Memory Configuration

AWS Lambda supports multiple runtimes, including Java, Node.js, Python, and .NET, among others. Choosing the right runtime for your application can have a significant impact on performance. Additionally, Lambda allows you to configure the amount of memory allocated to your function, which directly affects the CPU power and performance. It's essential to strike a balance between allocating enough memory for your function to run efficiently and avoiding over-provisioning, which can lead to higher costs.

For instance, if you initially assign 128 MB of memory to your Lambda function and observe an overall duration of 1 second, but then increase the memory to 512 MB and notice a reduced overall duration of 0.3 seconds, the latter configuration with higher memory would be more cost-effective and performant.

The **AWS Lambda Power Tuning** tool is a powerful solution that streamlines the process of optimizing Lambda function performance by automating memory allocation testing. Instead of manually running tests with different memory allocations and measuring execution times, this tool leverages AWS Step Functions to concurrently execute multiple versions of a Lambda function with varying memory configurations. The tool runs the target function within your AWS account, mimicking a live production environment by making actual HTTP calls and interacting with AWS SDKs. This approach ensures that the performance measurements accurately reflect real-world scenarios.

Once the Lambda Power Tuning tool completes its analysis of the function invocations, it will present you with a visual representation indicating the optimal memory configuration for your Lambda function, considering both cost and performance factors.

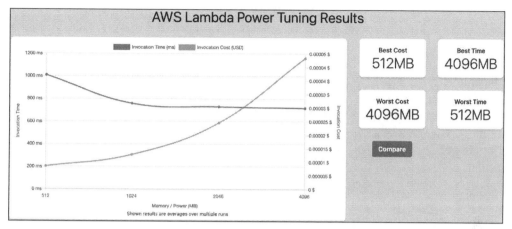

Figure 9.2: *Showing results from the AWS Lambda Power Tuning tool*

Figure 9.2 illustrates the Power Tuning results for the `NewOrder` service that we created in *Chapter 3, Messaging with Amazon SQS and Amazon SNS*. According to the analysis, the most cost-effective memory configuration for our Lambda function would be 512 MB, which aligns with our current settings. However, for optimal performance, the recommended memory allocation is 4096 MB.

To learn more details about Lambda Power Tuning, you can refer to the AWS documentation here:

https://docs.aws.amazon.com/lambda/latest/operatorguide/profile-functions.html

Implement Efficient Code and Avoid Long-Running Tasks

Lambda functions are designed to handle short-lived, event-driven operations, making it essential to develop efficient code that minimizes execution time. Avoid long-running tasks or computationally intensive operations within your Lambda function, as they may result in timeouts or performance bottlenecks.

To optimize the performance of your Lambda functions, implement various optimization strategies. Minimize external dependencies by utilizing native libraries and modules, as external dependencies can increase the deployment package size and potentially introduce security vulnerabilities. Judiciously employ caching mechanisms to store and retrieve frequently accessed data, thereby reducing redundant computations and network requests. Additionally, carefully select appropriate data structures and algorithms tailored to your specific use case, as suboptimal choices can lead to inefficient memory usage and processing times.

Initialize Outside the Handler Method

Optimize resource utilization and enhance performance by initializing resource-intensive operations, such as database connections, external API calls, or object instantiations, outside the function's handler method. This approach ensures that these operations are executed only once during the function's initial invocation. Subsequent invocations can then reuse the pre-initialized resources, thereby minimizing overhead and maximizing efficiency. By adopting this best practice, you not only achieve significant performance gains but also foster code reusability, maintainability, and testability. The separation of initialization code from the main logic facilitates easier modification and independent testing, promoting a more robust and modular codebase. Ultimately, this practice contributes to a streamlined and efficient application, benefiting both the development process and the end-user experience.

Leverage Graviton

Leveraging **Graviton**, Amazon's custom Arm-based processor, can significantly enhance the performance and cost-effectiveness of AWS Lambda functions. Graviton processors are designed to deliver exceptional compute performance while consuming less power, making them an ideal choice for serverless environments like Lambda. By utilizing Graviton-based Lambda functions, you can benefit from improved execution speeds, reduced latency, and potentially lower costs due to the energy efficiency of these processors.

When creating your AWS Lambda function, if you wish to leverage the Graviton processor architecture, you should choose the **arm64** option instead of **x86_64** for the function's architecture. However, before opting for Graviton, it is essential to verify that your application is compatible with Arm-based processors to ensure seamless execution on the Graviton architecture.

Smaller Deployments

When it comes to deploying Lambda functions, it's crucial to minimize the deployment package size to its runtime necessities. This not only enhances performance but also reduces the overall cost of running the functions. By including only the required dependencies and code, the deployment package becomes leaner, leading to faster initialization times and more efficient resource utilization. Additionally, a smaller package size translates to quicker updates and deployments, enabling a more agile development cycle.

Using the Latest AWS SDK

When working with AWS Lambda, it's crucial to use the latest versions of the Software Development Kits (SDKs) provided by AWS. The SDKs are regularly updated with new features, performance improvements, and bug fixes. By utilizing the latest SDKs, you can take advantage of the most recent enhancements, which can lead to better performance, increased security, and access to the latest functionalities offered by AWS services. Additionally, newer SDK versions often provide better documentation, examples, and community support, making it easier to develop and maintain your Lambda functions efficiently.

Using Lightweight Dependencies

When working with AWS Lambda functions, it's crucial to use lightweight dependencies to optimize performance and minimize the deployment package size. Lambda functions have a limited deployment package size, and larger packages can lead to longer cold start times and increased execution costs. By carefully selecting and minimizing dependencies, you can reduce the overall package size and improve the function's efficiency. For example, using lightweight logging libraries like SLF4J SimpleLogger instead of Log4J2 can significantly reduce the package size. Additionally, lightweight data access frameworks like Spring Data JDBC, which is more lightweight than Spring Data JPA, can help minimize the dependencies required for database operations.

Additionally, lightweight dependencies often have a smaller memory footprint, resulting in faster execution times and lower memory usage, which can help minimize costs associated with Lambda function invocations. For instance, using a lightweight JSON parsing library such as Jackson or Gson instead of a more heavyweight XML parsing library can improve performance and reduce memory consumption.

Leverage Provisioned Concurrency

AWS Lambda's default concurrency management can sometimes result in cold starts, where a new instance of your function needs to be initialized, leading to increased latency. **Provisioned concurrency** allows you to pre-warm a pool of execution environments, eliminating cold starts and improving overall performance. However, provisioned concurrency comes at a cost, and it's important to monitor and adjust the provisioned concurrency levels based on your workload patterns to avoid unnecessary costs.

Let's now see how to set up provisioned concurrency for the `NewOrder` service we created in *Chapter 3, Messaging with Amazon SQS and Amazon SNS*. We will allocate 10 execution environments that will be ready to handle incoming requests, ensuring low-latency execution of the Lambda function:

1. From the **Lambda** dashboard of your Lambda function, go to the **Configuration** tab and click **Concurrency** from the left sidebar and click **Edit**.

2. In the **Provisioned concurrency configurations** section click **Add**.

3. Select **Version** for the **Qualifier type**, enter **10** for the *Provisioned concurrency* and click **Save**, as shown in *Figure 9.3*.

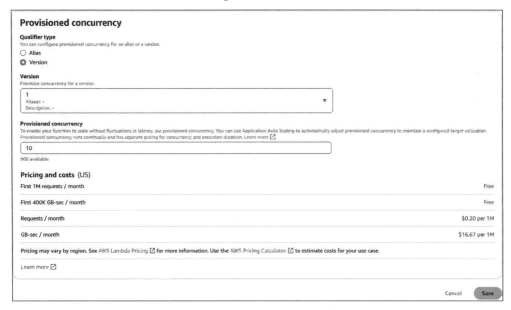

Figure 9.3: *Configuring provisioned concurrency for an AWS Lambda function*

After enabling provisioned concurrency, when the **NewOrder** service is invoked, and the current demand requires only 10 execution environments, there will be no cold start delays associated with them. However, maintaining provisioned concurrency incurs additional costs. It is highly recommended to utilize provisioned concurrency for applications that require low latency response times.

Leverage SnapStart

Lambda **SnapStart** is a feature that can significantly enhance the startup performance of latency-sensitive applications by up to 10 times, without incurring any additional costs or requiring changes to your function code. This is achieved through a process where Lambda captures a snapshot of the initialized execution environment's memory and disk state, encrypts it, and caches it for low-latency access. When you invoke the function version for the first time or as the invocations scale up, Lambda resumes new execution environments from the cached snapshot instead of initializing them from scratch, thereby reducing startup latency. Currently, SnapStart is only available for Java.

Let's now enable **SnapStart** for the **NewOrder** service:

1. From the **Lambda** dashboard of your **Lambda** function, go to the **Configuration** tab and click **General Configuration** from the left sidebar and click **Edit**.

2. In the **General Configuration** section click **Edit**.

3. Under **SnapStart** select **PublishedVersions** and click **Save** to apply the changes.

4. As soon as **SnapStart** is enabled, as shown in *Figure 9.4*, go to the **Versions** tab and click **Publish new version**.

General configuration Info   (Edit)

Description   **Memory**   **Ephemeral storage**
-                                  512 MB   512 MB

Timeout   **SnapStart** Info
0 min 15 sec   PublishedVersions

Figure 9.4: Enabling SnapStart for an AWS Lambda function

5. In the popup click **Publish**.

The **SnapStart** feature introduces a slight delay in the version creation process, requiring you to wait for a few minutes. Once the new version is created, any service you have configured as a trigger needs to be updated to utilize the new version. For instance, if you're using Amazon API Gateway, you will need to modify the integration settings to point to the new version.

When you invoke the Lambda function for the first time after the update, the CloudWatch logs will display a **restore** *duration* instead of an **init** *duration*, indicating that **SnapStart** has successfully restored the function from its snapshot.

Let's analyze the CloudWatch logs, both with and without **SnapStart** enabled, to determine the total execution time for the **NewOrder** service in each scenario.

SnapStart enabled:

REPORT RequestId: e5190e8a-e957-4b69-a178-0dd88e902286 **Duration: 1320.91 ms** Billed Duration: 1483 ms Memory Size: 512 MB Max Memory Used: 172 MB **Restore Duration: 733.56** ms Billed Restore Duration: 162 ms

SnapStart disabled:

REPORT RequestId: 0665ef7e-e0c6-475e-857d-d2c6affd2c2e **Duration: 2742.62 ms** Billed Duration: 2743 ms Memory Size: 512 MB Max Memory Used: 163 MB **Init Duration: 1773.77 ms**

By contrasting the overall execution time with and without SnapStart enabled, we observe a remarkable reduction in the total duration of the Lambda function, decreasing from 2.7 *seconds* to 1.3 *seconds* when SnapStart is activated.

Note: *Provisioned concurrency and SnapStart are two different features offered by AWS Lambda for improving the performance of Lambda functions. While provisioned*

concurrency helps in keeping a pool of warm instances ready to handle incoming invocations, SnapStart is designed to accelerate the startup time of newly created instances. However, these two features cannot be used together for a single Lambda function. When provisioned concurrency is enabled for a Lambda function, AWS automatically manages the pool of warm instances, ensuring that there are always instances available to handle incoming requests promptly. On the other hand, SnapStart leverages a snapshot of the function's code and configuration to significantly reduce the initialization time for new instances. Since provisioned concurrency already maintains a pool of warm instances, the need for accelerating startup times is diminished, making it incompatible with SnapStart. Therefore, AWS does not allow enabling `SnapStart` *for Lambda functions that have provisioned concurrency enabled, as it would result in redundant resource allocation and potential performance degradation.*

Implement Asynchronous Invocation and Batching

By leveraging **asynchronous communication**, applications can achieve improved scalability, resilience, and responsiveness. Increased throughput is one key benefit, as asynchronous communication eliminates the need for components to wait for responses, allowing them to process more requests concurrently. This leads to higher throughput and improved overall system performance.

Additionally, components in an asynchronous system are loosely coupled, meaning they can evolve and scale independently without impacting the entire system. This flexibility enables teams to develop, deploy, and scale individual components more efficiently. Furthermore, if a component fails or becomes unavailable in an asynchronous system, messages can be queued or buffered until the component recovers, minimizing the impact on the overall system and user experience, providing fault tolerance.

Asynchronous communication also facilitates horizontal scaling by allowing multiple instances of a component to process messages in parallel, distributing the load and improving overall capacity. This capability is crucial for applications that need to handle large volumes of traffic or computationally intensive tasks.

By adopting asynchronous communication patterns and leveraging event-driven services like Amazon SQS and Amazon EventBridge, you can build highly scalable, resilient, and responsive applications. These services abstract away the complexities of message queuing and event routing, allowing you to focus on delivering business value while ensuring their applications can scale seamlessly to meet growing demands.

Both Lambda and SQS support **batching**, as we saw in *Chapter 3, Messaging with Amazon SQS and Amazon SNS*, which can significantly improve performance and reduce costs for certain workloads. With SQS batching, multiple messages can be combined and sent to a Lambda function in a single invocation, reducing the overhead of invoking Lambda functions individually for each message. Lambda batching allows you to process multiple events or records within a single function invocation. This can be particularly useful when processing large datasets or when the overhead of individual invocations becomes significant.

Implementing batching with Lambda and SQS involves configuring the appropriate batch size and processing logic within your Lambda function. AWS provides SDKs and libraries that simplify the handling of batched events and messages.

In the following section, we will explore a sample architecture capable of accommodating an extremely high volume of traffic.

Sample Architecture to Handle Massive Load

Let's suppose that in our current microservices architecture, Amazon API Gateway serves as the entry point, routing incoming requests to 10 AWS Lambda functions for processing. Although API Gateway can handle up to 10,000 requests per second, Lambda has a limitation of 1,000 concurrent requests that can be processed simultaneously. Any requests exceeding this limit are throttled, potentially leading to request failures. Considering that each of the 10 Lambda functions receives 1,000 requests per second, we have reached a bottleneck in terms of the number of requests API Gateway and Lambda can receive and the number of microservices we can implement.

To enhance the system's ability to handle a higher volume of requests, we have two primary options:

- **Increase API Gateway rate limit quota**: We can open a ticket with AWS Support to request an increase in the service quotas for API Gateway and Lambda, allowing them to handle more concurrent requests.

- **Rearchitect with asynchronous communication**: Alternatively, we can introduce an asynchronous communication pattern by incorporating Amazon SQS between API Gateway and Lambda. This approach is similar to the messaging architecture discussed in *Chapter 3, Messaging with Amazon SQS and Amazon SNS*, where we utilized SQS. By introducing SQS, the system can decouple the request ingestion and processing stages, enabling SQS to handle an unlimited number of requests while Lambda processes them concurrently within its capacity.

By implementing this asynchronous architecture, we can leverage several additional features and optimizations:

- **Lambda Batching**: AWS Lambda supports processing multiple messages from SQS in batches. This capability can significantly boost the system's throughput and efficiency by maximizing resource utilization and minimizing overhead.

- **Dead-Letter Queues (DLQs)**: SQS Dead-Letter Queues provide a robust mechanism for capturing and handling failed or problematic messages. This feature enhances the system's resilience by enabling the retry or reprocessing of failed requests, ensuring that no data is lost due to transient errors or exceptional circumstances.

- **SQS Long Polling**: The SQS Long Polling feature optimizes resource utilization and reduces costs by minimizing the number of empty receive requests. Instead of continuously polling for new messages, Lambda waits for a specified period before returning an empty response. This approach results in more efficient resource utilization, lower latency, and reduced operational costs.

Additionally, Lambda functions can communicate with each other asynchronously via Amazon EventBridge, a serverless event bus service. EventBridge allows for decoupled and event-driven architectures, enabling microservices to publish and consume events in a reliable and scalable manner. This asynchronous communication pattern can help improve system resilience, reduce coupling between components, and facilitate event-driven workflows across multiple services.

EventBridge supports various event sources, including AWS services, custom applications, and third-party SaaS providers. It provides advanced filtering, routing, and transformation capabilities, allowing you to define rules and targets for handling events based on specific criteria. This enables microservices to react to relevant events in real-time, enabling efficient and responsive system behavior.

Fault Tolerance and Reliability

Building fault-tolerant and reliable event-driven systems can be challenging, as they involve asynchronous communication and distributed components. Next, we will explore best practices for building fault-tolerant and reliable event-driven microservices in AWS.

Implementing Retries

Ensuring resilience and fault-tolerance is paramount in event-driven architectures, where asynchronous messaging plays a pivotal role. **Retries** serve as a crucial safeguard against transient failures, enabling systems to recover gracefully from temporary disruptions. These transient issues can manifest as network glitches, service outages, or resource constraints, all of which can impede the successful processing of messages or events.

AWS services like Amazon SQS and Amazon Kinesis recognize the importance of retries and provide built-in capabilities to facilitate this mechanism. With these services, you can configure the number of retries and the delay between each attempt, allowing you to strike the right balance between resilience and resource utilization.

By implementing retries judiciously, event-driven systems can enhance their overall reliability and availability. When a message fails to process initially, the system will automatically attempt to retry the operation after a specified delay. This delay can be tailored to account for the nature of the failure and the expected recovery time, ensuring that resources are not overwhelmed while also minimizing the risk of data loss or inconsistencies.

Moreover, the retry mechanism can be combined with other strategies, such as Dead-Letter Queues or error handling workflows, to ensure that failures are properly handled and monitored. This holistic approach not only enhances the system's robustness but also provides valuable insights into potential bottlenecks or recurring issues, enabling proactive maintenance and optimization efforts.

Dead-Letter Queues (DLQs)

When messages encounter persistent issues, such as data corruption or application bugs, they may continue to fail despite multiple retries. In these scenarios, it becomes crucial to remove these problematic messages from the primary processing pipeline to prevent them from disrupting the normal flow of operations. This is where the concept of a **Dead-Letter Queue (DLQ)** comes into play.

A DLQ acts as a separate queue or storage destination for messages that have failed to be processed successfully after exhausting the configured number of retries. By diverting these failed messages to a DLQ, you can isolate them for further investigation and debugging without impacting the main processing flow.

Several AWS services, such as AWS Lambda, Amazon SQS, and Amazon EventBridge, support the use of DLQs. For example, with SQS, you can configure a DLQ at the queue level, allowing messages that have exceeded the configured maximum number of receives to be automatically moved to the designated DLQ.

Circuit Breakers

Circuit breakers are a resilience design pattern that aims to mitigate the impact of cascading failures in distributed systems. This pattern is inspired by the electrical circuit breakers used in homes and buildings. When a downstream service or component becomes unresponsive, overloaded, or experiences high latency, a circuit breaker can temporarily prevent new requests from being sent to that service or component. This *circuit open* state allows the downstream service to recover without being overwhelmed by additional requests.

During the open state, the circuit breaker can respond to incoming requests with a predetermined fallback response or error message. After a predefined time period, the circuit breaker may attempt to send a test request to the downstream service, and if successful, it can transition back to a *closed* state, allowing regular traffic flow.

AWS Step Functions, a serverless orchestration service, provides built-in support for implementing circuit breakers through its integration with AWS Lambda. In *Chapter 5, Orchestration with AWS StepFunctions*, we explored how Step Functions can leverage Lambda and DynamoDB to implement circuit breaker logic. This approach allows Step Functions to gracefully handle failures and prevent overwhelming downstream services, improving the overall resiliency of the distributed system.

Data Consistency

Ensuring data consistency is a critical aspect of distributed event-driven systems, where multiple services need to update data concurrently. In such environments, maintaining data integrity and preventing inconsistencies can be a daunting task. AWS offers robust serverless services like Amazon DynamoDB that provide built-in support for transactions, enabling you to perform atomic updates across multiple data stores. This feature ensures that either all updates are successfully applied or none are, preventing partial updates that could lead to data inconsistencies.

Moreover, you can leverage architectural patterns such as *Saga* and *Event Sourcing* to further enhance data consistency across microservices. The Saga pattern, that we saw in *Chapter 5, Orchestration with AWS Step Functions*, models business transactions as a sequence of local transactions, each updating data within a single service. If one local transaction fails, the Saga executes compensating transactions to undo changes made by preceding local transactions, maintaining data consistency across the system.

Event Sourcing, as we examined in *Chapter 4, Choreography with Amazon EventBridge*, on the other hand, involves capturing all changes to an application's state as a sequence of events. By persisting these events in an event store, you can reconstruct the application's state at any point in time, ensuring data consistency even in the face of failures or concurrent updates.

These architectural patterns empower you to build distributed event-driven systems that maintain data consistency, ensuring reliable and accurate data across multiple services and data stores. By leveraging these tools and techniques, you can mitigate the risks of data inconsistencies and provide a robust foundation for your mission-critical applications.

Design for Idempotency

Idempotency guarantees that an operation can be applied multiple times without changing the result beyond the initial application. This property is especially important in event-driven microservices, where events may be replayed, duplicated, or received out of order due to network failures, retries, or other factors.

When designing event-driven microservices in AWS, incorporating idempotency principles is essential to ensure data integrity and prevent unintended side effects.

Here are some strategies and best practices for achieving idempotency in AWS:

Unique identifiers and message deduplication

- **Generate unique identifiers**: Ensure data integrity and prevent duplicate processing by implementing unique identifiers for each event or message. These identifiers, such as UUIDs or message IDs, should be incorporated into the event payload of Amazon API Gateway or Amazon SQS. Leveraging these identifiers, you can detect and discard any duplicates, maintaining data consistency and avoiding redundant computations.

- **Deduplicate messages**: Leverage Amazon SQS FIFO queues, which offers built-in message deduplication capabilities. SQS can automatically deduplicate messages based on either the message content or the provided message identifiers. By utilizing SQS, you can offload the deduplication logic from your application, ensuring a more efficient and reliable data processing pipeline.

Idempotent Consumers

- **Design event consumers to be stateless**: Event consumers should not rely on internal state or external dependencies that might change between executions. Instead, they should rely solely on the event data and the current state of the system to perform their operations. This approach ensures that processing the same event multiple times will always produce the same outcome.

- **Implement idempotency checks and conditional updates**: Before executing any operations, your event handlers should verify the current state of the system or data. If the desired outcome has already been achieved, the event handler should skip the operation. This can be accomplished by maintaining idempotency keys or version numbers, allowing you to detect and ignore duplicate events.

- **Leverage transactional operations and versioning strategies**: When updating data, utilize database transactions or versioning mechanisms to ensure that updates are applied correctly, even if the same event is processed multiple times. Transactions ensure that all operations within a single event are treated as an atomic unit, preventing partial updates. Versioning strategies, such as optimistic or pessimistic locking, can help detect and resolve conflicts when multiple event consumers attempt to update the same data concurrently.

Idempotent Retries

- **Implement retry mechanisms**: To safeguard against unintended consequences and ensure data integrity, it is crucial to implement idempotent retry mechanisms when dealing with failures or retries. Idempotent operations guarantee that repeated attempts produce the same outcome as a single attempt, preventing duplicate processing and potential data corruption.

- **Implement exponential backoff strategy**: When retrying failed operations, adopt an exponential backoff strategy with jitter (random delay) to avoid overwhelming downstream systems with a surge of retries. This approach spaces out retry attempts exponentially, reducing the load on the target systems and allowing them to recover gracefully. The addition of jitter helps prevent synchronization issues that could arise if multiple clients retry simultaneously.

- **Leverage serverless services**: Leverage the power of serverless computing services like AWS Lambda and AWS Step Functions, which offer built-in retry mechanisms with configurable retry policies. These services abstract away the complexities of implementing and managing retry logic, allowing you to focus on your application's core functionality. AWS Lambda automatically retries failed invocations based on your specified retry policy, while AWS Step Functions provides robust state management and retry capabilities for long-running workflows.

Idempotent APIs

- **Embrace RESTful API design principles**: Leverage the inherent semantics of HTTP methods to promote idempotency. Utilize **PUT** and **DELETE** methods for modifying or deleting resources, respectively, as these methods are designed to be idempotent by nature. For safe, read-only operations, employ the GET method, which is inherently idempotent.

- **Implement idempotency keys or request deduplication mechanisms**: Incorporate unique identifiers or idempotency keys in your API requests to enable duplicate request detection and handling. These keys can be generated by the client and included in the request headers or payload. On the server-side, maintain a database or in-memory cache to store these keys and detect duplicate requests based on them, ensuring that only the first request is processed while subsequent duplicates are safely ignored or returned with a cached response.

- **Enrich your APIs with comprehensive error handling and response codes**: Provide clear and descriptive error messages and HTTP status codes to inform clients about the outcome of their requests. This feedback allows clients to make informed decisions about retrying failed requests or taking appropriate actions based on the specific error conditions.

Adopt an Event-Sourcing approach

In *Event-Sourcing*, all changes to application state are captured as a sequence of immutable events, which are persisted in a dedicated event store. This event store serves as the authoritative source of truth, enabling you to reconstruct the current state of your system by replaying the recorded events. For the event store, consider leveraging highly scalable and durable services like Amazon DynamoDB or Amazon Kinesis Data Streams.

By treating events as the system's source of truth, event sourcing inherently ensures idempotency and consistency. Since events are immutable and ordered, you can reliably replay them to rebuild the application state, eliminating the risk of data corruption or inconsistencies. This approach also simplifies auditing, as the complete history of state changes is preserved, enabling you to understand how the system evolved over time.

Event sourcing unlocks powerful capabilities beyond just persisting data. By capturing and processing events in real-time, you can enable event-driven architectures, where components react to events as they occur. This facilitates loose coupling, scalability, and responsiveness, as different parts of your system can independently subscribe to and process relevant events.

Furthermore, event sourcing lays the foundation for advanced patterns like *Command Query Responsibility Segregation* (CQRS) and event-driven microservices. CQRS separates read and write models, allowing you to optimize each model independently for its specific use case. Event-driven microservices leverage events as the communication mechanism between loosely coupled services, enabling greater autonomy, resilience, and scalability.

Monitoring and Observability

- **Implement observability**: Implement robust monitoring and observability solutions that provide end-to-end visibility into your application's behavior. Leverage powerful tools like Amazon CloudWatch for comprehensive monitoring, AWS X-Ray for distributed tracing, and AWS CloudTrail for auditing and logging. These solutions will enable you to proactively detect, diagnose, and troubleshoot issues related to duplicate events, retries, and idempotency violations, ensuring your application's consistent and reliable performance.

- Establish a comprehensive monitoring strategy that captures and analyzes relevant metrics, logs, and traces from various components of your application. Identify and define *Key Performance Indicators* (KPIs) and thresholds specific to idempotency-related concerns, such as duplicate event counts, retry rates, and idempotency violation frequencies. Implement automated alerting mechanisms to notify stakeholders when these KPIs deviate from expected values, enabling prompt investigation and resolution of potential issues. Additionally, leverage advanced analytics and machine learning capabilities to uncover patterns, correlations, and root causes of idempotency-related problems, facilitating proactive preventive measures and continuous improvement.

Next, we will explore a use case that demonstrates how to implement idempotency with Amazon API Gateway and AWS Lambda.

Design for Idempotency with Amazon API Gateway and AWS Lambda

To design for idempotency using Amazon API Gateway and AWS Lambda, you can implement a pattern where you generate a unique idempotency key for each request and store it in a database or cache. This idempotency key can then be used to identify and handle duplicate requests.

Here's an example of how you can implement this pattern:

1. Generate an Idempotency Key

In your client application (for example, a mobile app or a web application), generate a unique idempotency key for each request. This key can be a UUID (*Universally Unique Identifier*) or a combination of other unique identifiers, such as a timestamp and a client ID.

2. Include the Idempotency Key in the Request Headers

When making a request to your API Gateway, include the idempotency key in the request headers. For example, you can use a custom header like X-*Idempotency-Key*.

3. Handle the Request in Lambda

In your Lambda function, retrieve the idempotency key from the request headers and check if the request has been processed before.

```
@Override
public APIGatewayV2HTTPResponse handleRequest(APIGatewayV2HTTPEvent
event, Context context) {
        System.out.println("Received order request from API Gateway: " +
event);


        // get the idempotency key from the request headers
        var idempotencyKey = event.getHeaders().get("x-idempotency-key");


        // Check if the idempotency key is valid
        try {
                UUID.fromString(idempotencyKey);
        } catch (IllegalArgumentException e) {
                return APIGatewayV2HTTPResponse.builder()
                        .withStatusCode(HttpStatusCode.BAD_REQUEST)
```

```
            .withBody("Missing X-Idempotency-Key header")
            .build();
    }


    // get order event
    var order = toOrder(event);


    // save Order to DynamoDB
    HashMap<String,AttributeValue> itemValues = new HashMap<>();
    itemValues.put("idempotencyKey",  AttributeValue.build-
er().s(idempotencyKey).build());
    itemValues.put("orderId",  AttributeValue.builder().s(order.
getOrderId()).build());
    ...


    var request = PutItemRequest.builder()
            .tableName("orders")
            .item(itemValues)
            .conditionExpression("attribute_not_exists(idempotencyKey)")
            .build();


    try {
            ddb.putItem(request);
    } catch (ConditionalCheckFailedException e) {
            return APIGatewayV2HTTPResponse.builder()
                    .withStatusCode(HttpStatusCode.OK)
                    .withBody("Request already processed")
                    .build();
    } catch(Exception e) {
            System.err.println(e);
            return APIGatewayV2HTTPResponse.builder()
                    .withStatusCode(HttpStatusCode.INTERNAL_SERVER_ERROR)
                    .withBody("Internal server error")
                    .build();
```

```
    }

    // return response to APIGW
    APIGatewayV2HTTPResponse response = new APIGatewayV2HTTPResponse();
    response.setStatusCode(HttpStatusCode.CREATED);
    response.setBody(order.getOrderId());
    return response;
}
```

Here's how the code works:

a. The **handleRequest** method is the entry point for the Lambda function. It retrieves the **X-Idempotency-Key** header from the API Gateway request event.

b. If the **X-Idempotency-Key** header is missing, it returns a **400 Bad Request** response.

c. It calls the **PutItemRequest.conditionExpression** method, which tries to insert the idempotency key into DynamoDB with a condition that the key doesn't already exist.

d. If the **conditionExpression** method succeeds, it means the idempotency key is new, and the request is processed with a **200 OK** response.

e. If the **conditionExpression** method throws a **ConditionalCheckFailed Exception**, it means the idempotency key already exists, and the request is considered idempotent. In this case, it returns a **200 OK** response with a message indicating that the request has already been processed.

f. If any other exception occurs, it returns a **500 Internal Server Error** response.

4. Handle Errors and Retries

If there's an error or a timeout during the request processing, the client can retry the request with the same idempotency key. The Lambda function will detect that the idempotency key already exists and return the previously stored response, ensuring idempotency.

By implementing this pattern, you can ensure that your API Gateway and Lambda function handle duplicate requests correctly, preventing data inconsistencies and providing a reliable and idempotent service.

Caching, Data Partitioning, and Parallel Processing

In this section, we will explore three key techniques – caching, data partitioning, and parallel processing – that can enhance the performance and efficiency of event-driven microservices on AWS.

Caching for Improved Performance

Caching is a crucial technique that plays a pivotal role in enhancing the performance and minimizing the latency of serverless applications. AWS offers a comprehensive suite of caching services, including Amazon ElastiCache for in-memory caching, Amazon CloudFront for *Content Delivery Network* (CDN) caching, and Amazon API Gateway's caching feature, each tailored to address specific caching requirements.

ElastiCache, a high-performance, scalable, and cost-effective in-memory data store, supports both Redis and Memcached engines. By caching frequently accessed data in ElastiCache, serverless functions can retrieve data with lightning-fast speeds, eliminating the need for additional database queries or external API calls. This results in reduced latency and improved overall application responsiveness, providing a seamless user experience.

Amazon CloudFront, a global CDN service, takes caching to the next level by strategically positioning static and dynamic content closer to end-users. By leveraging CloudFront's distributed network of edge locations, serverless applications can efficiently serve content to geographically dispersed users, minimizing the distance data needs to travel and enhancing the overall user experience.

Moreover, Amazon API Gateway offers a powerful caching feature that significantly bolsters the performance and scalability of your APIs. This feature allows for the temporary storage of responses from backend services in a cache, reducing the need to fetch data from the origin with every request. When a request arrives, API Gateway first checks the cache for a matching response, and if found, it serves the cached response directly, bypassing the backend service altogether. This not only alleviates the load on your backend resources but also improves response times, resulting in a better user experience for your serverless applications.

Data Partitioning for Scalability and Parallel Processing

As serverless applications driven by events continue to expand, the ability to partition data becomes increasingly vital for effectively managing large datasets and enabling parallel processing, ultimately enhancing overall system performance. AWS offers a suite of services that facilitate seamless data partitioning, including Amazon DynamoDB and Amazon Kinesis.

Amazon DynamoDB, a fully managed NoSQL database service, employs an intelligent partitioning strategy by automatically distributing data across multiple storage nodes. This approach ensures high availability and seamless scalability, enabling serverless functions to access and process data with enhanced efficiency. By partitioning data based on access patterns or other predefined criteria, DynamoDB mitigates contention and bottlenecks, resulting in improved overall performance and responsiveness.

Complementing DynamoDB, Amazon Kinesis, a powerful data streaming service, introduces data partitioning capabilities through the concept of shards. Shards enable multiple serverless functions to concurrently process different partitions of the data stream in parallel. This parallel processing approach not only enhances throughput but also enables the creation of fault-tolerant and highly available data processing pipelines, ensuring continuous and reliable data ingestion and processing.

Parallel Processing with Lambda and Step Functions

Parallel processing with Lambda and Step Functions offers a powerful approach to accelerate computational tasks and enhance overall throughput. By leveraging the ability to invoke multiple Lambda functions concurrently, you can subdivide large workloads or data sets into smaller partitions, allowing for simultaneous processing across multiple execution contexts.

This parallel execution strategy is particularly beneficial for CPU-intensive or I/O-bound workloads, where the computational overhead can be effectively distributed across multiple Lambda instances. By harnessing the inherent scalability and on-demand nature of Lambda, the overall processing time can be significantly reduced, enabling faster completion of complex operations and improved responsiveness.

Furthermore, Step Functions simplifies the orchestration and management of parallel processing pipelines by providing a robust and scalable state machine construct. Through the use of parallel branches within a Step Function workflow, you can define and coordinate the concurrent execution of multiple Lambda functions, ensuring efficient resource utilization and fault-tolerant execution.

Step Functions' parallel branches allow for the specification of multiple paths that can execute concurrently, enabling seamless parallelization of tasks or data processing pipelines. This abstraction empowers you to focus on the logical flow and coordination of their applications, while AWS handles the underlying complexities of scheduling, monitoring, and managing the parallel execution of Lambda functions.

Moreover, Step Functions offers built-in error handling, retry mechanisms, and visibility into the execution status, ensuring reliable and resilient parallel processing pipelines. You can implement sophisticated error handling strategies, such as retrying failed executions or branching based on specific conditions, ultimately enhancing the overall robustness and fault tolerance of their applications.

Security and Access Control

With the rise of distributed systems, security and access control have become paramount concerns. Ensuring the confidentiality, integrity, and availability of data and services is crucial, especially in the context of AWS, where numerous services and components interact seamlessly. Next, we will explore best practices for security and access control.

Securing Your API

When using Amazon API Gateway as the front door for a microservices architecture, there are several best practices you can follow to enhance security, including:

- **API Keys**: Amazon API Gateway provides a robust authentication mechanism through the use of API keys. These keys serve as unique identifiers that allow you to control access to your APIs and enforce rate limiting policies. By associating API keys with specific clients or applications, you gain the ability to monitor and manage their usage patterns effectively. This feature enables you to implement throttling rules that prevent excessive or abusive consumption of your API resources, ensuring optimal performance and availability for all authorized consumers.

- **OAuth 2.0/OpenID Connect (OIDC)**: Seamlessly incorporate Amazon API Gateway with an Identity Provider (IdP) such as Amazon Cognito or an external IdP to enable robust authentication and authorization mechanisms. Leverage industry-standard protocols like OAuth 2.0 or OpenID Connect (OIDC) to ensure secure and controlled access to your APIs. This integration allows you to centralize user identity management, streamline the authentication process, and enforce granular access controls based on user roles, permissions, and attributes.

- **AWS Web Application Firewall (WAF)**: Implementing AWS Web Application Firewall (WAF) as a protective layer in front of API Gateway can fortify your application against a wide array of web-based threats and malicious bot activities. WAF acts as a robust gatekeeper, analyzing incoming traffic patterns and applying pre-defined or custom-tailored rules to identify and mitigate potential exploits, such as SQL injection, cross-site scripting (XSS), and distributed denial-of-service (DDoS) attacks.

- **SSL/TLS Encryption**: Implement robust transport layer security by mandating the use of SSL/TLS encryption protocols across all API endpoints. This measure fortifies data confidentiality by safeguarding sensitive information from unauthorized interception or eavesdropping during transmission over networks. The encryption process scrambles the data, rendering it unintelligible to anyone without the proper decryption key, thus mitigating the risk of data breaches and preserving the integrity of sensitive communications.

- **API Caching**: Leverage API Gateway's built-in caching functionality to enhance the performance and resilience of your application architecture. By caching frequently accessed responses at the API Gateway level, you can significantly reduce the load on downstream services, such as Lambda functions or other backend components. This caching mechanism acts as a buffer, absorbing traffic spikes and ensuring that your services are not overwhelmed by sudden surges in demand. Additionally, cached responses are served directly from the API Gateway, minimizing latency and improving the overall responsiveness of your application.

- **Least Privilege Access**: Adhere to the principle of least privilege by granting the necessary and minimal set of permissions to API Gateway's execution role and associated resources like Lambda functions or data sources. This approach helps to mitigate potential security risks and ensures that the resources have access only to the specific operations and data required for their intended functionality.

- **CloudWatch Logging and Monitoring**: Implement comprehensive logging and monitoring mechanisms for your API Gateway using Amazon CloudWatch. This approach empowers you to proactively detect and promptly respond to potential security threats or anomalous activities within your API ecosystem. CloudWatch provides valuable insights through various metrics, logs, and alarms, enabling you to maintain vigilance over your API's health, performance, and security posture.

- **API Throttling**: To safeguard your APIs from excessive usage or potential abuse, it is crucial to implement throttling limits in Amazon API Gateway. This approach establishes boundaries and restrictions on the number of requests that can be processed within a specified timeframe, thereby preventing resource exhaustion and ensuring the availability and performance of your APIs. By implementing throttling limits, you can define the maximum number of requests that a client can make within a certain time period, such as requests per second. This prevents any single client from overwhelming your API infrastructure and ensures fair resource allocation among all clients.

- **API Versioning**: Leverage the Amazon API Gateway stages feature to effectively manage and phase out obsolete API versions, ensuring clients seamlessly transition to newer, more robust, and secure versions. This approach enables you to introduce enhancements, bug fixes, and security updates while minimizing disruptions and maintaining backwards compatibility. By utilizing stages, you can deploy multiple versions of your API concurrently, each with its own configuration and deployment settings. This allows you to isolate changes, conduct testing, and roll out updates in a controlled manner before promoting them to production.

Securing Event Buses

Event buses are the backbone of event-driven microservices, enabling asynchronous communication and data exchange between different components. AWS offers several services for event bus, such as Amazon SQS, Amazon EventBridge, Amazon Kinesis and so on. To secure these event buses, it is essential to implement the following measures:

- **Authentication and Authorization**: Ensure secure access and control over event publishing and consumption by implementing robust authentication and authorization mechanisms. Leverage the granular access control policies provided by AWS Identity and Access Management (IAM) to meticulously govern permissions for event stream resources. This approach safeguards your event streaming infrastructure by allowing only authorized entities, be they individuals, applications, or services, to publish or consume events, mitigating the risks of unauthorized access and potential data breaches.

- **Encryption**: Ensuring the confidentiality and integrity of sensitive information is paramount in today's digital landscape. AWS provides robust encryption mechanisms that safeguard event data, both when it is stored (at rest) and when it is transmitted (in transit), shielding it from unauthorized access or interception. AWS offers two primary encryption options: server-side encryption and client-side encryption. Server-side encryption is a convenient and secure method where AWS manages the encryption keys and performs the encryption and decryption processes on your behalf. This option is suitable for scenarios where you want to offload the key management responsibilities to AWS while still benefiting from robust data protection. Alternatively, client-side encryption allows you to maintain complete control over the encryption process, including the generation, management, and safeguarding of the encryption keys. This approach is recommended when you have stringent security requirements or regulatory compliance mandates that necessitate retaining full custody of the encryption keys. With client-side encryption, the data is encrypted before it is transmitted to AWS, ensuring that only authorized parties with the correct keys can access and decrypt the information.

- **Access Logging and Monitoring**: Ensuring robust security measures for your event streams is crucial to safeguard against potential threats and unauthorized access attempts. By enabling access logging and monitoring, you can gain invaluable insights into activities occurring within your event streams, allowing you to promptly detect and respond to any security incidents or suspicious behavior. AWS CloudTrail and Amazon CloudWatch are powerful tools that can be leveraged to capture and analyze log data from your event streams. CloudTrail provides a detailed audit trail of API calls and events, enabling you to track user activity, monitor changes, and investigate potential security breaches. Amazon CloudWatch, on the other hand, offers robust monitoring and logging capabilities, allowing you to collect, analyze, and visualize metrics and logs from various AWS resources, including your event streams.

Implementing Access Controls

Microservices often interact with various AWS resources, such as databases, caching systems, and storage services. Implementing proper access controls is crucial to ensure that microservices can only access the resources they need and no more. AWS IAM roles and policies provide a powerful mechanism for managing access controls:

- **Least Privilege Principle**: The principle of least privilege advocates for a judicious and minimalistic approach to granting permissions. It underscores the importance of endowing entities, such as microservices, with only the bare minimum access rights and privileges necessary to fulfill their intended functions. By adhering to this principle, you can significantly reduce their attack surface, fortifying their defenses against potential security breaches and mitigating the risks associated with unauthorized access or inadvertent misuse of valuable resources.

- **Role-Based Access Control (RBAC)**: Embrace the principle of least privilege by implementing Role-Based Access Control (RBAC), facilitated by Identity and Access Management (IAM), to meticulously define and assign precise roles to your microservices. This approach enables fine-grained access control, tailored to the specific responsibilities and requirements of each microservice. By granting only the necessary permissions and restricting unauthorized access, you fortify the security posture of your distributed system, mitigating potential vulnerabilities and upholding data integrity across your microservices architecture.

- **Resource-Based Policies**: While Identity and Access Management (IAM) roles provide a powerful mechanism for controlling access at the user or application level, it is advisable to complement them with resource-based policies. These policies allow you to define granular access controls directly at the resource level, such as Amazon S3 bucket policies. By implementing resource-based policies, you can further enhance the security posture of your AWS resources by specifying precise conditions and permissions for various operations. This approach aligns with the principle of least privilege, ensuring that only authorized entities can perform specific actions on your resources, thereby reducing the risk of unauthorized access or unintended modifications.

Encrypting Data at Rest and in Transit

Encryption plays a pivotal role in fortifying the security posture of sensitive data within the AWS ecosystem, particularly in the realm of event-driven microservices architectures. By employing robust encryption techniques, you can safeguard your critical information from unauthorized access, ensuring the confidentiality and integrity of data at every stage of its lifecycle.

In the context of event-driven microservices, where data flows seamlessly across distributed components and services, it is imperative to implement encryption measures for data at rest and in transit:

- **Data at Rest:** Encrypting data at rest involves securing information stored in persistent storage systems, such as databases, object storage, or file systems, using industry-standard algorithms and secure key management practices. This proactive approach mitigates the risk of data breaches and ensures that even if unauthorized parties gain physical access to the storage media, the data remains indecipherable and protected.

- **Data in Transit:** Encrypting data in transit is equally crucial, as it safeguards sensitive information from interception and eavesdropping during transmission across networks or between microservices. By leveraging secure communication protocols like Transport Layer Security (TLS) or secure messaging queues, you can establish encrypted communication channels, preventing potential man-in-the-middle attacks and preserving the confidentiality of data as it traverses the cloud infrastructure.

AWS provides a comprehensive suite of encryption services and tools that facilitate the implementation of encryption best practices across various services and components. Services like AWS Key Management Service (KMS) offer robust key management capabilities, enabling you to create, manage, and control the lifecycle of encryption keys. Additionally, AWS services like Amazon SQS, and Amazon S3 natively support encryption at rest, while services like AWS Certificate Manager (ACM) and AWS Secrets Manager simplify the management of TLS certificates and secure storage of sensitive credentials, respectively.

Network Security

Event-driven microservices often communicate across different networks and environments. Implementing robust network security measures is crucial to prevent unauthorized access and protect against potential threats:

- **Virtual Private Cloud (VPC)**: Implement microservices in a dedicated and isolated Amazon Virtual Private Cloud (VPC), which offers a secure and highly controlled networking environment. This approach ensures that your microservices are logically isolated from other resources and networks, enhancing security, privacy, and regulatory compliance.

- **Security Groups and Network Access Control Lists (NACLs)**: To ensure a robust and secure network architecture for your microservices, it is crucial to implement layered security controls. Leverage the power of security groups and Network Access Control Lists (NACLs) to meticulously regulate inbound and outbound traffic flows to and from your microservices. By carefully defining granular rules, you can restrict network communication to only the essential channels required for your microservices to function efficiently, while mitigating potential security risks. Security groups act as virtual firewalls at the instance level, enabling you to specify inbound and outbound traffic rules based on protocols, ports, and source or destination IP addresses. These rules should be tailored to allow only the necessary network connections for your microservices to communicate with each other and with external services or clients. NACLs, on the other hand, operate at the subnet level, providing an additional layer of defense by filtering traffic to and from your subnets. These stateless rules can be used to further restrict or allow specific IP addresses, IP address ranges, or traffic protocols, ensuring that only authorized traffic is permitted to reach your microservices.

Continuous Security Monitoring and Auditing

Security is an ongoing process, and it is essential to continuously monitor and audit your event-driven microservices environment. AWS provides various tools and services to assist with this:

- **AWS Config**: Leverage AWS Config, a powerful configuration management service, to establish continuous monitoring and comprehensive assessments of your AWS resources' configurations. This service empowers you to proactively ensure adherence to your organization's stringent security policies and industry-recognized best practices. By automating the auditing process, AWS Config streamlines compliance efforts, enabling you to identify and remediate any deviations promptly. Additionally, it maintains a detailed record of resource configuration changes over time, facilitating comprehensive auditing and seamless troubleshooting. With AWS Config at the forefront of your cloud operations, you can confidently maintain a secure and compliant infrastructure, mitigating risks and fostering a robust governance framework within your AWS environment.

- **AWS Security Hub**: Optimize your cloud security posture with AWS Security Hub, a comprehensive security monitoring and management solution. Security Hub acts as a centralized command center, consolidating and prioritizing security alerts and findings from a wide array of AWS services. By seamlessly integrating with services like Amazon GuardDuty, Amazon Inspector, AWS Config, and AWS Firewall Manager, Security Hub provides you with a holistic view of your security landscape. With Security Hub, you can swiftly identify and address potential security risks, vulnerabilities, and compliance deviations across your AWS environment. Its advanced analytics and machine learning capabilities enable intelligent prioritization of security findings, ensuring that critical issues are brought to your attention promptly. Security Hub also offers automated remediation capabilities, allowing you to streamline and accelerate your incident response processes.

- **AWS CloudTrail**: AWS CloudTrail is a powerful service that facilitates comprehensive logging and monitoring of all API calls and activities occurring across your AWS environment. By enabling CloudTrail, you gain access to a detailed audit trail that meticulously records every action taken within your AWS resources, including API requests, console actions, and responses from AWS services. This audit trail is invaluable for enhancing security posture, ensuring compliance with industry regulations, and enabling effective incident response. CloudTrail captures a wealth of information, including the identity of the user or service that initiated the activity, the source IP address, the timestamp, and the details of the request itself.

By implementing these security and access control measures, you can effectively mitigate risks and ensure the confidentiality, integrity, and availability of your event-driven microservices in AWS. However, it is important to remember that security is an ongoing process, and regular reviews, updates, and adherence to best practices are essential for maintaining a secure and compliant environment.

Use Infrastructure as Code (IaC)

As the number of microservices and their associated resources grow, managing, and maintaining these resources manually can become a daunting task. This is where Infrastructure as Code (IaC) tools such as AWS CloudFormation and AWS Cloud Development Kit (CDK) come into play, providing a declarative and automated approach to provisioning and managing cloud resources.

AWS CloudFormation

AWS CloudFormation is a native AWS service that allows you to define and provision cloud resources using infrastructure-as-code templates written in JSON or YAML. With CloudFormation, you can define your entire infrastructure stack, including serverless components like Lambda functions, API Gateway endpoints, EventBridge rules, and SQS queues, in a single configuration file.

CloudFormation templates provide a consistent and repeatable way to deploy and manage your serverless microservices across multiple environments (for example, development, staging, and production). You can version control your templates, collaborate with team members, and automatically roll out changes to your infrastructure, ensuring consistency and reducing human error.

AWS Cloud Development Kit (CDK)

The AWS Cloud Development Kit (CDK) is an open-source software development framework that allows you to define and provision AWS resources using familiar programming languages like Java, TypeScript, Python, and C#. Unlike CloudFormation, which uses declarative templates, the CDK provides an imperative approach to defining your infrastructure using code constructs.

With the CDK, you can leverage the full power of programming languages, enabling you to write modular, reusable, and testable code for your serverless microservices. The CDK also integrates seamlessly with existing development tools and workflows, making it easier for you to adopt and maintain infrastructure as code practices.

Using IaC tools like CloudFormation or the CDK for managing serverless microservices in AWS offers several benefits:

- **Consistent and repeatable deployments:** IaC tools ensure that your infrastructure is consistently provisioned across different environments (development, staging, and production) by leveraging declarative configurations or code. This consistency minimizes the risk of misconfigurations and facilitates reliable deployments.

- **Version control and collaboration**: IaC configurations can be stored in version control systems like Git, enabling collaborative development, tracking changes, and rolling back to previous versions if needed. This promotes team collaboration and streamlines the infrastructure management process.

- **Automated provisioning and updates:** With IaC, you can automate the entire lifecycle of your infrastructure, from initial provisioning to updates and decommissioning. This automation reduces manual efforts, minimizes human errors, and accelerates the delivery of new features or updates to your serverless microservices.

- **Integration with CI/CD pipelines**: IaC tools can be seamlessly integrated into your Continuous Integration and Continuous Deployment (CI/CD) pipelines, enabling automated infrastructure provisioning and updates as part of your software delivery process.

- **Separation of concerns**: IaC promotes the separation of concerns by decoupling infrastructure management from application code. This separation improves maintainability, reduces complexity, and facilitates independent scaling and updates for both infrastructure and application components.

When deciding between AWS CloudFormation and the AWS CDK for managing your serverless microservices, consider the following factors:

- **Team skills and familiarity**: If your team is more comfortable with declarative templates and has experience with JSON or YAML, CloudFormation might be the better choice. If your team prefers an imperative, code-based approach and is proficient in programming languages like Java or Python, the CDK could be a better fit.

- **Complexity and requirements**: For simple infrastructure setups, CloudFormation templates might be sufficient. However, as your infrastructure becomes more complex, with intricate dependencies and custom logic, the CDK's programming capabilities might be more suitable.

- **Integration with existing tools and workflows**: If your team already uses programming languages supported by the CDK and has established development workflows, the CDK might integrate more seamlessly into your existing processes.

Regardless of your choice, both CloudFormation and the CDK provide powerful tools for managing serverless microservices in AWS using Infrastructure as Code principles. By adopting these practices, you can streamline deployments, ensure consistency, and effectively scale your event-driven serverless architectures on AWS.

Conclusion

This chapter provided a comprehensive overview of various optimization techniques, and best practices for building scalable, resilient, and secure event-driven microservices on AWS. By leveraging AWS Serverless Services like AWS Lambda, you can create highly scalable and cost-effective applications that respond dynamically to events. The chapter emphasized the importance of optimizing Lambda functions, implementing fault tolerance and reliability measures, ensuring idempotency, and leveraging caching, data partitioning, and parallel processing for enhanced performance and scalability.

Additionally, the chapter highlighted the significance of robust security and access control mechanisms, as well as the adoption of IaC practices for consistent and streamlined provisioning and configuration management across environments. By applying the principles and techniques discussed in this chapter, you can build highly efficient, event-driven microservices that can handle large workloads, recover gracefully from failures, and maintain data integrity and consistency, all while ensuring compliance with industry standards and best practices.

Overall, this chapter provided a solid foundation for architects and developers to design and implement event-driven microservices on AWS, equipping them with the knowledge and tools necessary to create scalable, resilient, and secure applications that can adapt to changing business requirements and evolving technological landscapes.

The concluding chapter of this book will delve into real-world examples of event-driven microservices use cases on AWS. We will explore how organizations have successfully built scalable, resilient, and secure event-driven microservices architectures within the AWS ecosystem.

CHAPTER 10

Real-World Use Cases on AWS

Introduction

In this chapter, we will delve into the practical applications of AWS event-driven services across six diverse industries: e-commerce, Internet of Things (IoT), financial services, media and entertainment, logistics and transportation, and healthcare and life sciences. We will explore how these powerful services, such as Amazon EventBridge, Amazon SQS, Amazon SNS, Amazon Kinesis, AWS Step Functions, Amazon API Gateway, and AWS Lambda can be leveraged to streamline operations and enhance customer experiences within each sector. We will embark on an exploration of real-world use cases, illuminating the ways in which event-driven architectures can revolutionize businesses. Throughout the chapter, we will provide concise overviews of the AWS event-driven services most suitable for each industry, empowering you to make informed decisions and leverage the full potential of these cutting-edge technologies.

Structure

In this chapter, we will discuss the following topics:

- Unleashing the Power of AWS Event-Driven Services for E-commerce and Retail Business
- Building an IoT and Sensor Data Processing Business with AWS Event-Driven Services
- Embracing AWS Event-Driven Services for Financial Services
- Revolutionizing Media and Entertainment with AWS Event-Driven Services
- Streamlining Logistics and Transportation through AWS Event-Driven Services
- Transforming Healthcare and Life Sciences with AWS Event-Driven Services

Unleashing the Power of AWS Event-Driven Services for E-commerce and Retail Business

In the realm of e-commerce and retail products, event-driven architectures play a pivotal role in delivering seamless and efficient operations. These architectures leverage the power of serverless computing, enabling you to react to real-time events with agility and scalability. AWS offers a suite of event-driven services that cater to various event-driven use cases, enhancing the customer experience and streamlining business processes.

Order Processing and Fulfillment

In the realm of e-commerce platforms, efficient order processing and fulfillment are paramount to delivering exceptional customer experiences. These critical components directly influence customer satisfaction levels. When a customer places an order, a series of intricate events are set in motion, encompassing payment processing, inventory management, and shipping coordination. AWS offers a robust suite of services that seamlessly integrate to facilitate event-driven order processing and fulfillment.

At the heart of this solution lies Amazon API Gateway, which acts as the entry point for customer orders received through the e-commerce website. This fully managed service securely exposes APIs, enabling smooth integration with other AWS services. When a customer submits an order, API Gateway triggers an AWS Lambda function, which serves as the business logic layer for order processing.

AWS Lambda, a serverless compute service, allows you to run code without provisioning or managing servers. This event-driven execution model ensures that order processing logic is executed only when needed, providing cost-effectiveness and scalability. The Lambda function can interact with various AWS services to orchestrate the order fulfillment process seamlessly.

For instance, the Lambda function can leverage Amazon SQS or Amazon SNS to coordinate the order fulfillment workflow. SQS offers reliable, scalable, and fully managed message queuing, enabling asynchronous communication between components of the order processing system. Alternatively, SNS provides a highly available, durable, and secure pub-sub messaging service, enabling fanout patterns for parallel processing of order fulfillment tasks.

Furthermore, Amazon EventBridge, a serverless event bus, can be employed to detect and respond to various events within the order processing lifecycle. This event-driven architecture allows for real-time processing and automation of order-related tasks, such as inventory updates, shipping notifications, and customer communication.

AWS Step Functions, a serverless function orchestrator, can be leveraged to coordinate complex order processing workflows, ensuring seamless integration and coordination between various microservices and external systems involved in the fulfillment process.

These services provided by AWS offer a highly scalable, cost-effective, and event-driven solution for order processing and fulfillment. Businesses can handle spikes in demand without worrying about provisioning and managing servers. Additionally, the event-driven nature of these services ensures near real-time order processing, ultimately improving customer satisfaction and fostering loyalty.

Real-Time Inventory Management

In the retail industry, inventory levels are subject to frequent changes due to customer purchases, restocking, or other business operations. Ensuring that inventory data is up-to-date and consistent across various systems and applications is crucial for accurate order processing and inventory management.

Amazon Kinesis can be an ideal solution for streaming real-time inventory updates from various sources, such as point-of-sale systems, warehouses, or online stores. Kinesis Data Streams can ingest large volumes of inventory data in real-time, allowing for parallel processing and scalability.

AWS Lambda functions can be triggered by Kinesis Data Streams to process and transform the incoming inventory data. These functions can perform operations such as data validation, enrichment, or aggregation before storing the processed data in a persistent data store like Amazon DynamoDB.

Amazon EventBridge can also play a role in this use case by capturing and routing inventory-related events to the appropriate downstream services or applications. For example, when inventory levels for a particular product fall below a certain threshold, EventBridge can trigger a notification to be sent to the supply chain management system or initiate a restocking process.

By leveraging these AWS services, you can maintain accurate and up-to-date inventory levels, minimize stockouts, and ensure efficient supply chain management. The event-driven nature of these services enables real-time visibility and agility in responding to inventory changes.

Customer Engagement and Notifications

In today's highly competitive e-commerce landscape, providing timely and personalized customer engagement is paramount for fostering brand loyalty and driving sales.

Event-driven architectures enable real-time notifications and targeted marketing campaigns tailored to customer actions and preferences, offering a seamless and contextualized experience.

Amazon SNS can be leveraged as a powerful tool to deliver various types of notifications to customers, such as order confirmations, shipment updates, or personalized promotional offers. AWS Lambda functions can be triggered by events from Amazon EventBridge or other services, allowing for custom logic to be executed before sending notifications through SNS.

For instance, when a customer places an order, an AWS Lambda function can be invoked to generate a personalized order confirmation message, incorporating relevant details such as the customer's name, order items, and estimated delivery date. The Lambda function can then publish the personalized message to an SNS topic specific to that customer. Amazon SNS allows you to create distinct topics for each customer or to use message filtering capabilities to ensure that only the intended customer receives their personalized notification. This way, customers subscribed to their respective topics or filters receive the notification via their preferred delivery channels, such as email or mobile push notifications, while ensuring that each customer receives only their personalized message.

Moreover, Amazon SQS can be employed to decouple the notification generation process from the actual delivery, ensuring reliable and asynchronous message handling. AWS Lambda functions can poll SQS queues and send notifications through SNS or other channels, providing a scalable and fault-tolerant solution for high-volume notification delivery.

By leveraging event-driven architectures and AWS services like Lambda, EventBridge, SNS, and SQS, you can elevate their customer experience by delivering timely and personalized notifications, fostering stronger customer relationships, and driving increased brand loyalty and sales.

Personalized Marketing and Recommendations

Personalized marketing and product recommendations are essential for enhancing the customer experience and driving sales in e-commerce and retail platforms. By leveraging event-driven architectures, you can deliver highly relevant and timely recommendations based on customer behavior and preferences.

Amazon EventBridge can capture events from various sources, such as website interactions, purchase history, and browsing patterns. These events can then be routed to AWS Lambda functions or AWS Step Functions for processing and analysis. Machine learning models can be integrated to generate personalized recommendations based on the customer's behavior and preferences.

For example, when a customer browses a particular product category or adds items to their cart, an event can be generated and routed to an AWS Lambda function via EventBridge. This function can analyze the customer's behavior, fetch their purchase history, and generate personalized product recommendations. These recommendations can then be displayed on the e-commerce website or sent to the customer via Amazon SNS, for email or push notifications.

Additionally, AWS Step Functions can orchestrate complex recommendation workflows, integrating multiple microservices and external systems. For instance, a Step Function can coordinate the retrieval of customer data, the generation of recommendations, and the delivery of personalized marketing campaigns through various channels such as email, push notifications, and targeted advertisements.

These are just a few examples of event-driven use cases in e-commerce and retail products, and the corresponding AWS services that can be employed to address them. The flexibility, scalability, and cost-effectiveness of these services make them ideal choices for building modern, event-driven architectures that enhance customer experiences and drive business success.

Building an IoT and Sensor Data Processing Business with AWS Event-Driven Services

In the era of digitalization, Internet of Things (IoT) and sensor data processing have become crucial components for businesses across various industries. With the increasing adoption of connected devices and the need for real-time data analysis, companies are seeking scalable and cost-effective solutions.

IoT and sensor data processing products often involve handling real-time events, orchestrating complex workflows, and processing large volumes of data. AWS offers a range of services that can effectively address these use cases. Here are some common event-driven use cases and the corresponding AWS services that can be leveraged.

Real-Time Data Ingestion and Processing

In the world of IoT and sensor data processing, real-time data ingestion and processing are crucial components. Imagine a scenario where thousands of sensors are continuously streaming data, capturing various metrics such as temperature, humidity, pressure, and more. To handle this massive influx of data efficiently, you need a scalable and reliable solution. To effectively handle this massive influx of data, a scalable, reliable, and secure solution is indispensable. This is where AWS IoT Core, combined with Amazon Kinesis Data Streams, comes into play.

AWS IoT Core is a managed cloud service that enables secure and seamless communication between IoT devices and the cloud. It provides a robust infrastructure for ingesting data from IoT devices, ensuring secure device authentication, data encryption, and device management capabilities. By integrating AWS IoT Core with Amazon Kinesis Data Streams, you can ingest and process large streams of sensor data in real time.

Amazon Kinesis Data Streams is a fully managed service designed to handle high-throughput data ingestion from numerous sources, including IoT devices, sensors, and applications. It seamlessly scales to accommodate fluctuations in data volume, ensuring that no data is lost or delayed, even during periods of high traffic. By leveraging Kinesis Data Streams, you can ingest sensor data as it arrives from AWS IoT Core, without the need to provision or manage servers.

The power of this combination lies in its ability to process and analyze the ingested data in real time. Kinesis Data Streams integrates seamlessly with other AWS services, such as AWS Lambda and Amazon Managed Service for Apache Flink, enabling you to build serverless data processing pipelines. These services can be configured to process and analyze the sensor data as it streams in, allowing for real-time insights, anomaly detection, and automated decision-making.

Data Transformation and Enrichment

Sensor data, originating from various devices and sources, frequently requires transformations and enrichment before it can be effectively analyzed or stored for further processing. This process might involve activities such as data filtering, aggregation, or combining data from multiple sources to derive valuable insights and uncover hidden patterns or trends.

AWS Lambda, a serverless compute service, emerges as an ideal solution for this use case. By seamlessly integrating AWS Lambda with Kinesis Data Streams, you can process and transform data in real time as it streams in from IoT devices and sensors. Lambda functions can be triggered by incoming data records, enabling you to perform complex transformations, data enrichment, or invoke other AWS services as needed, all within a highly scalable and event-driven architecture.

For instance, you could develop a Lambda function that filters and aggregates temperature readings from multiple sensors within a specific geographical area, providing a consolidated view of the environmental conditions. Alternatively, another function could enrich the data by adding contextual information, such as location coordinates or device metadata, enhancing the insights derived from the raw sensor data.

This powerful combination of AWS Lambda and Kinesis Data Streams empowers you to build robust, scalable, and efficient data processing pipelines, unlocking the true potential of sensor data and enabling real-time decision-making and actionable insights across various domains, from industrial automation to environmental monitoring and beyond.

Data Archiving and Analytics

In many IoT and sensor data processing scenarios, the need to archive vast quantities of data for long-term storage and future analysis becomes paramount. This archived data can be leveraged for batch processing, historical analysis, or training machine learning models to uncover valuable insights.

Amazon S3 (Simple Storage Service) emerges as a highly scalable and durable object storage service that excels in this use case. S3 offers virtually unlimited storage capacity and can store any type of data, making it an ideal destination for archiving IoT and sensor data. Its robust architecture ensures data durability and availability, providing a secure and reliable repository for your valuable data assets.

To streamline the archiving process, Kinesis Data Streams can be configured to automatically deliver data to a designated S3 bucket. This process can be further enhanced by leveraging AWS Lambda functions, which can perform additional data transformations or processing steps before securely storing the data in S3.

Once the data is safely archived in S3, you can harness the power of other AWS services for analytics and machine learning workloads. For instance, Amazon Athena enables ad-hoc queries and analysis on the archived data, empowering you to uncover valuable insights and patterns. Alternatively, Amazon EMR (Elastic MapReduce) provides a robust platform for running distributed big data processing jobs, allowing you to process and analyze large volumes of archived data efficiently.

Furthermore, AWS Glue can be employed to prepare and load the archived data into Amazon Redshift or other data warehousing solutions, enabling advanced analytics and business intelligence capabilities. This integrated approach allows you to leverage the full potential of your archived IoT and sensor data, unlocking new opportunities for data-driven decision-making and innovation.

Continuous Data Delivery and Streaming

In the realm of IoT and sensor data processing, there are often scenarios where continuous data delivery and streaming to various destinations, such as data lakes, real-time analytics platforms, or downstream applications, becomes a necessity. Amazon Data Firehose, a fully managed and serverless service, streamlines the intricate process of capturing, transforming, and delivering streaming data to diverse destinations.

With Data Firehose, you can seamlessly ingest data from many sources, including Kinesis Data Streams, and automatically route it to destinations like Amazon S3 for data lakes, Amazon Redshift for data warehousing, Amazon Elasticsearch Service for search and analytics, or even third-party services like Splunk. This service alleviates the complexities associated with managing resources and scaling infrastructure for continuous data delivery, as it dynamically scales to match the throughput of your data stream, ensuring reliable and consistent delivery without any data loss.

Moreover, Data Firehose seamlessly integrates with AWS Lambda, enabling you to perform data transformations or enrichment before delivering the data to its intended destination. This powerful capability proves invaluable when you need to process, reshape, or enrich the data to meet the specific requirements of downstream applications, analytics tools, or data processing pipelines. By leveraging this feature, you can ensure that the data is properly formatted, cleansed, and enriched, enhancing its value and usability for various analytical or operational purposes.

Overall, Amazon Data Firehose empowers organizations to effortlessly capture, transform, and deliver streaming IoT and sensor data to multiple destinations, while offloading the complexities of resource management and infrastructure scaling. With its seamless integration with AWS Lambda, organizations can unlock the true potential of their data by performing transformations and enrichments, enabling more informed decision-making and driving greater business value from their IoT and sensor data streams.

In summary, AWS provides a robust set of services that can effectively address various event-driven use cases in IoT and sensor data processing scenarios. By leveraging services like Amazon Kinesis Data Streams, AWS Lambda, Amazon S3, AWS Step Functions, and Amazon Data Firehose, you can build scalable, reliable, and cost-effective solutions for ingesting, processing, archiving, and delivering IoT and sensor data in real time or batch modes.

Embracing AWS Event-Driven Services for Financial Services

In the fast-paced and highly regulated financial services industry, event-driven architectures play a crucial role in enabling real-time processing, automation, and seamless integration between various systems. AWS offers a suite of services that can be leveraged to implement event-driven use cases effectively. Here are some common use cases and their corresponding AWS event-driven service recommendations.

Order Processing and Trade Execution

In the world of financial services, timely order processing and trade execution are critical. An event-driven architecture can streamline this process by triggering downstream actions based on order events.

AWS Step Functions is an excellent choice for orchestrating order processing workflows. It allows you to create state machines that define the steps and logic for processing orders. Each step can invoke AWS Lambda functions or integrate with other AWS services, enabling seamless execution of tasks such as risk assessment, compliance checks, and trade execution.

Amazon EventBridge can be used to capture and route order-related events from various sources (for example, trading platforms, APIs, or internal systems) to the appropriate AWS Step Functions state machine. This decoupled approach ensures that order events are handled in a scalable and reliable manner, reducing the risk of missed or delayed trades.

By leveraging AWS Step Functions and Amazon EventBridge, financial institutions can build robust and scalable order processing pipelines that adapt to varying workloads and provide real-time visibility into the order lifecycle.

Fraud Detection and Risk Management

Financial institutions must constantly monitor transactions and user activities to detect and mitigate fraudulent behavior and manage risk effectively. Event-driven architectures enable real-time fraud detection and risk management by analyzing events as they occur.

AWS Lambda, combined with Amazon Kinesis, can be used to build a real-time fraud detection and risk management system. Amazon Kinesis can ingest high-volume transaction data and user activity events from various sources, such as payment gateways, mobile apps, and web applications. These events can then be processed by AWS Lambda functions in real time, applying fraud detection algorithms and risk scoring models.

Amazon DynamoDB can be used as a low-latency and scalable data store to maintain user profiles, transaction histories, and risk scores. This data can be efficiently queried and updated by AWS Lambda functions during the fraud detection process, enabling real-time risk assessments and decision-making.

By leveraging AWS Lambda, Amazon Kinesis, and Amazon DynamoDB, financial institutions can implement event-driven fraud detection and risk management systems that can process high-volume data streams, adapt to changing patterns, and provide near real-time insights and alerts.

Regulatory Compliance and Auditing

Financial services organizations operate in a highly regulated environment, requiring strict adherence to regulatory guidelines and comprehensive auditing capabilities. Event-driven architectures can facilitate real-time monitoring, reporting, and auditing of critical events to ensure compliance.

Amazon EventBridge can be used to capture and route events related to regulatory compliance from various sources, such as transaction systems, user activity logs, and external data feeds. These events can then be routed to trigger AWS Lambda functions for further processing or auditing.

AWS Lambda functions can be triggered by EventBridge events to perform real-time compliance checks and generate audit logs. The audit logs can then be securely stored in Amazon S3 for long-term storage and analysis. Amazon S3 provides a durable and secure storage solution for maintaining audit trails and historical data required for regulatory compliance.

By combining Amazon EventBridge, AWS Lambda, and Amazon S3, financial institutions can build event-driven compliance and auditing systems that can capture and process critical events in real time, generate comprehensive audit trails, and maintain historical data for regulatory reporting and analysis.

Revolutionizing Media and Entertainment with AWS Event-Driven Services

In the rapidly evolving world of media and entertainment, delivering captivating content and ensuring seamless user experiences has become paramount. With the advent of cloud computing, businesses in this domain can revolutionize their operations and unlock new possibilities. AWS offers a suite of event-driven services that empower media and entertainment companies to build highly scalable, cost-effective, and responsive applications.

Video Transcoding and Post-Processing

In the media and entertainment sector, video transcoding and post-processing are crucial operations that demand efficient and dependable execution. When a new video is uploaded, it frequently requires conversion into various formats and resolutions to cater to diverse devices and platforms. Moreover, post-processing tasks such as watermarking, overlaying graphics, and generating thumbnails may be necessary.

For this use case, AWS Lambda and Amazon S3 can be employed in tandem with Amazon EventBridge and Amazon SNS. Upon uploading a new video to an S3 bucket, an EventBridge event can trigger a Lambda function to initiate the transcoding and post-processing tasks. The Lambda function can then leverage third-party libraries to perform the required operations. Once the tasks are completed, the processed files can be stored back in S3, and an SNS notification can be sent to downstream systems or users.

This event-driven, scalable architecture offers several advantages. It eliminates the need for provisioning and managing dedicated transcoding servers, ensuring efficient resource utilization and cost-effectiveness. Lambda functions automatically scale based on demand, allowing for seamless parallel processing of multiple videos simultaneously. Furthermore, this approach facilitates seamless integration with other services, enabling a streamlined and flexible workflow.

Live Streaming and Real-Time Analytics

Live streaming and real-time analytics are pivotal for broadcasters and content creators to engage with their audience dynamically. This includes ingesting live video streams, processing and distributing them across various platforms, and analyzing viewer metrics and engagement data.

AWS offers a suite of managed services that can be seamlessly integrated to create a robust and scalable solution for this use case. Amazon Kinesis, a fully managed data streaming service, can ingest live video streams and viewer engagement data in real time. AWS Lambda, a serverless compute service, can be triggered by Kinesis to process the video streams, perform real-time analytics, and store the data in Amazon DynamoDB, a fully managed NoSQL database, for further analysis or display on dashboards. Amazon API Gateway can expose APIs, allowing external systems or applications to interact with the live streaming and analytics platform.

This event-driven architecture provides the scalability and elasticity required to handle fluctuating loads during live events. Kinesis and Lambda can automatically scale up or down based on the incoming data volume, ensuring efficient resource utilization and cost-effectiveness. Additionally, the seamless integration between services enables real-time processing and analysis of data as it arrives, facilitating dynamic engagement with the audience.

Audience Engagement

Amazon EventBridge and AWS Lambda can be utilized to create a powerful solution for real-time audience engagement in live streaming and content delivery scenarios. EventBridge, a serverless event bus service, can ingest and route events from various sources, such as live video streams, user interactions, or content management systems. These events can then trigger Lambda functions, which are serverless compute resources, to perform custom logic and execute actions in response to the events.

For instance, when a new live stream starts or a viewer interacts with the content, EventBridge can capture these events and invoke a Lambda function. The Lambda function can then process the event data, perform real-time analytics, and trigger notifications or updates to be delivered to the audience. This could involve sending push notifications, updating dashboards, or even initiating dynamic content personalization based on viewer preferences or engagement patterns.

The combination of EventBridge and Lambda enables a highly scalable and event-driven architecture for audience engagement. EventBridge can handle high volumes of events without the need for provisioning or managing infrastructure, while Lambda functions can scale automatically to meet demand, ensuring efficient resource utilization and cost-effectiveness. This serverless approach allows for seamless integration with other AWS services, enabling real-time processing, analysis, and delivery of engaging content and experiences to the audience.

Usage Tracking and Metering

Amazon Kinesis and AWS Lambda can be effectively utilized for usage tracking and metering in media services. Kinesis, a fully managed data streaming service, can ingest real-time usage data from various sources, such as media players, content delivery networks, and other components of the media ecosystem. This data can include metrics like video playback duration, bitrate, user interactions, and more.

AWS Lambda, a serverless compute service, can be seamlessly integrated with Kinesis to process and analyze the incoming usage data in real-time. Lambda functions can be triggered by Kinesis data streams, allowing for efficient and scalable processing. These functions can perform data transformations, aggregations, and calculations necessary for accurate billing and metering based on the actual usage patterns.

By leveraging the power of Kinesis for data ingestion and Lambda for real-time processing, media services can implement a flexible and scalable architecture for usage tracking and metering. This approach ensures accurate billing and metering while optimizing resource utilization and cost-effectiveness, as both services automatically scale up or down based on the incoming data volume, eliminating the need for provisioning and managing infrastructure.

Streamlining Logistics and Transportation Through AWS Event-Driven Services

In the realm of logistics and transportation, event-driven architectures play a crucial role in enabling efficient and responsive systems. AWS offers a suite of services that can seamlessly integrate with event-driven workflows, providing scalable and cost-effective solutions. Here, we will explore several use cases in the logistics and transportation domain and the corresponding AWS services that can be employed.

Order Tracking and Notifications

In today's fast-paced logistics industry, providing real-time visibility into order status and seamless communication with customers is a critical differentiator. This use case leverages the power of serverless architecture to streamline order tracking and notification processes, ensuring a superior customer experience while optimizing operational efficiency.

At the core of this solution lies Amazon EventBridge, a fully managed event bus that ingests and routes events from diverse sources, such as order management systems, warehouse management platforms, and logistics partners. This centralized event hub acts as a unified entry point for capturing critical events throughout the order lifecycle, including order placement, shipment status updates, and delivery confirmations.

Tightly integrated with EventBridge are AWS Lambda functions, which act as event-driven compute engines, automatically triggered by relevant events. These serverless functions enable real-time processing and execution of custom business logic tailored to specific event scenarios. For instance, when a new order is placed, a Lambda function can be invoked to generate and send a personalized confirmation notification to the customer via Amazon SNS, keeping them informed at every step of the journey.

The serverless nature of this architecture ensures seamless scalability, automatically adjusting resources to accommodate fluctuations in demand, while eliminating the need for provisioning and maintaining dedicated infrastructure. This translates into significant cost savings and improved operational agility, allowing businesses to focus on their core competencies while delivering exceptional customer experiences.

Moreover, the modular design of this solution fosters extensibility and integration with other AWS services and third-party systems. For example, Lambda functions can interact with Amazon DynamoDB to store and retrieve order data, enabling real-time analytics and reporting. Additionally, Amazon API Gateway can be leveraged to expose secure APIs, facilitating integration with mobile applications or customer portals, and providing customers with a unified view of their order status and shipment details.

Supply Chain Optimization and Route Planning

Optimizing supply chain operations and route planning is a critical aspect of the transportation industry, as it directly impacts costs and efficiency. This use case revolves around leveraging real-time data streams from various sources, such as IoT devices, weather services, traffic updates, and more, to dynamically adapt routes and schedules on the fly.

Amazon Kinesis, a fully managed data streaming service, plays a crucial role in ingesting and processing these real-time data streams from diverse sources like GPS trackers, weather APIs, and traffic monitoring services. As new data arrives, AWS Lambda functions are automatically triggered, enabling real-time processing and analysis of the incoming information.

The processed data is then stored in Amazon DynamoDB, a high-performance, fully managed NoSQL database service, facilitating efficient querying and retrieval of the analyzed data. This allows for quick access to the most up-to-date information, enabling informed decision-making.

Based on the insights gained from the analyzed data, Lambda functions can invoke external APIs or services to dynamically update route plans, adjust schedules, and notify logistics partners and drivers about any changes. This event-driven approach enables agile supply chain optimization and route planning, adapting to real-time conditions and minimizing disruptions.

By leveraging the power of AWS services like Amazon Kinesis, AWS Lambda, and Amazon DynamoDB, this use case empowers transportation companies to enhance operational efficiency, reduce costs associated with delays and inefficient routing, and ultimately provide a better customer experience through timely and optimized deliveries.

Moreover, the serverless nature of AWS Lambda and the scalability of Amazon Kinesis and Amazon DynamoDB ensure that this solution can handle high volumes of real-time data and scale seamlessly as the business grows, without the need for manual provisioning or management of underlying infrastructure.

Shipment Exception Handling and Incident Management

In the logistics domain, exceptions and incidents are inevitable, such as delayed shipments, damaged goods, or lost packages. This use case involves capturing and responding to these events promptly to minimize disruptions and ensure customer satisfaction.

Amazon EventBridge can ingest events from various sources, such as warehouse management systems, transportation management systems, and IoT devices. These events can trigger AWS Step Functions, which orchestrate and coordinate the execution of multiple Lambda functions or integrate with external systems.

For instance, when a shipment delay event occurs, a Step Function can be initiated to notify relevant stakeholders using Amazon SNS, update the order status in the system, and potentially initiate alternative shipping arrangements. Step Functions provide a visual workflow management tool, enabling efficient coordination of complex processes and ensuring proper exception handling and incident resolution.

AWS services, such as Amazon EventBridge, AWS Lambda, Amazon Kinesis, and AWS Step Functions, offer a powerful combination for implementing event-driven architectures in the logistics and transportation domain. These services provide scalability, cost-effectiveness, and rapid deployment capabilities, enabling businesses to build agile and responsive systems that adapt to real-time events and optimize operations.

Transforming Healthcare and Life Sciences with AWS Event-Driven Services

In the dynamic world of healthcare and life sciences, event-driven architectures have emerged as a game-changer, enabling agile and responsive systems that can adapt to ever-changing requirements. AWS offers a comprehensive suite of services that seamlessly integrate with event-driven workflows, providing scalable and cost-effective solutions tailored to the unique needs of the healthcare and life sciences industry. From real-time patient monitoring to streamlined clinical trials, AWS services empower organizations to unlock the full potential of event-driven architectures in this mission-critical domain.

Patient Appointment Reminders

In the healthcare industry, it's crucial to ensure that patients don't miss their scheduled appointments. An event-driven approach can be employed to send automated reminders to patients before their appointments.

The process can be triggered by an event in Amazon EventBridge, such as a scheduled rule or an event from a third-party system like an Electronic Health Record (EHR) system. This event can initiate an AWS Step Functions workflow, which orchestrates the subsequent steps. The workflow can invoke an AWS Lambda function to retrieve patient contact information from a database like Amazon DynamoDB or a data lake like Amazon S3.

Another Lambda function can then be invoked to generate personalized appointment reminders based on the patient's preferred communication channel (for example, SMS, email, or push notification). For SMS and push notifications, the Lambda function can integrate with Amazon SNS, which handles the delivery of messages to the respective channels.

AWS Lambda functions are an excellent choice for this use case because they can be triggered by events, executed concurrently to handle high volumes of reminders, and scaled automatically based on demand. Amazon EventBridge and AWS Step Functions provide a robust and flexible event-driven architecture, enabling easy integration with other AWS services and external systems. Additionally, Amazon DynamoDB and Amazon S3 offer highly available and scalable data storage solutions for patient information and appointment details.

Real-Time Patient Monitoring

In critical care scenarios, it's essential to monitor patients' vital signs and health data in real time to detect any anomalies or urgent conditions promptly. An event-driven architecture can enable real-time processing and alerting systems for patient monitoring.

The data from medical devices and wearables can be ingested into Amazon Kinesis Data Streams, a real-time data streaming service. Kinesis Data Streams can then trigger AWS Lambda functions to process and analyze the incoming data streams. These Lambda functions can apply real-time analytics and machine learning models to identify patterns, detect anomalies, or trigger alerts based on predefined thresholds.

If an urgent condition is detected, the Lambda function can invoke an AWS Step Functions workflow to coordinate the necessary actions. This workflow can involve sending notifications to healthcare providers via Amazon SNS, updating patient records in a database like Amazon DynamoDB, or triggering automated responses such as dispatching emergency services or adjusting medication dosages.

The combination of Amazon Kinesis Data Streams and AWS Lambda is well-suited for this use case because it enables real-time processing of high-volume data streams while providing the necessary scalability and elasticity to handle varying workloads. AWS Step Functions adds orchestration capabilities, ensuring that the appropriate actions are taken in a reliable and coordinated manner. Additionally, Amazon SNS and Amazon DynamoDB provide reliable messaging and data storage solutions, respectively, for notifications and patient data management.

Clinical Trial Data Processing

Clinical trials in the life sciences industry generate vast amounts of data that need to be collected, processed, and analyzed. An event-driven architecture can streamline the data processing pipeline and enable efficient collaboration among researchers and stakeholders.

Clinical trial data can be collected from various sources, such as mobile apps, wearable devices, and electronic data capture (EDC) systems, and ingested into Amazon S3 buckets through Amazon Data Firehose. These data ingestion events can trigger AWS Lambda functions to perform data validation, transformation, and enrichment tasks. The processed data can then be stored in a data lake or a data warehouse for further analysis.

As new data becomes available or specific events occur (for example, trial milestones, data quality checks), Amazon EventBridge can be used to route these events to the appropriate AWS services. For example, an event can trigger an AWS Step Functions workflow to coordinate the execution of data analysis pipelines, generate reports, or initiate review processes. These workflows can involve invoking AWS Lambda functions, querying data stores like Amazon DynamoDB, and sending notifications to stakeholders via Amazon SNS.

The combination of AWS services provides a flexible and scalable event-driven architecture for clinical trial data processing. Amazon S3 and Amazon Data Firehose enable reliable and scalable data ingestion, while AWS Lambda and Amazon EventBridge enable event-driven processing and orchestration. AWS Step Functions simplify the coordination of complex workflows, and services like Amazon DynamoDB, and Amazon SNS, provide robust data storage, querying, and messaging capabilities. This architecture allows for efficient collaboration, automated data processing, and timely insights generation throughout the clinical trial lifecycle.

These are just a few examples of event-driven use cases in the healthcare and life sciences domain, showcasing the power and flexibility of AWS services. By leveraging these services, organizations can build scalable, responsive, and cost-effective solutions to address various challenges and improve patient care, research, and operational efficiency.

Conclusion

The versatility and power of AWS event-driven services have proven invaluable across a diverse range of industries. From streamlining e-commerce operations and enhancing customer experiences to enabling real-time monitoring and intelligent decision-making in IoT and logistics, these services have emerged as game-changers.

As we move forward, the potential applications of event-driven architectures will continue to expand, driven by the ever-increasing demand for real-time data processing, automated workflows, and intelligent decision-making. By embracing these powerful AWS event-driven services, organizations can future-proof their operations, staying ahead of the curve and maintaining a competitive edge in an ever-evolving digital landscape.

Index

Made in the USA
Middletown, DE
12 November 2024

64425124R00216